Intermediate microeconomics: a perspective on price theory

Intermediate microeconomics: a perspective on price theory

Frederick G. Hay,
Christine Oughton and Andrew S. Skinner

Manchester University Press
Manchester and New York
distributed exclusively in the USA by St. Martin's Press

Published by Manchester University Press
Oxford Road, Manchester M13 9NR, UK
and Room 400, 175 Fifth Avenue, New York, NY 10010, USA

Distributed exclusively in the USA
by St. Martin's Press Inc., 175 Fifth Avenue, New York, NY 10010, USA

British Library Cataloguing-in-Publication data
A catalogue record for this book is available from the British Library

Library of Congress Cataloging-in-Publication data applied for

ISBN 0-7190-4581-9 *hardback*
ISBN 0-7190-4582-7 *paperback*

First published 1996

00 99 98 97 96 10 9 8 7 6 5 4 3 2 1

Printed in Great Britain
by Redwood Books, Trowbridge

Contents

Preface

This brief study purports to convey an understanding of a number of key relationships which are essential to our understanding of the theory of price. To this extent it is a *textbook* - but it is also intended to be read as an *argument* for reasons which the Introduction should make plain: hence the significance of the title. The study is intended to be read as a *perspective* on price theory.

Readers who do not find the mathematical notes, which are integrated with parts of the argument, to be congenial, may omit them without damage to their understanding of the argument as whole. Others may find it useful to omit the various notes on particular topics which occasionally appear in the text and which are designed either to explore particular implications of the analysis or to address specific difficulties.

We have acknowledged obvious debts as the argument unfolds, but inevitably these acknowledgements are scarcely exhaustive. It is to be hoped that writers of other textbooks will forgive our occasional trespasses. But we owe a great debt to the patient forebearance of our students who have used variants of the text which follows from the 1988/89 session to the present.

F.G.H.
C.O.
A.S.S.

Glasgow, March 1996.

Introduction

I

Adam Smith (1723-1790) believed that the economy could be regarded as an organism, as a whole made up of a number of separate but inter-related parts. Even more influential (in the event at least) was the analogy of the machine, which owed a great deal to Newtonian physics. Newton had shown that the entire universe could be regarded as a single whole, made up of a number of separate components, connected in ways which can be explained, illustrating a pattern of movement which could be predicted.

Smith and his contemporaries applied this way of looking at phenomena to the study of man: society, too, Smith asserted, can be regarded as 'an immense machine, whose movements produce a thousand agreeable effects' resulting from the interaction of individuals who are unaware of the final impact of their own activities. Hence the analogy of the 'Invisible Hand' (or the modern doctrine of functionalism); the argument that men act in ways which produce results which were no part of their original intention.

Smith regarded the purpose of philosophy, by which he meant science, to be the elucidation of the forces behind these 'movements and effects'; the exposure of the 'connecting principles of nature'. The characteristic output of this type of perspective is the intellectual system, which Smith also described in terms of a mechanical analogy, and which was 'designed to connect together' in the mind 'those different movements and effects which are already in reality performed'.

A number of points are worth emphasising in this statement. First, it is apparent that the purpose of systematic thought is to provide us with the means of conceptualising a process or series of processes. Secondly, the intellectual effort concerned must involve an act of imagination; the creation of something 'ideal', in other words a 'theory'. Finally, it is to be observed that this effort of thought is concerned with movements 'already in reality performed' thus confirming the importance of relevance. Few, if any, of these propositions would be regarded as exceptional today.

The importance of the perspectives we have just been describing is nowhere more obvious than in Smithian economics, and especially in the theory of price itself. Readers of the *Wealth of Nations* (1776) will be aware that the main components of the 'system' to be explained were simple. Smith worked in terms of two sectors (manufacture and agriculture) where productive activity involved, in effect, the use of four distinct factors of production (land, labour, capital and entrepreneurship) and featured the creation of two types of commodity, consumption and investment goods. Corresponding to the four factors were certain forms of payment; payments which are required since these factors are productive and (in the short-run) scarce. Rent represented the payment for the use of the factor land; wages, the compensation for undergoing the fatigues (disutility) of labour; profit, the return for taking the risks attendant on combining the factors of production; interest, the payment required for the use of 'loanable' funds. In Smith's model it follows that total output, at any one time, will feature the use of all four factors; that these factors will require payment, thus generating a particular level of (aggregate) income which may be used by those to whom it accrues to purchase commodities (consumption and investment goods) at present or at some point in the future.

Thus specified, the argument points in two directions, both of which were followed by Smith: the first, macro, where he was concerned with the functioning of the economy during a given period as well as through time; the second, micro, where one problem to be considered was the allocation of a given aggregate stock of factors between competing uses. It is the latter problem which is of major interest in the present context, at least to the extent that Smith's treatment helps to isolate some of the important issues with which price theory still seeks to deal.

A characteristic of Smith's treatment of price is the assumption that output can be expanded or contracted under conditions of constant cost. He also assumed given rates of factor payment (the natural rates), which may obtain in a given time period. These rates (which he assumed to be stable in the context of a short-run model) define the producer's costs, and hence the position of the cost curve.

Initially, at least, the argument was developed in terms of a 'partial' case; i.e. the examination of the behaviour of a number of sellers marketing a single product. The concept of equilibrium was worked out in terms of a distinction between 'natural' and 'market' prices where the former corresponds to cost of production while the latter represents a price which may prevail at any given moment.

Smith noted that where the market and natural prices diverge, the rates of factor payment in the employment affected would either rise above, or sink below, their 'natural' levels – thus generating an inflow or outflow of resources to or from particular employments. The net effect is to increase or decrease the use of resources within particular employments with consequent effects on the rates of return to factors and on the supply (and hence the price) of the commodity itself. Three points follow: first, that a movement to equilibrium will involve inter-related responses in both the factor and the commodity markets (a theme followed in this book); secondly, that the 'natural price' must be the equilibrium or 'central' price 'to which the prices of all commodities are continually gravitating' (Smith 1976: I.vii. 15). Finally, it should be noted that where a commodity is produced under conditions of constant cost, the equilibrium price will correspond to costs of production, while the amount produced will be determined by the level of demand (see below, Chapter 3).

The argument leads directly to another result successfully stated by Smith, namely that if the processes outlined above hold good for all commodities taken separately (the partial view) they must also hold good for all commodities taken 'complexly' (the general view). It would appear that a position of equilibrium over the whole economy can only obtain where each commodity is sold at its 'natural' price and where each factor in each employment is paid for at its 'natural' rate. The economy can be said to have attained a position of 'balance' since where the above conditions are satisfied there can be no tendency for resources to move within or between employments. On the other hand, where these conditions are not satisfied some movement of resources in the system is likely, at least until the allocation of resources conforms to the structure of consumers' preferences.

Smith was careful to add that this result would only hold good where the owners of resources sought the best return for effort, where there was freedom of movement between geographical areas and different employments, and in the absence of monopoly powers (Smith 1976: I.vii. 27)

The analogies used, the method employed, even the problems dealt with by the modern theory of price, are in fact surprisingly similar to those faced by Smith. But important differences began to emerge in the aftermath of the first marginal revolution. These are usefully summarised in a quotation from W.S. Jevons (1835–1882) writing in the preface to his *Theory of Political Economy* (1871):

> In this work I have attempted to treat Economy as a calculus of Pleasure and Pain, and have sketched out, almost irrespective of previous opinions, the form which the science, as it seems to me, must ultimately take. I have long thought, that as it deals throughout with quantities, it must be a mathematical science in matter if not in language. I have endeavoured to arrive at accurate quantitative notions concerning Utility, Value, Labour, Capital, etc., and I have often been surprised to find out how clearly some of the most difficult notions, especially that most puzzling of notions, *Value,* admit of mathematical analysis and expression. The Theory of Economy, thus treated, presents a close analogy to the science of Statical Mechanics, and the Laws of Exchange are found to resemble the Laws of Equilibrium of a lever as determined by the principle of virtual velocities. The nature of Wealth and Value is explained by the consideration of indefinitely small amounts of pleasure and pain, just as the Theory of Statics is made to rest upon the equality of indefinitely small amounts of energy. But I believe that the dynamical branches of the Science of Economy may remain to be developed, on the consideration of which I have not at all entered (Jevons 1871: vii-ix)

The first point which arises from this statement relates to the emphasis which it gives to mathematics and especially to the techniques which are associated with the calculus. It must be remembered that the calculus, not to mention geometrical and algebraic techniques, were entirely familiar at the time that Smith wrote: what is unique about the first 'marginal revolution' is the perception that such techniques, and especially that of the calculus, could be applied to the solution of specifically economic problems; applications which at once made it easier to understand the analysis offered by Smith with regard to the determinants of price, and at the same time seemed to raise the analysis to a higher level of precision.

Secondly, it is interesting to note that the 'marginal revolution' was a revolution in respect of technique and in the choice of problem; that it was–at least historically–associated with a narrowing of the focus of attention as compared to that found in the *Wealth of Nations* – a point to some extent confirmed by Jevons' concentration on the 'statical' aspects of the subject while recognising that the dynamic branches still remained to be developed.

Third, it is worth observing that Jevons should have placed so much emphasis on analogies drawn from the laws of mechanics, in that such analogies present both a parallel and a contrast with Smith's usage:- a *parallel* in that the laws of mechanics, like the explanation of the solar system, were ultimately based on the (Newtonian) laws of motion; a *contrast* in that analogies drawn from theoretical mechanics make it possible to think in a useful and systematic way about *particular areas* of analysis rather than in terms of the Smithian vision of a more compendious or all embracing *system* of economics similar in conception to the Newtonian vision of astro-physics.

II

It would probably now be agreed that at least one aspect of the Smithian interest in competition and equilibrium was illuminated, not only by the advent of 'marginalism' but also by two rather different formal approaches to the subject, both of which owed a good deal to the analysis of the *Wealth of Nations*. The first approach was at one time the dominant Anglo-Saxon tradition; it is associated with W.S. Jevons , and Alfred Marshall (1842-1924, *Principles of Economics* 1890). The second line of argument is associated with Léon Walras (1834-1910) and Vilfredo Pareto (1848-1923), whose *Manuale di Economia Politica* (1906) is the work on which modern accounts of his analysis are based. These two lines of argument are not of course the same, a point which may explain G.L.S. Shackle's illuminating comment when introducing the work of one of Pareto's most informed expositors, Eraldo Fossati:

> Familiar problems appear in it from a slightly different and refreshing angle, and the jaded teacher finds new stimulation and valuable alternative approaches.[1]

1 *Theory of General Static Equilibrium* (1946, transl. 1957).

Shackle refers to a valuable *alternative* and to the point that problems familiar to the student of Marshallian economics appear in a *slightly* different light. There is no gulf in terms of analysis or objective, although there is, as Shackle also points out, a very considerable difference between the two traditions. The Marshallian focus is *partial*, that of Pareto is *general*: while Marshall's argument is designed to show the forces which generate movements *towards* equilibrium, Pareto was more interested in revealing the 'tableau of equilibrium' and in formulating the necessary efficiency conditions.

This rather unexceptional statement conceals another real difference. In Marshall's case, the interest shown in the return to equilibrium is reflected in the choice of analogy used; he speaks of the pendulum *returning* to rest and therefore concerns himself with processes which involve *time.*

In Paretian analysis, however, the process by which equilibrium is attained, following a disturbance, is much less emphasised; a fact which is reflected in Pareto's *exclusion* of time to all intents and purposes. Shackle makes this very point in a passage which confirms the different routes followed by Marshall and Pareto.

> Pareto's virtual exclusion of time is no accidental or incidental matter, it arises from a belief that the study of economic forces *in mutual balance* is a necessary foundation for all understanding of economic phenomena (*ibid.*: vii).

It would appear therefore that both approaches have certain strengths and weaknesses. The Marshallian argument derives its strength from the interest shown in *processes*, its apparent weakness from the formal concentration on the *partial* case. The Paretian argument, in contrast, apparently derives its strength from the formal concentration on *general equilibrium*, while its weakness may lie in the emphasis given to *results* rather than to the processes by virtue of which they are attained. Taken together, they supply a valuable and probably indispensable introduction to the theory of price.

As a means of illustrating this point, we begin, in Chapter 1, with the (Paretian) analysis of the logic of choice as it affects 'consumers' and 'producers' thus paving the way for a discussion of the fact that choices are interdependent. This analysis concludes with an account of Pareto-optimality (or efficiency) in the context of a simple hypothetical economic system.

Chapter 2 marks the beginning of our concern with 'partial' analysis, building on the technical results already established by extending the analysis of choice as it affects'households' and 'firms' in respect of specific areas. 'Households' are now presented as facing choices with regard to the purchase of commodities, but also as between work and leisure, and between consumption now and in the future. This discussion enables us to identify important (Marshallian) functions; for example those which relate to the demand for commodities and to the supply of services such as labour and saving.

The argument is then extended to the 'firms' which supply commodities and demand services, enabling us to identify an additional number of functional relationships. The purpose of this part of the argument is to identify a series of independent functions and the appropriate equilibrium conditions.

Chapter 3 then offers an analysis of the allocative mechanism under conditions of perfect competition. The thesis that resources will be allocated in such a way as to conform to the structure of consumers' preferences is supported by an analysis which emphasises the importance of interdependent adjustments in both factor and commodity markets.

The analysis which is developed in Chapter 3 emphasises the importance of the theory of the firm, a theme which is further developed in the passages which follow. In Chapter 4 we proceed to examine the model of monopoly, treating this model as the polar opposite of perfect competition in the context of a case where we confront a single seller of a commodity for which there are no close substitutes. The model is useful in the sense that it introduces the need to modify the average and marginal curves of costs and revenue which were established in the previous section.

The model of monopoly paves the way for an examination of the phenomenon of monopolistic competition where sellers have the opportunity to vary price, selling costs and product specification. Particular attention is given to the complex behavioural patterns which are likely to emerge where numbers are small and where the decisions taken by one firm may have a profound impact on others (oligopoly). Throughout this analysis the theme of interdependent factor and commodity markets is sustained.

Chapter 5 considers one possible response to the problems identified in the previous section in the form of an analysis of game theory. This is treated as an important subject in its own right, although particular attention is given to its application to oligopoly. Problems identified in the previous section, such as predatory pricing, limit price analysis and the meaning of rationality, appear here in new guises.

The study concludes with a chapter which considers some of the implications of the foregoing argument but which is primarily concerned with the contribution which was made by E.H. Chamberlin to the theory of the firm. It is Chamberlin's analysis which informs the treatment offered here, notably in Chapter 4. Chamberlin's contribution confirms the difficulties which confront attempts to establish unambiguous relationships between the prices of goods and services and the quantities offered. The same argument confirms the difficulties which are encountered in constructing general equilibrium systems in situations where knowledge is imperfect.

As Shackle has noted:

> When economic theory elects to bring in imperfect competition and to recognise uncertainty, there is an end to the meaning of general equilibrium. Economics thereafter is the description, piece by piece, of a collection of fragments. These fragments may fit together into a brilliant, arrestingly

> suggestive mosaic but they do not compose a pattern of unique, inevitable order.[2]

This perception suggests that mechanistic analogies are of limited relevance; it also explains the order in which the different parts of the present argument are placed.

2 *The Years of High Theory* (1967), p. 295.

Chapter 1

Paretian Analysis

Section A: The Consumer

The Logic of Choice

Production of a good or a service for the purpose of exchange rather than direct consumption by the producer necessarily implies the interdependence of the parties to the exchange, irrespective of the degree of complexity of the economy concerned. Where freedom of choice also exists this interdependence becomes complicated. For example, consumers face a problem of choice with respect to different goods; producers have to decide which goods are to be supplied and in what quantities. Solving one choice problem alters the situation for others, in varying degrees, and further reaction generates new choice situations. Our purpose here is to review the logic of choice, and see how much light it casts on the nature and implications of interdependence.

I. Indifference Curve Analysis

The equilibrium approach to the analysis of consumers' choice owes much to the work of F.Y. Edgeworth, whose *Mathematical Psychics* was published in 1881. But the modern exposition is based upon Pareto and owes a great deal to the re-statement of his results by J.R. Hicks, whose *Value and Capital* was first published in 1939. The approach has a number of particular features:

1. It postulates that consumer's satisfaction (utility) is a common denominator of different quantities of different 'goods' from which a choice is to be made, a condition which we shall term that of general substitutability.
2. It deals with combinations of different 'goods' rather than with single 'goods' taken in isolation.
3. It employs the concept of preference, which involves the comparative evaluation of the satisfaction to be derived from different 'goods'.
4. It requires only the ranking of preferences, and not their measurement.
5. It defines 'rational behaviour' as the selection of the combination of 'goods'

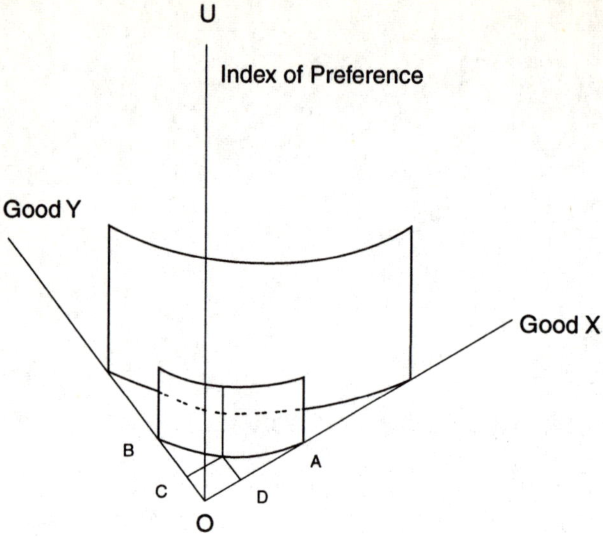

Figure 1.1

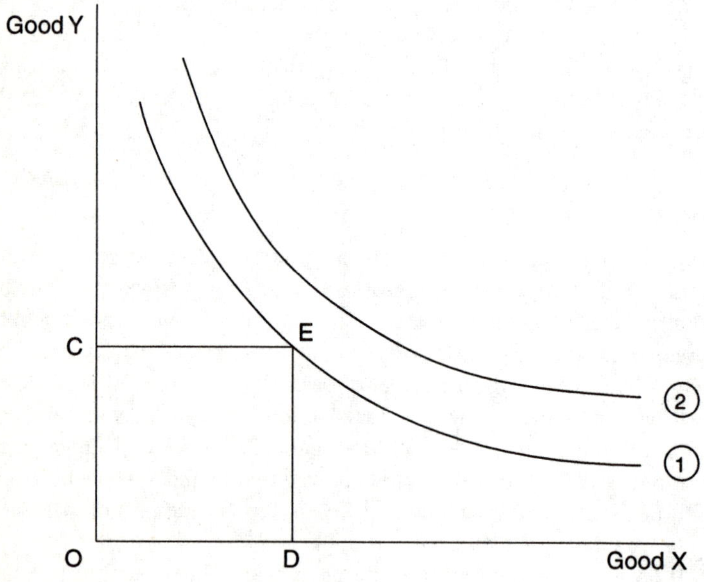

Figure 1.2

with the highest preference ranking, and assumes that 'realised satisfaction' is equal to the satisfaction expected from any specific act of choice.

6. It assumes the continuous divisibility of the 'goods' available to the consumer. This complex assumption permits us to draw functions which are smooth and continuous.[1]

The Concept of Indifference

Let us suppose that the consumer can review combinations of any quantities of different goods. Imagine a basket of given size, one of a set of different capacities, and assume that this basket can be filled with different combinations of quantities of two goods, X and Y. We also assume, so long as the basket is filled, that the consumer has attained a particular level of satisfaction. In this situation the basket might contain a great deal of X, and little of Y, or vice-versa, or equal amounts of each. Since each combination represents the same level of satisfaction we cannot diffferentiate among them on that basis: the consumer is literally indifferent as to which particular combination of quantities of the two goods is chosen.

A Diagrammatic Approach

We can examine the problems of preference and indifference by the use of diagrams. At the outset it was assumed that the satisfaction arising from exercising choice was a 'common denominator' of all such decisions, the relationship among the objects of choice being one of general substitutability. We can therefore entertain the possibility of a particular level of satisfaction being sustained by a change in the quantity of one good which offsets or compensates for a change in the quantity of the other.

We illustrate this in a simple diagram (Figure 1.1) depicting a three-dimensional relationship involving quantities of the two goods, X and Y, and the level of satisfaction. In this figure, quantities of the goods X and Y are placed on the corresponding axes with 'satisfaction' or preference ranking represented by the U axis.

Imagine a situation where the consumer could attain the same level of satisfaction with OA of X and no Y or OB of Y and no X or some combination intermediate between these extremes (such as OC and OD). If we erect an ordinate of given height from the locus of such points and join them, we can complete a 'utility surface'. The height of the ordinate it is to be emphasised gives us an index of preference ranking and not a (cardinal) measure of it.

The same diagram also shows the various levels of satisfaction which can be reached with various combinations of quantities of the two goods. Taken together

1. In using the term 'good' or 'goods' we refer to choices facing the 'consumer'. These may relate to choices between quantities of *commodities* or other opportunities such as the choices between work and leisure or between present and future 'goods'. See below, Chapter 2.

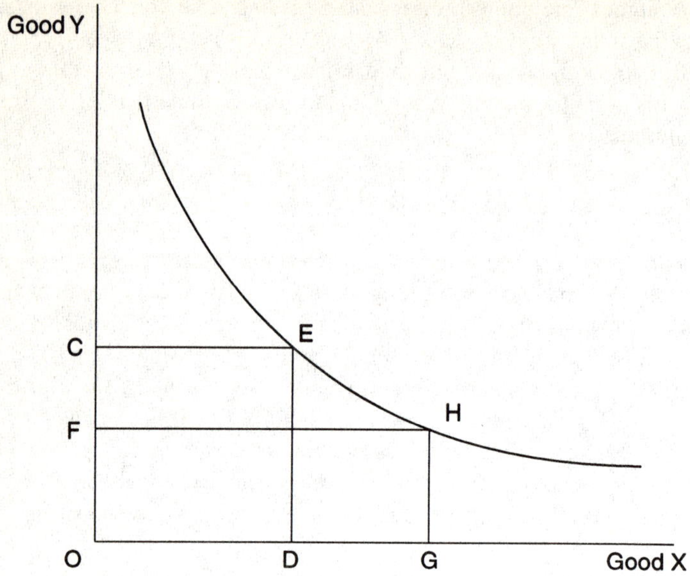

Figure 1.3(a)

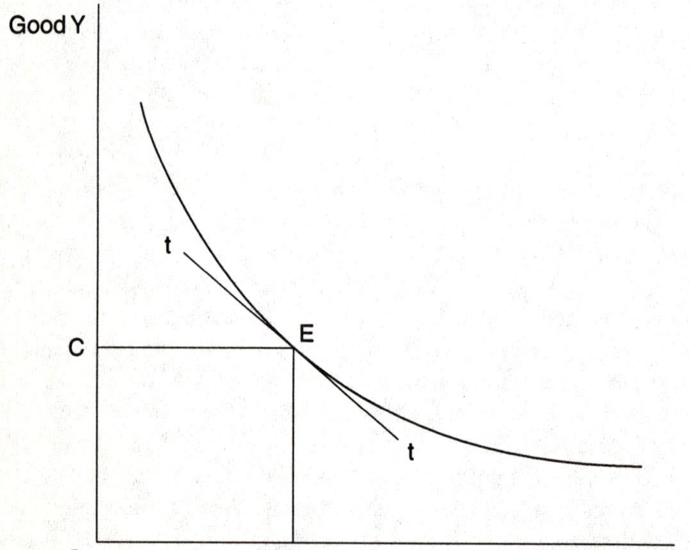

Figure 1.3(b)

these form a 'satisfaction hill' made up of a series of utility surfaces: each one of which represents a particular level of satisfaction.

In Figure 1.2 we have drawn 'contours', or lines of equal height (in this context equal rank), on the surface. Each contour therefore represents a particular value of the satisfaction index. If we project these contours on to the base of the diagram in such a way as to expose the X and Y axes only, we obtain a 'map' representing the three-dimensional surface on a one-dimensional plane similar in style to the topographical map of a hill. These contours can be labelled with a particular 'height' or satisfaction index.

Each of the contour lines represents a particular level of satisfaction so that the consumer must be indifferent as to which of the combinations is chosen. We can therefore label these curves 'Indifference Curves' and term the entire Figure 1.2 an 'Indifference Map'.

The Shape of the Indifference Curve

The shape of the indifference curve reflects the use of a number of assumptions.

First, it is assumed that indifference curves slope downwards from left to right, indicating that the consumer prefers (i.e. is not indifferent to) combinations offering greater quantities of both goods, or combinations offering greater quantities of one good and the same amount of the other. This rules out, respectively, indifference curves which slope upwards to the right, or those which are either horizontal or vertical (although the latter situation could obtain where the goods are perfect complements).

Note that our argument excludes the possibility that the consumer will ever reach a point of satiety, beyond which additional quantities of either good will reduce satisfaction. The assumption is not intended to infer that such states do not exist, nor that they cannot be successfully analysed by this approach; it is made simply to keep the argument concise. Finally, it should be noted that indifference curves will not intersect: two levels of satisfaction by definition different cannot at one point be the same.

The downward slope of the indifference curve gives rise to the concept of the Marginal Rate of Substitution. Technically the MRS is the measure of the slope of the indifference curve, and is defined as the ratio of the differences in quantities between two neighbouring points on the indifference curve. Or, more simply, *the MRS may be expressed as the ratio of the quantity of one good given up and the quantity of the other good obtained while the consumer remains on the same indifference curve*. For example, in acquiring an additional quantity of X, shown as DG in Figure 1.3(a) the consumer will be prepared to give up a particular quantity of Y, shown as CF, remaining on the same level of satisfaction but moving from E to H.

It will be apparent that the slope of the indifference curve will tell us how much of Y the consumer is prepared to give up in order to acquire a compensating amount of X, thus expressing the value of the MRS of X for Y at that point.

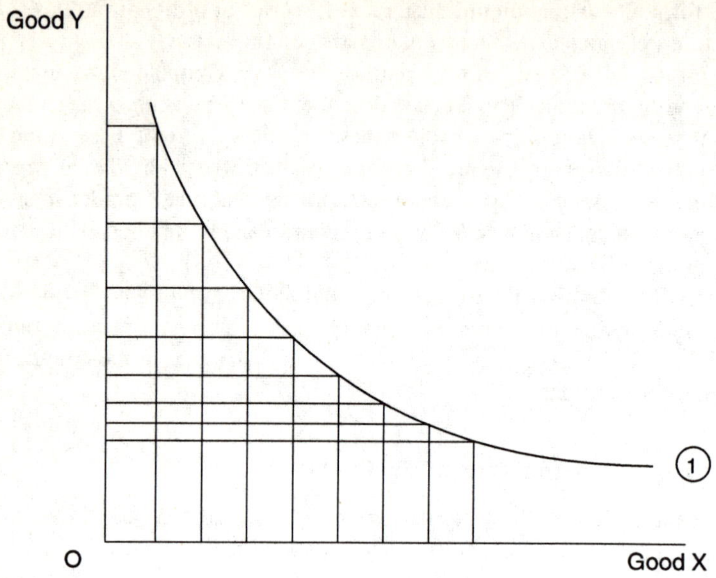

Figure 1.4(a)

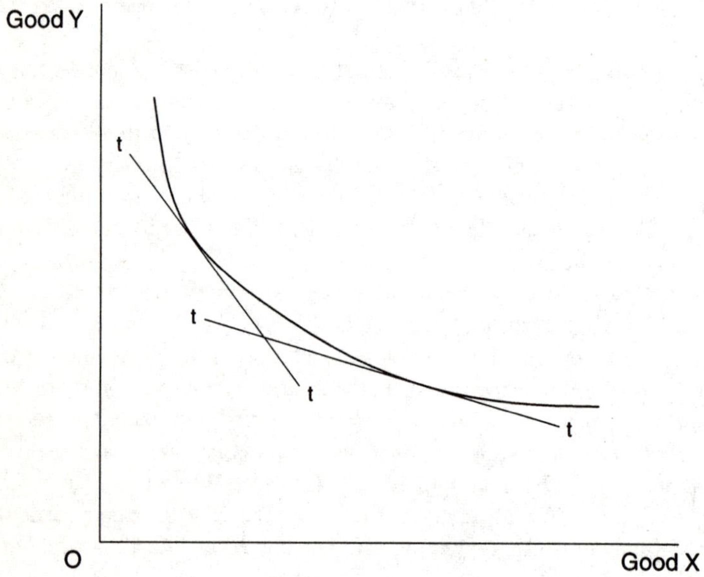

Figure 1.4(b)

Alternatively, we can state that if we take two points on an indifference curve which are very close, the slope of a tangent (tt) to the curve will express the value of MRS (Figure 1.3(b)).

Secondly, the curves are drawn consistently convex to the origin, becoming flatter at the extremities. This indicates that the slope of the curve changes as we move along it in any direction and therefore that the value of the MRS must be changing. More specifically, it will be seen (in Figure 1.4 (a)) that as we move along the curve from left to right (progressively choosing more and more of X) we reach a situation where we are prepared to give up less and less of Y if we are to remain on the same level of satisfaction. As we might expect, additional quantities chosen of X diminish in significance in terms of Y while successive units of Y forgone increase in significance in terms of X. Alternatively it can be stated that as we move along the indifference curve, the MRS will consistently move against the good the quantity of which is augmented and in favour of the good the quantity of which is relinquished. In graphical terms (Figure 1.4(b)) this means that the slopes of a series of tangents drawn to the indifference curve become progressively flatter as we move from left to right along the curve. As more X is chosen convexity means that the MRS increases (becomes less negative).

We can use the rate of increase of the MRS as an index of substitutability between the two goods, perfect substitutability being defined as zero rate of increase in MRS, i.e. a constant MRS or a straight line indifference curve. The fact that our indifference curve is consistently convex to the origin indicates that the goods considered are imperfect substitutes for each other.

[A Mathematical Approach

The diagrams used so far are representative pictures of a general relationship between quantities of two goods and an index of satisfaction. This can be written mathematically and then used very readily to obtain some useful results. The indifference map is a set of contours on a smooth continuous surface or Utility Function expressed mathematically as

$$U = f(X,Y) \quad \text{where } U, X, Y \geq 0, \frac{\partial U}{\partial X}, \frac{\partial U}{\partial Y} > 0 \text{ and } \frac{d^2Y}{dX^2} > 0$$

The variables are constrained not to be negative (assuming that to be meaningless in an economic context). The always-positive partial derivatives define the Marginal Utilities of the two goods - the incremental variation in preference in response to incremental variation in the quantity of one of the goods, the quantity of the other held constant - and signal the assumed non-satiety of preferences, i.e. always-downward-sloping indifference curves. The positive second-order total derivative, U held constant, indicates the assumed convexity of the indifference curves, i.e. imperfect substitutability.

The ratio of a change in Y to a change in X amounts to the slope of this function in the X-Y plane. If the changes in Y and X are limited to those necessary for satisfaction to remain constant, i.e. for U to remain constant, then the ratio of these changes in Y and X becomes the slope of the indifference curve. Such change in Y and X with U remaining constant can be related to the total differential (which shows the general way U could change as both X and Y change: see Appendix) to obtain a useful result:

$$dU = \frac{\partial U}{\partial X}dX + \frac{\partial U}{\partial Y}dY \qquad \text{the total differential}$$

but dU = 0 along an indifference curve so

$$0 = \frac{\partial U}{\partial X}dX + \frac{\partial U}{\partial Y}dY$$

whereupon the slope of the indifference curve (which lies in the X,Y plane) is found by re-arrangement to be:

$$\frac{dY}{dX} = -\frac{\frac{\partial U}{\partial X}}{\frac{\partial U}{\partial Y}} = -\frac{MU_X}{MU_Y}$$

The right-hand side then defines the Marginal Rate of Substitution. The result has therefore been obtained that the MRS equals the negative of the ratio of the marginal utilities.

Given that the second order total derivative is assumed to be positive, signifying the convexity of the indifference curve, it follows that, as X increases and Y decreases along the indifference curve, the MRS increases, i.e. the marginal utility of Y increases relative to the marginal utility of X. So convexity carries no implications for the independent behaviour of the two marginal utilities, a point of some importance later in the argument.]

II. Constraints

So far we have only dealt with the consumer's preferences, making no mention of the opportunities which are actually available, or the constraints to which the consumer is subject. Let us suppose:

1. that the consumer has allocated a particular Budget (R) to be spent on goods X and Y whose prices are known,
2. that the consumer has no influence on the prices of X and Y,
3. that all other prices are given and constant.

Figure 1.5 illustrates the attainable choices open to the consumer in the light of these constraints. The consumer could spend all of R on good Y, purchasing OA units, or spend it all on X, purchasing OB units, or spend it in purchasing some

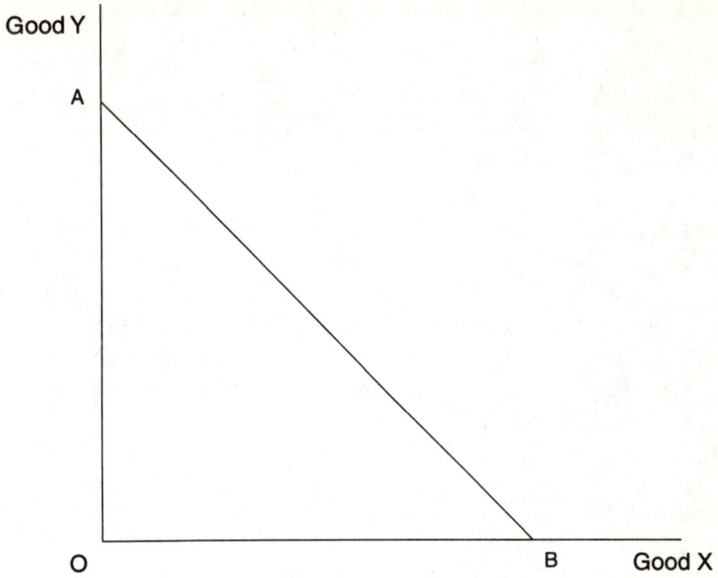

Figure 1.5

combination which is intermediate between these extremes. The line AB represents the set of all attainable combinations of goods X and Y. A point closer to the origin than AB leaves some of R unspent; a point beyond AB requires a larger budget than R.

The line AB, showing the attainable combinations of the two goods for the given expenditure R, has a slope which is equivalent to the ratio of the prices of the two goods:

$$\text{Slope AB} = \frac{OA}{OB} = \frac{\frac{R}{P_y}}{\frac{R}{P_x}} = \frac{R}{P_y}\frac{P_x}{R} = \frac{P_x}{P_y}$$

AB is termed the Price Opportunity Line (or Budget Line). As long as the ratio of the prices of the goods X and Y remains constant the position of the Price Opportunity Line will depend solely on the magnitude of R, the fund allocated to the expenditure on the two goods. If R were to increase (with the price-ratio constant) the line would move out from the origin, parallel to the existing price-opportunity line; similarly it would move closer to the origin if R were to be reduced in size, other things remaining equal.

[Mathematics of the Constraints

Initially the budget R can be thought of as a three-dimensional function of quantities of X and Y, mathematically similar to the Utility Function:

$$R = g(X,Y) \quad \text{where } R, X, Y \geq 0, \frac{\partial R}{\partial X}, \frac{\partial R}{\partial Y} > 0$$

Again values of the variables are constrained to be non-negative, and increasing the quantities of X and Y causes the values of R to increase i.e. requires a larger budget.

In general the ratio of a change in Y to a change in X defines the slope of this function in the X-Y plane. If the changes in Y and X are constrained to be those necessary for the budget (R) to remain constant, then the relevant ratio of changes in Y and X becomes the slope of the Price Opportunity Line. As Y and X change in this way R remains constant; this can be employed via the total differential to obtain the equivalent result:

$$\frac{dY}{dX} = -\frac{\frac{\partial R}{\partial X}}{\frac{\partial R}{\partial Y}}$$

But we know rather more about the budget function than the utility function: it is linear in the assumed given prices of the two goods, Px and Py. That is, the budget function is

$$R = PxX + PyY$$

That being so,

$$\frac{\partial R}{\partial X} = P_x \text{ and } \frac{\partial R}{\partial Y} = P_y$$

It follows that the slope of the Price Opportunity Line is

$$\frac{dY}{dX} = -\frac{\frac{\partial R}{\partial X}}{\frac{\partial R}{\partial Y}} = -\frac{P_x}{P_y}$$

While this is true of any Price Opportunity Line on the budget function, we assume that a given budget has already been allocated to the purchase of quantities of the two goods. That is, we have selected a given value of R, so we confront a single contour line on the budget function, which can be projected as a single line in the X,Y plane (AB in Figure 1.5).]

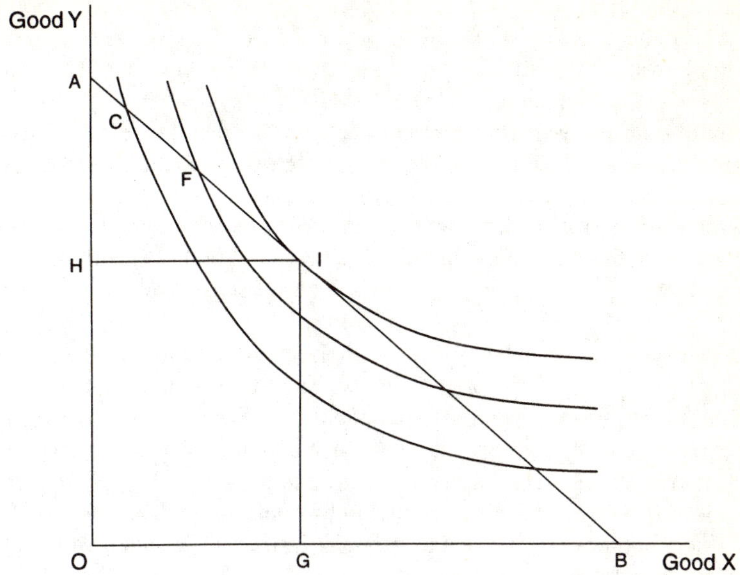

Figure 1.6

Preferences and Constraints

It should be evident that the preferences of the consumer, and the constraints under which choice is exercised, have been presented in a way which makes them logically distinct. However, both elements contain information relevant to the rational consumer who is seeking to obtain as much satisfaction as possible. The discussion of preferences tells us that the consumer reviews the levels of satisfaction yielded by all conceivable combinations of quantities of the two goods, but not which level will actually be attained, or which combination of quantities of X and Y will be acquired.

The discussion of constraints only shows the attainable combinations of quantities of X and Y. Both sides of the discussion have to be integrated to find the equilibrium position for the consumer: This may be illustrated by superimposing the Price Opportunity Line on the consumer's Indifference Map, as in Figure 1.6. The combination with the highest value of the satisfaction index among those which are attainable is shown at point I, where the "contour" or indifference curve is just tangent to the Price Opportunity Line AB, indicating that it is the highest attainable level of satisfaction. C and F are less preferred combinations.

Let us consider this point in terms of the substitution of one good for the other. The nature of the constraint - a fixed amount of expenditure to be devoted to the purchase of two goods whose prices are also given – only permits the substitution of quantities of the two goods in a fixed ratio, that is, the ratio of their prices. The nature of preference, in contrast, indicates the possibility of substitution (as we move along an indifference curve) at a ratio which varies in a particular manner. It will be recalled that this is a consequence of the assumption of convexity, that the goods in question are imperfect substitutes for each other.

Equilibrium is reached at that combination of quantities of goods X and Y where the rate at which the consumer is permitted to substitute quantities of the two goods in the market, i.e. the price ratio, equals the rate at which the consumer is willing to substitute them with no loss of satisfaction; a position which is reached when the slope of the indifference curve and of the price-opportunity line are the same. In this case the consumer will purchase OH units of Y and OG units of X.

Consumer equilibrium may thus be defined (as at point I in the diagram) in terms of the equality of the price ratio and the MRS. The consumer will not be in equilibrium at any other point, for example C or F, where the price-opportunity line intersects an indifference curve. At such points the consumer would be willing to substitute one good for the other, since the consumer can become better off (i.e. move to a higher indifference curve) by doing so. In the same way, the consumer will not move to the right of the point I, since this would involve a move to a lower level of satisfaction.

[A Mathematical Solution

The mathematical procedure for combining the utility function and the budget function is to create a third function combining both of them (known as the Lagrangean Expression), through the involvement of a new variable (known as the Lagrangean Multiplier), and then to operate on this new function in accordance with standard mathematical procedures for finding the highest value of this new function. In so doing a constrained maximum of the utility function will have been found, i.e. the highest value of the preference index attainable with the given budget. (See Appendix, Note 3).

Maximise $U = U(X,Y)$
Subject to $R = PxX + PyY$ [The budget constraint]
So $R - PxX - PyY = 0$ [Rearranging]
Then the Lagrangean Expression is

$$L = U(X,Y) + \lambda(R - PxX - PyY)$$

We now differentiate this function partially with respect to the three variables, X, Y and λ. (The new variable λ does have economic significance, as it can be shown to be the marginal utility of the budget). We obtain the following first derivatives, and set them equal to zero to satisfy the first-order condition for a relative extremum, a maximum or a minimum:

$$1. \quad \frac{\partial L}{\partial X} = \frac{\partial U}{\partial X} - \lambda P_x = 0$$

$$2. \quad \frac{\partial L}{\partial Y} = \frac{\partial U}{\partial Y} - \lambda P_y = 0$$

$$3. \quad \frac{\partial L}{\partial \lambda} = R - P_x X - P_y Y = 0$$

Note that when equation (3) is satisfied the Lagrangean Expression itself collapses to the Utility Function.

Dividing (1) by (2) and rearranging we obtain

$$4. \quad \frac{\frac{\partial U}{\partial X}}{\frac{\partial U}{\partial Y}} = \frac{MU_x}{MU_y} = \frac{P_x}{P_y} \qquad [\lambda \text{ disappears in the quotient}]$$

Earlier we established that the ratio of the partial derivatives of the Utility Function (the marginal utilities) was the Marginal Rate of Substitution and established that it was the (negative) slope of the indifference curve. In addition we established that the ratio of the prices of the two goods was the (negative) slope of the Price Opportunity Line. We can now see that at the quantities of X and Y which satisfy the conditions for a relative extremum these two ratios are equal. In diagrammatic terms the slope of the indifference curve equals the slope of the Price Opportunity Line.

But is it a maximum or a minimum? It can be shown that the assumption of convexity of the indifference curve (or the convexity of preferences), a condition on the relative changes of marginal utilities of the two goods, is sufficient to ensure that this solution is indeed a maximum rather than a minimum.

One useful insight follows immediately by re-arrangement of equation 4: in equilibrium the consumer equates the price-weighted marginal utilities of the two goods.

$$4a. \quad \frac{MU_x}{P_x} = \frac{MU_y}{P_y}$$

This will be of some significance later in the argument.]

III. Changes in the Position of Equilibrium

Let us now consider the consequences of changes in the constraints under which the consumer must make decisions: i.e. changes in expenditure on the two goods,

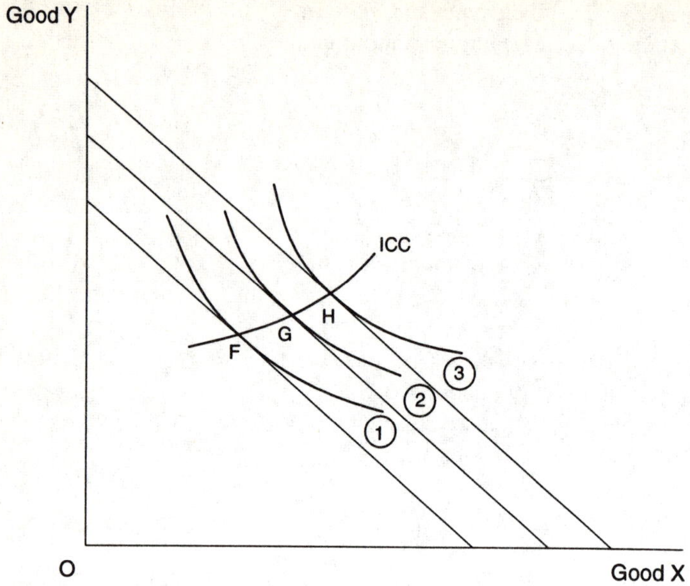

Figure 1.7

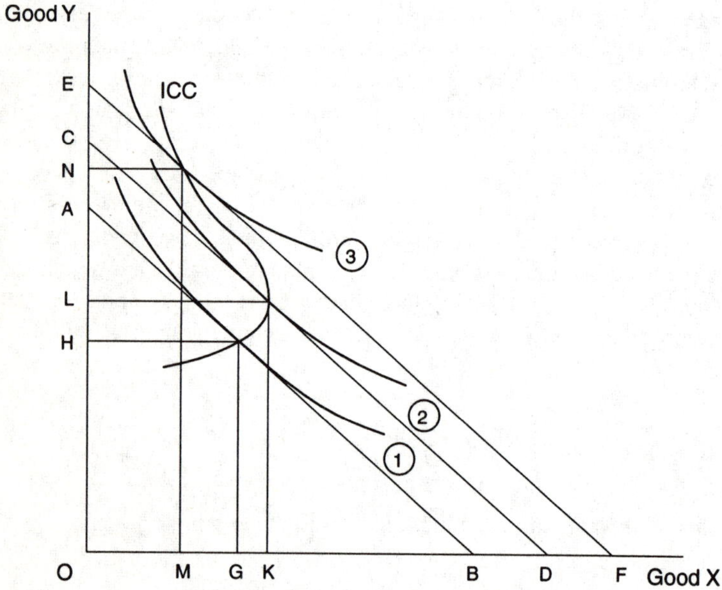

Figure 1.8

and changes in their relative prices.

Expenditure Changes

In introducing the Price Opportunity Line we noted that different levels of expenditure devoted to X and Y could be represented graphically by parallel Price Opportunity Lines.

Our discussion of consumer equilibrium has just indicated that for a given level of expenditure, other things remaining equal, the consumer will purchase the combination of quantities of the two goods where the price ratio and the Marginal Rate of Substitution are equal. It follows that there will be a position of equilibrium corresponding to each level of expenditure: a situation illustrated in Figure 1.7. A line linking the equilibrium points for many different levels of expenditure is termed the Income Consumption Curve, since it traces out the consumer's response to changes in the level of expenditure on the two goods, their prices being given. The movement between two points on the Income Consumption Curve (for example F and G in the diagram), which is a movement from one indifference curve to another, we define as the Income Effect of the expenditure change which has given rise to the movement.

In Figure 1.7 the Income Effect involves increasing the quantities purchased of both goods X and Y: from F to G to H as expenditure on them increases. This need not be the case, since the precise outcome depends on the consumer's preferences. It could be that the quantity chosen of one or the other remained unchanged, or indeed that the structure of the consumer's preferences exhibited such a degree of imperfect substitutability as to result in less of one of the goods being purchased, that is, a negative income effect. This situation would be depicted by a backward (or downward) sloping Income Consumption Curve. In such a case, the relationship between the two goods concerned is termed one of inferiority. This is illustrated in Figure 1.8. Initially a rise in expenditure reveals a positive income effect (i.e. purchases of both goods rise), which is followed later by a negative effect in terms of good X at higher levels of expenditure. At that point X becomes an inferior good with respect of Y. In Figure 1.8 the lines AB, CD and EF are price-opportunity lines corresponding to three levels of income. At the first point of equilibrium the consumer purchases OG of X and OH of Y; at the second, OK of X and OL of Y. In the third position the purchases of Y have increased to ON, but those of X have decreased (OM).

Price Changes

Suppose now that the level of expenditure remains constant, while the price ratio changes. If we start from a position of equilibrium then an alteration in purchases will ensue, since the change in the price ratio will disturb the equality between that ratio and the Marginal Rate of Substitution. In Figure 1.9 the position of the Price Opportunity Line has changed because of a fall in the price of X. One end of the

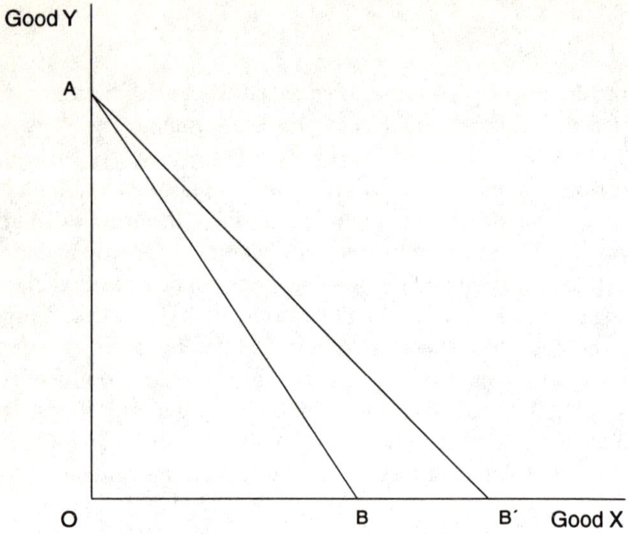

Figure 1.9

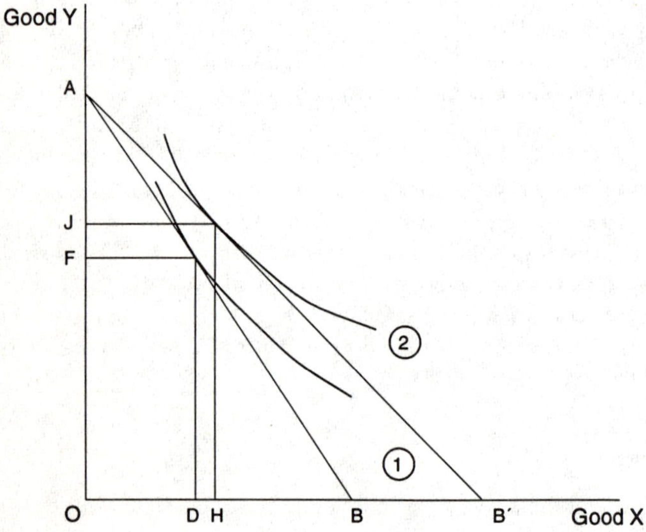

Figure 1.10(a)

line moves outwards since with a lower price of X it is now possible for the consumer to purchase more of X if all available resources were to be devoted to this commodity (OB′ rather than OB units).

The consumer can now reach a higher level of satisfaction, moving to a new indifference curve. But a movement between indifference curves is our definition of an income effect. In the illustration Figure 1.10(a) we observe that the consumer can purchase more of both X and Y as a result of the change in the price of X (an increase of DH in the case of X, and of FJ in the case of Y). Since an income effect is involved, the problem is to separate this from a specific effect related to price.

We have to abstract the income effect from the overall movement. We can do this by considering the behaviour of the consumer in relation to the original level of satisfaction and the new price ratio. Consider Figures 1.10(a) and (b). The original Price Opportunity Line AB is tangent to indifference curve 1. The new price line AB′ is tangent to indifference curve 2. We now draw an additional price line CC′ parallel to AB′ (to represent the now-prevailing price ratio), but tangent to indifference curve 1 in Figure 1.10(b). By returning to the original indifference curve we have abstracted from the income effect and are able to see the specific effect of the change in price. This effect, called the Substitution Effect, then appears as a departure from the original point of equilibrium, I (where the new price ratio no longer equals the Marginal Rate of Substitution), and a move down

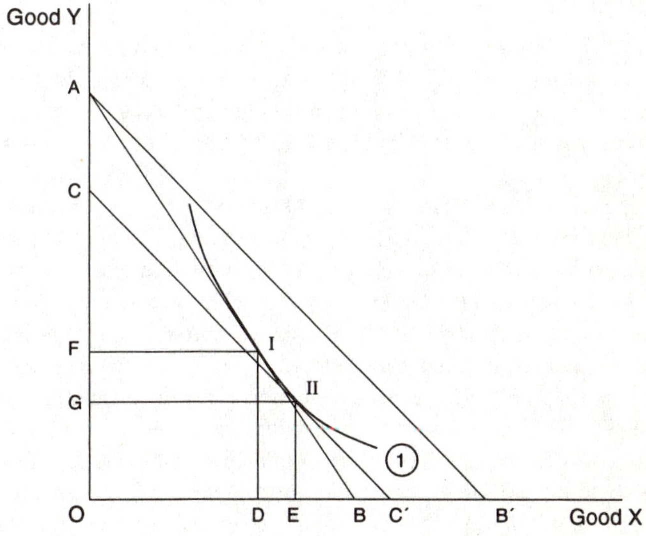

Figure 1.10(b)

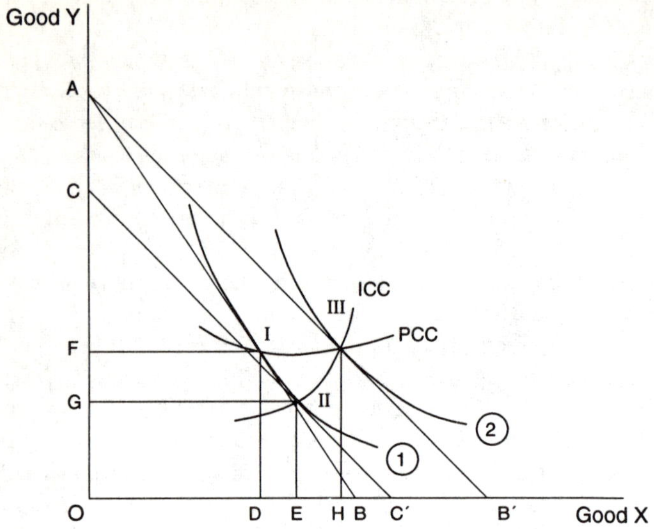

Figure 1.11

the indifference curve until the equality which signifies equilibrium is re-established at II – a substitution effect of DE in terms of the quantity of X.

The substitution effect involves the purchase of more of the good whose price has declined (DE), and less of the good whose price remains unchanged and is thus relatively dearer (FG); thus defined the substitution effect is always positive. The size of the effect will of course depend on the preferences of the consumer (i.e. on the characteristics of the indifference curve which has been chosen to illustrate the effect).

(Strictly speaking, from the mathematical point of view, the substitution effect is negative, involving as it does an increase in the quantity chosen of the good in response to a decrease in its price. However, the convention of terming it positive helps to avoid confusion where an income effect which acts in the opposite direction is correctly termed negative. It is then convenient to talk of a negative income effect offsetting a positive substitution effect).

Suppose now that the consumer is permitted to enjoy the benefit of an increase in the value of real income arising from a reduction in the price of X. The argument developed so far implies that the effect of a change in the price of one of the two goods which the consumer is considering will involve a movement to a new equilibrium by way of an income effect and a substitution effect. In Figure 1.11, DE extra units of X represents the substitution effect and EH extra units of X, the income effect. The whole response to the change in price – the move from the original to the new position of equilibrium – may be defined as the Price Effect.

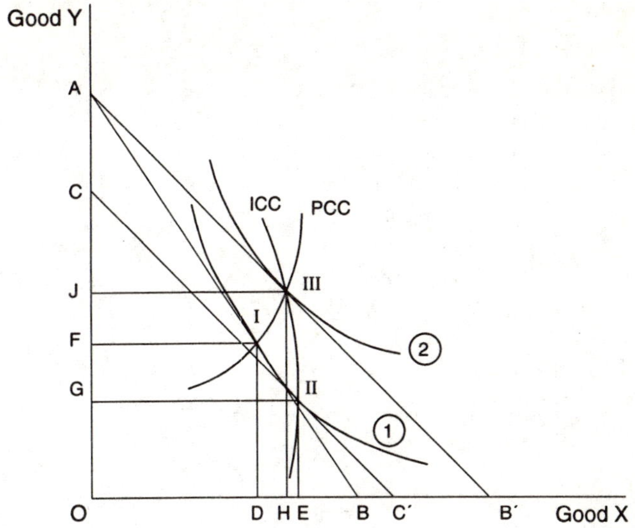

Figure 1.12(a)

The locus of points of equilibrium established in response to changes in the price of one of the goods is termed the Price Consumption Curve.

The Price Effect is then the sum of the Income Effect and the Substitution Effect. But while the substitution effect is always positive, the income effect may range from negative to positive values. There are four representative outcomes:

1. Income effect negative but insufficient to outweigh the positive substitution effect;
2. Income effect negative and exactly counterbalancing the substitution effect;
3. Income effect negative and sufficient to outweigh the substitution effect;
4. Income effect positive and augmenting the substitution effect.

The fourth case has already been illustrated in Figure 1.11; the others are depicted in Figure 1.12 (a) – (c).

Case 1 – Figure 1.12 (a) shows a net increase in the quantity of X purchased, DH, composed of a positive substitution effect of DE and a negative income effect of EH. There is therefore a positive response to the fall in price; in this case the Price Consumption Curve is sloped positively while the Income Consumption Curve is sloped negatively.

Case 2 – Figure 1.12 (b) shows no change in the quantity of X taken; the substitution effect and the income effect are the same magnitude of DE but opposite in sign. The Price Consumption Curve is vertical, while the Income Consumption Curve is again sloped negatively.

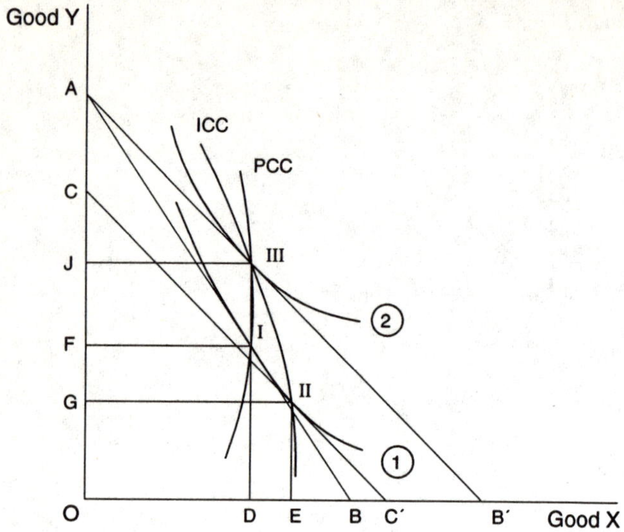

Figure 1.12(b)

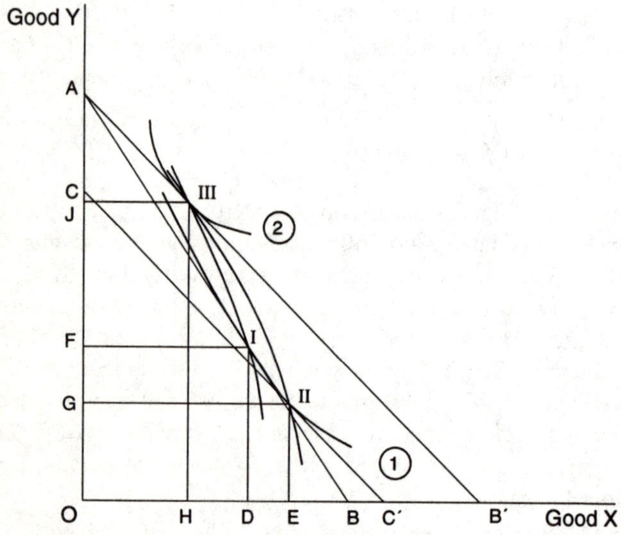

Figure 1.12(c)

Case 3 – Figure 1.12 (c) is the special case of the inferior good named after Sir Robert Giffen (1837–1910), where the size of the negative income effect (EH) is sufficient to swamp the positive substitution effect (DE) resulting in a reduction in the quantity of X taken, despite the fall in its price. In this case both the Price and Income Consumption Curves will be negatively sloped.

To sum up this section, we observe –

1. The equilibrium position for the consumer is the combination of quantities of goods X and Y at which the Price Ratio equals the Marginal Rate of Substitution of X for Y.
2. A change in the constraints confronting the consumer will shift the equi librium position by:
   (i) an income effect alone in the case of a change in expenditure, and
   (ii) a price effect – that is, a combination of an income effect and a substitution effect – in the case of a change in price.
3. The relationship between the two goods within the structure of the consumer's preferences may result in the price and quantity being positively rather than negatively related.

[A Note on the Slutsky Equation

The Slutsky Equation, named after the Russian mathematical economist Eugen Slutsky (1880-1948), states mathematically that the overall Price Effect is composed of a Substitution Effect and an Income Effect, and shows that while the former is always mathematically negative - given the assumption of convexity which is customarily made about the Utility Function - the latter may be positive or negative. The manipulation and the resulting equation form a mathematical proof of the relationship, to parallel that previously established geometrically.

The objective is to find out mathematically what happens to the quantity chosen of one of the two goods when its price changes, the price of the other good and the budget remaining constant. The starting-point is the assumption that the quantities initially chosen of both goods are those which satisfy the conditions for the highest attainable level of preference; accordingly the first-order conditions for a maximum set out on page 12 are satisfied. These equations, each now containing the solution values of all three variables X, Y and λ, are then differentiated totally. The resulting equations are then solved simultaneously for the change in X in respect of the change in Px, incorporating the further assumptions that Py and R have remained constant. (Without the use of linear or matrix algebra the manipulation is cumbersome; it is reproduced in the Appendix.)

Defining the Price Effect as

$$\frac{dX}{dP_X}$$

(bearing in mind, however, that Py and R are assumed to have remained constant) the manipulation produces the following result, the Slutsky Equation:

$$\frac{dX}{dP_X} = \frac{\partial X}{\partial P_X} + \frac{\partial X}{\partial R}\frac{dR}{dP_X}$$

The first term is the Substitution Effect; the second is the Income Effect. Some interpretation is required to establish their significance. The first term on the right-hand side shows the direct effect on X of a change in Px holding all else constant, including the preference ranking (or level of utility). The second term is the Income Effect, showing the indirect effect on X of the change in Px via its effect on the budget R. Although R has not changed in itself the change in the price of X has produced an equivalent effect. Thus the second term breaks down into the direct effect on X of that equivalent change in R (holding Px and Py constant), and the equivalent change in R due to the change in Px.

The first term is definitely negative, given the convexity of the indifference curve (see *Appendix*). The latter component of the second term is also definitely negative, given the constraint: the purchasing power of a given R falls if Px rises. However, the former component of the second term is of indeterminate sign. Consequently, depending on the sign and magnitude of this term the overall value of the Price Effect may be negative, zero or positive.]

Section B: The 'Producer'

Our hypothetical system assumes the presence of 'firms' as well as 'consumers'. Let us suppose that each 'firm' in the 'system' operates under conditions of given technique and manufactures a single product by virtue of the combination of two inputs, X and Y.

I. Isoquants

The firm faces a choice with regard to the inputs to be used in achieving a particular level of output; a problem which is conceptually similar to that faced by consumers as considered in the previous section. There are important differences, however: output, for example, is measurable (unlike satisfaction) and empirical data may be obtained with regard to the relationship between the use of factors and the level of output attained.

With these points borne in mind, the three dimensional structure used earlier (above Figure 1.1) may be re-constituted (Figure 1.13). We now measure output on the vertical axis and replace commodities with the inputs X and Y on the appropriate axes. Seen in this light, the diagram reveals that a particular level of output (say 10 units per unit of time) may be obtained with a number of combinations of X and Y. For example, this level of output could be attained by using OB units of input Y and no X; or by using OA units of X and no Y; or by using OC units of Y and OD units of X.

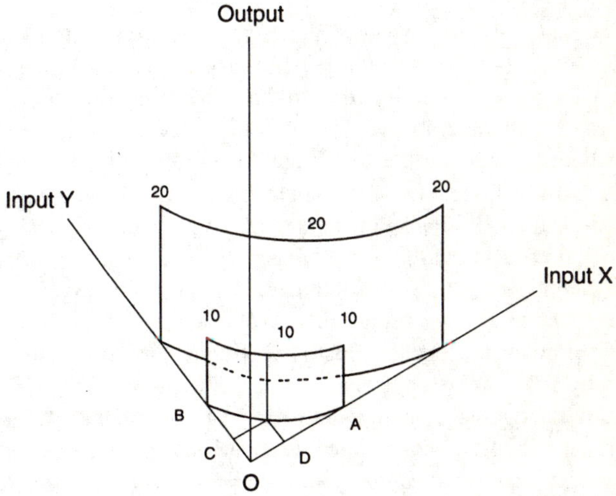

Figure 1.13

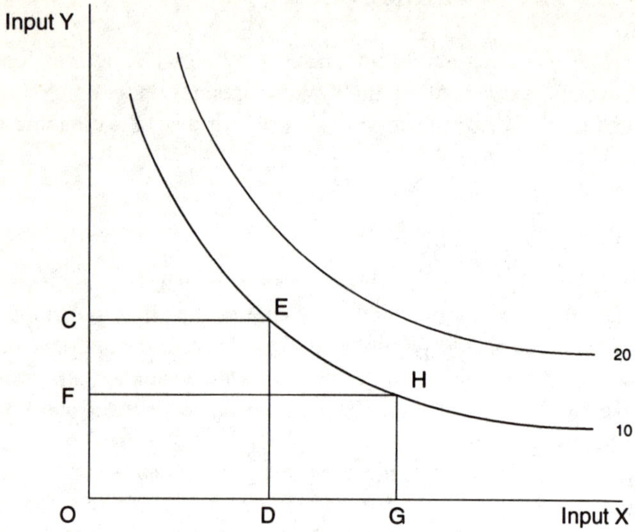

Figure 1.14

We now rotate the diagram (as before) to expose the factors X and Y on the relevant axes and the tops of the production surfaces, thus yielding lines of equal output, that is, isoquants (Figure 1.14).

General Characteristics of Equal Product Curves:

Each isoquant is defined as showing the possible combinations of factors which may be used to attain a particular level of production of a single commodity.

In drawing the isoquant, we refer to the possible combinations of inputs which may be used, without employing more of either than is necessary.

The isoquants will not intersect since it is unlikely that a given combination of inputs X and Y will yield two different levels of output – where used subject to the same technical conditions and where employed efficiently.

The equal product curve will be negatively sloped since we refer to a situation where a given level of output is obtained. If this condition is to be met, a decision to increase the use of one input must involve a decision to decrease the employment of the other. In the case illustrated (Figure 1.14) a decision to increase the use of X by DG, involves a decision to decrease the use of Y by CF.

The latter judgement enables us to identify the Marginal Rate of Technical Substitution, which may be defined as *the reduction in the quantity of one input which must be compensated for by an increase in the other, if the level of output is to remain the same.*

The Isoquants illustrated are not only negatively sloped, they are also drawn

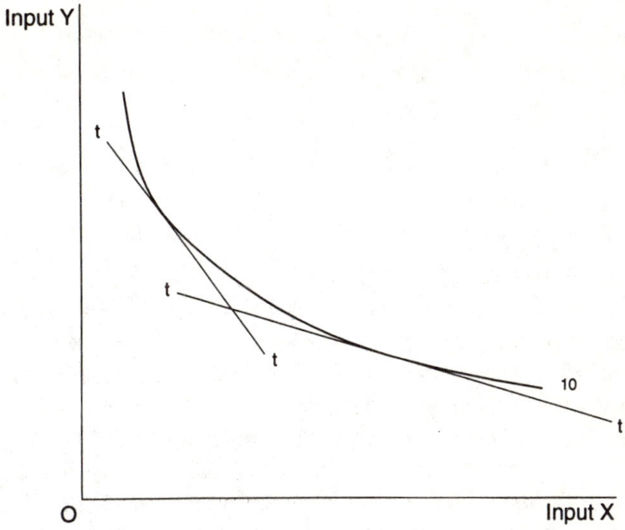

Figure 1.15

consistently convex to the origin thus illustrating the assumption that the two inputs are imperfect substitutes for one another and that they are perfectly divisible.

The marginal rate of technical substitution involves the measurement of a ratio; the ratio of the input given up to the quantity of the input which must be increased if output is to remain the same. If we take two points on an isoquant which are very close together they will lie on a tangent drawn to the curve at a particular point. It will be evident from inspection that the slopes of a series of tangents will change as we move up or down a particular isoquant, becoming progressively flatter, for example, as we increase the quantity of X which is used and decrease that of Y (Figure 1.15).

This illustrates a case where as we increase the use of X, we can give up progressively smaller amounts of Y while remaining at the same level of output. This suggests in turn that where the inputs are imperfect substitutes the marginal rate of technical substitution must move progressively against the input which is augmented and in favour of the input which is relinquished. To put the matter in another way, the example suggests that the marginal product of X in terms of Y is progressively diminishing as the use of the former increases and the latter diminishes.

We now define the slope of a tangent drawn to a particular isoquant as the marginal rate of technical substitution at that point. Moreover, in the light of the formal similarity between the isoquant map and the indifference map we can employ the procedure already used on pages 7 and 8 to derive the result that

$$MRTS_{xy} = \frac{MPP_x}{MPP_y}$$

That is, the MRTS will be equal to the ratio of the marginal physical productivities of the two inputs X and Y.

II. Constraints

Like the consumer, the producer will confront constraints, represented by the level of resources which is available for the purchase of inputs and by their prices.

Let us assume as before that the available resources are given by R and that the prices of X and Y are known and fixed. This permits us to construct an *iso-cost line* which shows the choices open to the firm in the market. For example, under the conditions illustrated (Figure 1.16) the firm could purchase OA of Y and no X, or OB of X and no Y or any combination of X and Y which is intermediate between these extremes (such as OD of Y and OC of X). All the possible combinations shown involve the same level of expenditure on factors. It also follows that the position of the iso-cost line will be determined by the level of resources available for the purchase of inputs, while the slope of the line will be determined by the price ratio, Px:Py (see above, p. 9).

III. Equilibrium

The *isoquant map* reveals different production possibilities but does not of itself reveal the level of production which will be chosen, nor the particular combination of inputs to be used. On the other hand, the *iso-cost line* reveals information as to the choices of inputs which may be made in the market, but not the specific decision with regard to the purchase of inputs. In short, we have to confront possibilities *and* constraints before a position of equilibrium can be identified. This is illustrated in Figure 1.17.

The isoquants indicate the different levels of output which may be attained using different combinations of X and Y; the line AB is the iso-cost line. Given the assumption of rationality, the firm will not operate within the line AB and is unable to operate outside it. Suppose that the first isoquant represents a level of output which can be obtained by using OA of Y and no X. It will be apparent that this would not be efficient since the firm could move down the iso-cost line (keeping costs constant) while progressively increasing the level of output. Maximum output will be obtained, for a particular level of expenditure on factors, where the iso-cost line is tangent to the highest available isoquant. The equilibrium condition thus requires that firms use OC units of X and OD units of Y in obtaining an output (in this case) of 30 units of the commodity produced per unit of time.

We have already established that the MRTS may be expressed in terms of the

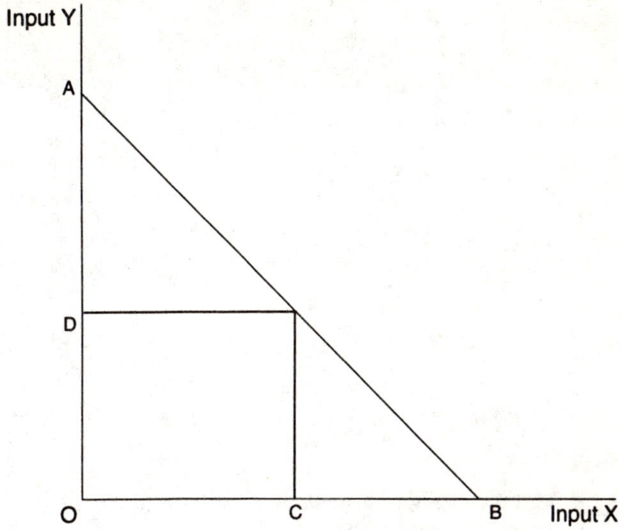

Figure 1.16

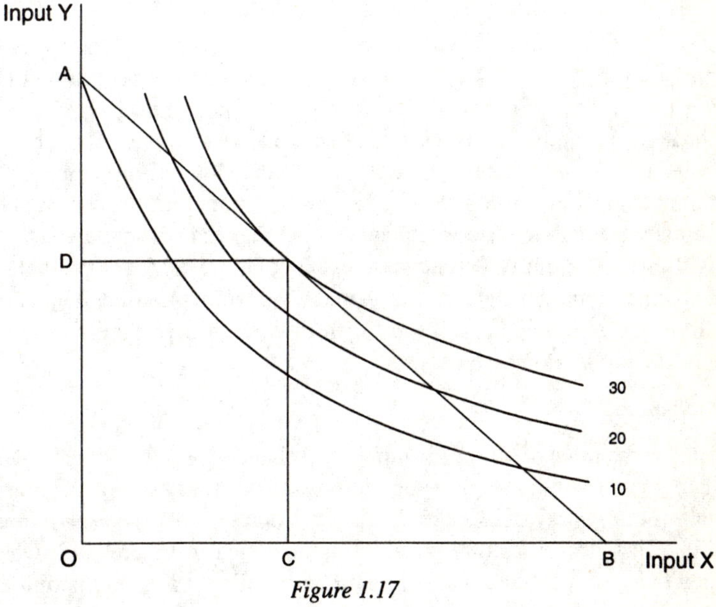

Figure 1.17

slope of a tangent drawn to the isoquant, and that the iso-cost line has a slope which is determined by the prevailing price ratio. It therefore follows that in a position of equilibrium,

$$MRTS_{xy} = \frac{P_x}{P_y}$$

Given that

$$MRTS_{xy} = \frac{MPP_x}{MPP_y}$$

it follows that

$$\frac{MPP_x}{P_x} = \frac{MPP_y}{P_y}$$

That is, at equilibrium the efficient firm can be said to arrange the purchase and use of the inputs X and Y in such a way as to bring into equality their price-weighted marginal productivities.

Changes in the Position of Equilibrium

Outlay Changes

A decision to increase the level of output from the original position will require more of the necessary inputs. Various levels of outlay on the purchase of inputs are represented graphically by a series of parallel iso-cost lines. The locus of their associated equilibrium positions we shall term the Output Employment Curve; a movement along this curve is then defined as the Output Effect, i.e. the shift from one isoquant to another as a consequence of the change in the outlay on the inputs. This is shown in Figure 1.18 which is a repeat of Figure 1.7 (p. 14) with the appropriate changes in nomenclature. The shape of the Output Employment Curve will depend on the technical possibilities open to the producer, that is to say, on the shape of the production surface.

Price Changes

A change in the price of one of the inputs will change the slope of the iso-cost line. By analogous reasoning from the previous discussion we can expect two separate effects to be at work, one of them being the output effect just considered. The other, the Technical Substitution Effect, is identified in Figure 1.19, where it is assumed that although the reduction in the price of input X would permit a higher level of output to be reached the producer decides to remain at the original level of production, thereby eliminating the output effect.

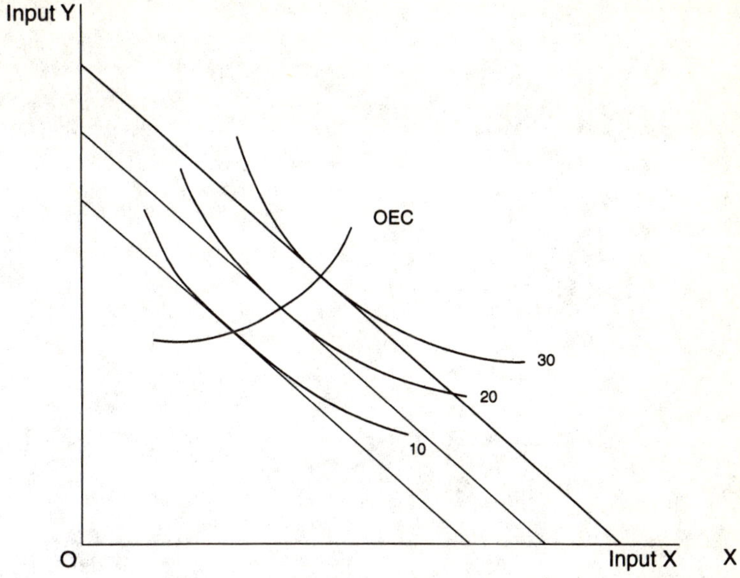

Figure 1.18

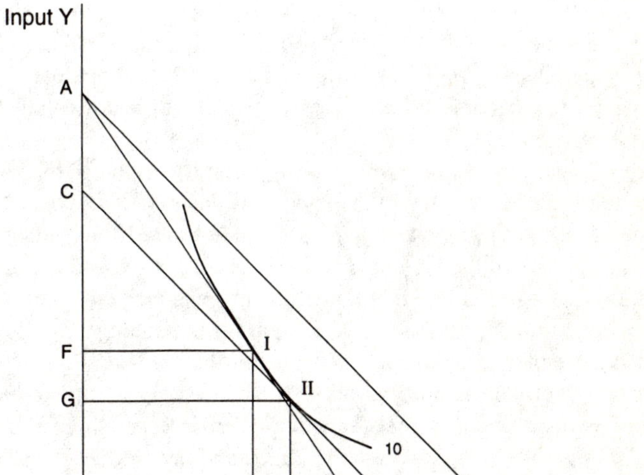

Figure 1.19

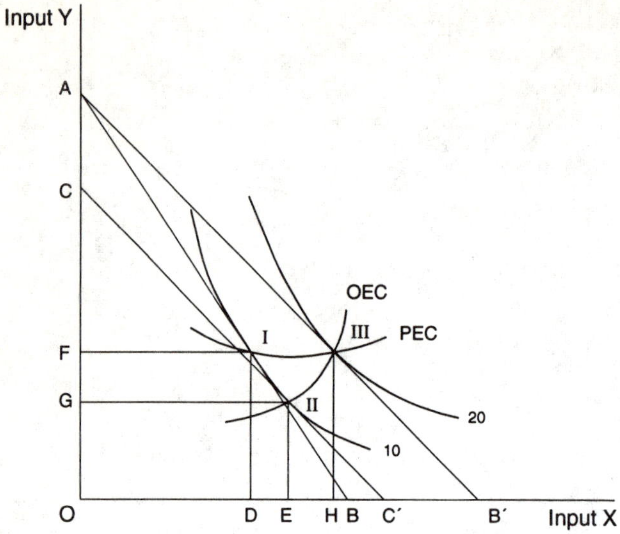

Figure 1.20

In the case supposed, the producer must confront an iso-cost line (CC′) which has the same slope as AB′ and which is tangent to the original isoquant. The example indicates that the level of output (10 units per unit of time) is maintained by using DE more units of the factor X and OG units of the factor Y (a reduction of FG). The producer, acting rationally would be expected to substitute in favour of the input which has become relatively cheaper (X) and against that which has become relatively dearer (Y).

In Figure 1.20 we depict a case where the opportunity to change the level of output as a consequence of a reduction in the price of the input X has been taken, and separate the two effects. Suppose that the price of X has fallen as indicated by the change in the position of the iso-cost line from AB to AB′. To isolate the reaction to price, draw CC′ parallel to AB′ to meet the original isoquant at II. As before, the producer substitutes in favour of X, increasing the quantity used by DE and decreasing the use of Y (FG); the *technical substitution effect.*

If we now allow the possibility of an increase in output, as the producer takes advantage of an increase in the real value of the resources, arising from the fall in the price of X, output will be increased to 20 units of the product per unit of time. At point III in the diagram, this level of output is attained by using OF units of Y and OH units of X. In this case, the technical substitution effect in respect of X is DE, and the *output effect* is EH.

The overall consequence is a movement along the curve termed the Price Employment Curve, being the locus of points of equilibrium relevant for different values of the price of one of the two inputs. Since the Output Effect can be either positive or negative (or zero) the Price Effect can exhibit the same range of possibilities which we encountered in the discussion of positive and negative income effects (Figures 1.12(a)–(c), pages 19 and 20).

To sum up this section we observe:

1. The equilibrium position for the producer is represented by the quantities of inputs X and Y at which the Price Ratio equals the Marginal Rate of Technical Substitution of X for Y.
2. A change in the constraints confronting the producer will shift the equilibrium by
   (i) an output effect alone in the case of a change in outlay, and
   (ii) a price effect – that is a combination of an output effect and a technical substitution effect – in the case of a change in the price of an input.
3. The relationship between the two inputs within the structure of the technical possibilities open to the producer may result in the price and quantity of an input being positively rather than negatively related.

IV. The Firm: A Choice of Products

In the case just examined, we considered a firm which had already decided to produce a single product and now faced the choice of inputs to be used. In the present case, we consider the firm facing a choice of products having already decided on what factor or bundle of factors is to be employed.

Suppose that the firm has already decided on a particular level of expenditure on factors and that their prices are known. This establishes the size of the factor bundle to be used and means that the firm may face a choice between devoting all the available input to the production of Y, or all of it to X – the amounts OA and OB in Figure 1.21, or some combination within these extremes.

It is to be noted that the distances OA and OB need not be the same and that they are very unlikely to be so where the products in question are different. The points A and B represent the possible boundaries of choice, and the line joining them the various possible combinations of the two products which can be created with a given bundle of factors. The curve represents the *production frontier* or *Production Possibility Curve* facing the firm and will remain constant in respect of shape and position provided there are no changes in the size of the factor bundle or in the technical conditions under which the two products are created.

The Production Possibility Curve identifies the choices which the firm may make with regard to the distribution of the available factor bundle as between different products. The same function also identifies the concept of opportunity cost, that is, the measurement of the quantity of one product which must be relinquished given a decision to increase the output of the other. In Figure 1.21 for example, a decision to increase the output of commodity X from OC to OD units requires a reduction in the output of Y from OE to OF units. This distance EF represents the opportunity cost which must be met in deciding to increase the output

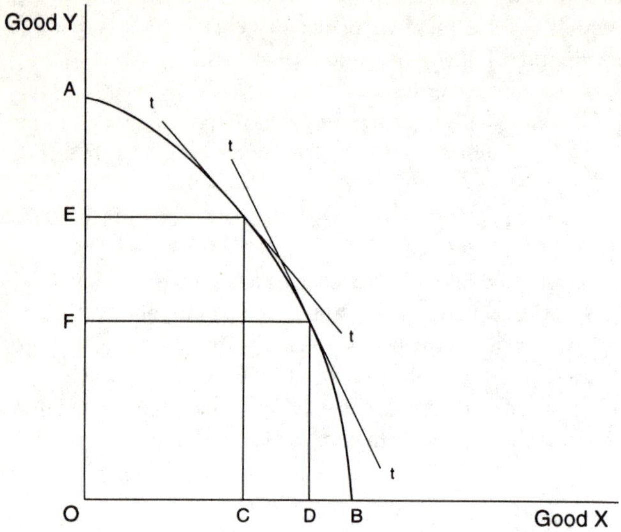

Figure 1.21

of X.

Two points on a Production Possibility Curve which are very close together will lie on a tangent drawn to the curve at a point.

The Transformation Curve

The Production Possibility Curve may also be defined as a Transformation Curve in the sense that in moving along it, the firm keeps its production costs constant and in effect transforms one product into the other. In the example illustrated, it will be noted that the transformation curve is consistently convex when seen from the origin, indicating that as the production of X progressively increases, the marginal rate of transformation (expressed by the slope of the curve at a point) is moving against the product augmented, and in favour of that relinquished. This is a plausible assumption in the case of goods which are not perfect substitutes in production.

It will be noted that every combination of outputs represented by a given Transformation Curve can be produced by the same total quantities of inputs. If the prices of the inputs are given, then each Transformation Curve can be viewed as a contour line on a function connecting costs to combinations of the quantities of the two outputs:

$$C = f(X,Y)$$

From this we can obtain the total differential

$$dC = \frac{\partial C}{\partial X} dX + \frac{\partial C}{\partial Y} dY$$

where the partial derivatives are the marginal costs of X and Y respectively.

Along the Transformation Curve costs are constant, i.e. dC = 0. Thus by re-arrangement:

$$\frac{dX}{dY} = -\frac{\frac{\partial C}{\partial X}}{\frac{\partial C}{\partial Y}}$$

Since the left-hand term is the MRT between X and Y we have obtained the further result that

$$MRT_{xy} = \frac{MC_x}{MC_y}$$

That is, the MRT equals the ratio of the marginal costs of the two outputs. This result will prove significant later in the argument.

The Iso-revenue Line

As drawn, the transformation curve only isolates a number of possible combinations of X and Y attainable for a given level of expenditure on the factors. To know the specific choice made, we need more information, e.g. with regard to the envisaged level of sales (a point not unconnected with a decision to purchase factors) and especially the price ratios of the two goods.

Given such knowledge, we can establish the iso-revenue line which indicates the possible organisation of sales of different combinations of quantities of the two outputs which will yield a given revenue, the prices of X and Y being known. When superimposed on the relevant transformation curve, we can establish a point of equilibrium where the iso-revenue line is just tangent to the transformation curve and where, therefore, the MRT of X for Y is equal to the price ratio of the two goods. Alternatively, we can say that in equilibrium the producer will choose a combination of products such that the prevailing price ratio is equal to the ratio of their marginal costs.

The equilibrium solution is illustrated in Figure 1.22. Here the line AB represents the transformation curve and the line CD the iso-revenue line. A point such as E where the iso-revenue line intersects a transformation curve is not a point of equilibrium since the firm can move down the iso-revenue line (keeping total receipts constant) thus attaining the same level of income while deploying a smaller factor-bundle. In the case shown the firm brings the MRT of X for Y to equality with the ratio of Px: Py, deciding to produce OF of X and OG of Y.

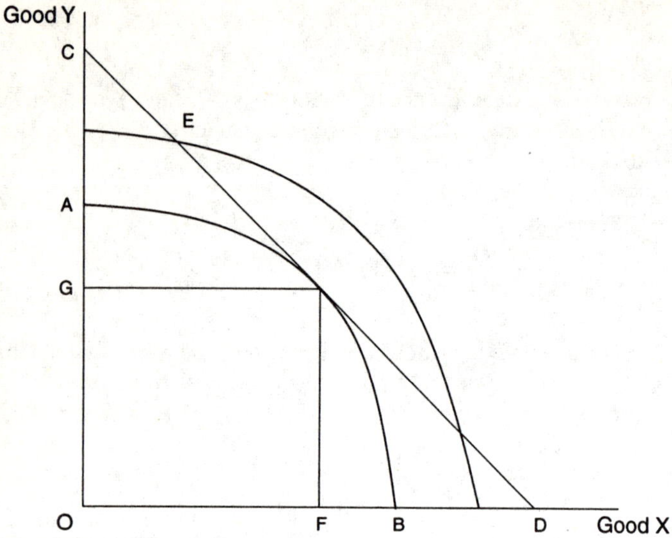

Figure 1.22

The argument can be extended to take account of changes in the position and shape of the transformation curve and of changes in the position and slope of the iso-revenue line.

Section C: General Interdependence

Efficiency Conditions

So far we have considered separately consumers who confront choices between two goods and producers who confront choices between two inputs in the production of a single good. It is evident that these decisions are potentially interrelated: consumers' choices of quantities of goods have implications for what producers can dispose of and thus for the level of employment of inputs; producers' choices of quantities of inputs have implications for the quantities of goods produced from which consumers may choose. More significant from this point of view are the applications of indifference curve analysis which follow in Chapter 2. For the moment we may state that through these applications we are able to appreciate that consumers not only choose to demand goods but also choose to supply inputs - precisely those inputs demanded by the producers in order that they, in turn, may supply goods demanded by the consumers. Thus when we contemplate not just the choices of isolated agents, be they consumers or producers, but also an entire system (albeit hypothetical) comprising numbers of such consumers and producers, a central characteristic of such a system is the general interdependence of choices made, whether by consumers or by producers.

In preceding sections we have shown what conditions need to be satisfied for the isolated agent to be in a position of equilibrium, and what consequences follow from any disturbance to the circumstances of an agent initially in a position of equilibrium. It is now necessary to set out the equilibrium conditions which apply to a complete system of interdependent agents. The simultaneous satisfaction of these conditions defines a Pareto-efficient state of the system, in which these interdependent decisions of consumers and producers are completely harmonised: quantities of goods chosen by consumers are precisely those which producers offer, and the quantities of inputs provided by consumers are precisely those required by producers to provide the same chosen quantities of goods. The system can then be said to be in general equilibrium. While these conditions are interesting in their own right, they also carry significant implications for subsequent parts of the argument. The conditions are first represented geometrically, and then mathematically.

From the geometric perspective there are four conditions required for a Pareto-efficient system.[2]

I. The Marginal Rate of Substitution for any pair of goods must be the same for all consumers of those goods

The need for this condition to be satisfied can be illustrated by examining a case where it is not met. Suppose our system consists of two individuals, G and R, and

2 The examples which follow are based in part upon G.B. Richardson, *Economic Theory* (1964), chapter 2.

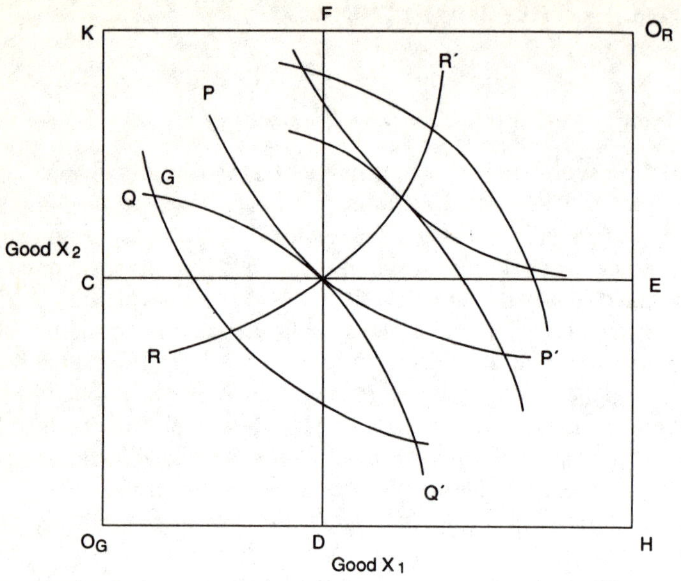

Figure 1.23

quantities of two goods X_1 and X_2. Suppose that G is prepared to give up one unit of X_1 for three of X_2, while R is prepared to give up one unit of X_1 for two of X_2 while remaining on the same level of satisfaction. In this case, if one unit of X_1 were taken from R and given to G, three units of X_2 would be released into the system. In such a situation it would be possible to compensate R for the loss of one unit of X_1 and to economise on X_2. Alternatively, we could say that by redistributing units of X_1 and X_2 between G and R, R could be made better off while G was left no worse off.

The case can be illustrated diagrammatically. Consider a two-consumer, two-good model, operating at a particular point in time. Let us assume there already exist particular stocks of goods X_1 and X_2 to be allocated between the two consumers G and R, noting in passing that we are abstracting, for the moment, from the process by which these stocks came into being. (The diagrammatic approach requires this independent or partial treatment of elements which in terms of the system as a whole are really interdependent; the focus for the moment falls on the interdependence between the two consumers, in that less allocated to one means that more is available for allocation to the other, at the expense of other forms of interdependence).

In Figure 1.23, we represent the total amount of X_1 (O_GH) and X_2 (O_GK) which is already available for distribution between two persons (G and R). We show G's indifference map viewed from the origin O_G, and R's indifference map viewed from the origin O_R. In effect we have taken two indifference maps and rotated one of them through 180 degrees in order to form a *box diagram*.

The equilibrium condition requires that the MRS for each consumer should be the same. In the example shown this occurs where the indifference curves PP' and QQ' are tangent: here G has OGC of X_2 and OGD of X_1, while R has ORE of X_2 and ORF of X_1.

There are a number of points worth noting on the basis of the argument so far:

1. There will not be a position of equilibrium or optimal efficiency where the indifference curves intersect. It will be evident from inspection that in this case it would be possible to make one individual better off while leaving the other at the same level of satisfaction.

2. There are many possible allocations which satisfy the condition and are therefore efficient. Collectively they form a locus termed a *Contract Curve* (RR'), the shape of which depends on the preferences of one consumer relative to those of the other. While any point on the Contract Curve is as efficient as any other, it will be obvious that movement from one efficient point to another will be in favour of one consumer but against the other. Movement along RR' towards the top right corner will favour G (a higher indifference curve being attainable) but at R's cost (a lower indifference curve being the limit to R's preferences); movement in the reverse direction would have the opposite effect. Thus efficiency in this context (i.e. an allocation being a point on rather than off of the Contract Curve) is independent of the particular distribution of the available quantities of the two goods between G and R (i.e. the allocation being one point rather than another on the Contract Curve) and of their relative preferences.

3. Subject to the above restrictions, it will be noted that the assumptions previously used when dealing with consumer equilibrium ensure that the results stated above will obtain. For example, it will be recalled that our consumers were held to face the same price ratios, i.e. price opportunity lines which have the same slope, and that in equilibrium the price ratio of the two goods must be equal to their marginal rate of substitution.

4. Note that the sum of the quantities of the two goods allocated to each consumer exactly equals the total available stocks of the two goods. There is neither a surplus unallocated, nor an unsatisfiable excess demand for one good or the other, or both. Neither would be compatible with the concept of efficient allocation. That the allocation between G and R does exhaust the available stocks is related to the point already made, namely that we have ignored for the moment the need to explain how these stocks came into being. A pointer in that direction is that evidently the stocks are precisely what can be purchased at the given prices with the combined budgets of the two consumers, budgets derived from the proceeds of supplying inputs to the producers of the goods themselves.

II. Our second condition requires that *the marginal rate of technical substitution between any two factors must be the same in the production of any commodity in which they both co-operate.*

Suppose the two goods X_1 and X_2 are both produced by combining the same two

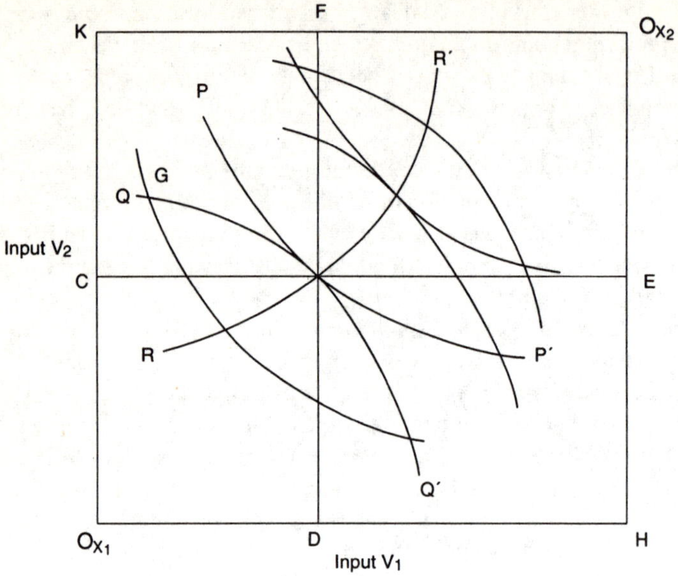

Figure 1.24

inputs, V_1 and V_2. Let us assume there already exist particular stocks of inputs V_1 and V_2 to be allocated between the production of X_1 and X_2. Suppose to start with that the marginal rates of technical substitution between V_1 and V_2 in the production of X_1 and X_2 are not equal; that the producer of X_1 could replace one unit of V_1 by three units of V_2 while still remaining on the same level of output, while the producer of X_2 could replace one unit of V_1 by two of V_2. Then if one unit of factor V_1 were taken from the production of X_2 and used to produce X_1, it would be possible to release three units of V_2 into the system, only two units of which are needed to allow the production of X_2 to remain at its current level. In short, it would be possible to economise on one unit of the input V_2.

Our efficiency condition therefore requires that the MRTS should be the same for the two producers. This can be illustrated in terms of Figure 1.24. Here X_1 and X_2 are the two goods, and PP' and QQ' refer to isoquants (rather than indifference curves). The quantities $O_{X1}H$ and $O_{X1}K$ refer to the available stocks of the inputs V_1 and V_2 which are to be distributed between production of the two goods.

In the position of equilibrium shown, good X_1 uses $O_{X1}D$ of V_1 and $O_{X1}C$ of V_2; good X_2 uses $O_{X2}E$ of V_2 and $O_{X2}F$ of V_1, and the MRTS is the same in the production of the goods in which they both co-operate. The parallel with the first condition is such that similar implications follow: equilibrium cannot exist where isoquants intersect since at any such point there are opportunities to increase the production of either good without reducing the production of the other, or indeed increase the production of both, with the available inputs; a *Contract Curve* (RR')

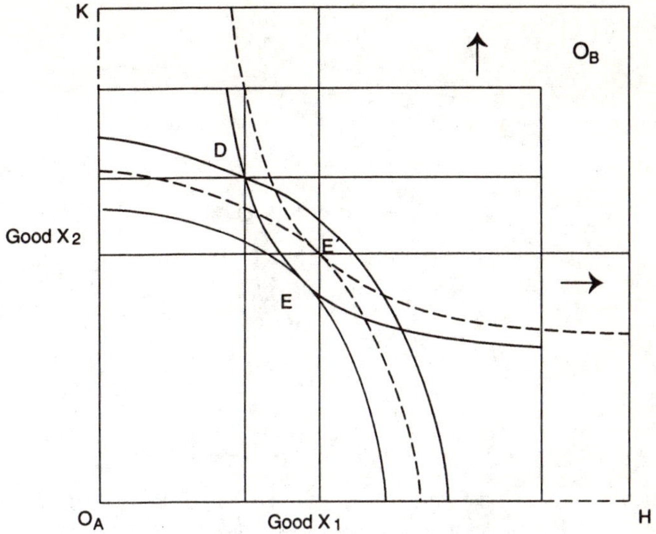

Figure 1.25

again exists, its characteristics being dependent on the relative technical possibilities concerning X_1 and X_2. The required condition will be satisfied if producers are price-takers with respect to the prices of V_1 and V_2, since they will then confront isocost lines with the same slopes; the allocation of V_1 and V_2 between the production of X_1 and X_2 is such that the available stocks are exhausted.

III. We may now state our third 'optimality' condition, which requires that: *the marginal rate of transformation of one commodity to another must be the same for all those who produce these goods.*

Suppose we have two producers A and B; that A can make two units of X_1 with factors released by forgoing one unit of X_2, and that B could make three units of X_1 with factors released by forgoing production of one unit of X_2. Under these circumstances it would pay to have A produce one more unit of X_2 (which B forgoes) leaving B to produce three units of X_1. This is illustrated in Figure 1.25, which shows the transformation curves confronting A and B. The equilibrium condition can be represented by a point where the transformation curves have a common tangent such as at E. This result will follow from our assumption that each producer was a price taker in dealing with the choice with regard to products; they therefore face the same price ratios and thus iso-revenue curves of identical slope. Accordingly their marginal rates of transformation will be equal through their response to the opportunities afforded by the price ratios.

IV. The final condition requires that: *the marginal rate of substitution of goods*

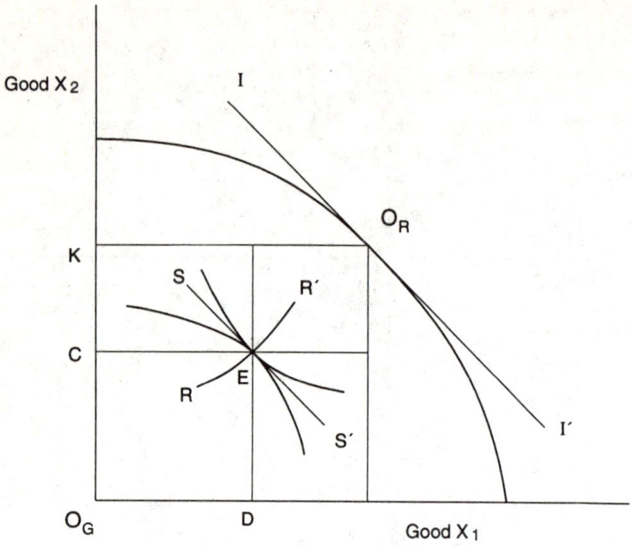

Figure 1.26

X and Y in consumption must be the same as their marginal rates of transformation in production.

To illustrate this case, suppose that consumer G could substitute two units of X_1 for one of X_2 without loss or gain, and that producers could efficiently substitute one unit of X_2 for three of X_1 without changing the total quantity of factors used. Then, if producers gave up the output of one unit of X_2 and produced three of X_1, consumer G could be compensated for the loss of one unit of X_2 with only two of the units of X_1 released into the system, i.e. we can economise on one unit of X_1.

Once again the necessary equilibrium condition can be illustrated graphically (Figure 1.26). Here a Transformation Curve assumed to incorporate the possibilities of efficient allocation of inputs between the producers concerned is combined with a box diagram constructed within the Curve in relation to a particular point on the curve at which it is tangential to a given iso-revenue line; that point then indicates the available (and efficiently produced) quantities of the two goods to be allocated between the two consumers. That point also signifies the origin of the indifference curves of one of the consumers, the other being the overall origin of the diagram. The box diagram corresponds in all respects to that employed in Figure 1.23. A Contract Curve constructed within the box diagram then shows all the efficient allocations of these given quantities of the two goods between the two consumers. Any such allocation at which the Marginal Rate of Substitution (given by the slope of the common tangent to the consumers' indifference curves) is equal to the Marginal Rate of Transformation (given by the slope of the iso-revenue curve) will satisfy this fourth condition. This is illustrated at point E in Figure 1.26. At that point II' is assumed to be parallel to SS'. At that point the particular combination of quantities of the two goods is both produced efficiently and allocated efficiently; the system as a whole is at equilibrium, with producers and consumers making mutually consistent decisions.

Once more the result will follow from the assumptions we have made: each consumer is assumed to face the same given price ratio for the two goods, and that this price ratio will be the same as that faced by producers. Both interdependent groups will respond in their own ways to the same set of opportunities thereby defined, the outcomes being a mutually consistent equilibrium.

We have now identified four conditions collectively necessary and sufficient to define a Pareto-efficient state of an hypothetical economic system, a state which is also a general equilibrium in relation to the preferences and the technical possibilities assumed to be given. Of importance to the subsequent argument is the association between the satisfaction of these conditions and a state in which:

1. All producers and all consumers face the same prices for each of the inputs and goods which they purchase and sell; and
2. The quantities of all inputs and goods supplied exactly equal the quantities of all inputs and goods demanded at these prices.

Satisfaction of these properties ensures equality of the relevant ratios at allocations of quantities of goods and inputs which exactly exhaust available supplies.

[*Note 1*: There are underlying complications which have to be exposed. One is a consequence of extending consideration to a world involving (at least) two producers. Despite the close parallel between the arguments supporting Conditions I and II there is a potential inconsistency which has to be resolved if we are to establish the possibility of harmonising the interdependent decisions taken by consumers and producers, an inconsistency which is not directly resolved by Condition III. The Contract Curve in Figure 1.23 shows all possible efficient allocations of *given* quantities of two *goods* between two consumers; the Contract Curve in Figure 1.24 similarly shows all possible efficient allocations of *given* quantities of two *inputs* between the production of two goods. However, movement along the latter Contract Curve involves *changing* quantities of the two goods; e.g. movement from bottom left to top right along RR' in Figure 1.24 involves increasing the production of X_1 and reducing the production of X_2. This is so even although the given quantities of the inputs used remain unchanged. It is evident that consistency requires more than efficiency: it requires not just the efficient production of *any* combination of quantities of the goods by the producers concerned, but the the efficient production of the *particular* combination shown being allocated efficiently between the two consumers in Figure 1.23. That is, in diagrammatic terms, the lengths of the sides of the box in Figure 1.23 have to be the same as those of the box in Figure 1.25. Now each producer acting individually within the constraint of given quantities of the two inputs can vary the combination of goods produced, moving along the corresponding Contract Curve and Transformation Curve. But the quantities of the two goods can also be varied by *redistributing the inputs between the producers*. Consequently, now there are two producers we have to consider whether inputs are allocated efficiently *between producers* of the same goods in addition to being allocated efficiently *by each producer individually*.

The consequences of redistribution of inputs can be examined with the aid of Figure 1.25, which shows the Transformation Curves of the two producers arranged in a box diagram format. If we initially assume each produces an arbitrary combination of quantities of the two goods then their Transformation Curves may be arranged around the resultant point, such as D. Since their marginal rates of transformation are not equal at D this is not an equilibrium. Following the procedure of the earlier analysis the attainment of equilibrium would seem to involve movement from D to E (where the Transformation Curves have a common tangent). Following the point just made this could involve transferring quantities of the two inputs from one producer (A) to the other (B). But each transfer of inputs generates a new Contract Curve for each individual producer (in terms of Figure 1.24) and for each new Contract Curve a new Transformation Curve. The box diagram in Figure 1.25 is thereby affected. The new Transformation Curve for the producer who loses inputs is closer to the relevant origin and that for the producer who gains inputs is further from the other origin. Since the consequences of the transfer of inputs between them differ in terms of changes in the quantities of the goods produced (their marginal rates of transformation initially assumed to be unequal), movement to the new equilibrium thus involves displacement of the origin of one of the producers (that is, B), and the attainment of a final equilibrium such as E'. This signifies, as anticipated in the preceding paragraph, that the overall quantities of the two goods produced have changed as a result of re-allocating the given quantities of the inputs between the two producers. The lengths of the sides of the box are thus not given from the outset but are the result of the process of re-allocating inputs between the two producers. The box diagram in Figure 1.25 differs conceptually from the others in that the lengths of its sides are a *consequence* of the decisions of the two producers, not a given feature of the circumstances confronting them. Their decisions determine the particular combination of quantities of the two goods to be produced, and a relevant factor in these decisions is the quantities of inputs which are available to each of them. While any point on an individual Transformation Curve denotes the efficient exhaustion of the particular input combination underlying it, only a point of mutual tangency will indicate an efficient combination of quantities of the two goods in the two distinct senses of efficiently deploying the total available quantities of the inputs *and* exhausting the opportunities to maximise (in some sense) the production of the two goods by re-allocation of the inputs between the two producers.

Where each producer operates within the constraint of given quantities of the inputs, movement from a point like D towards equilibrium, and the satisfaction of Condition III, merely involves the given Transformation Curve of one producer sliding round the given curve of the other producer to attain a position of mutual tangency with. This would be an interpretation of both producers reacting to the same given price ratio; their marginal rates of transformation will indeed be equal through their response to the opportunities open to them. Where this constraint is relaxed and the inputs can be redistributed between them, it will follow that there will be many points at which this condition will be satisfied, in the form of an equivalent to a Contract Curve within Figure 1.25. But of relevance to the matter of consistent decision-making is the requirement already mentioned, that the box formed around the equilibrium combination of quantities of the two goods has the dimensions corresponding to those of the box in Figure 1.23: the quantities produced are the same quantities as those allocated between the consumers.

Note 2: There is a further complication. Underlying our present specification of the Pareto-efficient system is the assumption that there already exist given quantities of the two inputs which the producers will choose employ, alhough we have noted already the possibilities for redistribution of these quantities between the producers concerned. Yet at the outset we noted that the interdependence between consumers and producers involved not only the former choosing quantities of goods produced by the latter, but also the former choosing to supply quantities of inputs employed by the latter. Properly, then, the quantities of inputs available should not be assumed given but should be explained in terms of consumer choice, terms similar to those used in connection with the choice of quantities of goods.

This matter concerns a feature of Figure 1.26. At point E II' is parallel to SS', signifying that at that point the Marginal Rate of Substitution is equal to the Marginal Rate of Transformation, since both equal the prevailing ratio of the prices of the two goods. However, there is no guarantee that in relation to any given point on any such Transformation Curve a point like E exists; nothing has been assumed so far to ensure that somewhere along the length of the Contract Curve there will be a common tangent to the indifference curves which has a slope equal to that of the given iso-revenue curve at the point which presently forms the top right-hand corner of the box diagram. Nor can it be assumed that a change in the relative price ratio - which would then select a new point on the given Transformation Curve and generate a new box diagram - would of itself be sufficient to create such a point. However, it can be accepted that if no such point initially exists then the system is not yet in equilibrium in relation to all the opportunities which confront the agents; moreover it can be surmised that in the subsequent movements towards equilibrium the Transformation Curve itself could change its shape, as well as the price ratio changing. Now given that this Transformation Curve already represents efficient allocations of *given* quantities of inputs between producers, any change in the curve itself must come from changes in the total available quantities of the two inputs (rather than further reallocations between the producers). It seems reasonable to argue that if inputs are supplied by the consumers themselves then substitution possibilities between goods and inputs are relevant to the explanation of the quantities of inputs available to producers; in turn, the ratio between the price of a good and the price of an input should enter into the specification of the efficiency conditions of such a system. If that is so, the absence of a relevant overall equilibrium point from a diagram such as Figure 1.26 signifies scope for further substitutions between goods and inputs, and further adjustments in relative prices. Together these ensure that the quantities of inputs supplied by the consumers change. Consequently, the Transformation Curve - as well as the ratio of the prices of the goods, and implicitly of goods to inputs - changes in such a way that an overall equilibrium (a point such as E) does come into being. The formal derivation of this aspect of the equilibrium solution has to await its mathematical representation, since there are too many variables for diagrammatic treatment.

[A Mathematical Statement of the Conditions

The principal advantage of a mathematical approach over the diagrammatic approach is that it can cope with the number of variables necessary to deal not only with the problem just described, but also with the generalisation of the hypothetical system beyond a model comprising two consumers, two producers, two goods and two inputs to one comprising an unspecified but potentially very large number of agents, goods and inputs. It is also possible to dispense with the distinction between the two classes of agents (consumers and producers) by replacing producers as choosing agents with a very general relationship which summarises the technical possibilities of transforming inputs into goods. Thus only consumers remain, and the need to consider a number of complex issues regarding the nature and behaviour of producers or firms can be sidestepped.

Consider an hypothetical economic system comprising *s* consumers. Each has a utility function of the following specification:

$$U^g = U^g(x_i^g; v_j^g) \text{ for all } g = 1,\dots, s; \text{ all } i = 1,\dots, n \text{ and all } j = 1,\dots, m$$

where the arguments (in brackets) are the amounts of the *i*-th good and j-th input chosen by the *g*-th consumer. There exist *n* goods and *m* inputs. The production possibilities of the system, governing the transformation of inputs into goods can be summarised in an implicit transformation function, as an alternative to making numerous explicit assumptions about the ways in which individual inputs and outputs are related:

$$T(X_1, \dots, X_n; V_1, \dots, V_m) = 0.$$

The aggregate quantities of inputs and goods which appear in the transformation function are related to the quantities which appear in individual consumers' utility functions via the following sums:

$$\sum_{g=1}^{s} x_i^g = X_i \text{ for } g = 1,\ldots, s; \text{ all } i = 1,\ldots n$$

$$\sum_{g=1}^{s} v_j^g = V_j \text{ for } g = 1,\ldots, s; \text{ all } j = 1,\ldots m$$

Given these features it is now necessary to establish the implications of allowing one individual to attain maximum preference subject to the technical possibilities confronting the system. There is, however, one further consideration: it is apparent that one individual can always attain a higher level of preference at the expense of another or indeed all other individuals. For example, returning to Figure 1.23 it is apparent that one individual attains the highest level of preference if the other individual has no share at all of the available quantities of the two goods. i.e. the points at the bottom left and top right of the box diagram. However, we are interested here not in the distribution of the available quantities of goods among individuals but the efficiency of any given distribution - in diagrammatic terms not in movement along the Contract Curve but in movement from off of the Curve to a position on it. Consequently we need to limit the improvements in one individuals' preferences to those attainable by improvements in efficiency, not reductions in others' preferences. So we need to build in the constraint that others' preferences are set at given levels. That is,

$$U^r(x_i^r;v_j^r) = U^{r0} \text{ for } r = 1,\ldots, s, r \neq g$$

In other words the value of the utility functions of all individuals other than g (which is what *r* signifies) is held constant. Given all these features of the model the Lagrangean Expression becomes:

$$L = U^g(x_i^g;v_j^g) + \sum_{r=1}^{s}\lambda_r[U^r(x_i^r;v_j^r) - U^{r0}] + \sum_{i=1}^{n}\theta_i[(x_i^1 + \ldots + x_i^s) - X_i]$$

$$+ \sum_{j=1}^{m}\rho_j[(v_j^1 + \ldots + x_j^s - V_j] + \pi[T(X_i,V_j)]$$

Note that this Lagrangean incorporates (s – 1) + n + m + 1 constraints, and so requires the same number of Lagrangean Multipliers: $\lambda_r + \theta_i + \rho_j + \pi$.

The next step is to differentiate the Lagrangean partially with respect to the quantities of goods and inputs, and set the derivatives equal to zero:

$$\frac{\partial L}{\partial x_i^g} = \frac{\partial U^g}{\partial x_i^g} + \theta_i = 0$$

$$\frac{\partial L}{\partial v_j^g} = \frac{\partial U^g}{\partial v_j^g} + \rho_j = 0$$

$$\frac{\partial L}{\partial x_i^r} = \lambda_r \frac{\partial U^r}{\partial x_i^r} + \theta_i = 0$$

$$\frac{\partial L}{\partial v_j^r} = \lambda_r \frac{\partial U^r}{\partial v_j^r} + \rho_j = 0$$

$$\frac{\partial L}{\partial X_i} = -\theta_i + \pi \frac{\partial T}{\partial X_i} = 0$$

$$\frac{\partial L}{\partial V_j} = -\rho_j + \pi \frac{\partial T}{\partial V_j} = 0$$

Manipulating these for pairs of goods (say h and i) and pairs of inputs (say j and k) we can obtain

$$\frac{\dfrac{\partial U^g}{\partial x_i^g}}{\dfrac{\partial U^g}{\partial x_h^g}} = \frac{\dfrac{\partial U^r}{\partial x_i^r}}{\dfrac{\partial U^r}{\partial x_h^r}} = \frac{\dfrac{\partial T}{\partial X_i}}{\dfrac{\partial T}{\partial X_h}} \quad \text{and}$$

$$\frac{\dfrac{\partial U^g}{\partial v_j^g}}{\dfrac{\partial U^g}{\partial v_k^g}} = \frac{\dfrac{\partial U^r}{\partial v_j^r}}{\dfrac{\partial U^r}{\partial v_k^r}} = \frac{\dfrac{\partial T}{\partial V_j}}{\dfrac{\partial T}{\partial V_k}} \quad \text{and}$$

$$\frac{\dfrac{\partial U^g}{\partial x_i^g}}{\dfrac{\partial U^g}{\partial v_j^g}} = \frac{\dfrac{\partial U^r}{\partial x_i^r}}{\dfrac{\partial U^r}{\partial v_j^r}} = \frac{\dfrac{\partial T}{\partial X_i}}{\dfrac{\partial T}{\partial V_j}}$$

The left-hand and middle terms are marginal rates of substitution; the others are marginal rates of transformation between goods or between goods and inputs, and a marginal rate of technical substitution. Thus:

$$MRS^g_{ih} = MRS^r_{ih} = MRT_{ih} \quad \text{and}$$
$$MRS^g_{jk} = MRS^r_{jk} = MRTS_{jk} \quad \text{and}$$
$$MRS^g_{ij} = MRS^r_{ij} = MRTS_{ij}$$

Satisfaction of these conditions signifies the existence of a Pareto efficient state of the hypothetical economic system (assuming the second-order conditions have also been satisfied). Note that given the way in which the model has been specified substitution possibilities between goods and inputs have been addressed, thus dealing with the final aspect of interdependence of the economic system.

At this point it is instructive to recall that these various marginal rates have been defined earlier in specific ways, which have a significance for later stages of the argument. The Marginal Rates of Substitution between two goods are ratios of marginal utilities of the goods in question (see page 8), the Marginal Rates of Technical Substitution relate the marginal physical products of pairs of inputs in a similar way (see page 26) while the Marginal Rates of Transformation between two goods are the same thing as the ratios of their marginal costs (see page 33). Recall also that equilibrium for each individual agent involves equality between these marginal rates and the corresponding ratios of prices, while Pareto efficiency for the system as a whole requires equality of these marginal rates for all agents. When these conclusions are combined it follows that

$$\frac{MU_{Xi}}{MU_{Xh}} = \frac{P_{Xi}}{P_{Xh}} = \frac{MC_{Xi}}{MC_{Xh}} \quad \text{and}$$

$$\frac{MU_{Vj}}{MU_{Vk}} = \frac{P_{Vj}}{P_{Vk}} = \frac{MPP_{Vj}}{MPP_{Vk}}$$

From the first of these comes the conclusion that Pareto efficiency involves equality between prices of goods and their marginal costs, as well as marginal utilities being in the same ratio as that of marginal costs; from the second comes the conclusion that it also involves marginal (dis)utilities from the provision of inputs being in the same ratios as their marginal products. Moreover it also involves the inputs being paid their marginal products (which becomes evident if the numerator and denominator of the ratio of the marginal products are each multiplied by the given price of a good in which the particular inputs are incorporated). These conclusions will provide a useful link with the argument of the following chapter, where the focus falls on the process yielding equilibrium of resource allocation, rather than the state of equilibrium in itself.]

Chapter 2

The Marshallian Functions

Section A: The Consumer: The Demand for Commodities and the Supply of Services

The argument so far has identified conditions which, if they are satisfied, permit us to say that our hypothetical system of consumers and producers is in an optimal state. However, the argument has not yet examined the processes necessary for the achievement of such a state; processes which, by their operation, will ensure that these conditions will hold, and that resources will be allocated and employed efficiently.

As the discussion proceeds it will become apparent that we are essentially looking at the same issues from a different vantage point, namely the Marshallian position; and that while the perspective may be quite different the substance of the view is essentially the same. As a first stage in this appreciation we show the way in which the functional relationships relevant to our present purpose may be derived from the previous argument. It will be convenient to begin with the analysis of consumer behaviour.

I. Demand as a Function of Price

When W.S. Jevons published his *Theory of Political Economy* in 1871, he believed that the theory of consumption had been neglected, and indeed Alfred Marshall made the same complaint nearly two decades later. Jevons believed that: 'Economics must be founded on a full and accurate investigation of the conditions of utility; and, to understand this element, we must necessarily examine the wants and desires of mankind' (Jevons 1871:45).

In order to illustrate the point at issue Jevons plotted units of a commodity on the (horizontal) x-axis and erected a series of rectangles, each of which may be assumed to represent the satisfaction which accrues from the possession of each unit, where satisfaction is 'measured' on the (vertical) y-axis (Figure 2.1)

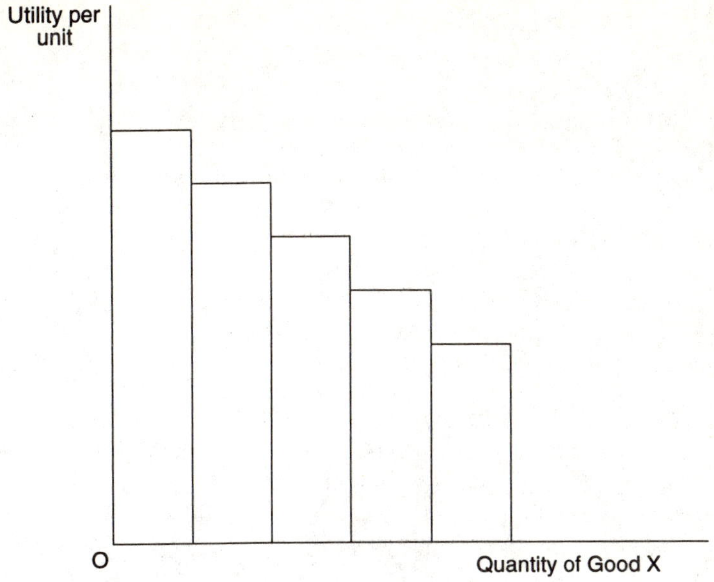

Figure 2.1

Total utility is expressed in terms of the sum of the rectangles, while marginal utility expresses the addition to total utility which accrues from the possession of the final unit making up a particular quantity. Three points follow:

1. If the commodity is highly divisible, the tops of successive rectangles will in effect form a smooth continuous curve.
2. It was suggested that a curve which expresses utility per unit will fall within a category of shapes:

   'We may state as a general law, that the degree of utility varies with the quantity of the commodity, and ultimately decreases as that quantity increases' (*ibid.*:53). This is shown in Figure 2.2.
3. It follows that the curve which expresses utility per unit must determine the shape of the demand curve for a commodity since it is reasonable to infer that the consumer acting rationally will be prepared to pay a particular price only if the utility expected from the acquisition of the marginal unit justifies the expenditure involved (Figure 2.3).

This was the procedure followed by Alfred Marshall in explaining the demand curve for a commodity, such as tea, where he related quantities taken to prices paid in a way which suggests that the shape of the demand curve must reflect the content of the Law of Diminishing Marginal Utility. Marshall added that since a particular quantity is associated with a particular price, the decision to acquire that quantity must imply that there is a relationship between the last (marginal) unit which is taken and the price paid. For example, if 6lbs of tea are taken at a price

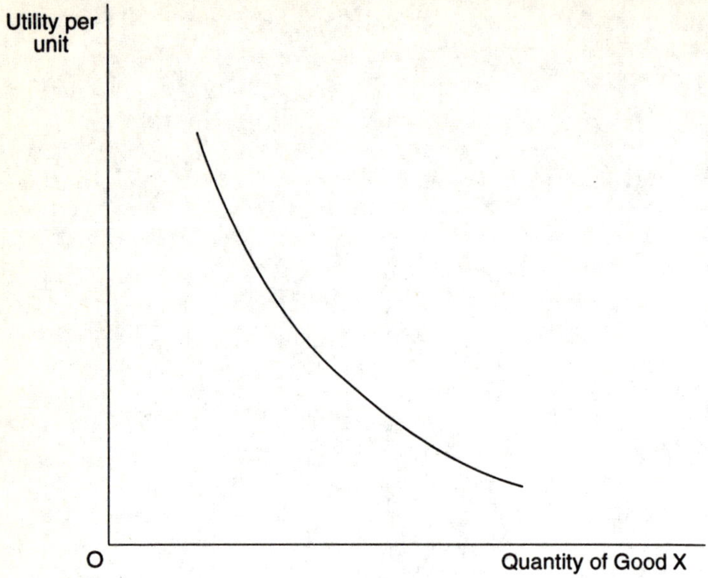

Figure 2.2

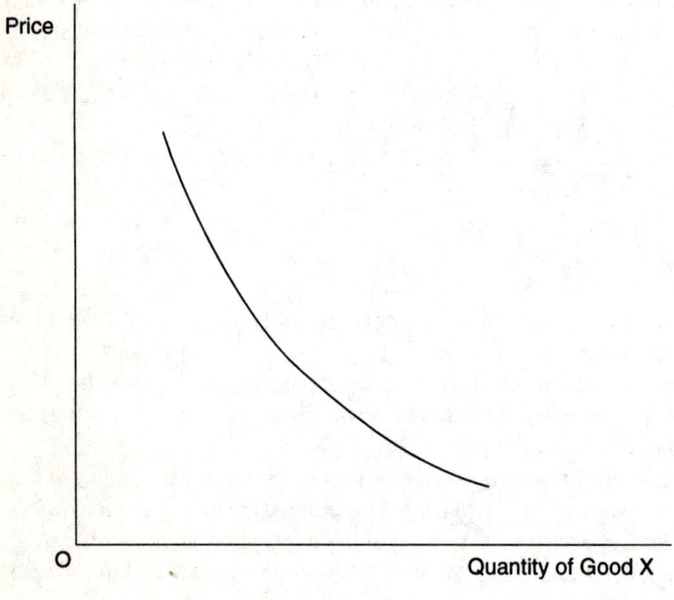

Figure 2.3

of 50p, 7lbs at 40p, 8lbs at 30p and 9lbs at 28p, then the utility expected from the acquisition of the seventh pound (and subsequent pounds) must justify the price paid. Marshall also noted that if we take a series of prices and quantities then the price actually paid when taking 9 units at 28p means that in taking this quantity the consumer is actually paying less per unit than he would have been prepared to pay for the seventh, eighth and ninth units taken separately - a gain which Marshall described as 'consumer's surplus' (Marshall 1890: chapter 6).

Marshall added that the demand curve would be stable only when satisfaction expected equalled satisfaction obtained; when tastes remained constant; when there were no changes in the prices of competing goods (e.g. in this case coffee); and when the marginal utility of money remains the same.

We can now assess the extent to which we require to modify or amplify our understanding of the demand relationship as a result of the indifference curve approach reviewed in the preceding sections. Recall that the indifference curve gives us information as to the consumer's preferences, while the price opportunity line summarises the objective constraints which confront the consumer.

One modification can now be introduced: units of income are now shown on the *y*-axis in Figure 2.4, so that the indifference curve shows the various combinations of quantities of good X and income – the power to purchase any other goods and services - which will provide the consumer with the same level of satisfaction. The price opportunity line, whose slope is now determined by the price of good X, tells

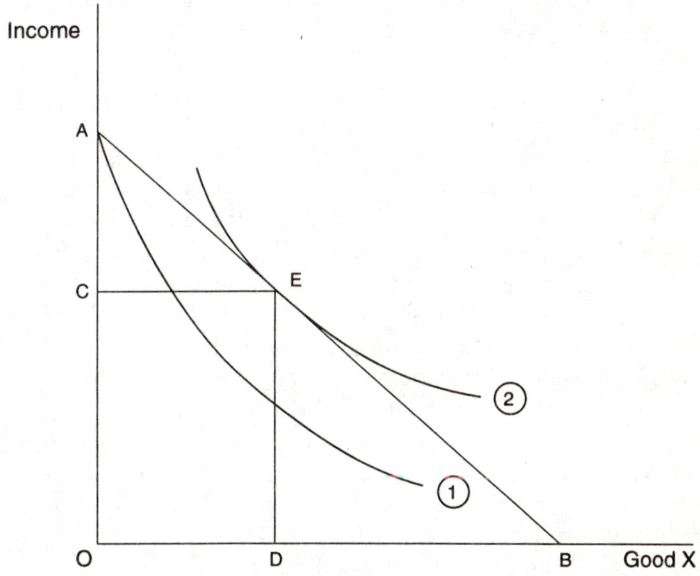

Figure 2.4

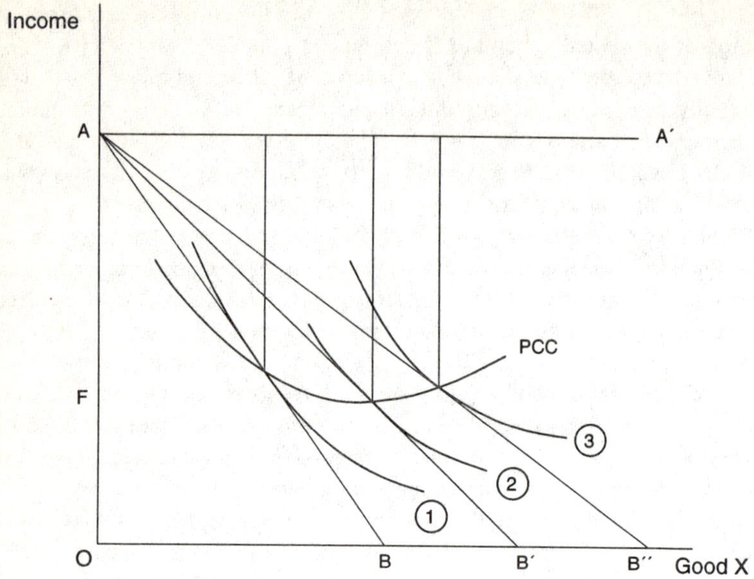

Figure 2.5

us that the consumer may, at one extreme, retain all the income for other purposes, spend it all on the good X, or adopt some intermediate course by moving along AB. Equilibrium will be attained in the already-established manner at E. In this position the consumer spends AC units of income in purchasing OD units of X, retaining OC units of income for other purchases.

In terms of the previous discussion, it will be recalled that the Price Consumption Curve was the locus of equilibrium positions generated in relation to variations in the price of one of the two goods then being considered. In the present context, where income has replaced one of the goods, points on such a locus arising from variation in the price of good X represent combinations of levels of income and quantities of good X, looking at the situation from the normal origin O. But as the consumer's income is given, expenditure on good X plus what is allocated to other unspecified uses must always sum to that income. So if we look at the situation from the point A rather than from the origin, the distance from A to another point on the y-axis will represent the level of total expenditure on the good X. The price consumption curve becomes a total expenditure path as a consequence of viewing the diagram from the point A rather than from the origin. We can observe that total expenditure on good X increases over a certain range as price falls, reaches a maximum, and thereafter declines. This is represented more clearly in Figure 2.5.

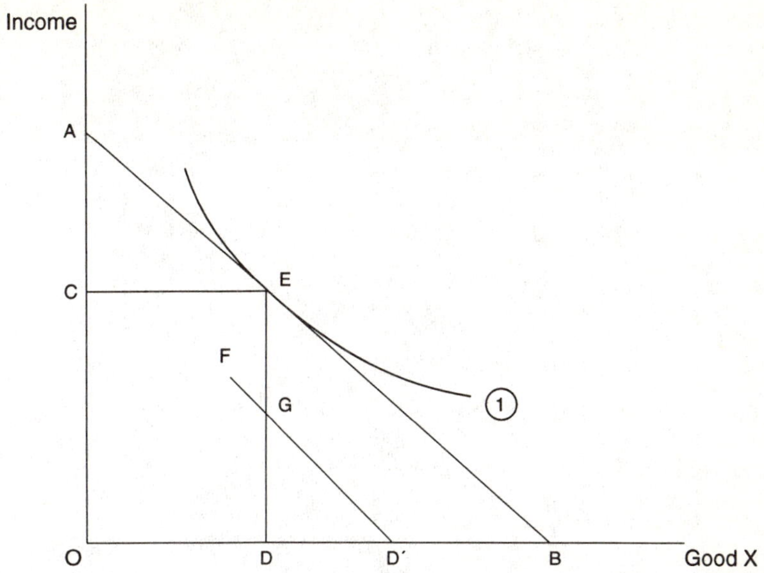

Figure 2.6

The Demand Curve

The total expenditure curve contains the information necessary to derive the demand curve, since various expenditures at various prices are paired with various quantities of the good X.

Consider the point E on the price consumption curve in Figure 2.6. At the given price of good X represented by the slope of AB the consumer purchases OD units of X, spending AC units of income.

Mark off to the right of D a distance DD´ to represent one unit of X. From D´ draw D´F parallel to AB to meet DE, the vertical from D, at G. The distance of DG now represents expenditure on one unit of good X, that is, the price of good X. Point G is therefore a point on the demand curve for good X appropriate to this particular consumer. Every point on the price consumption curve can be similarly treated yielding a smooth demand curve, shown in this instance to be downward-sloping (dd in Figure 2.7).

The shape of the demand curve is determined by the shape of the price consumption curve from which it is derived and of course this in turn depends on the preferences of the consumer, represented by variation in the size of the income and substitution effects. This can be illustrated in terms of the distinction between 'normal', 'inferior' and 'Giffen' goods considered in Chapter 1. There we observed that due to variations in the relative magnitude and sign of the two effects, the quantity consumed might increase, remain the same, or even decrease,

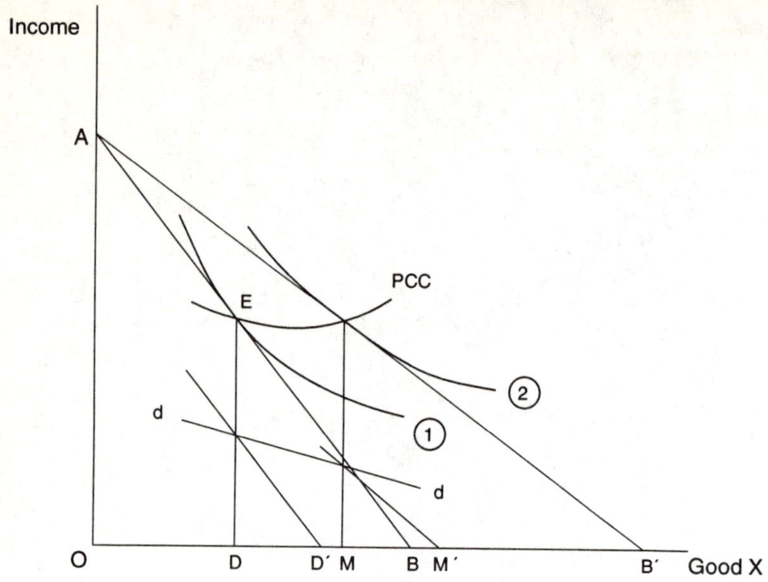

Figure 2.7

in the face of a reduction in its price. These possibilities involved different shapes of price consumption curves, and consequently different shapes of demand curves: downward sloping in the case of 'normal' and 'inferior' goods (except where the two effects cancel out yielding a vertical demand curve), and backward-sloping in the case of the 'Giffen' good (Figures 2.8(a) and 2.8(b)).

In Figure 2.8(a), the first price-opportunity line is AB; the second, corresponding to a lower price of X is AB´. Draw FF´ parallel to AB´ to meet indifference curve (1) at the point II. This isolates the substitution effect (DE which is always positive). Given the assumption of no net change in the quantity taken despite a reduction in price, this indicates that the negative income effect (ED) exactly counterbalances the positive substitution effect (DE).

We may now establish points on the demand curve. In Figure 2.8(a) the first price level is represented by the slope of the line AB. Drop a perpendicular from the point of tangency at I to meet the *x*-axis at D. Mark off to the right of D a distance DD´ to represent one unit of the commodity X. Draw D´G to meet the perpendicular at H, thus establishing the first point on the curve. The second price level is represented by the slope of the line AB´ and the second point of tangency is vertically above the first. We then draw the line D´K parallel to AB´ to meet the perpendicular at L, thus establishing a second point on the demand curve which is directly below the first.

In Figure 2.8(b) the process is repeated save that in this case the second point on the demand curve will be established below and to the left of the first while the

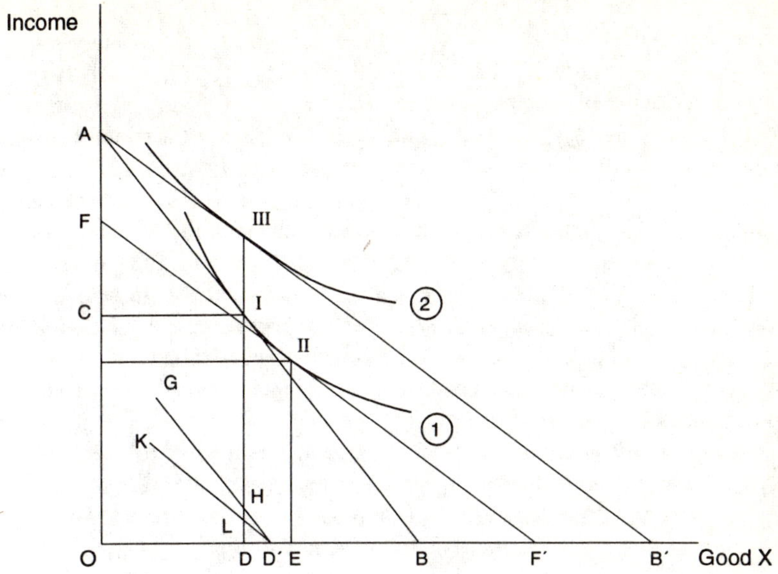

Figure 2.8(a)

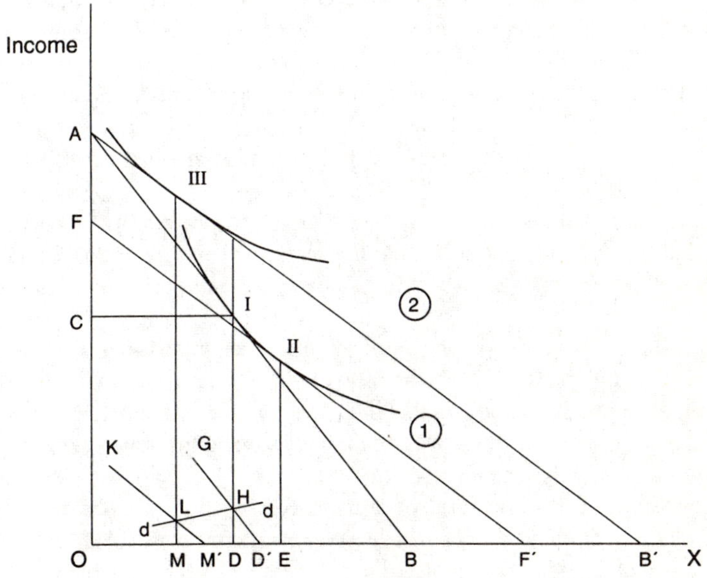

Figure 2.8(b)

demand curve is represented by the distance HL.

While the shape of the demand curve follows from the relative importance of the income and substitution effects, its position will be stable provided there is no change in the level of income, no change in the prices of other goods, and no change in tastes. The last point is especially interesting since the structure of tastes determines the shape of the indifference map. A change in tastes and preferences will therefore be reflected in a change in the indifference map, and a consequential alteration in the position and perhaps also the shape of the demand curve.

It will be noted that the argument just considered explains the nature of individual points on the demand curve (since at each such point the marginal significance of the last unit purchased equals the price paid), the pattern into which such points fall, and also indicates that the curve will be stable under identifiable conditions (such as given and stable preferences). It is therefore natural to ask whether or not the derivation of the demand curve from the PCC has any advantages over the alternative argument stated at the outset of this section, especially since we appear to have merely re-stated results which were there expressed in a simpler form. However, even if the approach does have the disadvantage of relative complexity, its advantages more than compensate.

Advantages of the Indifference Curve Approach

First, we recall that no assumptions are needed about the measurability or other attributes of utility – we express levels of preference in ordinal (rather than in cardinal) terms. Second, we can substitute a more general relationship for the Law of Diminishing Utility which involves looking at two or more goods simultaneously in terms of their relative attractiveness. (Mathematically it is the *ratio* of the marginal utilities of each pair of goods, rather than the absolute value of each, which becomes important). Third, the argument has a number of important technical advantages:

(a) it establishes that movement along the Price Consumption Curve involves logically separate income and substitution effects; it therefore follows that the same effects must be involved in moving along a demand curve – an important clarification;

(b) since the indifference curve approach helps us to distinguish between income and substitution effects it also helps to clarify the terms 'normal', 'inferior' and 'Giffen' as applied to goods. It also indicates that these distinctions relate to the particular structures of preferences embodied in the indifference maps, rather than the qualities of the goods themselves;

(c) for the same reason the form of argument clarifies those concepts which involve comparison of points on a demand curve. If we define elasticity as a measure of response to a change in price depicted in a demand curve, then given the interaction of the income and substitution effects, it follows that price elasticity must be the resultant of the elasticity of substitution and of income elasticity.

Thus in general:

$$e = f(ei, es)$$

In particular, price elasticity may be given as follows:

$$e = KX.\,ei + (1 - KX)\,es,$$

where e = price elasticity;
ei = income elasticity;
es = elasticity of substitution; and
KX = proportion of consumer's income spent on the good X[1].

[Notes on Elasticity

It is evident that in measuring elasticity we take account of the extent to which the consumer purchases different quantities as a result of a change in price. We are then concerned to examine a proportion or a rate of change, so that elasticity may be given by:

$$e = \frac{\text{proportionate change in amount demanded}}{\text{proportionate change in price}}$$

$$= \frac{\text{change in amount demanded}}{\text{amount demanded}} \div \frac{\text{change in price}}{\text{price}}$$

Symbolically, with dq and dp representing the respective changes in quantity and price:

$$e = \frac{dq}{q} \div \frac{dp}{p} = \frac{dq}{q} \cdot \frac{p}{dp}$$

In terms of Figure 2.9, the latter may be expressed:

$$\frac{dq}{q} \cdot \frac{p}{dp} = \frac{RH}{DR} \cdot \frac{AN}{RN} = \frac{AB}{OA} \cdot \frac{OC}{DC}$$

We can discover elasticity at a point N by drawing TNV tangent to the demand curve at this point and measuring the ratio NV/NT (Figure 2.10). Take the point N and another point on the tangent TV in Figure 2.10 and represent them as N and H in Figure 2.11.

1. This statement is taken from A.W. Stonier and D.C. Hague. *A Textbook of Economic Theory*, Longmans, London, 1953, p. 75.

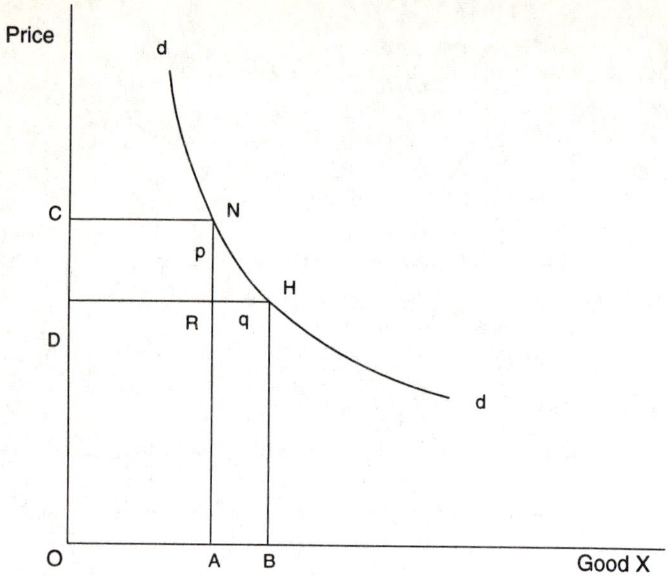

Figure 2.9

$$e = \frac{dq}{q} \cdot \frac{p}{dp} = \frac{AB}{OA} \cdot \frac{OC}{DC} = \frac{RH}{OA} \cdot \frac{AN}{RN} = \frac{RH}{RN} \cdot \frac{ON}{OA}$$

In Figure 2.11 triangles NRH and NAV are similar, therefore:

$$e = \frac{AV}{AN} \cdot \frac{AV}{OA} = \frac{AV}{OA} = \frac{AV}{CN}$$

That is, at the point N e equals the ratio between the two segments into which OV is divided by a perpendicular from N. Since triangles NAV and CNT are similar:

$$\frac{AV}{CN} = \frac{VN}{NT}$$

Elasticity is then given by the ratio between VN and NT where N is any point on the DD curve.

Note that the choice of a point on a given DD curve will determine both the slope of the line TV (the tangent to the curve) and the relevant ratios (see Figure 2.10); that is, the elasticity depends on the point chosen. In general no DD curve will have a single elasticity throughout its length, even if it is a straight line sloping down from left to right. However, there are exceptions: a demand curve which is a rectangular hyperbola, or a vertical or horizontal straight line.[2]

2. The above argument is drawn from E. Fossati, *The Theory of General Static Equilibrium*, ed. G.L.S. Shackle, Oxford, Blackwell,1957, pp. 88-92.

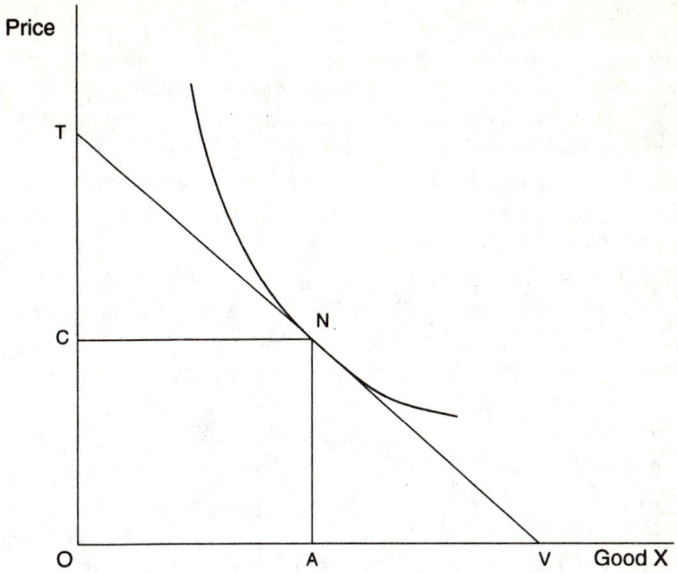

Figure 2.10

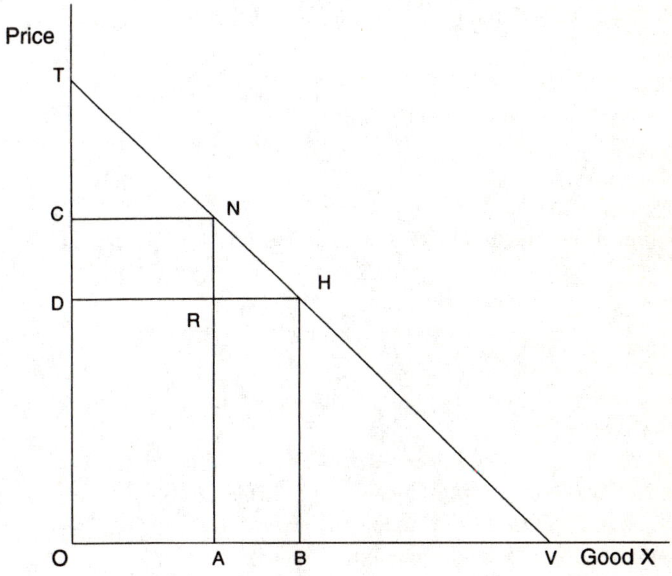

Figure 2.11

Arc Elasticity

The conclusion that the value of price elasticity of demand varies continuously along the length of demand functions (except in the special cases just referred to) is important. If, for example, our only information is two combinations of values of price and quantity which are 'far apart' (such as A and B in Figure 2.12), then it is evident that such points could lie on one of any number of curves passing through these points. It then follows that not only do the values of the elasticities at A and B differ because they are indeed different points on any given curve, but also the values differ according to which curve is considered. Without knowledge of the entire curve the values of elasticity at A and B are inaccessible. If we nonetheless use these discrete differences in values of price and quantity in the formula for elasticity - thus computing what is known as arc elasticity - we are in effect presuming that A and B lie on a straight-line demand curve (dd' in Figure 2.12). We then face the choice of evaluating arc elasticity in relation to a movement from A to B, (i.e. a fall in price) or in relation to a movement from B to A, (i.e. a price rise); these measures differ. That the value of price elasticity of demand should depend on the direction of change of price is an additional complication, on top of the possibility that neither is a 'true' measure given that the demand curve may not be linear.

In a case where we only have information about two combinations of price and quantity we can find an approximate measure of point elasticity which is equivalent to drawing a straight line between the two combinations and calculating elasticity midway between them. Arc elasticity in this respect may be given as:

$$\eta = \frac{q_0 - q_1}{q_0 + q_1} \cdot \frac{p_0 + p_1}{p_0 - p_1}$$

where p_0 and q_0 are the first price and quantity and p_1 and q_1 are the second price and quantity.[3]

The Mathematics of Elasticity

The complications surrounding arc elasticity arise from it having been defined in respect of discrete (or 'large') changes in price and quantity. In the mathematical treatment, employing calculus, elasticities are re-defined in terms of incremental change in the variables, represented by the differentials ∂Px, ∂Py, ∂R and ∂Q. Otherwise the concepts are the same. However, the results can be obtained very conveniently through the use of calculus.

3. This illustration is taken from G.J. Stigler, *The Theory of Price*, New York, Macmillan, 1952, p.350.

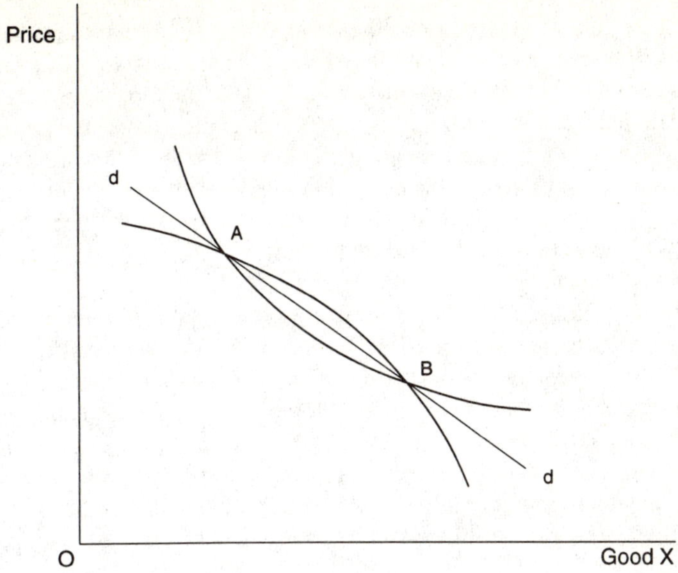

Figure 2.12

Given that the quantity demanded of a good is a function of its own price, the price of the other good and the available budget, this can be represented as

$$Qx = Q(Px, Py, R)$$

Given the presence of three independent variables we can define three elasticities:

Own Price Elasticity of Qx: $$\varepsilon_{XX} = \frac{\partial Qx}{\partial Px} \frac{Px}{Qx}$$

Cross Price Elasticity of Qx: $$\varepsilon_{XY} = \frac{\partial Qx}{\partial Py} \frac{Py}{Qx}$$

Income Elasticity of Qx: $$\varepsilon_{XR} = \frac{\partial Qx}{\partial R} \frac{R}{Qx}$$

The own price elasticity is evidently the product of the slope of the own-price demand function and the slope of the ray from the origin in Qx, Px space to the point on the function at which elasticity is evaluated:

$$\left(\frac{\partial Qx}{\partial Px}\right) \left(\frac{Px}{Qx}\right)$$

If, however, the function is linear the first term will be a constant; the value of the elasticity will then depend solely on the value of the second term. But variation in the slope of the ray from the origin to a point on the function simply means that, in diagrammatic terms, the point in question is sliding along the demand function. The elasticity therefore changes along the length of the linear demand curve. Moreover, as movement of the point along the demand curve controls the ratio of the lengths of the two parts into which the point divides the linear function, it follows that the elasticity is related to this ratio - precisely what was established previously through the use of geometry.

There will exist similar elasticities in respect to the quantity demanded of Y. The two cross price elasticities (one for Qx, the other for Qy) recall that the demands for the two goods are related to each other, which suggests that there will exist relationships among these elasticities. Moreover, links are also suggested with the Slutsky equation (given that it formally breaks the price effect on quantity demanded into a substitution effect and an income effect), and with a measure of the manner in which quantities of one good are substituted for quantities of the other, as relative prices change - the elasticity of substitution referred to on page 57.

First, given the budget constraint PxX + PyY = R the total differential is

$$dPxX + PxdX + dPyY + PydY = dR$$

Assuming only Px changes (i.e. dPy = dR = 0) then

$$dPxX + PxdX + Py\,dY = 0$$

Multiply both sides by $\frac{Px}{dPx}\frac{1}{R}\frac{XY}{XY}$ to enable some re-arrangement to proceed:

$$dPxX\frac{Px}{dPx}\frac{1}{R}\frac{XY}{XY} + PxdX\frac{Px}{dPx}\frac{1}{R}\frac{XY}{XY} + Py\,dY\frac{Px}{dPx}\frac{1}{R}\frac{XY}{XY} = 0$$

With selective cancelling we obtain

$$X\frac{Px}{1}\frac{1}{R} + PxdX\frac{Px}{dPx}\frac{1}{R}\frac{X}{X} + Py\,dY\frac{Px}{dPx}\frac{1}{R}\frac{Y}{Y} = 0$$

and by re-arrangement we obtain

$$\frac{PxX}{R} + \frac{PxX}{R}\frac{dX}{dPx}\frac{Px}{X} + \frac{PyY}{R}\frac{dY}{dPx}\frac{Px}{Y} = 0$$

whence

$$\frac{PxX}{R}\frac{dX}{dPx}\frac{Px}{X} + \frac{PyY}{R}\frac{dY}{dPx}\frac{Px}{Y} = -\frac{PxX}{R}$$

Then with α_X and α_Y representing the proportions of the budget devoted respectively to X and Y we obtain the result that

$$\alpha_X\varepsilon_{XX} + \alpha_Y\varepsilon_{YX} = -\alpha_X$$

In a similar manner we obtain

$$\alpha_Y\varepsilon_{YY} + \alpha_X\varepsilon_{XY} = -\alpha_Y$$

Adding the equations together and noting that $\alpha_X + \alpha_Y = 1$ we obtain

$$\alpha_X(\varepsilon_{XX} + \varepsilon_{XY}) + \alpha_Y(\varepsilon_{YY} + \varepsilon_{YX}) = -1$$

Returning to the total differential of the budget but this time setting $dPx = dPy = 0$ to get

$$PxdX + PydY = dR$$

multiply both sides by $\frac{R}{R}\frac{1}{dR}\frac{XY}{XY}$ to allow re-arrangement; by selective cancellation we obtain

$$\frac{PxX}{R}\frac{dX}{dR}\frac{R}{X} + \frac{PyY}{R}\frac{dY}{dR}\frac{R}{Y} = \frac{dR}{dR}$$

That is,

$$\alpha_X\varepsilon_{XR} + \alpha_Y\varepsilon_{YR} = 1$$

Thus the own price, cross price and income elasticities in respect of the two goods are closely related to each other.

Second, the Slutsky Equation can be manipulated (see Appendix) to yield the following:

$$\varepsilon_{XX} = -(\varepsilon_{XY} + \varepsilon_{XR})$$

The negative of the own price elasticity in respect of one good equals the sum of the cross price elasticity and the income elasticity of the same good.

Third, the substitution between quantities of the two goods along the indifference curve can be expressed in terms of the elasticity of substitution, which in turn is related to the price and income elasticities. The elasticity of substitution expresses change in the ratio of the chosen quantities of the two goods in relation to change in the Marginal Rate of Substitution, that is, the slope of the indifference curve. In the Appendix it is shown that as well as the relationship already referred to (see above, p.57), the elasticity of substitution is linked to the compensated price elasticities and the marginal utility of income (or the budget).

This emphasises that these elasticities are merely particular perspectives on the form of the consumer's preference function.]

II. Applications of Indifference Analysis

As far as consumers are concerned, the remaining problems relate to the issues of choice between work and leisure, and between present and future goods.

A. Work and Leisure:

The choice between work and leisure is in reality a choice between leisure (which is a good in its own right) and income (strictly speaking, real income) where the latter represents an ability to command certain utilities (goods and services) which compensate the disutility involved in work. In fact the individual will face a complex series of choices in this field. First it is necessary to decide what will be sold, that is, the kind of service which the 'consumer' will offer. Here the choice (e.g. of skill or profession) will be complicated by such things as opportunity, education and any trade-off between income and status. In what follows we will confine our attention to the simpler problem represented by the individual who has already decided what skill to offer and now faces the problem of choice with regard to the conditions under which this 'service' will be sold – the problem of how much to sell.

Preferences:

The indifference curve now represents a number of possible combinations of leisure and income which will give the individual the same level of satisfaction and between which the individual is therefore indifferent. As before, these curves will not intersect or coincide; nor will they slope up from left to right, or have the characteristics of vertical or horizontal straight lines. Again, the curves will be consistently convex to the origin, since leisure and income are unlikely to be perfect substitutes for one another. The fact that the curves are drawn consistently convex to the origin implies that the MRS is consistently moving against the good augmented and in favour of that relinquished – a very plausible assumption when we consider the choices involved. We would normally expect the relative marginal valuation of leisure (expressed by the slope of the indifference curve at a point) to increase as the number of hours of leisure remaining to us is progressively reduced by substituting income (work) and vice-versa.

Constraints:

The constraints are represented by the number of hours available for work or leisure, the price level of the parcel of goods which is available, and by the prevailing money wage-rate. Assuming that the individual is a price-taker, let us suppose that the constraints are such that at one extreme all of the available hours may be enjoyed in the form of leisure. At the other extreme, no leisure

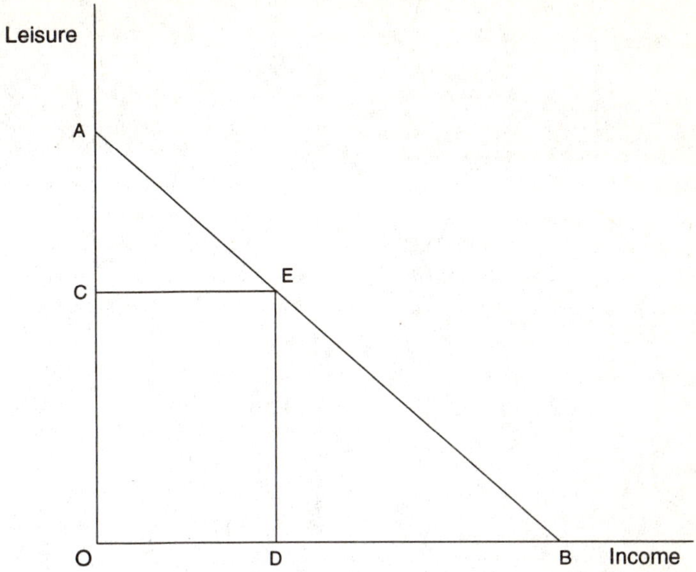

Figure 2.13(a)

hours are chosen while a level of income is earned determined by the total number of hours available and the wage rate.

In Figure 2.13(a) the constraints are such that the individual could have OA hours of leisure and no income, or OB units of income and no leisure, or some intermediate combination. For example the individual might work AC hours, retaining OC hours of leisure and thus acquire OD units of income. As before, the slope of the line AB will be determined by the ratio of OA/OB. Any change in the number of hours available for work or leisure will change the position of the constraint line (where the wage rate is assumed to be constant) while any change in the real wage rate (hours constant) will affect its position and slope. In the latter case, such a change could come about if there was any alteration in the general price level or in the value of the money wage. A fall in the wage rate (prices constant) would cause the line AB to become relatively steeper, and vice-versa.

Equilibrium:

As before, a position of equilibrium can only be established by taking in conjunction the logically separate issues of preference and constraint – that is, by superimposing the constraint line on the individual's indifference map. In this case, equilibrium requires that the constraint line is just tangent to the highest available indifference curve, i.e. that the marginal valuation of leisure in terms of income is brought to equality with the prevailing wage rate (Figure 2.13(b)).

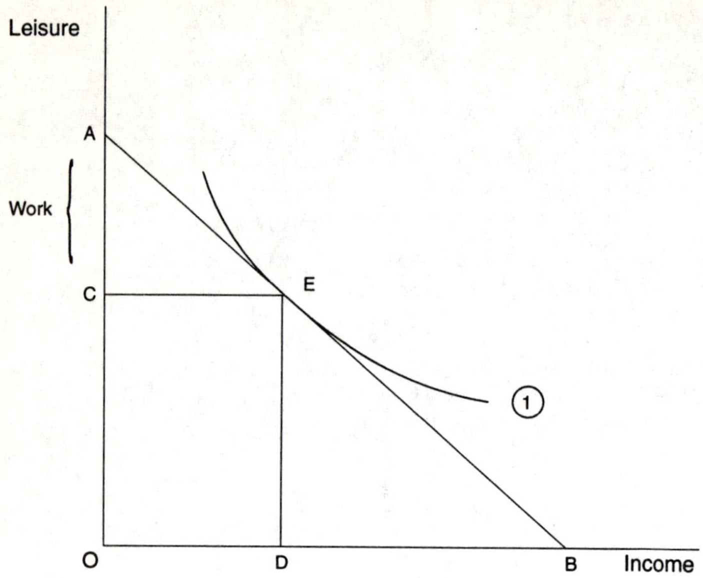

Figure 2.13(b)

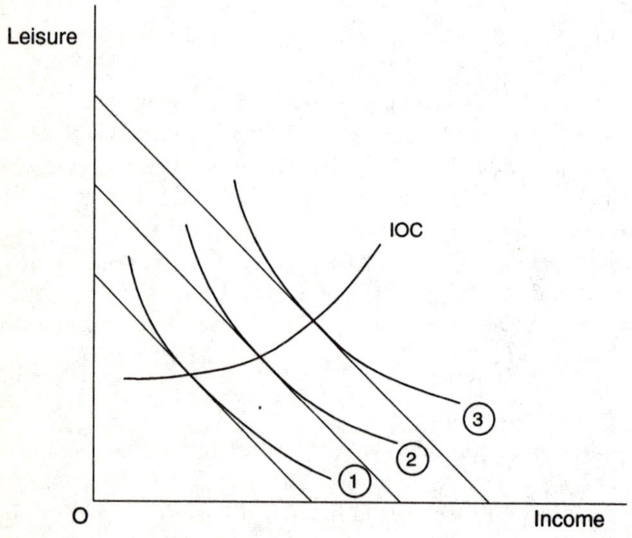

Figure 2.14

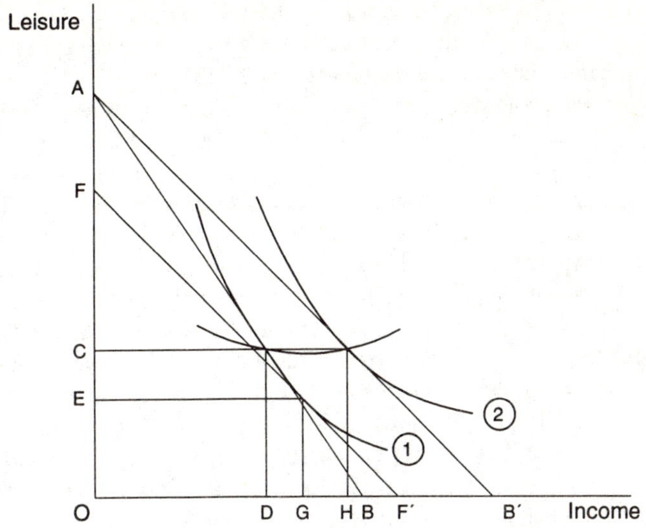

Figure 2.15

Changes in the Position of Equilibrium:

Any change in the number of hours which the individual would be prepared to devote to work and leisure, other things remaining equal, will alter the position of the constraint line, and yield a number of positions of equilibrium which establish the Income Offer Curve (Figure 2.14).

It is not easy to make valid generalisations about the shape of this curve. However, it will not slope downwards from left to right if leisure is a normal good (and thus work an inferior good). It is nonetheless quite possible that over some ranges at least it may slope upwards from right to left (since income, relative to leisure, may be an inferior good).

Any change in the wage rate will alter the position of the constraint line. In Figure 2.15 we illustrate the case of an increase in the wage rate. AB therefore pivots to AB′. As the result the individual is able to move from a lower to a higher indifference curve. There must therefore be an income effect (represented by the movement between indifference curves) and a substitution effect.

In order to isolate the substitution effect a constraint line FF′ is drawn parallel to AB′ (thus representing the same wage rate) and tangent to the original indifference curve (thus eliminating the income effect). In this case we can represent the substitution effect as a movement down the indifference curve as a result of which the individual re-establishes an equality between the marginal valuation of leisure (in terms of income) and the new wage rate. In the case shown, fewer hours of leisure are chosen, OE instead of OC hours) since as a result of the increase in the wage rate work is now relatively cheaper and leisure more expensive. As we would expect, the individual will substitute in favour of the relatively cheaper 'good', thus acquiring a level of income represented by OG.

A change in the wage rate which does not involve a compensating variation of the kind which we have just considered will feature both an income effect and a substitution effect. In Figure 2.15 we represent the movement from one position of equilibrium to another as compounded of first, a substitution effect which leads to a decrease in leisure (OE instead of OC hours) and an increase in income (from OD to OG). Secondly, there will be an income effect as a result of which the individual restores the leisure hours chosen to their former level (in the case illustrated) while acquiring a further increase in income (which rises to OH units). In this case the substitution effect (which moves against hours retained for leisure) is exactly balanced by the positive income effect with respect to leisure where the income effect (measured this time on the *y*-axis) is given by the distance EC.

In the case illustrated it is suggested that there is no net change in the number of hours worked as a result of the increase in the wage rate. This can be expressed more directly by establishing a link between two wage rates and the supply of labour. If we plot the wage rate on the *y*-axis and the supply of labour on the *x*-axis, then the curve connecting the two observations would be vertical. However, the shape of the curve may vary a great deal. For example, it is quite supposable, as a result of a change in the wage rate, that the income effect with respect to leisure is such as to lead to a net increase in the number of hours worked, i.e. a net fall in the number of hours retained for leisure. It is equally supposable, that at very high levels of income the consequence of an increase in the wage rate may cause a net fall in the number of hours worked (i.e. a net increase in the number of hours retained for leisure). These cases would yield positively and negatively sloped supply curves of labour. In terms of Marshallian analysis it is usual to illustrate the relationship between the wage rate and the supply of labour in terms of a positively sloped function (Figure 2.16). Supplying labour is assumed to involve a disutility which must be compensated by the capacity to acquire utility; this is determined by the real wage rate. As the supply of labour increases, so too does the disutility involved, meaning the real wage must progressively increase if the effort is to be made. The significance of each point on the supply function is that the supply of labour is established where the disutility involved in the last (marginal) unit of effort is exactly compensated by the real wage.

B. Present and Future Goods:

Several subjective factors lead us to abstain from present consumption. These factors include, for example, the desire to create a reserve for unforeseen circumstances, to provide for future needs, or for an anticipated change in the relation between future need and future income. The proportion of a given income which we save may also be responsive to changes in the level of the rate of interest.

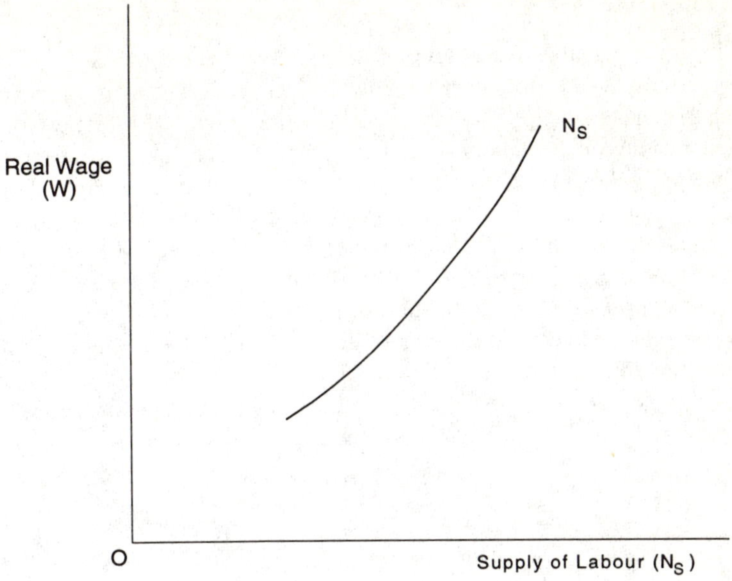

Figure 2.16

Preferences:

We can represent the choice between consumption and saving as one which involves a choice between consumption now and consumption in the future: in short, as a choice between present and future goods. Here the indifference curves represent various combinations of present and future goods which would yield the same level of satisfaction, with each drawn consistently convex to the origin since we are still dealing with goods which are not perfect substitutes for each other.

Constraints:

The constraints facing the consumer are: income, the prices of goods now and in the future, and the rate of interest. Interest may be defined, for the moment, as a rate payable by those who seek command over present resources, to those willing to forego present consumption for the sake of a greater future benefit. Looked at from this point of view the individual who borrows will be prepared to pay a premium in the expectation of being better off in the future, while the individual who lends is held to accept a disutility (the limitation on present consumption) for which some reward (interest) is required.

As before, we can only explain the nature of equilibrium by considering the individuals preferences and constraints in conjunction. It will be convenient to do so in three different ways:

1. Income Payable in the Period T:

Suppose income is payable in the period T and at the very outset of that period. In this case the individual will have the following options: to spend all of current income on present goods, purchasing an amount OA (Figure 2.17(a)) which is determined by the value of income and the current price level. At the other extreme, the individual may choose to forgo present consumption completely for the sake of consumption in the future (i.e. in the period T + 1) and buy an amount of future goods equal to OB. The quantity OB will be determined by the price level in the future (i.e. the period T + 1) and by the future value of present income.

Given our suppositions, the future value of present income will be determined by the value of that income plus the interest due on it, i.e. Y(1 + i) where Y is the level of income and i the rate of interest. The gradient of the line AB (Figure 2.17(a)) is given by the ratio OA/OB, which, assuming prices to remain constant between periods T and T + 1 may be expressed as:

$$\frac{OA}{OB} = \frac{\dfrac{Y_T}{P_T}}{\dfrac{Y_{T+1}}{P_T}} = \frac{Y_T}{P_T} \cdot \frac{P_T}{Y_T(1+i)} = \frac{1}{(1+i)}$$

Any change in income, other things remaining equal, will then cause a change in the position, but not the slope of the budget line, while any change in the rate of interest will cause it to pivot about A.

A position of equilibrium is shown in Figure 2.17(b): the individual has arranged purchases to maximise satisfaction, buying OC present goods with the intention of buying OD future goods: a quantity which will be determined by saving out of present income, plus the interest due, divided by the price level.

Changes in Positions of Equilibrium:

Any change in the level of income will yield a series of positions of equilibrium and will reveal a relationship between changes in the level of income and changes in the volume of saving which are forthcoming. Equally, we can examine changes in the rate of interest which would make the slope of the line OA either steeper or more shallow. For example if the rate of interest were to rise this would extend the command over future goods by increasing the future value of present income. In this case we can distinguish between the income and substitution effects in the manner already established in Figure 2.15 and repeated in Figure 2.18. The size of the substitution effect is given as DG – the individual substituting in favour of future goods which have now become relatively cheaper by virtue of the increase in the rate of interest, and against present goods, which have now become relatively dearer.

Note that in the case shown, the result of an increase in the rate of interest, allowing for the income effect, is to leave the demand for present goods unaffected at

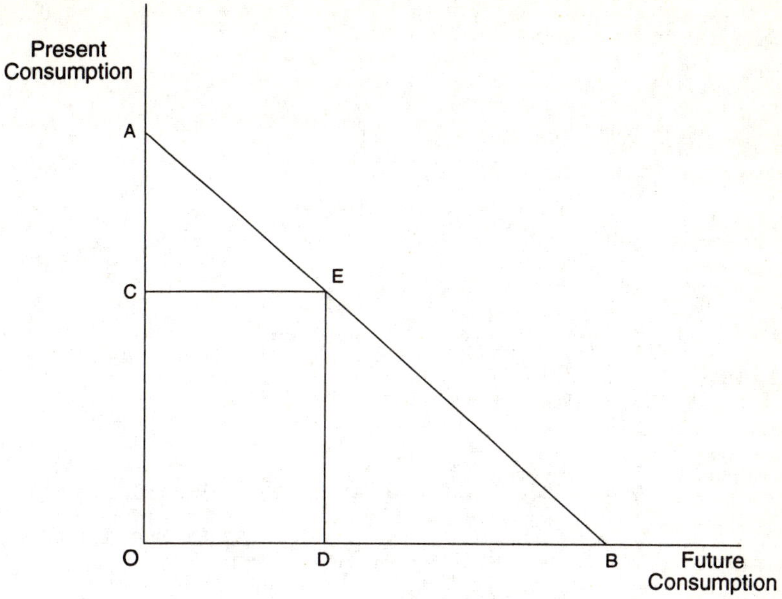

Figure 2.17(a)

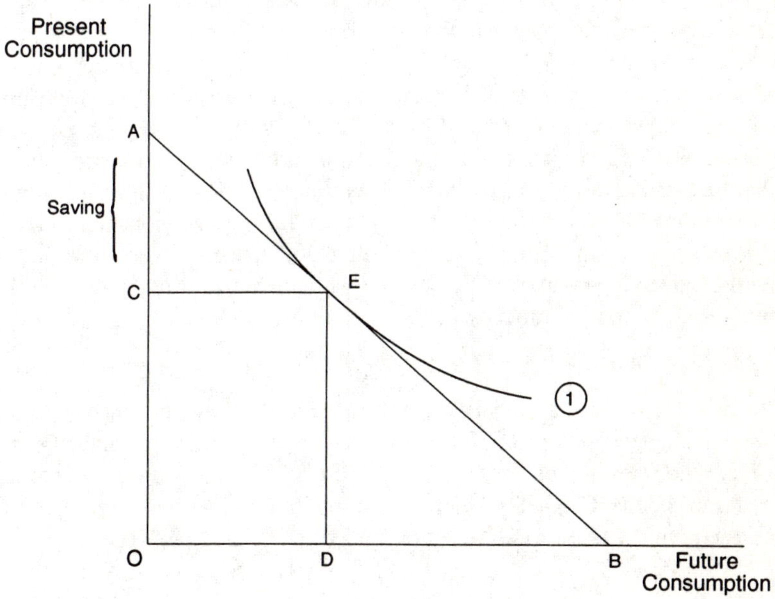

Figure 2.17(b)

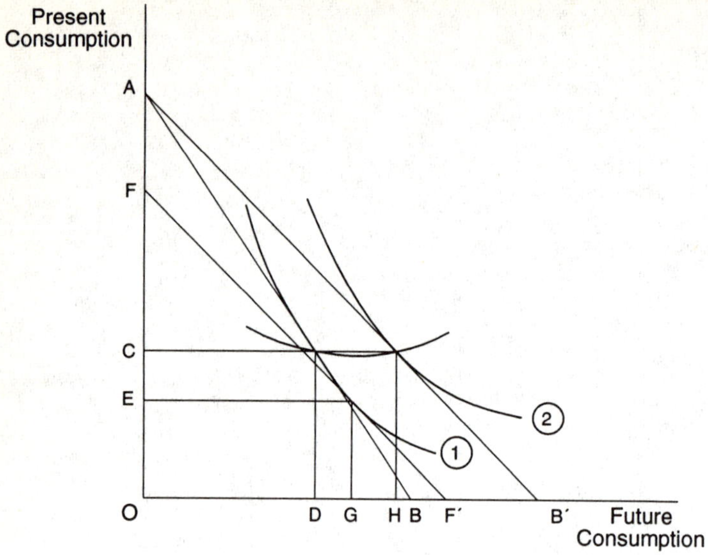

Figure 2.18

OC. There has thus been no change in the level of saving out of the given level of income in response to the change in the rate of interest. If we plot the rate of interest on the *y*-axis and the supply of saving on the *x*-axis, it is apparent that the function relating saving to the rate of interest (S(Y) = f(i)) is a vertical straight line (Figure 2.19). In Marshallian terms it is usual to illustrate a saving function with a positive slope. A curve like this (Figure 2.20) incorporates the assumption stated earlier that saving (a decision to defer consumption) involves a disutility which progressively increases as saving increases, thus requiring a progressively higher rate of interest by way of compensation. The significance of each point on the function is that saving is taken to the level at which the disutility involved in the last unit is exactly compensated by the prevailing rate of interest.

2. *Income Payable in the Period T + 1:*

Exactly the same form of argument might be used to illustrate the reaction of the individual to changes in the rate of interest where income is payable in the Period T + 1. Here the relevant constraints are the value of future income and the price level of future goods. On the assumption that the individual spent nothing in the present (the period T) OB of future goods could then be purchased, i.e.

$$\frac{Y_{T+1}}{P}$$

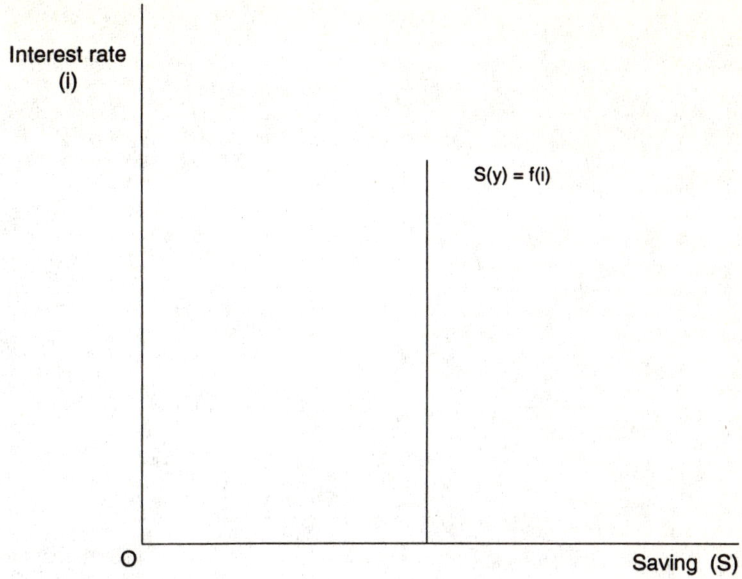

Figure 2.19

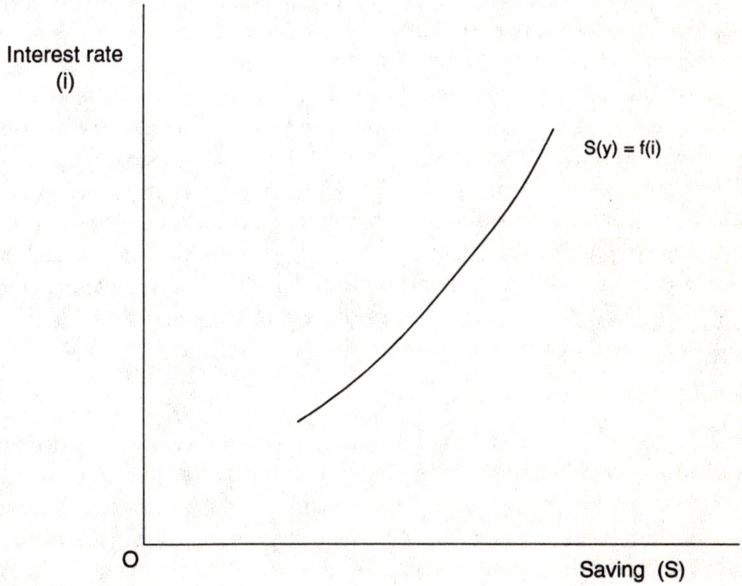

Figure 2.20

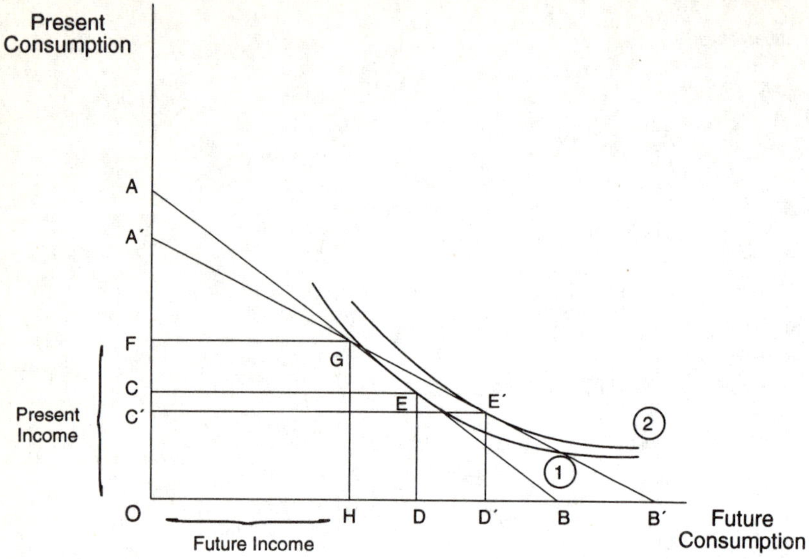

Figure 2.21

(Figure 2.17(b)). At the other extreme the individual might buy OA present goods, where that amount is determined by the present value of future income, and the current price level. In this case the individual is a borrower, not a lender, and in using future income in the present must be prepared to pay back both capital and interest when it becomes due. The present value of future income may be expressed as future income discounted by the current rate of interest. Our budget constraint line will then be as shown in Figure 2.17(b). The command over present goods, OA, however, is now determined by the present value of future income and the present price level; while OB is determined by the value of future income and the future price level. In this case a rise in the rate of interest will decrease the present value of future income and thus our command over present goods, while a fall in the rate of interest will increase that command.

3. Income Payable in Both Periods

In Figure 2.21 point G indicates the combination of present and future consumption attainable without any transfer of purchasing power between the present and the future periods. A budget line passing through this point (such as AB) indicates the additional combinations attainable either by borrowing against future income (the segment AG) or saving present income for future use (the segment GB), at the prevailing interest rate. An increase in the interest rate will reduce the present value of future income, and increase the future value of present income; AB will pivot about G to A'B'. (A reduction in the interest rate will pivot AB in the other direction). Given the consumer's preferences the original equilibrium is at E, where CF of present income (OF) is saved. With the increase in the interest rate the new equilibrium is E', increasing present saving to C'F. As before, however, this result is ambiguous, being dependent on the particular preferences of the consumer:saving could just as well have decreased. Indeed the initial equilibrium could have been on the segment AG (borrowing rather than saving in the present period). Given that consumption in only two periods is being considered, in the present and in the future, the equilibrium cannot involve borrowing or saving in both periods. This model focusses only on the transfer of purchasing power from one period to the other and does not apply to the accumulation (or decumulation) of assets in relation to other periods.

A Note on The Demand for Investment Goods:

Although this note anticipates results which are established later in the argument it may be useful to introduce a tentative discussion of the demand for investment at this stage if only because it provides a certain continuity with the topic just considered.

In the previous section it was suggested that interest could be regarded, when seen in one light, as a payment made to those who accept the disutility of forgoing present consumption, by those who wish to command present resources.

Looked at in this way there may be an inducement to invest where the rate of return expected exceeds the rate of interest which is payable at least until a point is reached where the two rates are equal.

We begin by supposing that the rate of return is treated as an indicator of the efficiency or earning power of a particular type of asset, which may be defined as the rate of return expected from the use of an additional (or marginal) unit of the type of asset in question.

The calculation of marginal efficiency will involve a judgement as to the cost of an asset on the one hand, and as to the yields expected on the other. The assumption of perfect knowledge, which we continue to employ, would suggest that the returns expected are identical to those actually realised. The returns in question would be calculated after deducting the expenses incurred in producing the output which the firm proposes to sell. In Figure 2.22(a), the rate of return illustrated progressively declines as investment takes place.

This reflects the assumptions:

(a) that the cost of the marginal unit of the asset will increase as the output of it increases, and

(b) that yields will fall as the output of commodities generated in part through the use of the type of asset concerned increases.

A number of points follow:

a) There will be an inducement to invest so long as the present value of an additional asset exceeds its cost. Here cost will be determined by cost of production of the (capital) asset, while present value of the returns expected over the

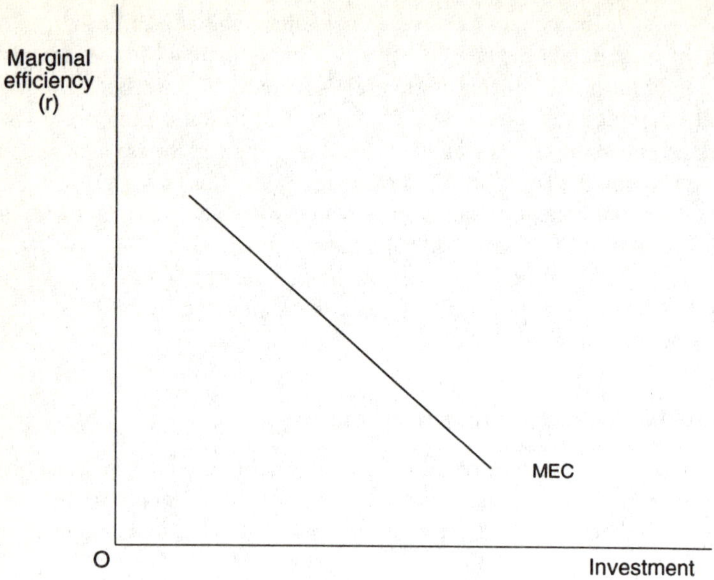

Figure 2.22(a)

life of the asset will be established by using the current rate of interest as a rate of discount.

In this case, present value is determined as follows:

$$PV = \frac{Q_1}{(1 + i)} + \frac{Q_2}{(1 + i)^2} + \ldots + \frac{Q_n}{(1 + i)^n}$$

where Q represents the yields expected in each time period, (n) represents the life-span of the asset, and (i) the rate of interest. So long as the present value, thus calculated, exceeds the cost of the asset it will pay to invest at least until that point is reached where the two are equal.

(b) Alternatively, we can make the same point in terms of a comparison between the marginal efficiency of an asset and the rate of interest. In his *General Theory of Employment, Interest and Money* (1936), J. M. Keynes defined the marginal efficiency of capital as being equal 'to that rate of discount which would make the present value of the series of annuities given by the returns expected from the capital asset during its life just equal to its supply price'.

If we represent this rate of discount as (r) and supply price as (SP) the point can be expressed in the form:

$$PV = \frac{Q_1}{(1 + r)} + \frac{Q_2}{(1 + r)^2} + \ldots + \frac{Q_n}{(1 + r)^n} = SP$$

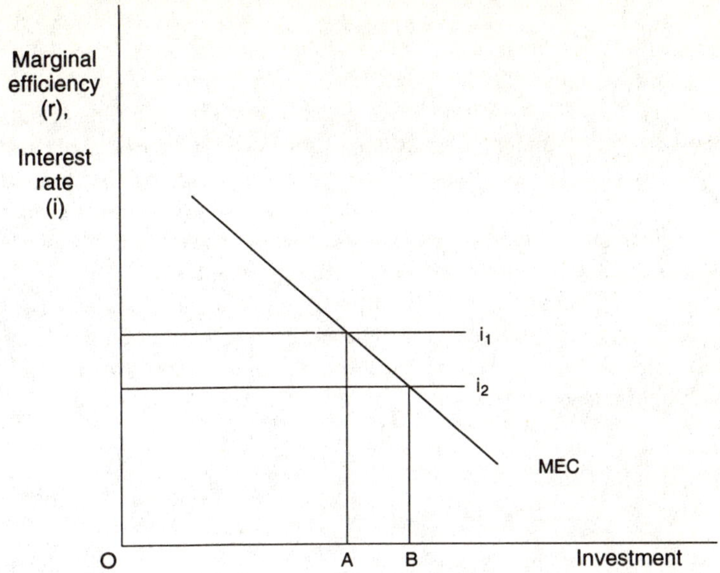

Figure 2.22(b)

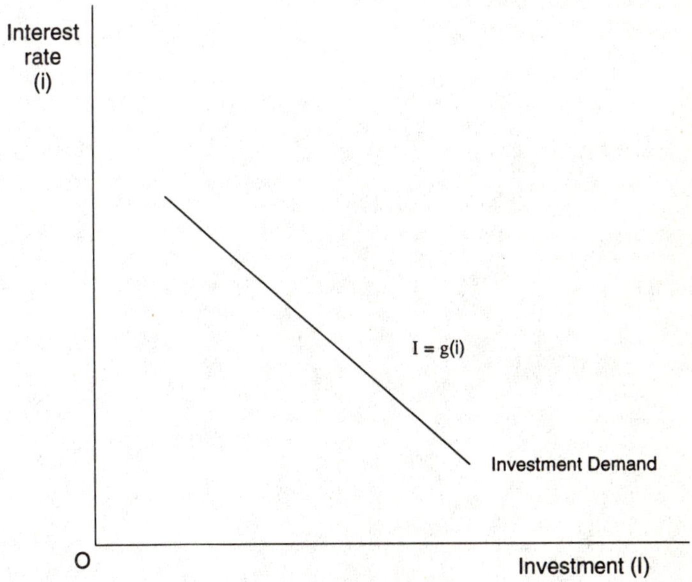

Figure 2.22(c)

So long as the marginal efficiency of the asset (r) exceeds the rate of interest (i) it will pay to invest in the type of asset in question at least until the two rates of discount are equal, (Figure 2.22(b)).

(c) In Figure 2.22(c) this information is given in the form of a direct relationship between the rate of interest (i) measured on the Y axis and the level of demand for the capital asset in question. In short, the argument yields another functional relationship which may be expressed in the statement that investment is a function of the rate of interest, i.e. that I = f (i). It should be emphasised that the shape of the investment demand function is affected by the shape of the MEC function, and that the relationship between the two will only be identical if we assume that expected yields are equal to those actually realised. Each point on the function indicates that investment is taken to that level where the rate of interest and the MEC are brought into equality.

Section B: The Producer: The Supply of Commodities and the Demand for Services

I. Supply as a Function of Price

Let us now return to the discussion of isoquants and isocost lines on pages 23-28 above. As before, let us assume that the producer cannot influence input prices, and that they do not change. If the producer changes the outlay on the two inputs, given the technical opportunities summarised in the isoquant map, we would obtain a series of positions of equilibrium tracing out the Output Employment Curve, analogous to that considered in Chapter 1, Figure 1.18. Let us now redefine this as the Expansion Path or Scale Line. Note the important fact that it is drawn on the assumption of constant input prices; there will be a different Scale Line for each complex of input prices.

It will be observed that both inputs are treated as open to variation in terms of quantities employed, and that returns to scale may also vary – equal movements along the Scale Line may yield unequal changes in the level of output. One case which may be isolated is that of constant returns to scale. This labels the case where if the quantities of both inputs are changed in a given proportion, output will change in the same proportion. The production function – the formal expression of the relation between output and the use of inputs – in such a case is linearly homogeneous, or homogeneous of the first degree. In terms of the isoquant map, the distance between successive isoquants will be the same (so long as they occur at equal output intervals as well). Under such circumstances we can employ the terms returns to scale and returns to outlay inter-changeably, since with constant input prices it follows that as we double the amounts employed of each input, we necessarily double the outlay on them.

The Short Run:

Let us now re-examine the same ground from a different viewpoint, introducing a distinction between the short and long run. We shall define these in terms of restrictions on the producer's freedom of choice rather than in terms of time periods.

In our simple two-input model we define the short run as a 'period' within which choice is restricted to variation in the level of employment of only one of the two inputs, the other being assumed fixed at a particular positive level. The long run will then be a 'period' where this condition is relaxed. It will be observed that the isoquant map is given in each case; we could describe this as a given "technology". Our task is now to examine the short run case, and show its relationship with the long run model, using a new technique of argument.

In our discussion of isoquants, their shape was attributed to the nature of the relationship between the inputs in the production process; a relationship which we

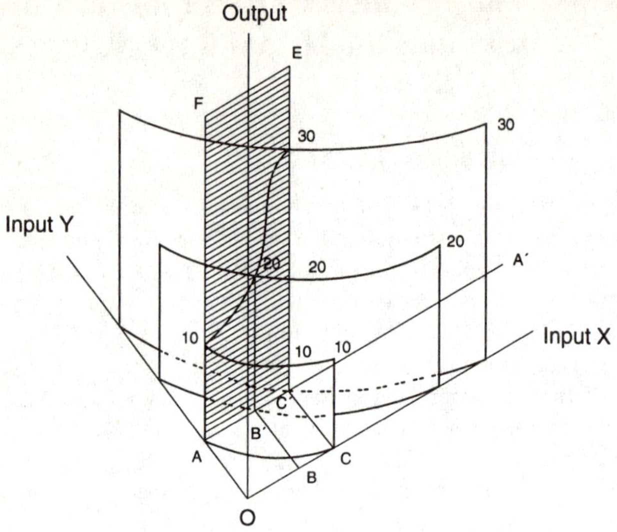

Figure 2.23

term as one of imperfect substitutability. In order to avoid some technical difficulties in the ensuing argument we now assume that this relationship is more strictly defined, as being subject to the Law of Variable Proportions, which holds that: *increasing the quantity of a variable input combined with a fixed amount of another input will initially yield more than proportionate increases in output, but subsequently less than proportionate increases, for a given technology.*

Under these circumstances, total product will increase at an increasing and then at a decreasing rate. The producer faces a total product curve belonging to a particular class of shapes. For example, if the amount of Y were fixed at OA in Figure 2.23 various levels of output could be attained by employing various quantities of X in conjunction with the fixed employment of Y (OA) such as OB or OC (generating 20 or 30 units of output). By taking a cross-section of the isoquant map along the line (AA´) we can illustrate the total product curve, shown in Figure 2.24. In effect we have taken a cross-section of the isoquant map and rotated the diagram so as to expose the axes on which quantities of output and the input X are measured. Output is now represented on the *y*-axis, thus exposing the relationship between changes in the level of output and changes in the use of the variable input X, the latter being used in conjunction with a fixed quantity of input Y.

If the total product curve has the general characteristics depicted in Figure 2.24, then output per unit of variable input, that is average product, will behave in a particular manner, increasing to a certain value, then diminishing. This can be checked by inspecting the increasing then decreasing slopes of the lines drawn

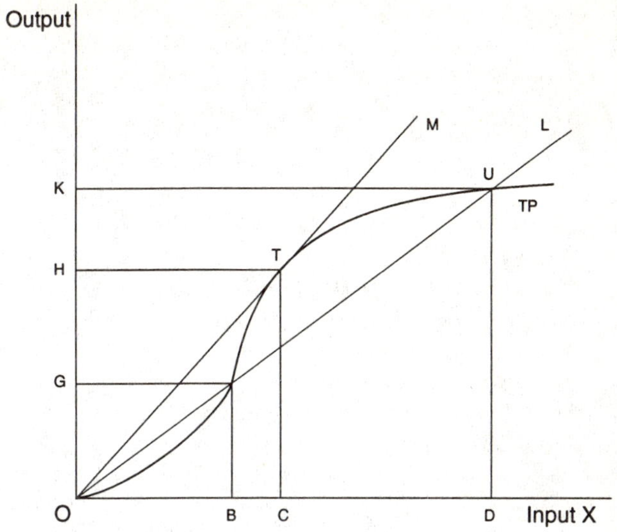

Figure 2.24

from the origin to successive points on the total product curve, such as OM and OL. Average product will reach its maximum value where a line drawn from the origin (OM) is tangent to the total product curve at the point T, (average product is given by the ratio TC/OC). As the use of the variable input increases up to this point, total product continues to rise, but average product declines. Where OD units of the variable input are employed, total product is DU, but average product is given by the slope of the line OL (i.e. by the ratio UD/OD).

Product and Cost:

Let us assume that the input prices are known. Given the characteristics of the total product curve we would expect that as average product increases, the cost per unit of output would decline, and vice versa. In short, given the assumptions so far used, the producer would encounter decreasing, and then increasing, unit cost. This is illustrated in Figure 2.25. With output OA (now plotted on the *x*-axis) the total cost of the variable input used to generate this level of output is AD (on the *y*-axis). Average cost is therefore AD/OA and is expressed in terms of the slope of the line OD. When output is OB total variable cost is BE and average cost is determined by the ratio BE/OB. Beyond that level of output average cost must be increasing. Thus, where output is OC and total variable cost CL, the value of average variable cost is given by the slope of line OL- steeper than OE (so a higher unit cost) and the continuation of line OD indicating that the unit cost is the same as at the level of OA).

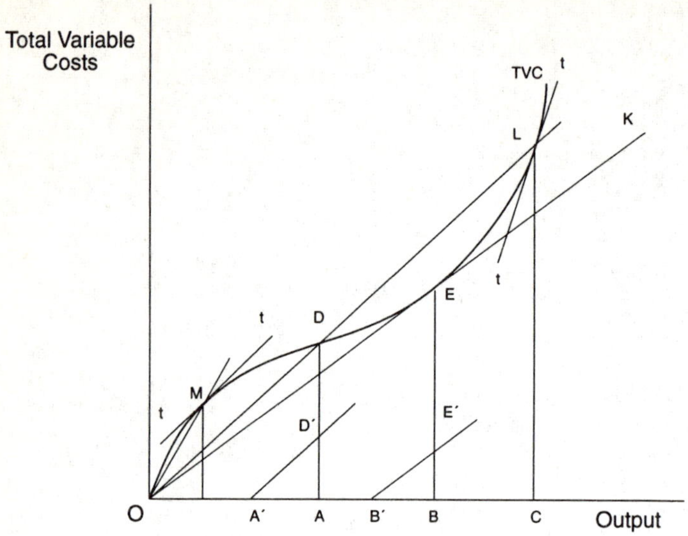

Figure 2.25

It will be evident from the nature of the discussion so far that the shape of the total variable cost curve (itself determined by the shape of the total product curve) must also determine the shapes of the average variable cost curve. Looking at Figure 2.25 the slopes of successive lines drawn from the origin to meet the total variable cost function must initially decrease, reach a minimum value at the point E (where the line OK is tangent to the curve) and increase thereafter - thus giving the curve of average variable cost (AVC) a distinctive U-shape.

Marginal Cost is the addition to total cost incurred by producing an additional or marginal unit of output, and is expressed in terms of the slope of a tangent drawn to the total variable cost curve at a particular point. It is evident from Figure 2.25 that the slope of such tangents must initially decline as we move away from the origin, attain a minimum value at the point of inflection (where the function ceases increasing at a diminishing rate and commences increasing at an increasing rate), and increase thereafter. In short, the curve of marginal cost will have the same U-shape as the curve of average costs.

The relationship between the two curves should be apparent from Figure 2.25. Consider the four points on the TVC function,: M, D, E and L. At the point M average cost is given by the slope of the line OM; marginal cost must be less given the lesser slope of the tangent at M. Given that D is the point of inflection, by definition marginal cost must have attained its minimum value, but average cost must exceed it since the slope of OD is clearly steeper. At E marginal cost must be higher than at D (the tangent at E being steeper) but equal to average cost since

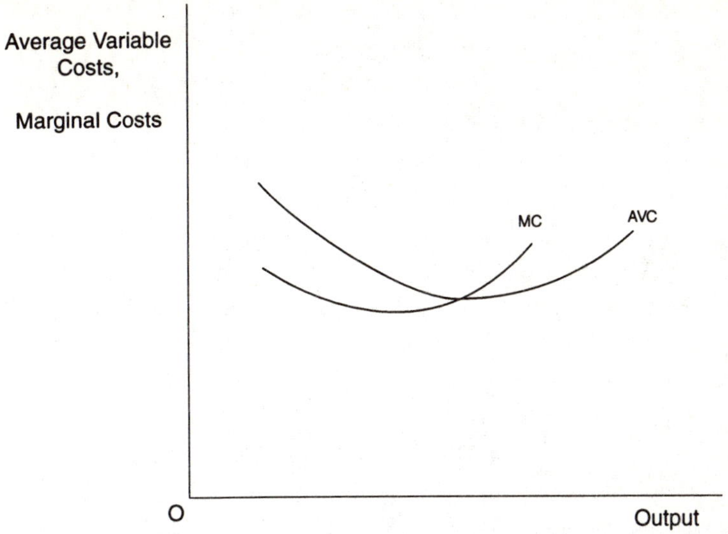

Figure 2.26

OE is both a line from the origin and a tangent at E. At L average cost is given by the slope of OL, but marginal cost must exceed it since the slope of the tangent to AVC at L is necessarily steeper.

In short, as marginal cost declines so must average cost. Marginal cost reaches its minimum value before average cost. As marginal cost begins to increase average cost continues to decline, but more slowly. The two values converge, becoming equal where average variable cost attains its minimum value. Thereafter, marginal and average variable cost both increase, the former increasing at a greater rate than the latter.

The relationships are summarised in Figure 2.26.

A formal geometric derivation of the two curves confirms the relationship between them. For convenience consider point E in Figure 2.25. Output is given by OB and average variable cost by the ratio BE/OB, i.e. by the slope of the line OE. Using the same technique as before (see derivation of the demand curve, p. 53) mark off to the left of B a distance BB´ to represent one unit of output, and draw from B´ a line parallel to OE to intersect BE at E´. Since the triangles OEB and B´E´B are similar their sides are in proportion; E´ is therefore a point on the producer's average variable cost curve, indicating the level of cost of one unit of output (B´B). Applying the same technique to other levels of output we obtain the complete U-shaped AVC curve.

Marginal cost, indicated by the slope of the total variable cost curve at different levels of output can be obtained in a similar manner. At the point E, for example,

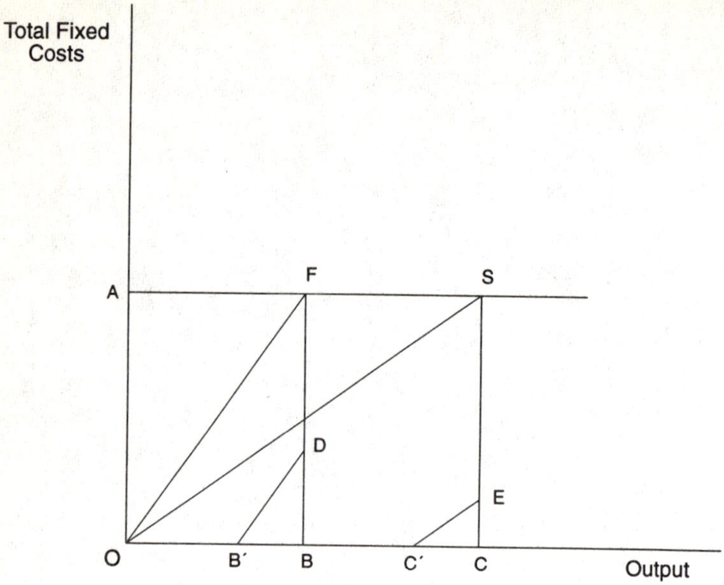

Figure 2.27(a)

the slope of the line OE gives us the value of marginal cost. Since the same line gives us the value of average cost it is apparent that average and marginal cost have the same value at this point. These relationships necessarily follow from the shape of the total product curve which we have introduced and from the assumption of a constant input cost.

Average Variable and Average Total Cost:

Up till now we have ignored the costs of the other fixed input, looking only at those attributable to the variable input. When no output is produced no variable costs are incurred and so costs are shown as zero. However, the fixed amount of the other input has to be paid for, even although the payment does not vary with output – the level of employment of it is fixed, and since its price has also been assumed fixed, there must be a fixed cost to be met by the producer. As output increases the average fixed cost must decline, as a given charge is spread over an increasing number of units of output. The Average Fixed Cost Curve (AFC) will therefore be a rectangular hyperbola. In Figure 2.27(a) we plot total fixed costs on the y-axis and output on the *x*-axis. The y-axis now has a positive intercept indicating the value of total costs. Take two levels of output, OB and OC. At OB total fixed costs are BF and the average value is given by the ratio BF/OB, i.e. by the slope of the line OF. As before, mark off the distance BB´ to represent one unit of output and draw a line from B´ to meet BF at D - thus giving us a point on the

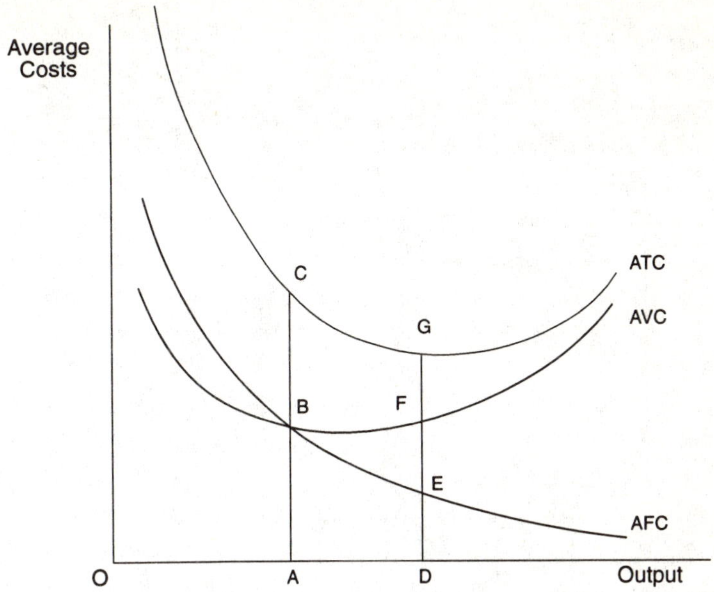

Figure 2.27(b)

curve of average fixed cost. In the same way we can establish a point such as C′ drawing from that point a line parallel to OS, thus providing a second point on the curve of AFC at E.

To obtain the Average Total Cost curve, we need to add the AFC curve vertically to the curve of AVC (Figure 2.27(b)). At the level of output OA average variable cost is AB and so too is average fixed cost. If we add AFC to AVC we obtain a point C on the average total cost curve. (The distance AB = BC). At the level of output OD we add DE to DF (the distance FG = DE), thus obtaining a second point on the curve of ATC. Note that as output increases the ATC curve gets closer to the AVC curve as a result of the fact that the AFC curve is necessarily declining.

It is useful to derive the various cost curves by the geometric means already used. In Figure 2.27(c) we employ the same TVC as before, only now it has a positive intercept with the y-axis to allow for total fixed costs. The excess of total costs over fixed costs (the latter given by the horizontal line through A) is by definition total variable costs. Thus the slope of a line from A to a point on TC gives the value of AVC. Given that AD is also a tangent to TC its slope gives MC, necessarily equal to AVC at that level of ouput. But at D, AVC is also minimised, a conclusion already established. Now consider the line OF. As a line from the origin to a point on TC its slope indicates the value of ATC. But as a tangent to TC its slope indicates both the value of MC, and the fact that ATC is at its minimum value at output level OC. Just as MC equals AVC at the latter's minimum so MC equals

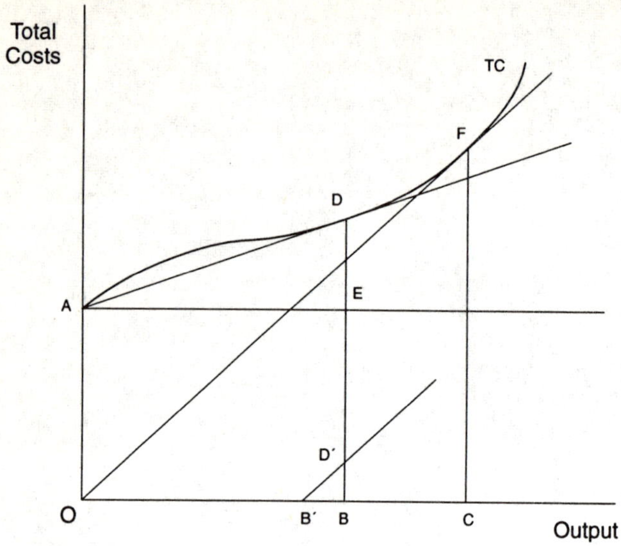

Figure 2.27(c)

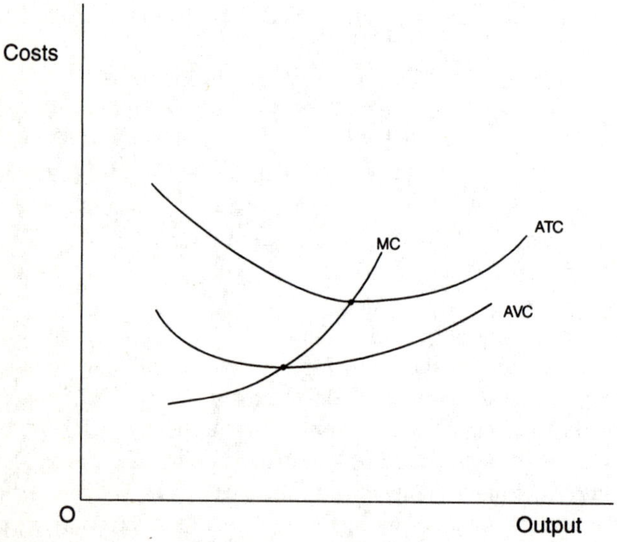

Figure 2.28

ATC at the minimum of ATC. However, note that the AVC curve will reach its minimum at a lower level of output compared to the attainment of the minimum of the ATC curve. The minimum of AVC is at D, at an output of OB, while the minimum point of ATC is attained at F, at an output of OC. Finally it is apparent that any line from the origin to a point on TC will have a steeper slope than a line from A to the same point, offering further proof that the AVC curve lies consistently below the ATC curve. The relationships are summarised in Figure 2.28.

The Relation between the Short Run and the Long Run:

Earlier we defined the 'short run' as a 'period' within which the producer was restricted to a single variable factor which may be used in conjunction with a fixed factor within the context of the same technical opportunities.

In the 'long run' it is clear that everything may vary; for example, the level and type of capital equipment may change over time, together with methods of production and even the managerial input. But we can progress the discussion by restricting the areas of choice open to the producer.

Let us assume for the moment that in the long run the producer confronts a given set of technical conditions and further that the managerial input is fixed. In effect this means that in this period the firm may vary both capital equipment and labour, i.e. the firm may change the scale of its operations by using increasing or decreasing amounts of a particular type of capital asset.

In a sense, the curve of long run average cost can be seen as being made up of a series of short run curves, each one of which corresponds to a particular time period. Let us assume (as in Figure 2.29) that SAC_1 is relevant in the period 't', SAC_2 in the period 't + 1' and that SAC_3 obtains in the period 't + 2'. In each of these time periods, the producer would confront a particular scale of operations and would be confined to the appropriate cost curve. For example a decision to produce OE units of a commodity would incur average cost of EB in the period 't'. A decision to increase output to OF units would generate average costs of FG in the same time period, although the producer would have the option in the period 't + 1' of incurring a lower level of costs of FH by moving to SAC_2, i.e. increasing the scale of operations. A decision to change the level of output in this time period would incur costs determined by SAC_2 although the producer would have the option of incurring a lower level of costs by a further change in the scale of operations in the following time period.

So far we have examined three different cost structures which relate to particular scales of operations and to particular periods of time. But if we now change the perspective we may examine the options which are open to the producer *through time*, and consider the cost structures which are perceived when looking into the future from the standpoint of the opening of the time period 't'. The curve of long run average costs when seen in this light *involves a projection into the future* (we assume for the moment that the cost structure which is anticipated corresponds to that actually realised). Seen in this light, the producer would not consider a point such as G to be relevant, because a change in the scale of operations would allow

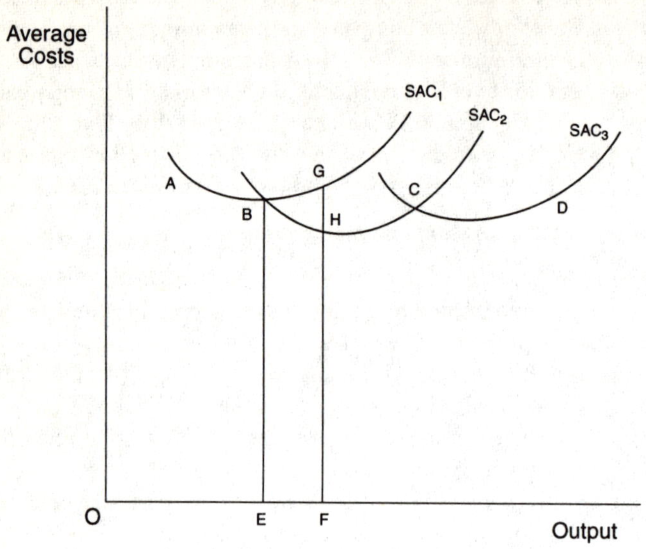

Figure 2.29

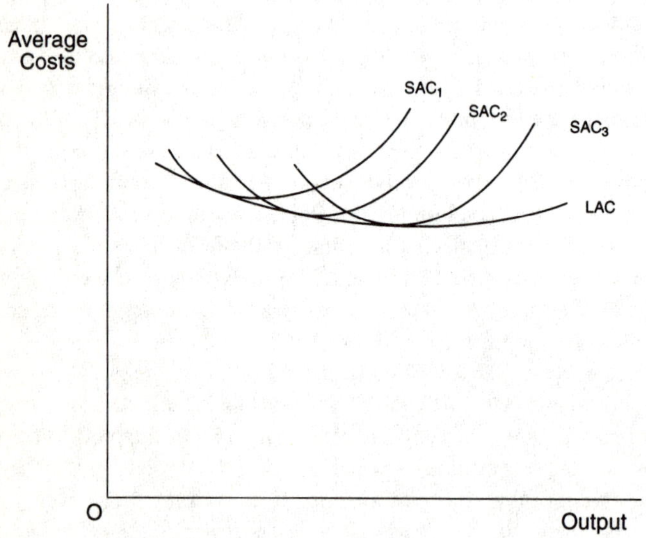

Figure 2.30

access to a more favourable structure of costs. In other words when seen as a projection the curve of long run average costs is perceived to be composed of those sections of the component short run curves which are relevant – the range ABCD in the figure.

A number of points should be noted:

(1) As drawn the curve of LAC is still 'U' shaped – a property which follows from the assumption that the method of production or technology used has not changed. It will also be observed that we have referred to the same producer facing short and long run curves, meaning that the managerial input has remained the same. We thus have still a fixed factor, making it possible to ascribe a particular shape to the curve.

(2) The curve shown in Figure 2.29 is not a smooth continuous curve, suggesting that quite large changes in the scale of operations would have to be envisaged before the firm would feel justified in moving from, say, SAC_1 to SAC_2. However,if it is assumed that capital equipment is readily divisible, (i.e. that it is of such a type that a change in the quantity of the asset used would be consistent with quite small changes in scale)then the succession of SAC curves whose relevant sections make up the curve of LAC would lie very close together relative to the *y*-axis.

(3) The LAC curve may be constructed (Figure 2.30) by drawing a smooth continuous line touching each of the relevant sections of the component SAC curves at just one point (thus comprising an 'envelope' curve). Where this curve is 'U' shaped, as here assumed, the LMC curve will stand in the same relationship to LAC as does the SMC curve to that of SAC – lying below AC as it declines, equal to AC at its minimum value and increasing as AC increases but more rapidly.

(4) Given that the LAC is an envelope curve it follows that at the point of contact between one SAC curve and the LAC curve their slopes are equal (they share a common tangent). In addition, short-run and long-run total costs are necessarily equal. It follows that at the corresponding level of output SMC = LMC.

Two cases are illustrated in Figures 2.31(a) and 2.31(b). In the former the selected SAC contacts LAC on a declining section of the curve. Here the level of output is OA and both SAC and LAC are given by AB. Under these conditions SMC and LMC will be equal with the curves intersecting at the point C.

In Figure 2.31(b) we have the interesting case where the point of contact between LAC and SAC occurs at the minimum point of both curves. Here

$$\text{LAC} = \text{SAC}$$
$$\text{and} \quad \text{SMC} = \text{LMC}$$

- in a unique solution where the average and marginal values are the same (the optimal scale of production). Although SMC and LMC are the same at this point, the curve of LMC will necessarily be less steep than that of SMC.

(5) The highly restrictive nature of the assumptions should be noted especially since the long run curves which we shall use in the argument to follow are typically drawn as smooth and continuous, with a single level of output at which cost per unit has attained its minimum value. But the curve is U-shaped only because

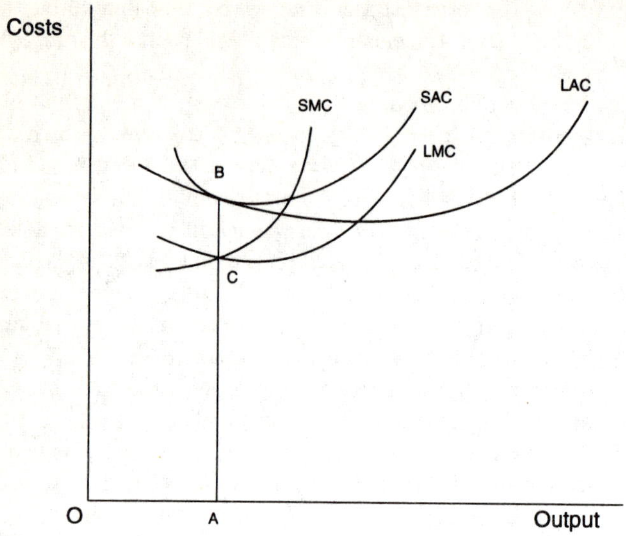

Figure 2.31(a)

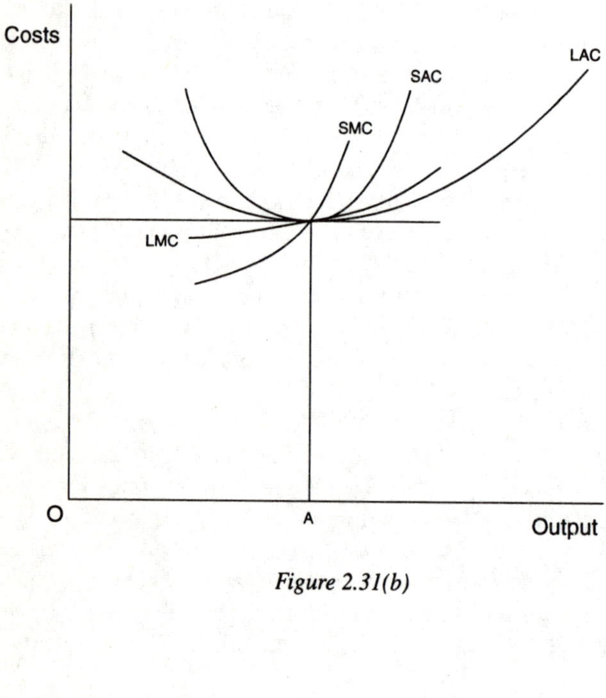

Figure 2.31(b)

we assume that the fixity of technique and managerial input ultimately require costs to rise. It is smooth and continuous only because we have abstracted from the problem of indivisibility with respect to the type of capital asset used. The notion that there is a single level of output at which cost per unit has attained a minimum value is a further simplifying (and frequently an implicit) assumption. It is quite possible that the curves of SAC and LAC might attain a minimum value over a range of output. Where an average cost curve is horizontal over a certain range the curve of MC will necessarily coincide with it.

[The Mathematics of Costs

In the short run the quantity employed of only one input (V_1) may be varied; the quantity of the other is fixed (V_2). Outlays on the inputs are given by the product of the quantities employed and their prices, assumed to be constant (P_1 and P_2). The quantity employed of V_1 is a function of output produced ($V_1(Q)$); thus $P_1V_1(Q)$ are Variable Costs and P_2V_2 Fixed Costs. So total costs are as follows:

$$TC = P_1V_1(Q) + P_2V_2$$

Average Total Costs (ATC) and Marginal Costs (MC) can be obtained respectively by dividing through by Q and by differentiating TC:

$$ATC = \frac{TC}{Q} = \frac{P_1V_1(Q)}{Q} + \frac{P_2V_2}{Q} \quad \text{(i.e. ATC = AVC + AFC)}$$

$$MC = \frac{d(TC)}{dQ} = P_1\frac{dV_1}{dQ} + 0 \quad \text{(i.e. MC is independent of Fixed Costs)}$$

The relation between MC and ATC can be established by differentiating ATC with respect to Q:

$$\frac{d(ATC)}{dQ} = \frac{Q.P_1\frac{dV_1}{dQ} - P_1V_1(Q)}{Q^2} - \frac{P_2V_2}{Q^2}$$

$$= \frac{1}{Q}\left(P_1\frac{dV_1}{dQ} - \left(\frac{P_1V_1(Q) + P_2V_2}{Q}\right)\right)$$

$$= \frac{1}{Q}(MC - ATC)$$

So ATC has zero, positive or negative slope according as MC is equal to, greater or lesser than ATC.

Now the Law of Variable Proportions places conditions on $V_1(Q)$ such that, apart from V_1, V_2 and $Q \geq 0$,

$$\frac{dV_1}{dQ} > 0, \; \frac{d^2V_1}{dQ^2} = 0 \text{ for } Q = Q' \text{ and } \frac{d^3V_1}{dQ^3} > 0$$

This guarantees that the derivative of $V_1(Q)$ has a minimum and that AVC (and ATC) also has this characteristic. That being so,

$$\frac{d(ATC)}{dQ} = \frac{1}{Q}(MC - ATC) = 0$$

i.e at the minimum of ATC, MC = ATC
and

$$\frac{d^2(ATC)}{dQ^2} = \frac{Q.P_1 \frac{d^2V_1}{dQ^2} - P_1 \frac{dV_1}{dQ}}{Q^2} - \frac{Q^2.P_1 \frac{dV_1}{dQ} - (P_1V_1(Q) + P_2V_2)2Q}{Q^4} > 0$$

Rearranging, multiplying both sides by $\frac{Q^2}{2}$

$$P_1 \frac{d^2V_1}{dQ^2}\frac{Q}{2} + \frac{(P_1V_1(Q) + P_2V_2)}{Q} > P_1 \frac{dV_1}{dQ}$$

$$P_1 \frac{d^2V_1}{dQ^2}\frac{Q}{2} + ATC > MC$$

But, at the relative extremum of ATC, ATC = MC, so

$$P_1 \frac{d^2V_1}{dQ^2}\frac{Q}{2} > 0$$

Given $Q > 0$ the inequality requires

$$P_1 \frac{d^2V_1}{dQ^2} > 0$$

That is, MC is upward-sloping. Or in other words MC cuts ATC from below at the minimum point of ATC. This is also true of the relationship between MC and AVC.]

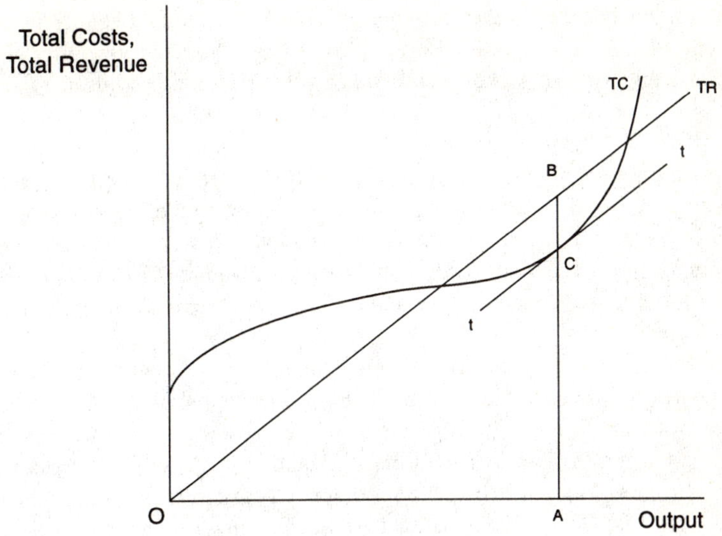

Figure 2.32

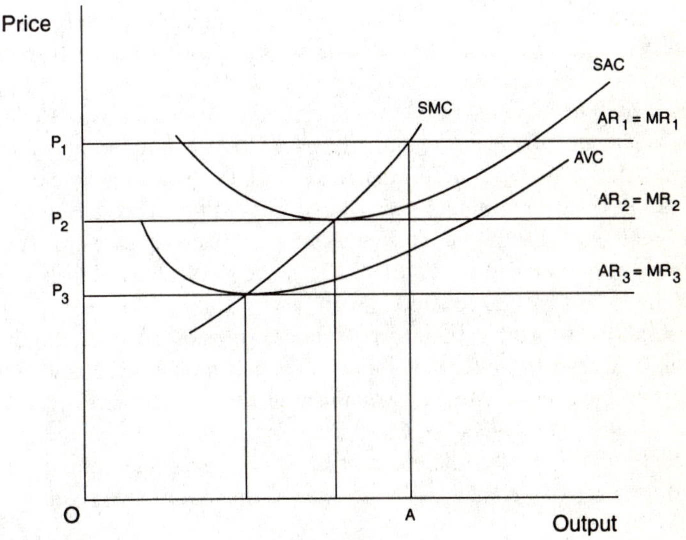

Figure 2.33

Supply as a Function of Price, the Short Run

So far the argument has shown that average cost changes as output changes in the short run, but we still do not know the level of output which the producer will choose. To find this we need to know something of the revenue conditions facing the producer.

Let us suppose that the producer can sell as much as is wished at a given price. In this case the total revenue (TR) curve confronting the producer will be represented by a straight line through the origin, its slope indicating the prevailing price (Figure 2.32). As long as the price remains constant so too will the revenue per unit of output, or average revenue (AR). The marginal revenue (MR) will also be constant and equal to AR (MR being the addition to total revenue from the sale of an additional unit).

We can relate price and output by taking cost and revenue conditions in conjunction. Suppose we revert to the total cost curve and establish that TR stands in the position shown in Figure 2.32. Under these circumstances, given the hypothesis of rationality, it can be established that the quantity OA will be produced, since the producer will then maximise the difference between total cost and total revenue (AC and AB). The vertical distance between them will be at a maximum where their slopes are the same, so our general rule is that profits are at a maximum where MC equals MR.

It is evident from inspection that given the prevailing price, no other level of output could yield as much profit. The same level of output is illustrated in Figure 2.33, this time in terms of average and marginal cost and revenue curves. At price P_1, the producer would not choose a level of output lower than OA since by increasing output additional revenue will exceed additional costs (MR lies above MC), nor will the producer offer an amount greater than OA, since beyond that level more will be added to costs than to revenue (MC lies above MR). By taking a series of values for AR we obtain a series of levels of output, or, in other words, a positive relation between supply and price; such that when the latter rises the former is increased. The producer's MC curve dictates this response, and so may be used to generate the supply curve. This curve will have a lower limit determined by the lowest point on AVC (Figure 2.33), since at still lower levels of price not even variable cost will be covered.

If we assume that other producers of the same good have similar curves, the short run industry supply curve will have a shape which is determined by the cost structures of the producers making up the industry. The *position* of the curve will be determined by the number of firms in the industry.

In exactly the same way the curve of LMC can be used to generate the supply curve of the firm where changes in the scale of operations are possible.

[The Mathematics of Profit Maximisation

With Profit (Π) defined as total revenue (TR) less total costs (TC), then, assuming the price of the good being produced is given (P_Q)

$$\Pi = TR - TC$$
$$= P_Q Q - (P_1 V_1(Q) + P_2 V_2)$$

where P_1 and P_2 are the prices of the variable input V_1 and the fixed input V_2

For a maximum of profit

$$\frac{d\Pi}{dQ} = 0 \quad \text{and} \quad \frac{d^2P}{dQ^2} < 0$$

$$\frac{d\Pi}{dQ} = P_Q - P_1 \frac{dV_1}{dQ} = 0$$

$$P_Q = P_1 \frac{dV_1}{dQ}$$

That is, MR = MC since in this context the given price is the MR. Also,

$$\frac{d^2P}{dQ^2} = -P_1 \frac{d^2V_1}{dQ^2} < 0$$

That is,

$$P_1 \frac{d^2V_1}{dQ^2} > 0$$

which concludes that where price equals marginal cost the latter is rising. Given these results it follows that the supply function of the good is the rising section of MC, where MC ≥ ATC.]

II. Short Run Demand for the Variable Input

Having established that the short run supply curve will have particular characteristics, let us now examine the nature of the producer's short run demand for a variable input.

We start as before with a total product curve consistent with the Law of Diminishing Returns. This shows a period of increasing returns to further additions of the variable input, followed eventually by a period of decreasing returns, each expressed in physical terms. Another way of saying the same thing is that average product, or physical output per unit of variable input, rises over a certain range at a diminishing rate and eventually falls at an increasing rate. Again this can easily be demonstrated geometrically.

In Figure 2.34 consider three levels of employment of the variable input, A, B and C, with their corresponding levels of output D, E and F. At A average physical product (APP) is output divided by the number of units of input, AD/OA. Mark

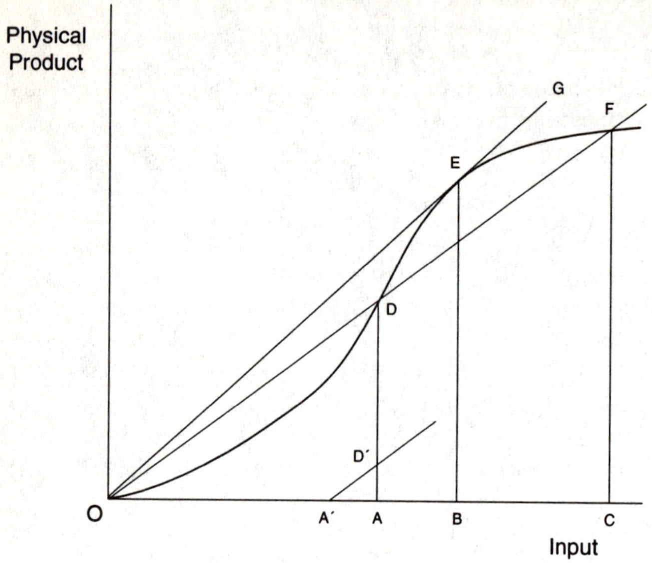

Figure 2.34

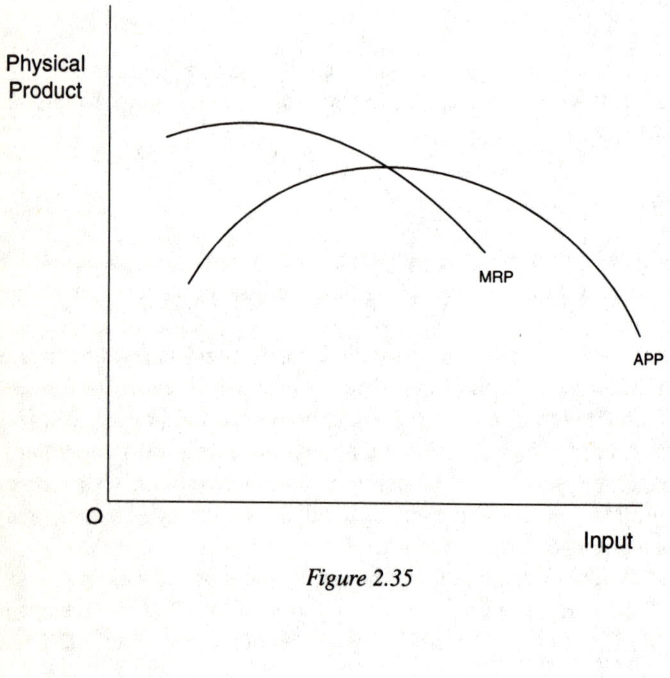

Figure 2.35

off to the left of A the distance AA′ representing one unit of the input. From A′ draw A′D′ parallel to OD (the slope of which represents APP) meeting AD at D′. D′ lies on the APP curve. Repetition of this procedure yields other points on the curve. To the right of D, APP increases until it reaches a maximum at E, declining thereafter. So the APP curve is an inverted U-curve, the reverse of the AC curve obtained earlier. In the same way we can obtain the marginal physical product curve (MPP), using the fact that the slope of the total product curve at a point indicates the value of MPP. Inspection of the slopes of tangents to various points on the total product curve reveals that MPP is at a maximum at the point of inflection of the total product curve, thereafter declining.

The MPP curve has the same characteristics as the APP curve and stands in a particular relationship to it: as APP rises MPP must rise more rapidly reaching its maximum prior to that of APP; MPP and APP will be equal at the maximum point of the latter; thereafter MPP declines more rapidly than APP. At point E, the slope of the line OG which expresses the value of APP also gives the value of MPP, since it is tangent to the Total Product Curve at E. The relationships between APP and MPP are shown in Figure 2.35.

Factor Demand and Revenue Product

Since the objective is profit maximisation, the producer will be interested in the relationship between the outlay on the inputs and the revenue gained through selling their product, rather than in their physical productivity. We can make the transition to this relationship if we retain the assumption that the producer takes the product price as given. By simply multiplying physical product by the product price we obtain revenue product. With the product price constant the average revenue product curve (ARP) will have characteristics determined by the APP curve.

We have a complication, however, which arises from the need to allow for the cost of the input whose level of employment is fixed – our assumption of the short run. So just as we made the distinction earlier between variable costs and total costs (the difference being termed fixed costs) we make the distinction between gross revenue (the total value of output sold) and net revenue. We thus obtain average gross revenue product (AGRP) and average net revenue product (ANRP). The ANRP curve consistently lies below the AGRP. This deduction, however, has no effect on the position and shape of the MRP curve.

Now we have to consider the ANRP in conjunction with the cost of the variable input in order to establish how much of the variable input the producer will use. Again, let us assume that the price of the input is given. In this case the average input cost (AIC) or price does not vary with the level of employment, and is equal to the marginal input cost (MIC); graphically represented in relation to quantities of the variable input, they coincide in a straight line. In Figure 2.36 the two sets of curves are brought together, and given the profit maximisation objective, the producer will hire OA units of the variable input where the wage rate is W_1. Using a series of values of the MIC we can obtain a series of values for the level of

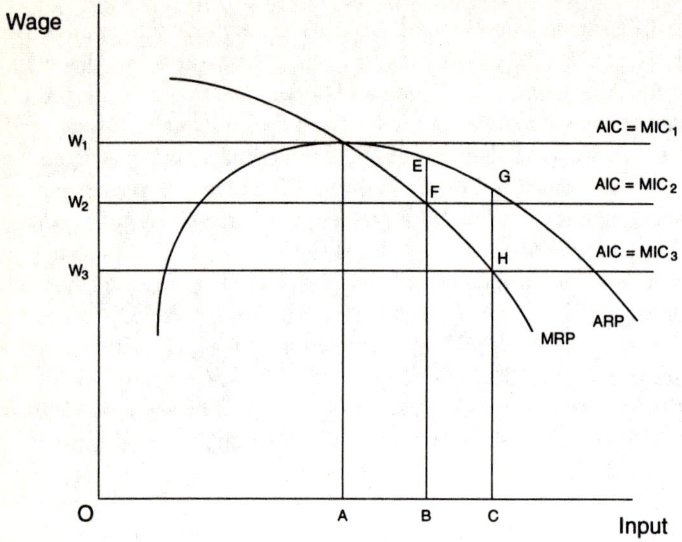

Figure 2.36

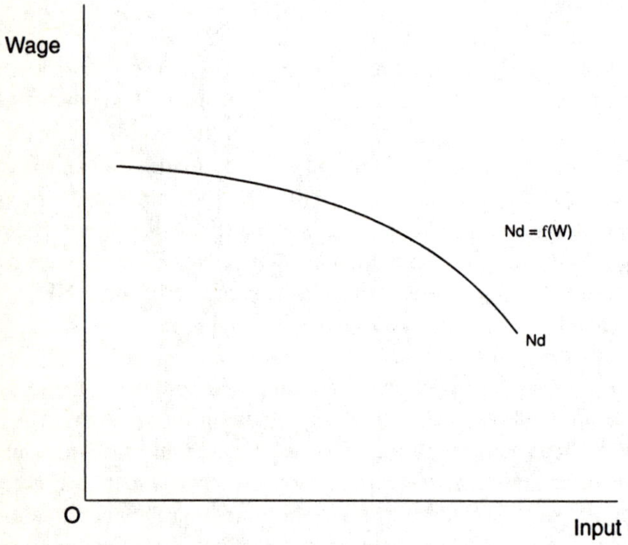

Figure 2.37

employment of the variable input (OA, OB, OC corresponding to W_1, W_2 and W_3).

The MRP curve therefore emerges as determining the producer's demand curve for the input (Figure 2.37) where employment levels and wage rates are directly related. Given this we can establish the position and shape of the market demand for the input by the same process of aggregation as was employed earlier.

It must be emphasised that the positions of the curves we have employed are inter-dependent. Average and marginal cost relationships were derived on the assumption of fixed input prices, that is a constant MIC (or AIC). Average and marginal revenue product relationships were derived on the assumption of fixed product prices, that is a constant MR (or AR). If either price were to change then the curve depending on its value would shift in position.

For example, if the product price rose the ANRP curve would shift upwards; if the product price fell the ANRP curve would shift downwards. But the same is true for changes in MIC of the kind we have just visualised, this time with respect to the average and marginal cost curves. An increase in MIC leads to an upward shift in the MC and AC curves, a reduction to a downward shift in the position of MC and AC curves. But if the product price is in the meantime constant it will be apparent that these cost curves are shifting their position in relation to that given price, so that as MIC falls, for example, an increasing gap arises between the product price and AC at the level of output which satisfies the profit maximising rule. Variation in the profit-maximising level of output is of course the counterpart of variation in the level of employment of the variable input in response to variation in its price.

[The Mathematics of Factor Demand

Cost functions and revenue product functions are both derived from the function linking inputs and outputs, i.e. the production function, by viewing it from different perspectives. Viewing inputs as a function of output, marginal cost is found to be the product of the input price and the derivative of the input (variable in the short run) with respect to output. Viewing outputs as a function of inputs, marginal revenue product is found to be the product of the output price and the derivative of output with respect to the input. These two views involve the inversion of the function, which is permissible given the constraints placed on the production function by the Law of Variable Proportions; these ensure that as long as inputs increase so too does output, and vice versa. That being so the average and marginal revenue product functions are in one respect in the same relationship to one another as are average and marginal cost, and in one respect in a different relationship.

First, defining revenue as the price of the product times output, which in turn is a function of the input which is variable in the short run, $P_Q Q(V_1)$, it follows that ARP and MRP are as follows:

$$\text{ARP} = \frac{P_Q Q(V_1)}{Q} \qquad \text{and} \qquad \text{MRP} = P_Q \frac{dQ}{dV_1}$$

Then by the same procedure as that employed to examine the relation between ATC and MC on page 82 the similarity emerges in that ARP has zero, positive or negative slope according as MRP is equal to, greater or lesser than ARP.

Second, the difference arises from the fact that while inversion of the function involves

$$\frac{dV_1}{dQ} = \frac{1}{\frac{dQ}{dV_1}}$$

the signs of higher derivatives are reversed, so one condition enforced by the Law of Variable Proportions becomes

$$\frac{d^3V_1}{dQ^3} > 0 \quad \text{but} \quad \frac{d^3Q}{dV_1{}^3} < 0$$

It then follows that while the derivative of the input with respect to output has a minimum, the derivative of output with repect to the input has a maximum. Consequently the relationship between MRP and ARP is such that the former cuts the latter from above at its maximum, found in a similar manner to that employed on page 82.

It was previously established that a necessary condition for profit maximisation was that product price equalled marginal cost:

$$P_Q = P_1 \frac{dV_1}{dQ}$$

Now given that

$$\frac{dV_1}{dQ} = \frac{1}{\frac{dQ}{dV_1}}$$

$$P_Q = P_1 \frac{1}{\frac{dQ}{dV_1}}$$

hence

$$P_Q \frac{dQ}{dV_1} = P_1$$

That is, MRP equals MIC, given that the price of the input is assumed given and so MIC = AIC. Given the conclusion above that the MRP will have a maximum value, it follows that the second order condition for profit maximisation will require MRP to be declining where MRP = MIC. In turn the demand function for the input will be the declining section of the MRP where MRP ≤ ARP.]

Summary: The Marshallian Functions

We have now established a number of separate functional relationships which are however inter-connected.

(1) The quantity demanded of a commodity is a function of its price, i.e. that Qd = f (P); cf. pp. 49–56 above.

(2) The quantity supplied of a commodity is a function of its price, i.e. that Qs= g(P); cf. pp. 79–95 above.

(3) The quantity demanded of a variable factor (labour) is a function of its price (wage), i.e. that Nd = f (W); cf. pp. 95–101 above.

(4) The quantity supplied of labour is a function of its price, i.e. that Ns = g(W); cf. pp. 64–69 above.

(5) The supply of saving from a given level of income is a function of the interest rate, i.e. that S (Y) = f (i); cf. pp. 69–75 above, and finally that:

(6) The demand for investment goods is a function of the rate of interest, i.e. that I = g(i); cf. pp. 75–78 above.

Chapter 3

Equilibrium and the Allocation of Resources: Perfect Competition

I. The Single Industry

We can approach the problem of equilibrium by examining a single industry (the partial equilibrium case) which is composed of a number of firms.

Let us assume that all firms work with the same factors of production, the same methods and techniques and that they are all of the same size. We also assume that each firm produces a single product, and that these products are indistinguishable from one another so that the pairing of buyer and seller is completely random. In addition we assume that there are large numbers of buyers and sellers so that neither the individual purchaser of the product nor the firm which makes it can influence the price at which it is sold – in short, the two parties are price takers. On the input side, we assume that there are large numbers of buyers and sellers of the variable input (labour), that its price is known, and that firms can acquire varying quantities of the input at that given price and without variation in quality. We shall also abstract from the problems of space.

Now it will be observed that these assumptions have certain consequences as far as our argument is concerned. For example, the assumption that all firms are of the same size means that we can work in terms of a single set of cost and revenue curves, and that we can treat these as representative of all firms which are members of the industry. The fact that we have taken as given the technical conditions of production, and the cost of the variable input, also allows us to establish the shape and position of the representative cost curves.

We can also establish the shape and position of the AIC line, which must of course be horizontal, since the firm is a price-taker with respect to the inputs. The assumptions made so far also allow us to establish the shape, but not the position, of the representative AR and ANRP curves. For the sake of simplicity let us now assume that the price at which the product is bought and sold is known and that it is compatible with profits in excess of normal (i.e. *in excess of that generally available rate of return which is in effect the supply price of entrepreneurship and for which allowance must now be made in constructing the firm's cost curves*).

The situation is illustrated in Figure 3.1. In this case the price charged is P and the rational firm thus offers the amount Ob (where MC = MR). Under the condi-

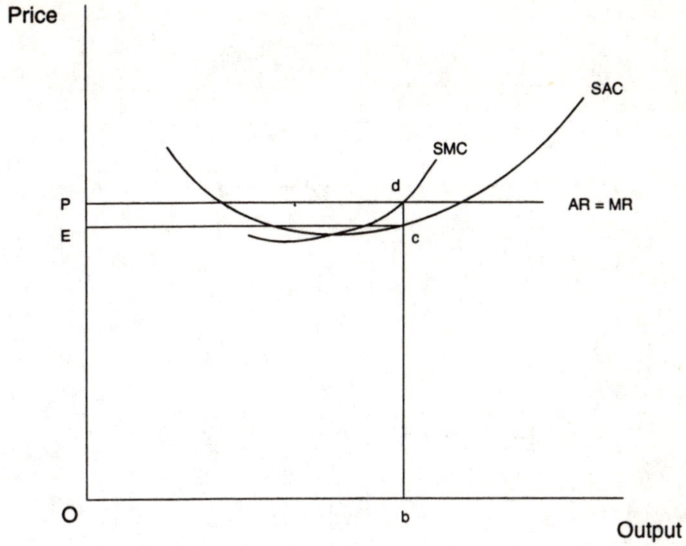

Figure 3.1

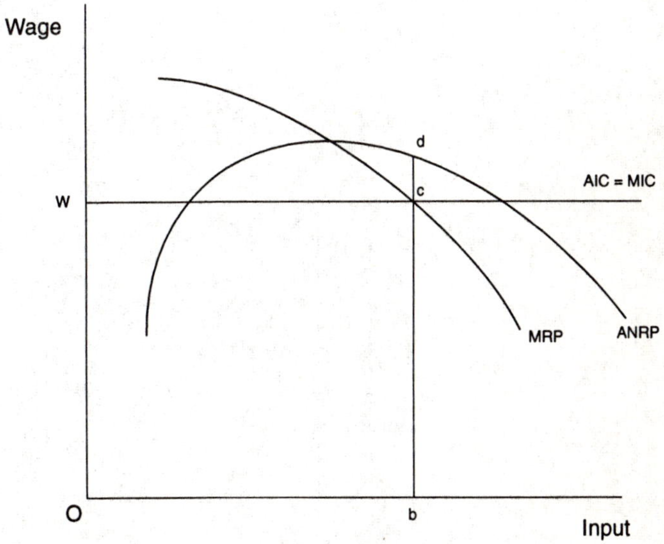

Figure 3.2

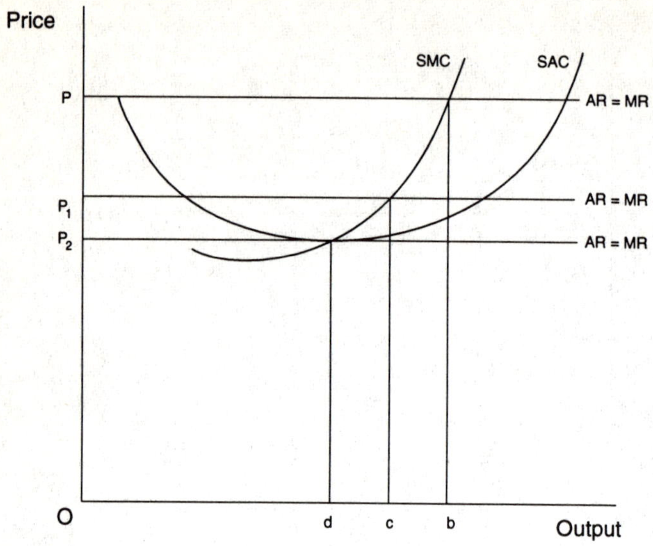

Figure 3.3

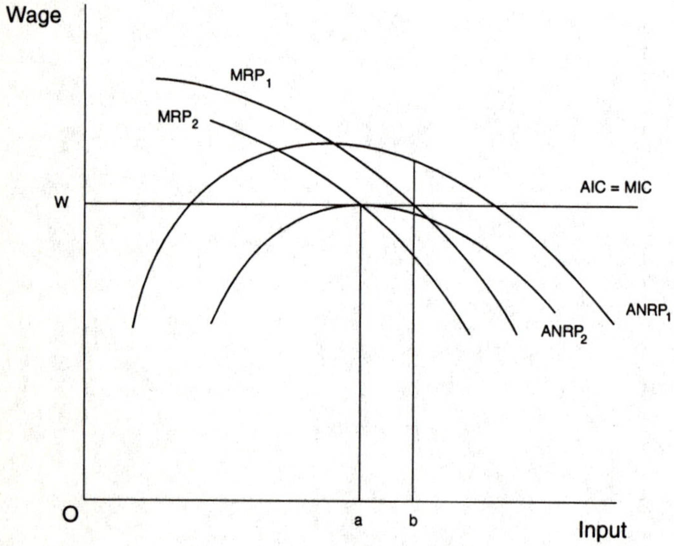

Figure 3.4

tions of cost and revenue shown, excess profit per unit is cd and total profit is expressed by the area cdPE. It will be noted that total revenue is represented by the area ObdP and that total cost is represented by ObcE. Output in the aggregate will be given by the contribution of each firm multiplied by the number of firms in the industry.

On the input side, the same situation is shown in Figure 3.2. Here the employment offered by each firm is Ob (MRP = MIC) and employment in the aggregate is once again determined by that offered by each firm multiplied by the number of firms involved. The existence of excess profits in this case is signalled by the fact that at the level of employment Ob, ANRP (bd) exceeds the cost of hiring the factor (bc) for each firm.

Now in a short run situation, this case represents the equilibrium attained by the firm, in that under the conditions prevailing it would not be in its interest (and not, therefore, in the interest of any other member of the industry) to change either the level of output or the level of employment offered.

Let us now assume that new firms can enter this employment in the long run and that they may do so under conditions of cost identical to those faced by existing members. With this assumption, it will be evident that the position of 'equilibrium' which we have just outlined cannot be regarded as stable since firms may decide to enter this employment, attracted by the excess profits which are available.

Our knowledge of the general characteristics of the aggregate demand and supply functions would lead us to expect that the increased number of firms would result in an increase in the level of output and, therefore, a reduction in the price at which it is sold. In Figure 3.3 a situation is considered where as the result of new entry, price has fallen to P_1, thus lowering the position of the AR curve facing the firm. In this case the output of our (initial) firm has fallen to Oc (MC = MR), while output in the aggregate has increased as a result of the change in the number of firms.

But once again, this cannot be regarded as a position of equilibrium, at least at the industry level, since the price charged is still compatible with profits in excess of normal. It therefore seems reasonable to conclude under the conditions assumed, that new entry will continue to take place until a situation is reached where the price charged (P_2) is just equal to cost, i.e. where the AR curve is forced down to a position where it is tangent to the AC curve and the firm is producing Od at minimum cost. Under these circumstances, MR = MC and AR = AC; there is therefore no tendency for firms within the industry to change the level of output and no tendency for firms to enter this employment since under the conditions shown the only profit available is the 'normal' or generally available level.

On the input side, the same situation is shown in Figure 3.4. It will be evident here that the process which altered the position of the AR curve must also lower the ANRP curve until a situation is reached where excess profits have been eliminated. In equilibrium for this market, the ANRP curve is forced down to a position of tangency with AIC so that AIC = ANRP and MIC = MRP. It will be observed that our representative firm now offers less employment than previously (Oa instead of Ob) but that employment in the aggregate must have increased due to the change in the number of firms.

Changes in the Position of Equilibrium

Using the same model, we can also consider the consequences of changes in demand conditions and by this means throw some light on the working of the allocative mechanism. Let us suppose that we start from a position of equilibrium in both the commodity and factor markets and examine the consequences of an upward shift in the position of the market demand curve. For the sake of simplicity we will initially abstract from the complication presented by scale changes on the part of member firms, and continue to assume that in the long run changes in the level of output will be generated by a change in the number of firms.

Consider Figures 3.5(a) and (b). In part 'a' we examine the position of the typical firm and in part 'b' the situation faced by the industry. In the initial position of equilibrium the price prevailing is P_1 and the aggregate quantity sold OA. In this situation, the aggregate demand curve (DD_1) intersects the industry supply curve (SR_1). In Marshallian terms the demand price and the supply price are equal. Each firm produces Oa units of the commodity where the AR curve corresponding to the price P_1 is tangent to the AC curve at the point c (Figure 3.5(a)). The demand curve now moves to position DD_2.

In the market period the only result is a change in the price charged, since this period is normally defined as being so short as to preclude any response from the member firms in terms of quantity supplied. In Figure3.5(a), the change in price alters the position of the AR curve facing the firm (to P_2) with the level of output constant at Oa so that profit per unit is dc. The demand price now exceeds the supply price.

This situation cannot be one of equilibrium for the firm in the short run where it is possible to change output within the constraints of a given scale of operations. In this period, each firm will obviously find it in its interest to expand the level of output since where price is P_2 and output is Oa, MC is not equal to MR. However, the consequence of each firm seeking to expand the level of output at the same time must be an expansion in aggregate supply and a reduction in market price. This case is represented in Figure 3.5(b) where the new DD curve intersects the short run industry supply curve at E, indicating a price of P_3 and a level of output of OB. It will be evident that this level of output will be made up of the contribution of each firm (Ob) multiplied by the number of firms (which has so far remained constant) and that in this case the excess profit per unit per firm is ef, (Figure 3.5(a)). Again, the demand price exceeds the supply price.

The consequence of this situation in terms of the labour market is shown in Figure 3.5(c) where the position of the ANRP curve has altered as a result of the price prevailing (P_3) and with it the level of employment offered. Once again the existence of excess profit is signalled in this market by the fact that the ANRP (bd)

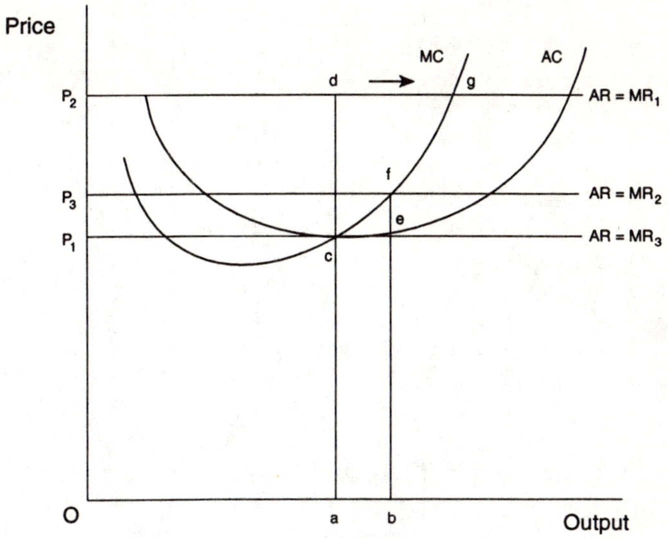

Figure 3.5(a)

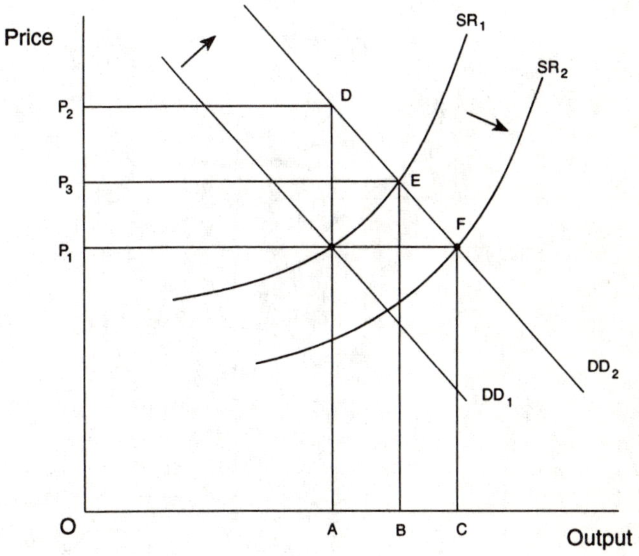

Figure 3.5b)

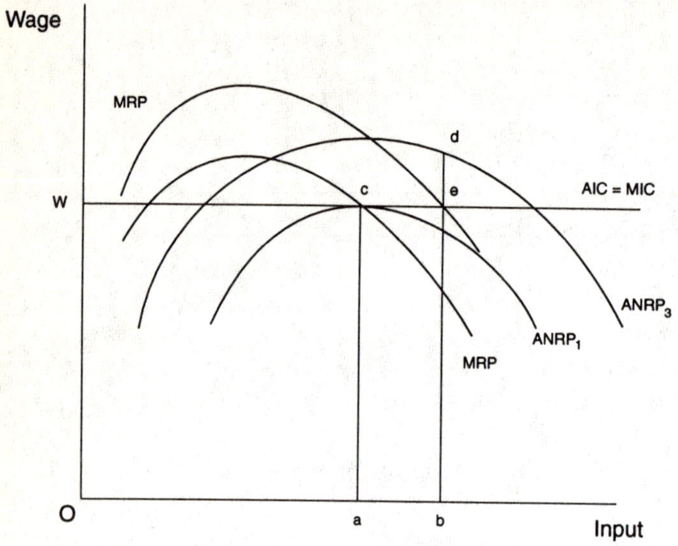

Figure 3.5(c)

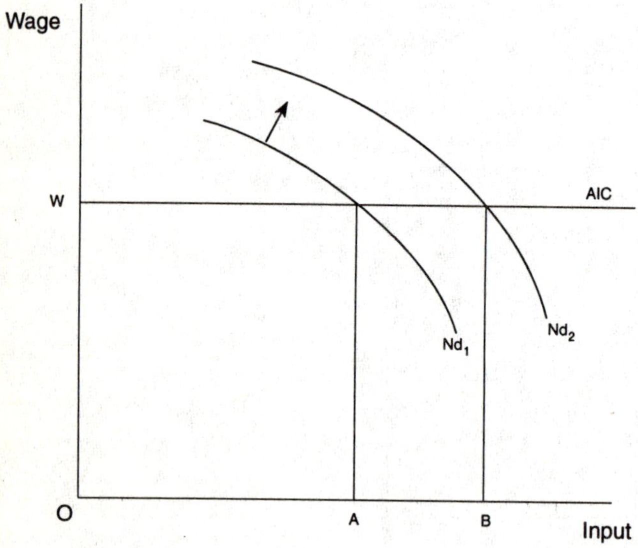

Figure 3.5(d)

at the level of employment Ob is greater than the cost of hiring the factor AIC (be).

In the long run, however, the situation as a whole cannot be stable since new firms will enter the industry attracted by excess profits, thus forcing the price down. As we have seen, the lower limit to this process is reached where as a result of expansion in supply, price settles at a level where the AR curve facing each firm is tangent to the AC curve, i.e. where AC = AR = MC = MR. In this case the contribution of the representative firm has fallen from Ob to Oa (Figure 3.5(a)) but aggregate supply has expanded as a result of the increase in the number of firms. In the labour market the same process results in a downward movement of the ANRP until once again the AIC line (which we have assumed to remain constant) is tangent to it, and where each firm offers a level of employment of Oa (Figure 3.5(c)). Here ANRP = AIC = MRP = MIC.

It will be noted, therefore, that the initial shift in the demand curve has some interesting consequences. In the commodity market for example, the consequence of this change must be a shift in the position of the short run industry supply curve from SR_1 to SR_2. The shape of this curve remains the same because it is determined by the shape of the SMC facing our representative firm, but its position must alter because of the change in the number of firms.

On the input side, our assumption that labour is freely available at constant cost means that we can employ a horizontal supply curve of labour. But it will be evident that the demand curve for labour must have altered in position due to the change in the number of firms 3.5(d)), moving from Nd_1 to Nd_2. Once again, our assumptions preclude change in the shape of this curve, which is determined by the shape of the MRP curve facing the firm.

In the case illustrated, each firm offers Oa units of the commodity; the price prevailing is once again P_1 and total output is OC. On the input side each firm offers Oa units of employment; aggregate demand for the factor is OB.

It may also be instructive to consider the reverse case, i.e. the consequence of a downward shift in the position of the market demand curve. Suppose as before that we begin from a position of equilibrium in both the factor and commodity markets, but abstract from the complication of the market period. In Figures 3.6(a) and (b) the initial position is such that at price P_1 total output is OA and the contribution of each firm Oa. Given a downward shift in the DD curve, the price falls to P_2 and the position of the AR curve with it, thus generating losses for the member firms. In the case chosen, output sinks to Ob (where MC = MR) but losses are involved since the selling price of the commodity (bc) is less than the average cost of producing this level of output (bd).

In the factor market (Figures 3.6(c) and (d)), the fall in the selling price of the commodity causes the ANRP curve to move downwards, thus leading to a contraction in the level of employment (Ob rather than Oa) with losses signalled by the fact that the ANRP (bc) is less than the cost of hiring the factor (bd). In both cases the marginal rule is satisfied (MC = MR and MRP = MIC).

In the short run then, we have a determinate result and a certain response to the change in demand conditions, but this cannot be a position of equilibrium in the

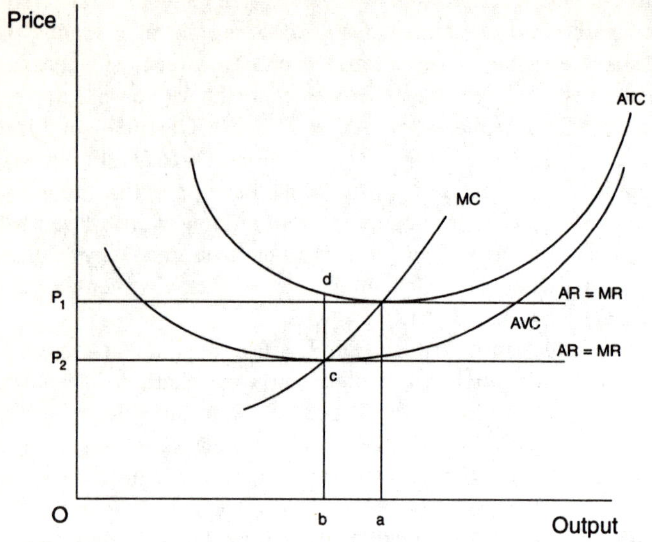

Figure 3.6(a)

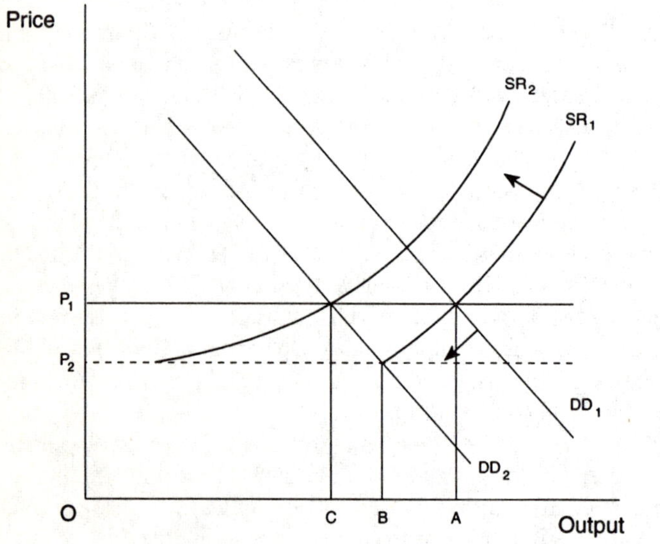

Figure 3.6(b)

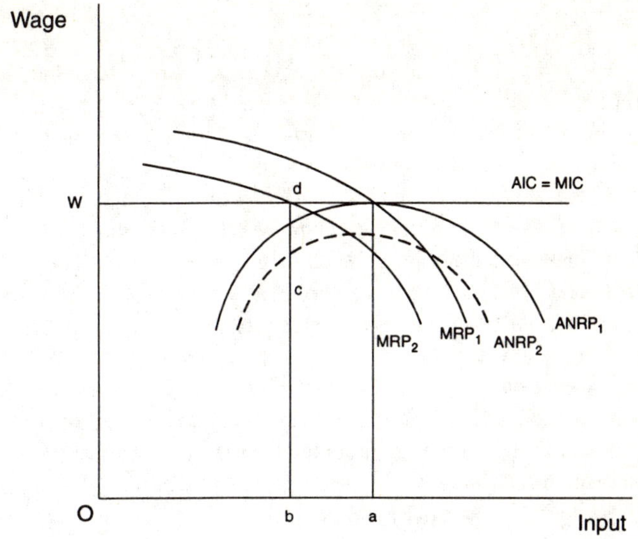

Figure 3.6(c)

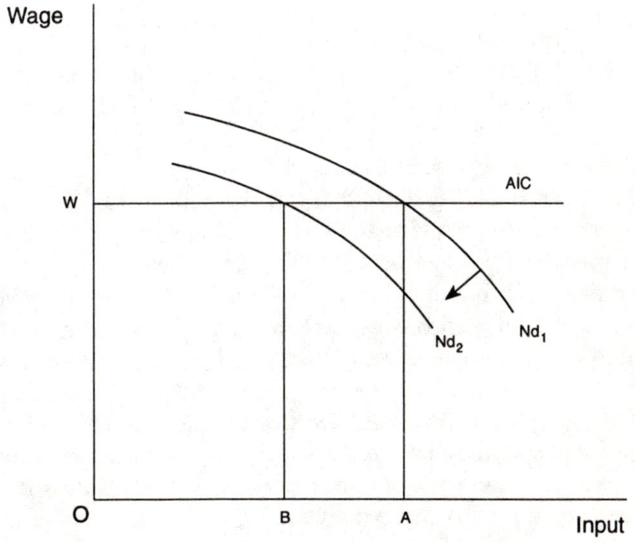

Figure 3.6(d)

long run in view of the losses which are being made. Firms must therefore leave this employment, driven from it by the losses incurred. There will thus be a reduction in aggregate supply which will allow prices to rise enabling the remaining firms to narrow the gap between cost and price. Evidently, this process will continue until each remaining firm is once again able to earn normal profits, i.e. where the fall in the number of firms has reduced output to such an extent as to allow price to rise to a level compatible with normal profits.

On the input side, the same process means that the position of the ANRP curve gradually rises until the tangency solution once more obtains (Figure 3.6(c)).

Once this process has worked itself out, each firm will be offering Oa units of the commodity (Figure 3.6(a)) but aggregate supply will now be OC units, reflecting the fall in the number of firms (Figure 3.6(b)); a change which causes the short run supply curve to move to the left.

Aggregate employment has now sunk to OB units, with each of the (reduced number of) firms once again taking Oa of the variable input (Figure 3.6(c)). Here again, it will be evident that the change in demand for the commodity has introduced certain consequential changes; this time in the position of the industry demand curve for the variable factor (Figure 3.6(d)).

Now these examples are separate and are really designed to illustrate the working of a process in terms of a simple competitive case. It will also be evident that they are examined in isolation: and that the firms which flow into, and out of, the two industries, come from, or go to, unknown destinations, although it is obvious that their arrival or departure must have repercussions not all of which we have examined here.

At the same time, however, it will be evident that our two partial examples do provide us (albeit indirectly) with the means of understanding the nature of the allocative process, and that they do illustrate the meaning of consumer sovereignty.

For example, suppose our hypothetical economy is composed of a number of buyers and sellers of goods and services; that total output and employment is known, and that there are only two industries (A and B) between which factors may move freely and without loss of efficiency. Suppose also that we start from a position of equilibrium in each industry and that there is a change in the direction of demand. We assume that the reduction in demand for the products of one industry is exactly balanced by the increase in demand for those of the other. In this situation our first example shows a rise in demand for industry A, and our second, a fall affecting industry B. Under these very restricted circumstances we can represent the process of re-attainment of equilibrium as involving a simultaneous movement to one employment and from the other in respect of both the commodity and factor markets. As the processes work themselves out, the net result is that the allocation of resources conforms to the (new) structure of consumer preferences. If we define equilibrium for our hypothetical system taken as a whole as a position which involves a state of rest, it will be evident that the following conditions must be satisfied:

1. Each consumer must purchase goods in such a way as to bring into equality the weighted marginal utilities of the last units of each of the (two) goods which are bought – otherwise some adjustment in demand patterns must take place.
2. Each producer must adjust the use of the factors used (plant and labour) in such a way as to bring into equality their weighted marginal productivities.
3. Each commodity must be sold at a price equal to its cost of production, where MC = MR = AC = AR, thus ensuring that there is no tendency for firms to adjust the level of output within a given employment.
4. Each factor in each employment must be paid according to its marginal revenue product such that MIC = MRP = ANRP = AIC, thus ensuring that there is no tendency for factors to move between employments.

In short, it is essential that there must be no movement within or between industries if our hypothetical system is to attain a position of rest. Such an argument is not of course very precise, although it does provide us with a means of visualising the inter-related processes which are involved in the allocative mechanism and an alternative perspective on the earlier (Paretian) discussion of the logic of choice (above, Chapter 1).

A Digression on the Long Run

It will also be observed that we have so far abstracted from the distinction between short and long run curves, and therefore the problem of scale changes on the part of member firms. The point is important in that the definition so far offered is not strictly adequate as a statement of equilibrium conditions which requires that MC = MR, where SMC = LMC.

The position is summarised in Figure 3.7. In part 'b' we have the aggregate situation showing that in the market as a whole the price charged is OP_1 and the amount offered OA. In part 'a' we show the contribution of the individual firm, Oa. It will be noted that in equilibrium the market demand curve will pass through the short and long run industry supply curves. The shape of these curves is determined by the short and long run marginal cost curves facing the representative firm, and their position by the number of firms which make up the industry.

This argument enables us to elaborate on our previous account. If we revert to the original example of an upward shift in the demand curve for industry A (Figure 3.7(b)), it will be evident that the movement to a new position of equilibrium may involve a short and a long run response on the part of the member firms, followed by an inflow of new firms. In Figure3.7 this process is represented as involving first a short run response, taking output as before to OB 3.7(b)) and the contribution of each firm to Ob (3.7(a)). This is followed by a long run response where the member firms seek to expand output through changing the scale of operations and with a view to bringing into equality LMC and MR – thus taking output to the level OC and the contribution of each firm to Oc at the price P_3.

In this case we may expect a further adjustment since the member firms are still earning excess profit per unit of ke thus attracting new entry which will in

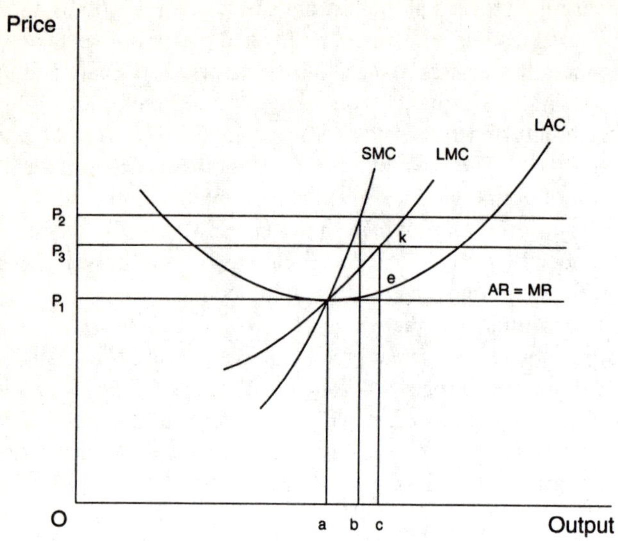

Figure 3.7(a)

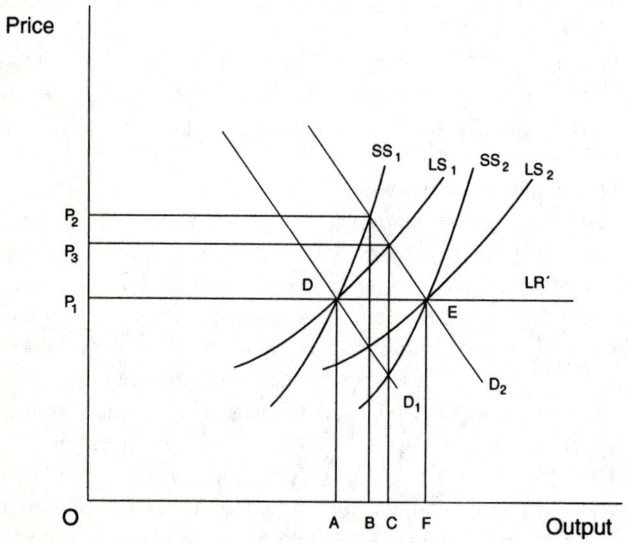

Figure 3.7(b)

turn further increase supply. We have in effect two long run supply curves: the long run curve which shows the way in which output will change on the assumption that the number of firms remains the same (LS), and the long run curve which shows the way in which the industry can expand through a change in the number of firms (LR′). A change in the position of the demand curve can now be seen to generate changes, with respect to the position of both the short and long run curves (i.e. SS_1 to SS_2 and LS_1 to LS_2).

The argument also confirms that the perfect competitor will necessarily operate (in equilibrium) at the 'optimal' level of production, i.e. at that point where the AR curve is tangent to the lowest point on the curve of long run average costs. As we have noted (above, p. 90, Figure 2.31(b)), in this situation LAC = SAC and SMC = LMC. Equilibrium for the firm thus requires that all the average and marginal values are equal, i.e. that AR = SAC = LAC = SMC = LMC = MR. Under these circumstances the ANRP curve will be forced back into a position of tangency with AIC.

II: Some Observations on the Argument

1. It will be observed that our outline of the allocative process was developed in terms of the simplest possible situation where in effect we took as given and fixed the shapes and positions of the AIC and AC curves facing the firm and only examined the consequences of change in the position of the AR and ANRP curves. In short, we abstracted from the presence of a positively sloped supply curve for the factor and therefore from the problem presented by the fact that in the short run a firm may face increased labour costs as it seeks to expand output in response to a change in demand. This situation complicates matters to the extent that a rise in demand for the factor may cause a rise in the value of AIC and therefore an upward shift in the position of the AC curve. It is evident that the difference between selling price and cost, or between cost of the factor and revenue product would be narrowed under these circumstances. It will also be evident that the result could be simultaneous pressure on both markets: new firms moving into the industry attracted by profits in excess of normal and labour attracted into the employment in question by the higher wages paid.

The result of both sources of change may then be a simultaneous pressure on the position of the AR and AC curves, matched by a like pressure on the position of the ANRP and AIC curves. This would seem to be a more realistic way of visualising the working of the process and one which also reminds us that the consequences of a change in the position of the aggregate demand curve will include a shift in the position of the (positively sloped) supply curve of labour which may face the industry in the short run.

2. It will be noted that the argument of this section has worked in terms of a particular hypothesis (rationality) and taken as its premisses certain results which were established elsewhere (e.g. with regard to the shapes of the cost curves). It will also be obvious that we have used two different kinds of assumption: those

necessary to define the market type (e.g. large numbers, homogeneous products) and those which enabled us to simplify the analysis (e.g. that all firms are exactly the same and face identical cost conditions). It therefore follows that the specific conclusions which we have reached are only valid within the framework which we have specified and that they inevitably follow from it.

At the same time, it will be evident that we can vary some of the assumptions without stepping outside our competitive model, and that when we do so some modification of results is to be expected. For example, the cases we have so far used all work in terms of a long run supply curve for the industry (LR′) which is a horizontal straight line, thus enabling us to say that a change in demand conditions will in the long run produce a situation where more or less of the commodity in question is sold at the original price.

Such a conclusion is not essential to the perfectly competitive case: it merely follows from the simplifying assumption made. It will be evident that in practice the industry may face diseconomies of scale thus giving both forms of long run curve a positive slope. Similarly, we have assumed that all firms are identical: in practice it may well be that some have superior entrepreneurs, or particular advantages arising from position (the problem of space) so that in equilibrium the contribution of each firm need not be the same. (See Chapter 6, where we review Chamberlin's discussion of pure as distinct from perfect competition). This kind of difference between firms may also be of great importance analytically especially since it may help to explain why some firms are first to enter a new employment, and why some firms rather than others are forced to leave when losses emerge.

3. The final group of points to be made in this section relate to the problem of time. We suggested at the outset that Paretian analysis was essentially timeless in the sense of being concerned with the 'tableau of equilibrium'. In contrast, as we have seen, the Marshallian argument has a time dimension at least in the sense of formally examining the way in which the system responds to changes in certain parameters.

The problem of movement thus examined is essentially dynamic in character – as we have seen, it unfolds through time in terms of a series of inter-related and continuous movements which culminate in a new equilibrium position. This kind of situation is often defined as a 'once-over change', but the point at issue is simply to note that as the process of change unfolds it must necessarily have a dynamic quality. This is important in the present context precisely because this dynamic process has been examined in terms of comparative statics – a technique which has obvious advantages in terms of simplicity and which amounts to taking a series of still photographs of a process at a number of separate but inter-related points in time. It is not the problem but the technique used to solve it that has a static aspect.

4. While the 'time dimension' of Marshallian analysis is to be perceived in terms of a pre-occupation with movements back towards positions of equilibrium in the event of some disturbance from it, this should not be allowed to obscure the

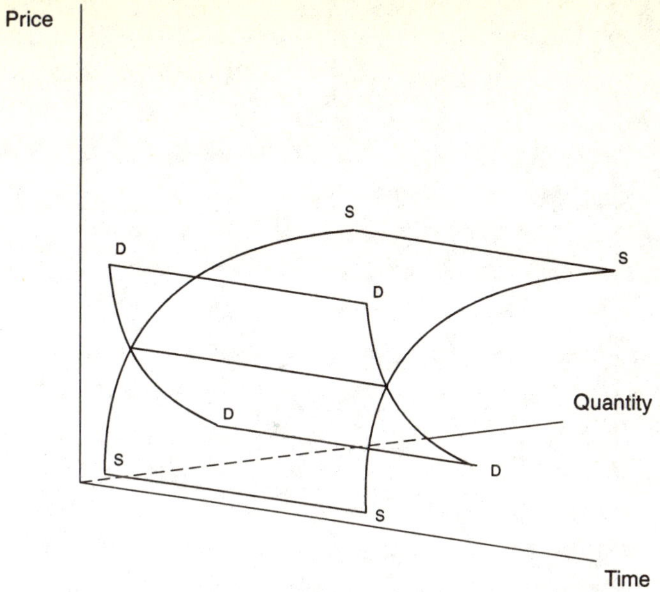

Figure 3.8

fact that a position of equilibrium once attained (and not just the process of attaining it) has a relationship with time. It will be recalled in this connection that in speaking of the output of firms we referred to a rate of output and in the same way referred to a rate of consumption on the part of the consumer – i.e. production or consumption per unit of time. The point is a simple one, namely that in a position of equilibrium the goods taken off the market at a particular price are used up by their consumers over time and continuously replaced, other things remaining equal. It thus follows that when we use a single set of demand and supply curves to illustrate a position of equilibrium we are in effect taking a time slice; we are examining a particular configuration of events at a specific point in time.

The matter can be put in another way by employing a diagram (derived from W. J. Baumol's *Economic Dynamics* (1962)) which adds a time axis to those expressing price and quantity (see Figure 3.8). It will be noted that looked at from this point of view our demand and supply curves become continuous surfaces.

5. Another aspect of time also examined by Baumol arises from the manner in which we treat the process of adjustment as we move between positions of equilibrium. It is evident that when we examine quantity adjustments we examine a situation which takes place over a period of time. But it will also be evident on reflection that implicit to this discussion is the assumption that such adjustments are simultaneous and immediate.

But there may be lags in the adjustment of supply to price in that it is not always easy immediately to put more or less of a commodity on the market.

Suppose a situation where there are lags in the adjustment of supply and that in consequence the SS curve now represents in effect the supply offered in period t + 1 in response to the currently prevailing price. Suppose further that there has been a reduction in supply perhaps in consequence of a dearth so that the quanti-

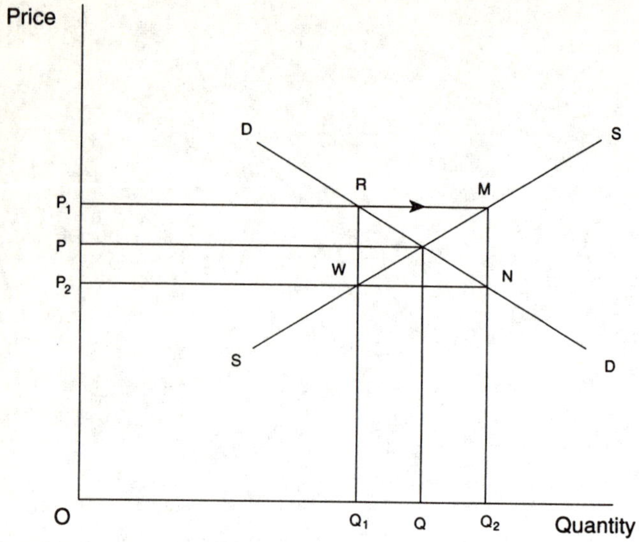

Figure 3.9(a)

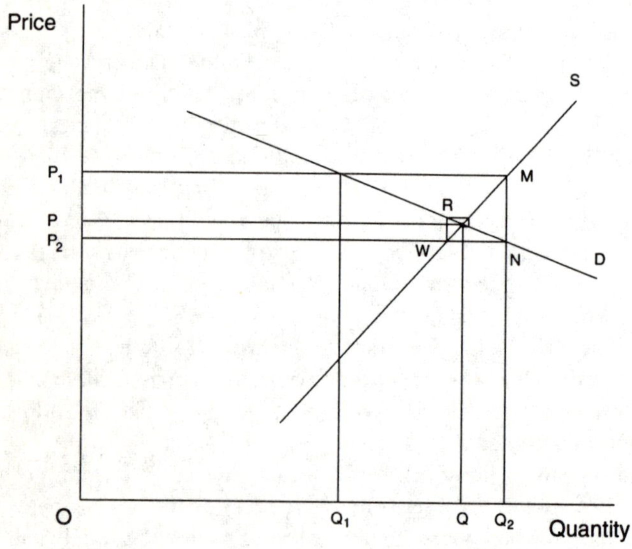

Figure 3.9(b)

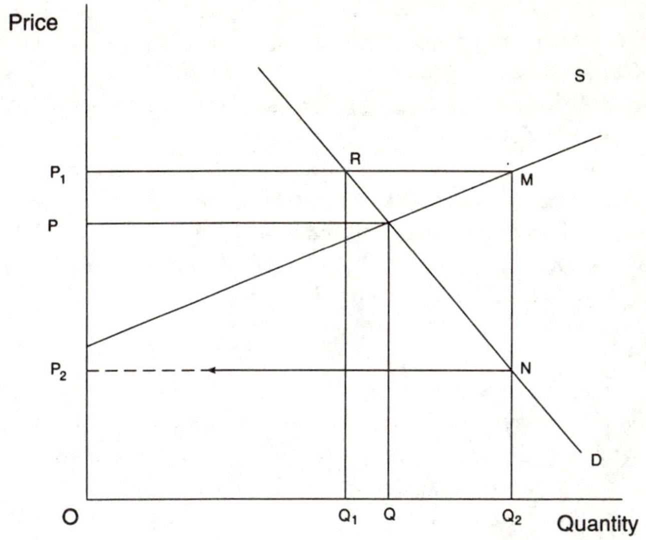

Figure 3.9(c)

ty offered is OQ_1 and the price P_1 (Figure 3.9(a)). In response to the price P_1 the quantity offered will be Q_2 in the second time period – but here the price sinks to P2 where the quantity supplied in the second time period will be once again Q_1 – thus restarting the whole cycle. Under these conditions our system would be moving continuously round the box RMNW – without ever actually attaining a position of equilibrium it would be constantly moving towards it. It should be observed that this situation will only obtain where the slopes of the DD and SS curves are equal but of opposite signs.

To take a second case (Figure3.9(b)) let us suppose that the slope of the DD curve is less than the slope of the SS curve. Assume once again a drop in the quantity available to OQ_1 so that the price rises to P_1. At the price P_1 the quantity offered is Q_2, causing the price to sink to P_2. It will be noticed in this case that even with lags in supply adjustment the equilibrium is necessarily stable, the requirement being that the slope of the DD curve is less than that of SS.

A further case can be examined where equilibrium is unstable as a result of the SS curve having a lesser slope than the DD curve – a further illustration of the Cobweb Theorem (Figure 3.9(c)).

6. It will be apparent that the discussion of time also raises problems of knowledge in that decisions taken at a given point in time generally involve expectations with regard to some 'future' period; expectations which may have to be revised. We have in fact already met one important example of this in the shape of the actions taken by firms when faced by a complex of factor and commodity

prices. As we have seen, this process of action and reaction only ceases when the 'equilibrium' level is reached – i.e. where the price which the firm takes as given does not alter in consequence of each firm so doing – that is, a case where expectations are in fact fulfilled.

Yet the type of decision taken by consumers and firms even within the framework of the simple model so far reviewed are of a kind which may make this unlikely, leading to a situation where our system undergoes a constant process of adjustment as expectations are revised – a point which does no damage to the concept of equilibrium or of the constant tendency towards it.

Problems of this kind are not difficult to find. For example, recall that the discussion of the logic of choice (when dealing with consumers) employed the assumption that realised satisfaction equalled that which was anticipated – an assumption which is unlikely to be completely valid especially when we allow for changes in taste through time. In the same way, consumers have to make choices regarding types of employment, as well as between work and leisure given the type of employment – all areas of choice where expectations may not be fully realised and where indeed information may not be entirely adequate.

In the same way we have noted that in the long run firms in effect make projections of costs and sales based on judgements as to the appropriate methods and scales of production – all of which may have to be revised in the light of actual events. In short, a competitive system (as distinct from a perfectly competitive system) is likely to be a system in movement for reasons inherent in its nature; (e.g. a market). It is a system with a number of objective features, which works by virtue of individual activities all of which reflect subjective judgements with regard to future events. The model of perfect competition which we have reviewed in this Chapter abstracts from problems of this kind by using the hypothesis of rationality and the assumption of perfect knowledge.

III. Observations on the Classical System

Before proceeding to the next stage of the argument, it will be useful to examine the relationship between the analyses of Chapter 2 and the content of the modern version of the classical system.[3]

The Basic Model of the System

1. It has been established (p. 80 above) that the output of a commodity in the short run will be subject to the Law of Variable Proportions. If we now suppose an economic system to feature constant technique, a fixed capital stock, and labour as the only variable input, we can state that aggregate real output (Y) is a function of the aggregate level of employment, i.e. that Y = f(N). Under these conditions

3. See G. Ackley, *Macroeconomic Theory*, New York, Macmillan, 1961, Part Two.

the marginal physical product of labour (the ratio of the increment of output to the increment of labour) will normally be positive but declining towards zero (Figure 3.10).

2. If the condition of perfect competition is satisfied, it has been established that the demand for a variable factor will be a function of its price, i.e. the demand for labour is a function of the wage, Nd= f(W) (pp. 95–101 above). The demand for labour at any moment will be determined by the marginal wage and the value of the marginal revenue product - the requirement being that the profit maximisation condition is met, i.e. that MIC = MRP. If we assume that there is perfect competition in all markets, output will be taken to the point where P = MC. Since labour is the only factor of production, MC = W/MPL (the marginal product of labour). Under these conditions P = MC = W/MPL so that MPL = W/P: - indicating that employment will be taken to the point where the marginal product of labour is equal to the real wage W/P (Figure 3.11). That is, Nd= f(W/P).

3. It has been established (pp. 64–69 above) that the supply of labour will be a function of its price, i.e. that Ns =g(W). The basic explanation of this relationship reflects the use made of the hypothesis of rationality, the argument being that the rational person will only undergo the 'fatigues of labour', i.e. the disutility involved, if this is compensated by the utilities received. In that money income represents the means of acquiring utilities it follows that the extent to which this compensation can be achieved must be determined by the real wage (W/P). That is, Ns =g(W/P). The curve is usually drawn with a positive slope, suggesting that the greater the disutility, the greater must be the real wage which is required to induce us to accept that disutility. The significance of each point on the schedule is that the supply of labour is taken to that level where the disutility involved in the last (and final)unit of work supplied is just compensated by the real wage (Figure 3.11).

The position and shape of the aggregate supply curve of the variable factor will be determined by the size of the working population and by the existence of a variety of opinion as to the disutility involved in supplying effort and the compensation required. In short, the aggregate supply function is obtained by adding together the separate functions which may be drawn for each individual in this hypothetical system.

4. If we now superimpose the Ns function on the Nd function (Figure 3.11) we can establish that the level of effort demanded and that supplied will be 0A at the real wage of W/P_1. It is also evident from Figure 3.10 that where the level of employment is 0A, the level of real output will be Y_1. Since output is generated by the use of factors of production, the model suggests that there must be a relationship between output and income.

5. The statement that the supply of saving will be a function of the rate of interest, i.e. that S = f(i) was discussed at pp. 69–75 above. This curve will normally have a positive slope, indicating that since the decision to forego present consumption involves a disutility, the greater the disutility incurred at a given level of income, the greater the compensation must be. As we have seen, the significance

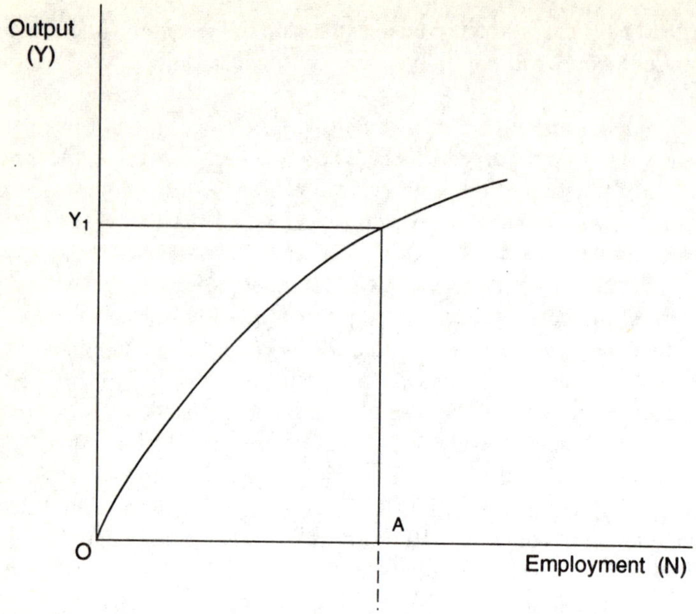

Figure 3.10

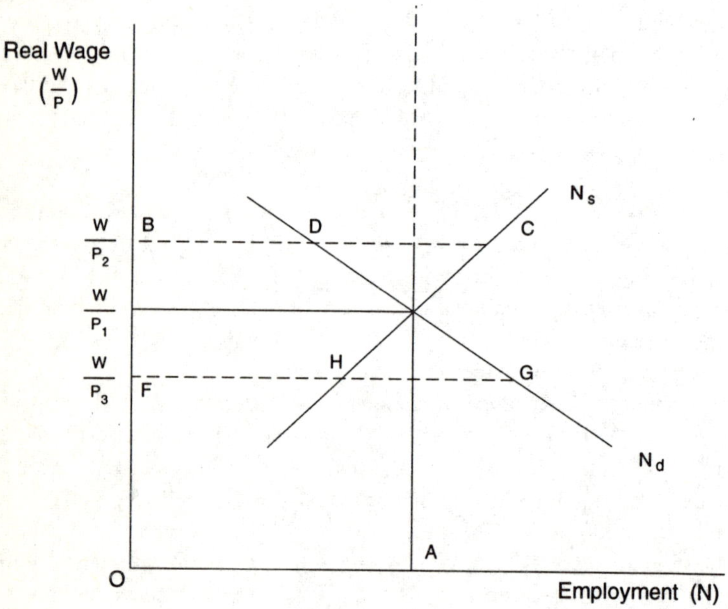

Figure 3.11

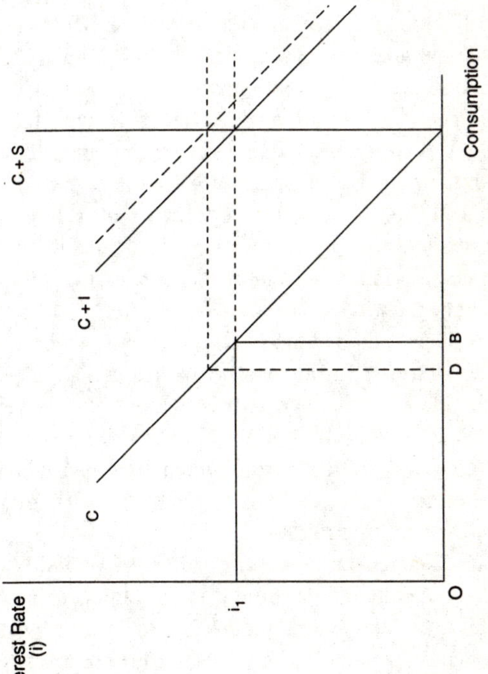

Figure 3.12(a)

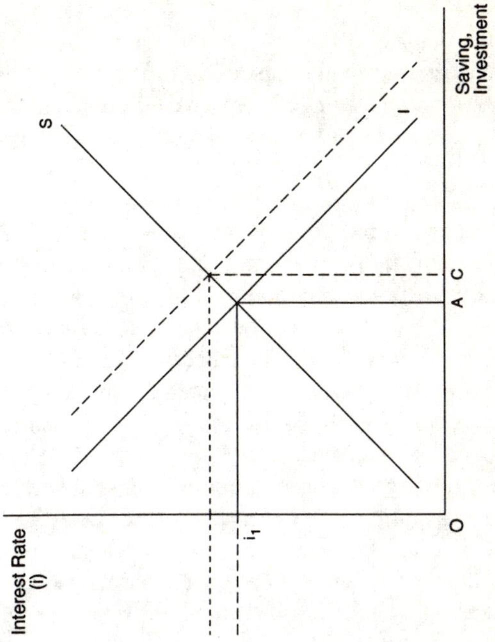

Figure 3.12(b)

of each point on the schedule is that saving is taken to that level where the disutility involved in effecting the last unit is just compensated by the rate of interest. The position and shape of the aggregate function will be determined by the level of income, its distribution, and by the existence of a variety of opinions as to the disutility involved and the level of compensation required. As in the case of the supply curve of labour, the corresponding aggregate function may be obtained by adding the saving functions of each individual in the hypothetical system (Figure 3.12(b)).

6. If saving out of a given level of income is a function of the rate of interest, it follows that consumption will also be a function of the rate, i.e. that C= c(i). The slope of this particular consumption function will be negative, suggesting that at high rates of interest the proportion of income devoted to consumption will be low (and saving high) and vice-versa. The outcome is summarised in Figures 3.12(a) and (b), indicating that various rates of interest will generate different levels of saving and of consumption. But since the level of income remains constant (by supposition) the saving and consumption functions must always sum to the same amount. If we add saving to consumption we obtain a vertical C + S line which summarises the possibilities at a given level of income (Figure 3.12(a)).

7. It has been established (see above, pp. 75–78) that the demand for investment goods will be a function of the rate of interest, i.e. that I = f (i). If we superimpose the aggregate investment function I on the saving supply function (Figure3.12(b)) we can establish that the level of saving and of investment will be 0A at the rate of interest i_1. Under these circumstances, the amount which it is intended to consume will be OB (Figure 3.12(a)). But since rational individuals working under conditions of perfect knowledge will translate an *intention* into an *act* of consumption, it follows that the level of demand for consumption goods will also be OB. If then we add the investment demand function to the consumption function, thus defined, it becomes apparent that we can obtain a C + I line which will intersect the C + S line at a point which is determined by the rate of interest, i.e. by the point at which the I and S functions intersect. Under these circumstances the equilibrium condition is met, i.e. that C + S = C + I.

We return now to the monetary sector.

8. If we look at the labour market (Figure 3.11) we have established that the equilibrium value of the real wage will be determined at the point at which the Nd and Ns functions intersect, i.e. W/P_1. It is evident that the real wage is provided by the ratio of W/P and that this ratio will hold good at a number of levels of W and P. The variety of values of W and P which are consistent with a given ratio of W/P are illustrated in Figure 3.13 where the slope of the line from the origin is determined by the prevailing ratio.

9. In order to discover the prevailing values of W and P we have to consider the supply of, and the demand for, money. Let us suppose that the supply of money is known and that it is exogenously determined. In our hypothetical system the only form of demand for money is for transactions purposes. With a given level of income, it follows that the demand for money will be a function of the physical

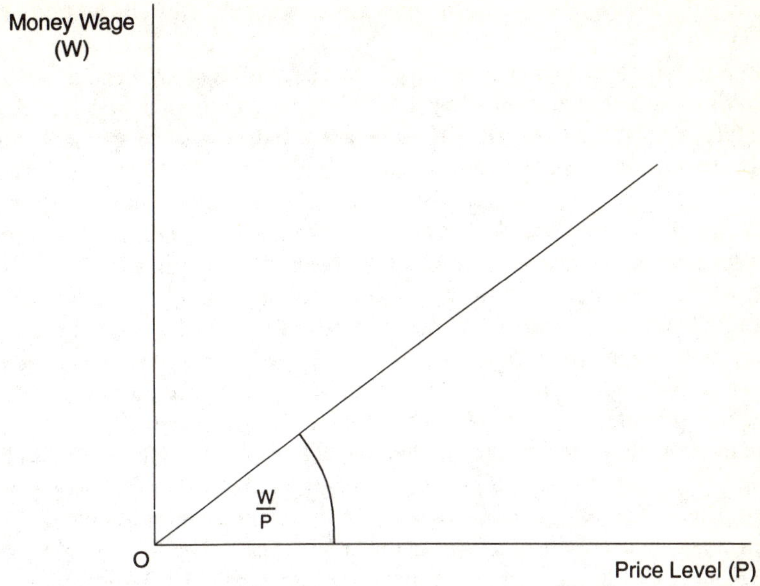

Figure 3.13

volume of transactions, the price level, and the velocity of circulation, i.e. that Md = f(T,P,V), where T represents the physical volume of transactions, P represents the general price level, and V represents the velocity of circulation.

10. Alternatively it may be stated that the supply of money will generate a series of levels of money income (Ym); a relationship which will be determined by the velocity of circulation. If then we assume that the supply of money is 0A (Figure 3.14) and that the level of income is Ym_1, and we know that the level of real output is Y_1 (Figure 3.10) we can establish the value of the price level and determine the associated value of W (Figure 3.13).

Manipulating the Model

Thus defined, the system can handle a number of changes without any damage to the relevant aggregates.

1. *The Price Mechanism*: We have already established that in a perfectly competitive environment, the demand for, and supply of, each commodity will be, respectively, a function of its price, i.e. that Qd = f(P) and Qs =g(P), (see pp. 49-56 and 79–95 above). We have also established that in a position of equilibrium each firm in each industry must operate at a point where AR = AC = MR = MC, while in addition ANRP = AIC = MRP = MIC (pp. 102–106 above). The argument also established that where there are movements in the positions of two market demand curves, price signals will be generated as a result of which the use of

resources will be adjusted to suit the prevailing preferences of consumers (pp. 106-113).

Let us return to the examples of industry A and industry B (above, pp. 112-113). Let us further assume that the aggregate level of consumption remains the same but that there has been a re-distribution in favour of industry A and against industry B. Under the circumstances illustrated, resources are attracted to industry A and impelled to leave industry B until a position of equilibrium is re-established.

2. *The Interest Mechanism*: We have established that in a position of equilibrium, the level of saving and of investment, together with the value of the rate of interest, will be determined by the intersection of the S and I functions (Figure 3.12(b)). If there is an upward shift in the position of the I function, this will generate a movement along the SY curve, resulting in a higher level of investment and of saving, and a reduction in the level of consumption. Saving have now risen to OC units and consumption has been reduced to OD units. Once again C + S = C + I, but with the C + I line now intersecting the C + S line at a higher point. It will be noted that the reverse movement in the position of the ID function will not result in a reduction in the level of income, but only in a redistribution of demand for investment and consumption goods as in the previous case. The price mechanism is once more of crucial significance in that any change in the level of demand for consumption and investment goods respectively, will generate price signals which will result in a redistribution of resources in a way which will reflect the current preferences of both producers and of consumers.

3. *The Labour Mechanism*: It was established above (Figure 3.11) that a position of equilibrium would be attainedwhere the Nd and Ns functions intersect, generating a level of employment offered and demanded of 0A and a real wage rate of W/P_1. Should there be a divergence from the prevailing value of the real wage rate, a competitive environment will enable the original position of equilibrium to be established. Let us assume that the position of the Nd function is likely to be stable (given the position of the production function) and that the Ns function is unlikely to change in the short run (reflecting a stable pattern of preferences). Should the real wage rate be higher than the equilibrium value, the supply of labour at the wage rate W/P_2 will be BC (Figure 3.11) and will exceed the demand (BD). In this situation those who are willing to work at a particular value of the real wage exceed the number required by employers. In a competitive environment the money wage rate would be bid downwards, allowing the supply of labour gradually to contract and the demand for labour gradually to expand until an equilibrium position was re-established.

Where the wage rate is below the equilibrium value (such as at W/P_3) the demand for labour will exceed the supply (FG and FH) respectively. In this case the money wage rate will be bid up, allowing the value of the real wage to increase until the equilibrium position is re-established.

4. *The Money Mechanism*: Where money can only be used for transactions purposes an increase in the quantity of money, other things remaining equal (i.e. the physical volume of transactions, and the velocity of circulation), will generate

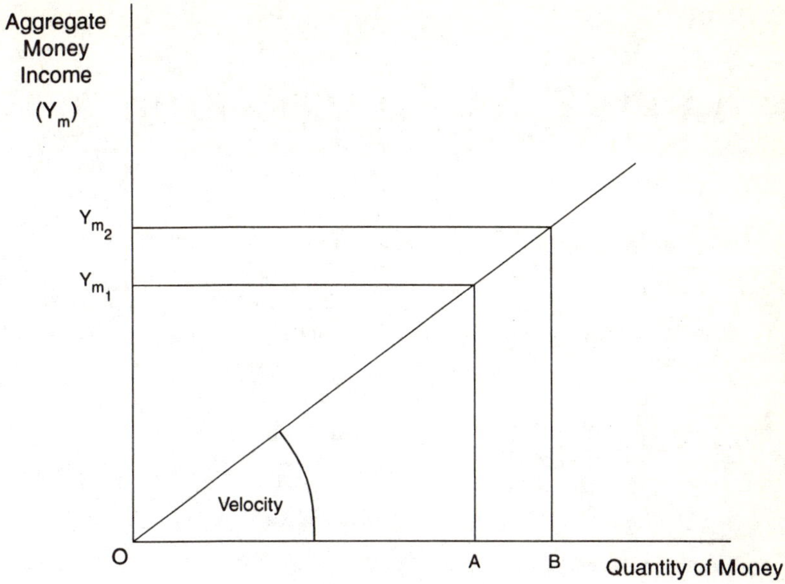

Figure 3.14

an increase in the level of money income, Ym (Figure 3.14). With output constant (Figure 3.10) the outcome will generate an increase in the general price level under the conditions assumed, and a corresponding change in the money wage.

Where the price level alters but money wages are slower to respond, the result is a fall in the value of the real wage (Figure 3.11). In this case the adjustment of the wage rate follows the reaction of the labour market as detailed above.

In sum, we have a system which is essentially self-equilibrating and capable of handling a series of changes without any damage to the relevant aggregates.

Thus presented, the system conveys very little as to the nature and content of classical political economy in either its pre- or post-marginal revolution forms. But abstraction that it is, the account does convey a view as to the self-equilibrating nature of a system based upon the key assumptions of perfect competition, and of perfect knowledge in all markets. This view of the economic process was to be attacked by J.M. Keynes, who dropped the assumption of perfect competition and explored the macroeconomic implications of a situation where decisions were taken against a background of uncertainty and of imperfect knowledge. The theory of monopolistic competition, broadly defined, followed the same path. Indeed it is no exaggeration to claim that the theory illuminates the nature of the competitive environment within which the Keynesian firm has to make investment decisions.

Before proceeding to the next stage of the discussion, it will be helpful to clear up some technical points by reference to the pure theory of monopoly.

Chapter 4

Monopoly and Competition

Section A: Monopoly

I. Output Analysis

Although Pure Monopoly would be established where a single seller manufactured a product on which the whole of the consumer's income was spent, we here confine attention to a simpler case: that of a single seller of a commodity which has no close substitutes so that cross-elasticity will be low (see page 61).

In addition, we can make a number of simplifying assumptions, namely that entry to the industry is blocked; that no buyer or group of buyers of the product can have a significant effect on price, and that there is a state of perfect competition in the labour market - the latter assumption being one which we will drop later in the argument. We continue to use the assumption of perfect knowledge with regard to the monopolist, and the hypothesis of economic rationality. We also take as given the shapes of, and relationships between, the short and long run AC and MC curves together with the assumptions employed when establishing these relationships - namely, that factors are available at a given price and quality and that the methods and techniques of production, together with the managerial input, remain fixed.

These assumptions allow us to work in terms of a single set of cost and revenue curves as distinct from using a representative set - the point being that the monopolist is the sole seller. We can also treat the cost and revenue conditions facing the firm as being independent of one another; that is, the monopolist takes the market demand curve (the AR curve) as given, so that the main area of choice relates to the level and scale of output.

However, before examining the rather restricted areas of choice open to the monopolist operating under the above conditions it may be useful to elaborate on certain features of the case:

1. When dealing with the consumer's demand for a particular product it will be

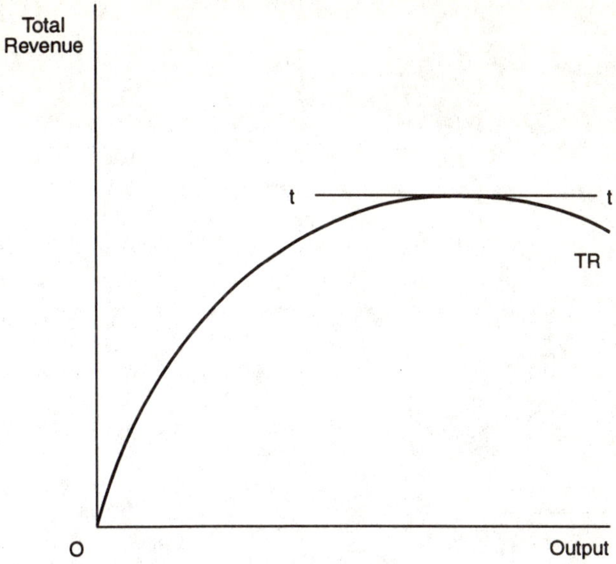

Figure 4.1

recalled that a specific shape was ascribed to the Price Consumption Curve; namely, that total expenditure would increase, reach a maximum point, and thereafter decline (see above, p. 52). It will therefore be evident that the single seller of a particular product will typically face a total receipts or total revenue curve which will rise over a certain range, reach a maximum point and thereafter decline. That is, while receipts increase as price falls total revenue will increase but at a diminishing rate until it reaches a maximum and thereafter declines. The situation is illustrated in Figure 4.1, where total revenue is measured on the *y*-axis, and output on the *x*-axis.

2. Profit maximisation can be illustrated by taking in conjunction the set of cost and revenue curves which face the firm. In Figure 4.2 the total (short run) cost curve is added to the total revenue curve. As in the earlier discussion of perfect competition, profits will be maximised where the vertical distance between the cost and revenue curves is greatest. Since at this point the slopes of the two curves will be the same, and since the slope of the curve at a point determines the relevant marginal value, the profit maximisation condition can once again be written in the form MC = MR. In Figure 4.2, the equilibrium level of output is OA; the maximum vertical distance between the curves is shown by BC.

3. Where the TR curve has the characteristics shown, the AR and MR curves which can be derived from it must have particular shapes and stand in a particular relationship to one another.

In Figure 4.3 where the level of output is OA, TR is AB and AR = AB / OA; that

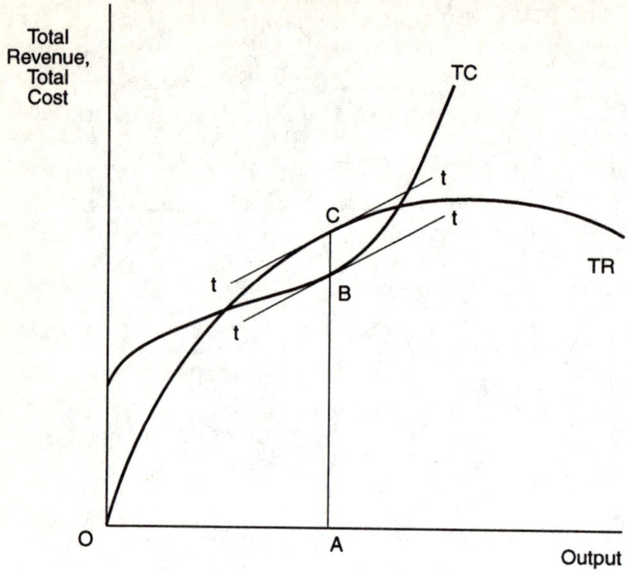

Figure 4.2

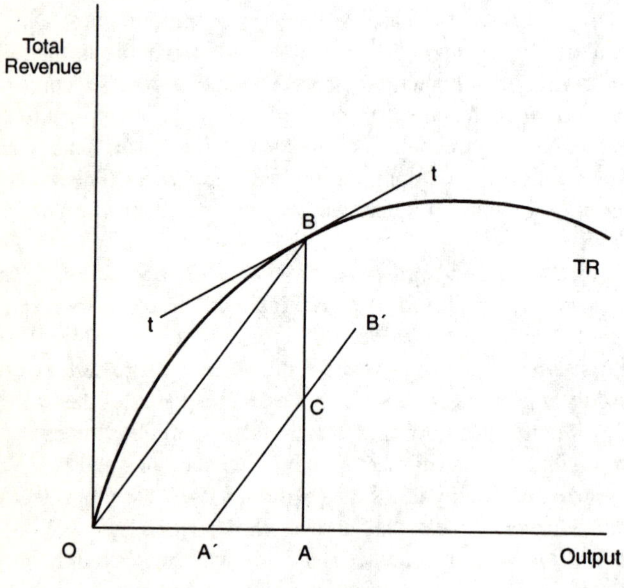

Figure 4.3

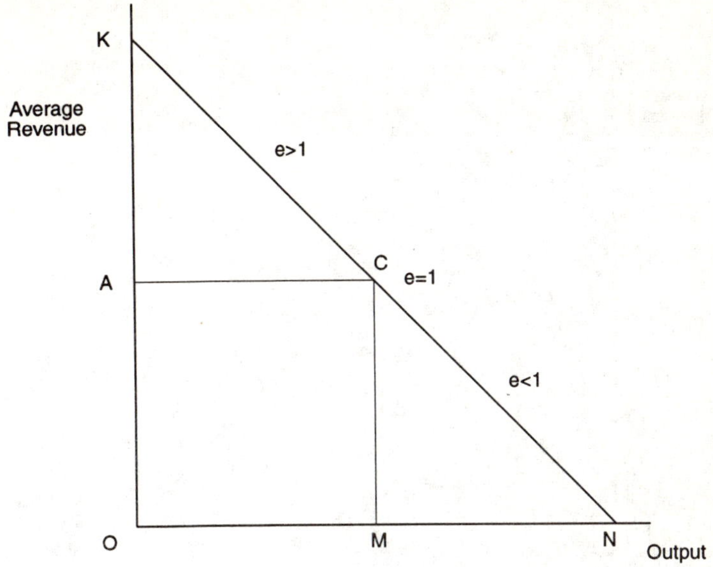

Figure 4.4

is, the value of AR at this level of output can be expressed in terms of the slope of the line OB. Using the now familiar technique, we can establish a point on the firm's AR curve by marking off to the left of A, a distance AA´ to represent one unit of the commodity. The line A´B´ drawn parallel to OB will then yield a point on the AR curve where it cuts the vertical AB at C. It will be apparent, if we take a series of levels of output beyond OA, that the value of AR must be progressively falling – i.e. that the AR curve will slope downwards to the right. This is, of course, exactly what we would expect given that the typical market demand curve has already been given this shape.

Marginal revenue can be handled in the same, again familiar, manner. The slope of the TR curve at a point determines the value of MR and it will be apparent that for a given value of AR, MR will necessarily be less. At the point B on the TR curve for example (Figure 4.3), the value of MR can be expressed in terms of the slope of a tangent drawn to the curve at that point – the slope of such a tangent being necessarily less than the slope of the line OB.

It will be evident that we can establish points on the MR curve using the same technique as for the AR curve; that such a curve will be negatively sloped and that it will lie consistently below the AR curve to which it corresponds. It will also be obvious from inspection of the curve, that where TR has reached a maximum, MR must be zero (the tangent drawn to the curve at that point will be parallel to the x-axis). This is illustrated in Figure 4.1.

4. In the case of a straight line AR curve such as that shown in Figure 4.4, total

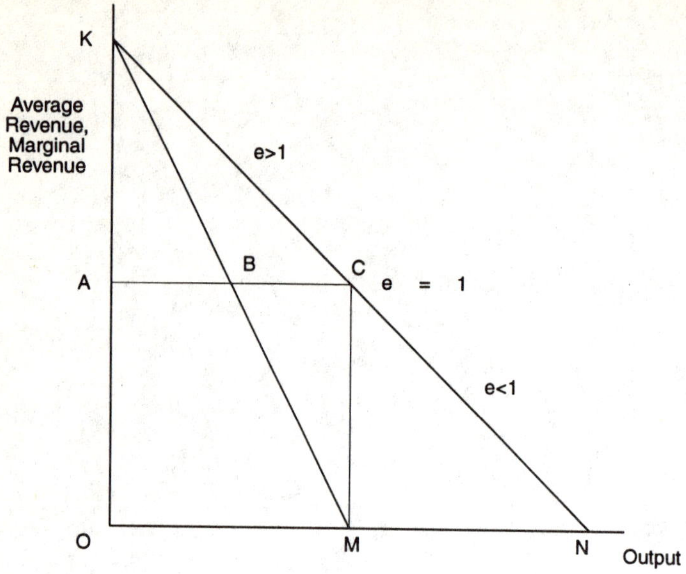

Figure 4.5(a)

revenue will be at a maximum at the level of output OM (where OM = MN, the rectangle OMCA is the largest which can be described in the triangle OKN). Where TR is at a maximum, elasticity is equal to 1: we may therefore conclude that over the range KC elasticity is greater than 1; equal to 1 at the point C and less than one over the range CN. This also means that as we move from N to C, TR is increasing until it reaches a maximum once again at C and thereafter diminishes as we move in the direction CK.

5. Consider now the curve of marginal revenue. Figure 4.5(a) reproduces Figure 4.4 with the addition of the MR curve. We have already established that MR will be zero where TR has reached its maximum value, so that the MR curve must pass through the point M. Two points follow:

(a) Given a linear AR curve the corresponding MR curve will bisect a horizontal line drawn from the y-axis to meet AR.

This can be established geometrically:

In terms of Figure 4.5(a), we need to prove that AB = BC.

Area ACMO = Area KMO (the first measures TR in terms of the product of output and price; the second sums the additions to TR).

Area ACMO = Area ABMO + ΔBCM

Area KMO = Area ABMO + ΔAKB

Δs BCM and AKB are equal in area; in addition

∠BAK = ∠BCM (right angles);

∠KBA = ∠CBM (vertically opposite)

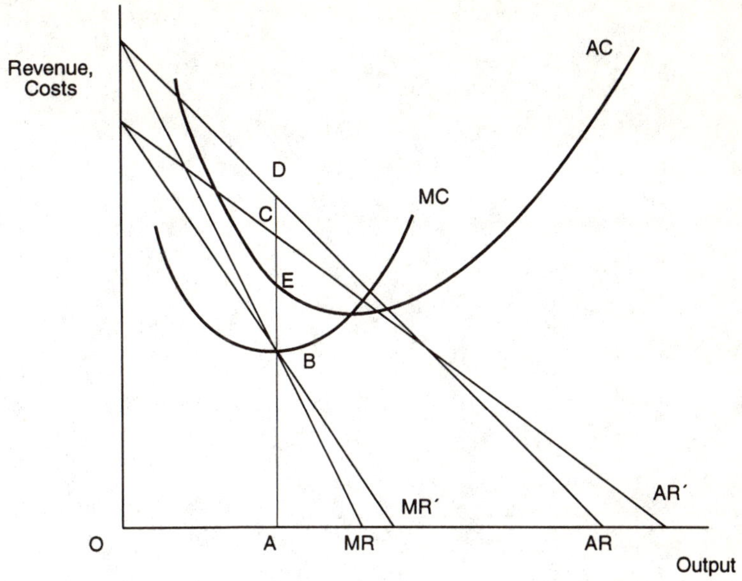

Figure 4.5(b)

The Δs are thus equal in all respects. It follows that

AB = BC.

(b) Where the elasticity of the AR curve is greater than 1, MR will be positive, where it is equal to 1 MR will equal zero and where it is less than 1, MR will be negative.

This can also be established geometrically:

We know that AB = BC (see above) and that elasticity at the point C is given by CN/CK (see pages 57–58). Since Δs AKC and CMN have equal angles, CN/CK = CM/KA. Since Δs KAB and BCM are equal in all respects (see above), then instead of writing elasticity as CM/KA it can be expressed as CM/MC, or as AR/(AR – MR). So, for example, at the point C, MR = 0 and consequently elasticity = 1.

This can be used to derive a useful result linking profit and elasticity, where two AR functions exist with their MR curves both intersecting MC at the same point. In Figure 4.5(b):

In general, elasticity = AR/(AR–MR)

Elasticity at C is AC/(AC–AB)= AC/BC = (AB + BC)/BC

Elasticity at D is AD/(AD–AB) = AD/BD = (AB + BD)/BD

But in addition, AD > AC, i.e. BD > BC; so AB/BC > AB/BD

So Elasticity at C > Elasticity at D

But CE < DE

∴ Profit per unit (DE) is greater at the point with the lower elasticity.

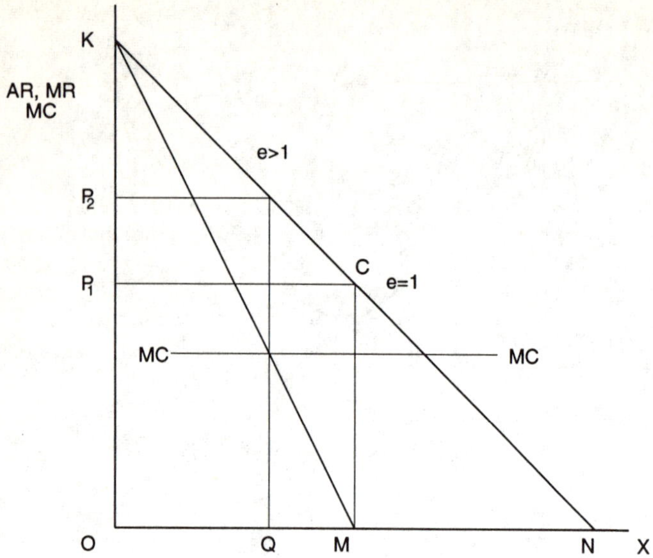

Figure 4.5(c)

Equilibrium

The points made so far enable us to establish some preliminary results with regard to the monopolist's choice of price/output.

1. For example: if we assume that MC is zero (Figure 4.5(a)) then given the hypothesis of rationality the output chosen will be OM, since at this level of output MR = MC (where both are zero) and TR is at a maximum. This means of course that where MC is zero, the monopolist will choose to operate at that point on the AR curve where elasticity is equal to 1. (Note that we obtain a single determinate position of equilibrium because it is assumed that there is a single point on the AR curve where elasticity equals 1. If there were a range over which TR was constant, there would be a range of the MR curve where MR equalled zero and therefore a number of levels of output which satisfied the profit maximising condition).

2. In the same way it will be evident that where MC is positive, the monopolist will operate on a section of the AR curve where elasticity is greater than 1. In Figure 4.5(c), for example, let us suppose that our single seller now faces positive marginal costs, here represented as a straight line. The output of OM which was chosen when MC was zero (price P_1) will no longer represent a position of equilibrium, and in consequence will be reduced to OQ (price P_2). It will be observed that in reducing output from OM, TR is decreasing, but not by as much as the decrease in costs. To put the same point in another way, it will pay to go on reducing output so long as MC exceeds MR, since by so doing the reduction in revenue

which comes from reduced sales is exceeded by the reduction in costs arising from falling output. By the same token, output will not be reduced beyond OQ since in this case the reduction in revenue would exceed the reduction in costs (the MR curve lying consistently above MC).

3. Given these results, it will be apparent that an equilibrium position under conditions of monopoly can be attained with a horizontal MC curve; an outcome which would not appear to be possible under conditions of perfect competition, at least where the MC and MR curves coincide. In the same way, an equilibrium solution can be found even where the MC curve is negatively sloped – the necessary condition being that the slope of the MC curve is higher in value than MR. These cases are illustrated in Figures 4.6(a) and 4.6(b).

4. A more conventional illustration of equilibrium is given in Figure 4.7 where average and marginal cost and revenue curves are used in conjunction. Here the level of output chosen will be OM, where MC = MR. Cost per unit will be MD and selling price MC, so that excess profit per unit is DC (we continue to make allowances for 'normal profit' in constructing the AC curve). Total Revenue is thus OMCB, Total Cost OMDA (cost per unit multiplied by the number of units sold) and Total (excess) Profit is represented by DCBA.

Finally, we should note that a position of equilibrium properly so called would not necessarily obtain where MC = MR if the MC curve in question is short run. For example, if MC = MR and the long run marginal cost curve lay below the SMC it would pay the firm, given the opportunity, to change the scale of operations – a process of adjustment which would continue (assuming stable demand conditions) until MC = MR where SMC = LMC (and thus SAC = LAC at the equilibrium level of output). In this situation the firm will have no incentive to change the level of output at a given scale of operations or that scale itself (Figure 4.8).

Conclusions

Given our assumption that entry to the industry is blocked, the model so far generates the following conclusions:

1. Given demand conditions over which the firm is assumed to have no control the most important area of choice relates to the choice of scale of operation.

2. Given the divergence between AR and MR, satisfaction of the profit maximisation condition necessarily results in price exceeding MC, though as we shall see this need not entail price exceeding AC (*i.e.* excess profits being earned).

3. Given the independence of revenue and cost curves, the existence of excess profits will depend on the relative positions of the AR and AC curves.

4. Given a particular profit maximising level of output (MC=MR), the extent of any excess profit could be said to be dependent on the elasticity of demand, such that the amount of profit is higher the lower is the elasticity, as is the rate of profit. (See above, Figure 4.5(b)).

5. Finally, there emerges from the discussion a technical complication regarding the status of the the statement that supply is a function of price. Where perfect

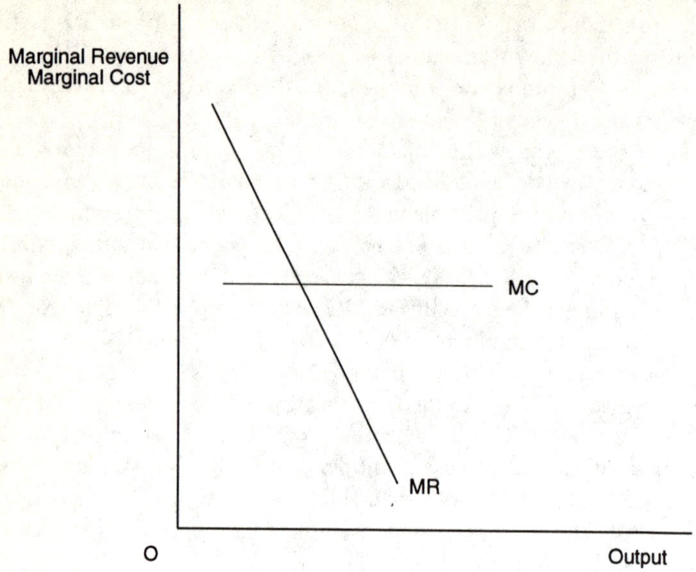

Figure 4.6(a)

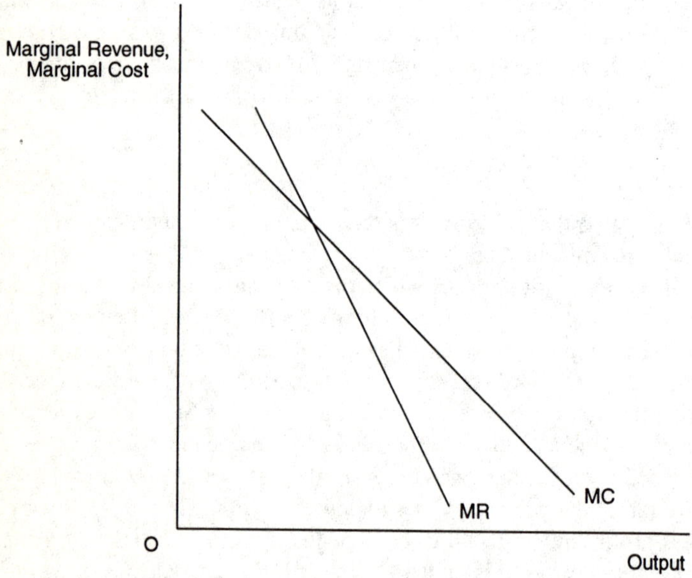

Figure 4.6(b)

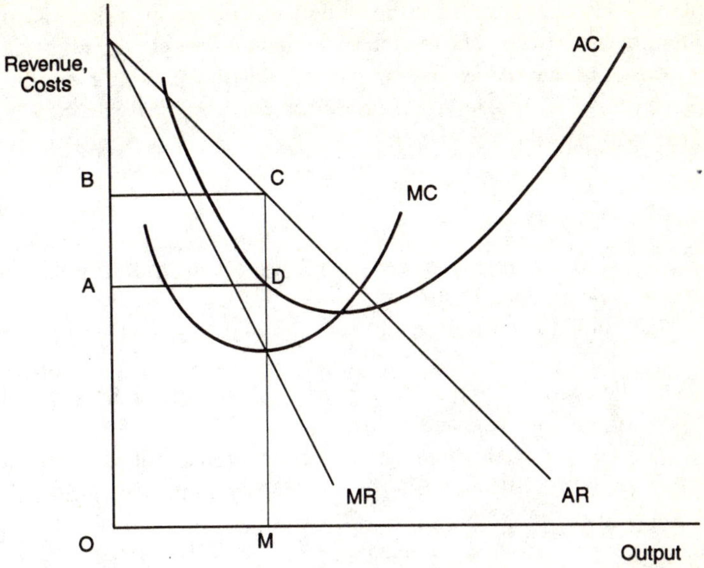

Figure 4.7

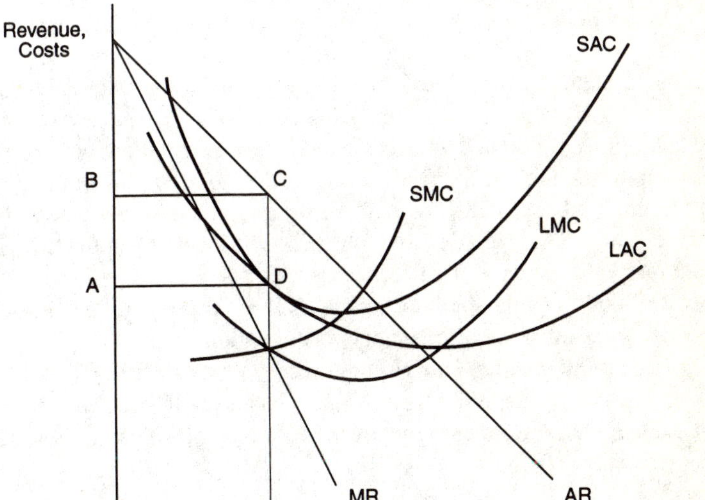

Figure 4.8

competition prevails there is an unambiguous continuous relationship between price and output. But under monopoly various prices can be associated with a given level of output, depending on the position and slope (*i.e.* elasticity) of the demand curve. Consequently, the supply curve as previously defined is restricted to perfect competition.

Further Possibilities

The examples so far employed seem to suggest a number of further possibilities which deserve comment; namely, that:

1. The level of output chosen will be 'sub-optimal' as that term was previously defined.
2. The maximisation of profit will be equated with the attainment of maximum profit in the long run, and,
3. The price charged and the level of output offered will be, respectively, greater and less, than those which would prevail under conditions of perfect competition.

All of these possibilities, which are apparently suggested by the previous argument, require, in fact, some qualification.

1. 'Sub-optimal' levels of output

'Sub-optimal' levels of output refer to the kind of comparison which is suggested by the previous treatment of perfect competition, where it was established that the typical firm would necessarily choose that level of output which was compatible with the lowest cost per unit. Conceptually, this could also be the case for the monopolist, although it will be evident that the most profitable choice of plant could correspond to any point on the LAC curve. This means in effect that under some conditions of demand and cost the monopolist could operate on the declining section of the LAC, the rising section of the curve, or, (as in Figure 4.9) at a level of output where the MR curve passed through the lowest point on the LAC curve, i.e. where SAC = LAC; SMC = LMC, at the level of output OM. The apparent contrast with the case of perfect competition thus appears to be not so much the level of output as the fact that such a level of output will be compatible with profits in excess of 'normal' in a monopoly situation. In the case illustrated, total costs are given by the area OMDA, total receipts are OMCB and total ('excess') profit by ADCB. On the other hand, while we can say that the 'perfect' competitor *will* operate on the lowest point of the LAC curve, we can only state that the monopolist *may* do so.

2. Maximum Profits

The choice of output may not be that which is consistent with maximum profits when allowance is made either for the threat of entry or for the possibility of external intervention, e.g. by the 'government' – a case which is often cited as 'limit

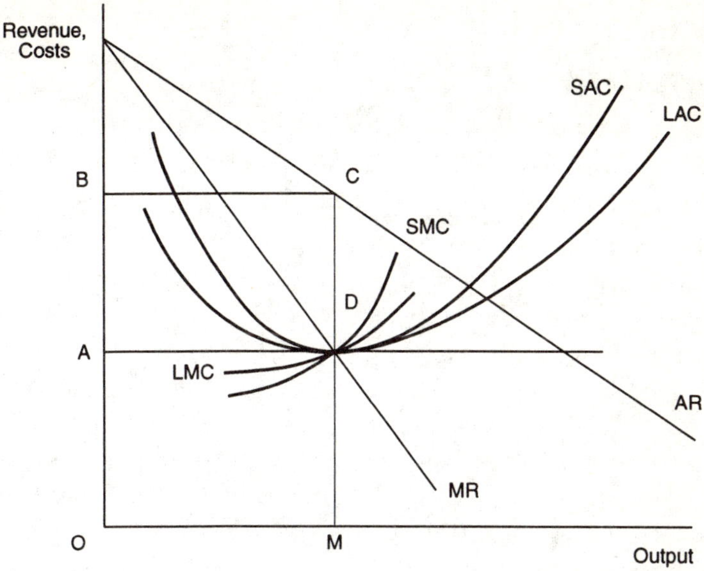

Figure 4.9

price analysis'. Suppose, for example, that a monopolist is in fact concerned that the profit levels attainable by a strict consideration of revenue and cost conditions might invite unwelcome attention of either kind. A calculation based only on a comparison of cost and revenue could lead the monopolist to conclude that the level of output Q_1 sold at the price P_1 would be the best, rational choice (Figure 4.10). But consideration of other factors, such as the possibility of government intervention, might lead the same monopolist (acting rationally) to select a greater level of output and a lower price, with a view to avoiding unwelcome attention. In Figure 4.10, for example, the single seller may decide to sell the quantity OQ_2 at the price P_2, so that P_2AD represents a range of the AR curve which the monopolist regards as relevant, thus yielding an MR curve composed of P_2A and BC – i.e. an MR curve with a discontinuous range, AB. With the (self-imposed range) of the MR curve represented by P_2A and BC, the firm will not offer more than OQ_2 since for such levels of output MC will lie consistently above MR (represented by BC).

There is, in short, a range of discontinuity in the MR curve (AB) and this in turn means that *so long as this range is perceived to remain stable*, a number of possible MC curves may pass through it, all of which are compatible with the same level of output and the same price. By the same token it will be evident that the position of the range of discontinuity would change if the choice of price to be charged in the market was to be lower than P_2. It would, therefore, appear that in cases where the monopolist seeks to attain objectives other than that of the earn-

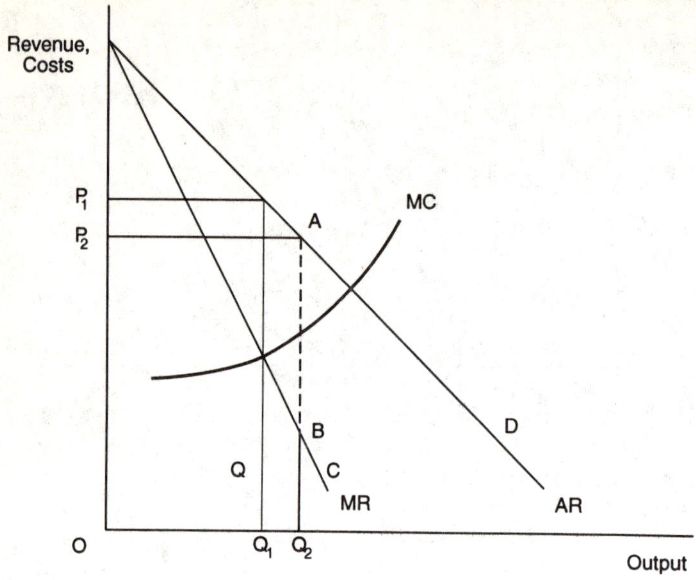

Figure 4.10

ing of maximum profits, 'maximisation' of profits may be consistent with a greater level of output sold at a lower price than that which might be expected under other, and simpler, conditions.

3. Competition and Monopoly Compared

In fact there is no valid way in which we can contrast a situation of monopoly and one of perfect competition, beyond saying that in the latter, equilibrium for the firm will normally feature a situation where MC = MR = AC = AR, while in the former MR will normally equal MC, with AR and AC diverging. At the level of pure theory, the only valid comparison would be in terms of a situation which was once perfectly competitive, but subsequently monopolised. In Figure 4.11, for example, we suppose a situation which initially involves an industry made up of a number of firms.

To begin with, an equilibrium position is established where output in the aggregate is ON, (Figure 4.11(a)), made up of the contribution of each firm (On) multiplied by the number of firms, (Figure 4.11(b)). If such an industry could be supposed to be monopolised, and if the monopolist could be assumed, as a single firm, to operate under the same cost conditions as an industry previously made up of a number of firms, then output would drop to OM in Figure 4.11(a) where the industry supply curve becomes the monopolist's MC curve and the industry demand curve the monopolist's AR curve, to which there corresponds a curve of

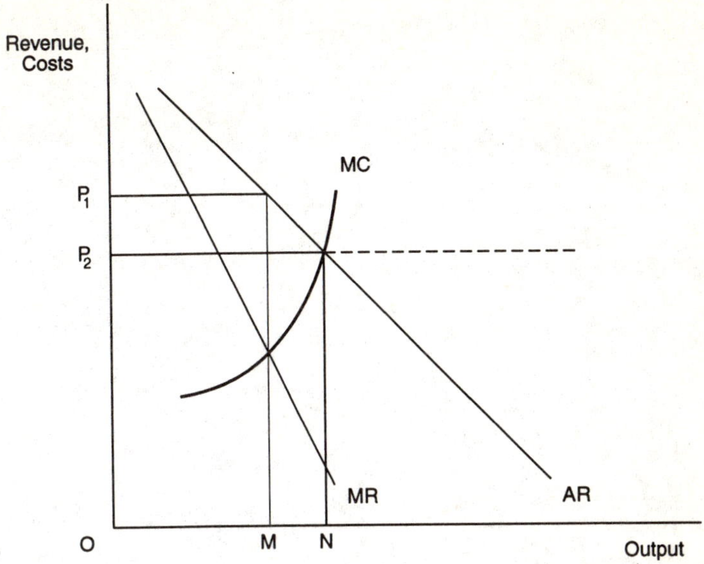

Figure 4.11(a)

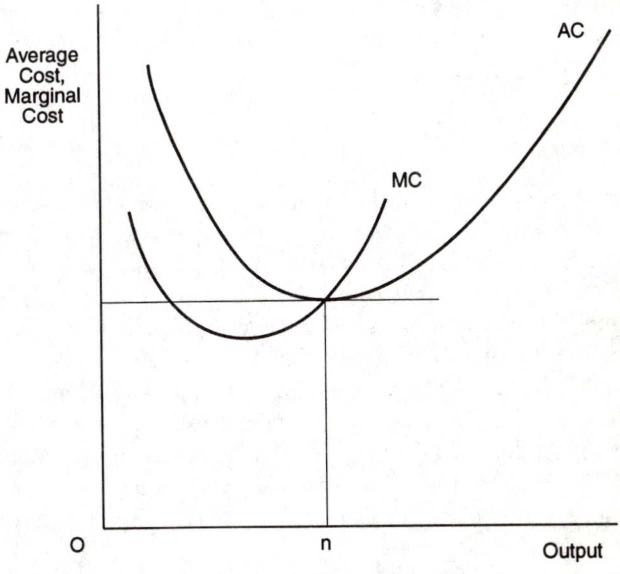

Figure 4.11(b)

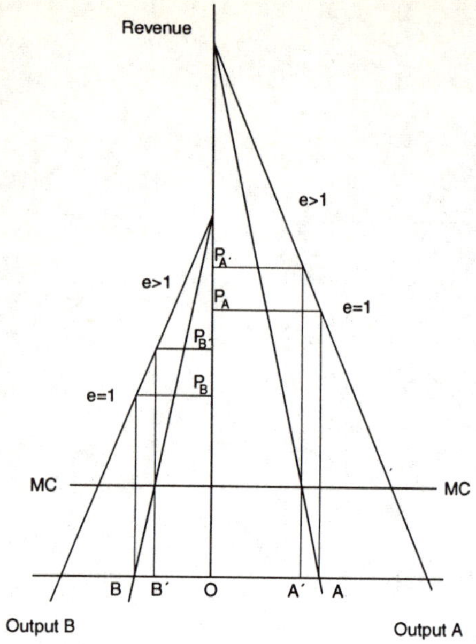

Figure 4.12

MR. Price would rise to P_1. Under such circumstances, and these alone, can we say that monopoly price will be higher and output lower than when the industry was perfectly competitive – neglecting of course the complications presented by the 'limit price' analysis considered above.

Discriminating Monopoly

The simple model outlined above may be extended to take account of the case of discriminating monopoly, i.e. the case of a single seller operating in two unrelated markets, with different elasticities of demand – conditions which are essential if discrimination is to be possible. Suppose, for example, a situation such as that illustrated in Figure 4.12 where the elasticities of demand differ in the two markets which face the monopolist, and where MC is zero in each case. Under these circumstances Total Revenue will be at a maximum where MR = MC in both markets and where MRa and MRb are equal. If we abstract from the problem of limit price analysis, the monopolist will choose to sell OA units in market A and OB units in market B. No other distribution of total output between the two markets could result in a greater profit since an increase in B and a decrease in A, or vice versa, would generate a decline in total receipts.

In a case where marginal costs were positive, OA´ units would be sold in market A and OB´ units in market B with MRa and MRb once again brought into equality, but with different selling prices in the two markets.

II. Demand for a Single Variable Input:

It was established earlier (see above, pages 95-99) that satisfaction of the conditions for short-run profit maximisation gives rise to a relationship between the level of employment of a variable input and its price. In the context of the model of perfect competition it was established that in equilibrium the level of employment offered by the firm would be taken to that point where ANRP=AIC=MRP=MIC.

Monopoly in the Product Market

Since our model of monopoly initially assumed that the input was available at constant cost we can continue to employ an AIC curve which has the characteristics of a horizontal straight line. In this situation AIC and MIC will be equal.

The differences as compared to the model of perfect competition involve the shape and the position of the curves of ANRP and MRP.

The *shape* differs under conditions of monopoly because the price at which different quantities of the product can be sold *varies continuously* – reflecting the fact that the monopolist's AR curve is in fact the industry demand curve. We have already established that such curves will have a negative slope. But where perfect competition prevails the firm will confront a *different* curve of ANRP for *each* price at which the product can be sold in the market.

Leaving aside the factors which determine the relative position of two ANRP curves, under conditions of monopoly, we would therefore expect that the curve of ANRP (and MRP) will slope downwards more rapidly than would be the case under conditions of perfect competition.

In equilibrium, the position of the curve of ANRP will also differ under conditions of monopoly, in the sense that in the model which we have specified entry is *blocked*. Thus whereas under conditions of perfect competition new entry forces the curves of AR and ANRP into a position of tangency with the curves of AC and AIC respectively, in monopoly equilibrium for the firm is likely to feature a situation where MC=MR but where 'excess' profits obtain.

Since AR is likely to exceed AC we would expect that on the input side employment would be taken to that point where MIC=MRP but where ANRP exceeds the value of AIC.

This outcome is summarised in Figure 4.13, where the level of employment offered is OM at the wage rate W.

Monopoly in the Product Market with Monopsony in the Input Market

The next case to which we now turn concerns the monopolist who is also a monopsonist, that is, the sole purchaser of the input in question. In this situation the monopsonist would face the industry supply curve for the factor – a curve which as we saw earlier is likely to have a positive slope (above, pages 64-69).

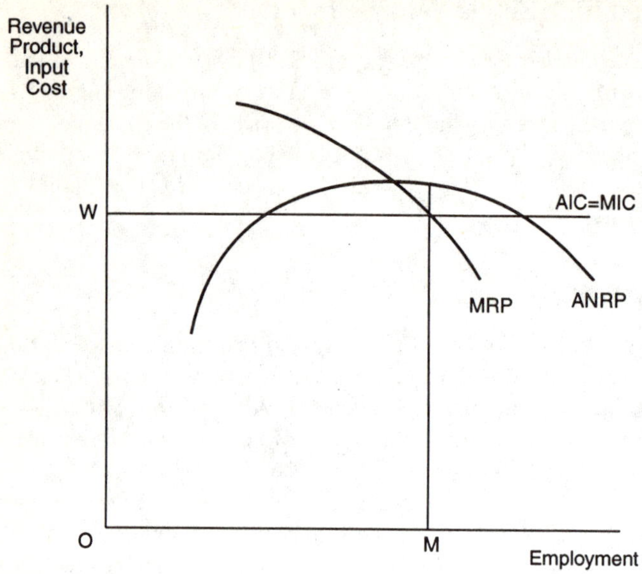

Figure 4.13

Where the AIC curve has a positive slope we confront a situation where the purchaser of the input can only obtain greater supplies at a progressively increasing price. Some interesting points follow:

1. Where input supply is an increasing function of the supply price, this must have an effect on the monopolist's cost curves. These were originally drawn on the assumption that AIC was constant; an assumption which helps to establish the position of the curve of AC. But where AIC has a positive slope, this means that additional units of the variable input can only be obtained at a price which progressively increases. Under such conditions, the monopolist's AC curve would slope upwards more rapidly in its increasing phase than where AIC was constant. In short, where the firm confronts a positively sloped AIC curve this must have an effect on both the position and the rate of change in the slope of the curves of AC and MC.

2. Where the curve of AIC is rising, the cost of the input at the margin must also be rising and will in fact lie consistently above the average input cost. This is simply the counterpart within the input market of the distinction between average and marginal costs within the output market. The geometric relationship between the curves of AIC and MIC is similar to that which we confronted in dealing with a negatively sloped curve of AR and of MR. Where the AIC curve is positively sloped and is also a straight line, the MIC curve will bisect a horizontal line drawn from the AIC curve to meet the y-axis. In Figure 4.14, the line AC is bisected by the MIC curve at B, so that the distance AB = BC.

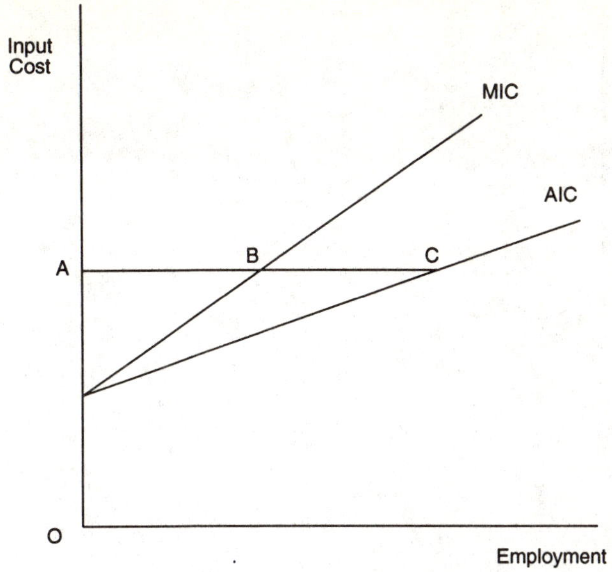

Figure 4.14

3. The modifications just introduced do not affect the principle by which the appropriate level of employment is determined. In Figure 4.15 we confront a positively sloped AIC curve and a positively sloped MIC curve. The curve of MRP will have a shape which is determined by the negatively sloped demand (AR) curve facing the firm. In equilibrium, the level of employment will be determined by the intersection of MRP and MIC. In the case illustrated, the employment level is OM and the wage rate, W. Here we face the interesting result that the equilibrium value of the wage rate lies below the point of intersection of MRP and MIC. The full set of average and marginal curves is summarised in Figure 4.16.

4. Although the intersection of the curves of MIC and MRP determines the profit-maximising level of employment of the variable factor, the input price can no longer be obtained from the MRP curve. The significance of this point is that the role of the MRP curve in delineating the relationship between the level of employment offered and the input price is curtailed. In short, we can no longer work in terms of an equivalence between the MRP curve and the input demand relationship. We no longer have an unambiguous relationship between MRP and the input price. Or to put the matter another way, the introduction of monopsony qualifies the statement that input demand is a function of its price, just as the introduction of monopoly qualifies the statement that the supply of a commodity is a function of its price.

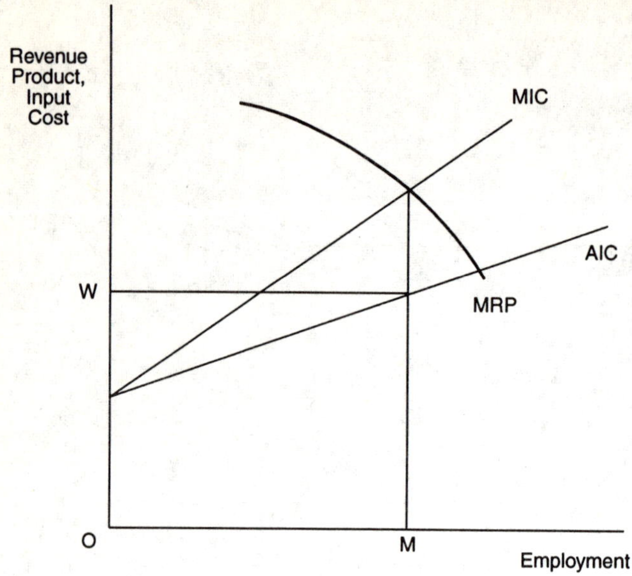

Figure 4.15

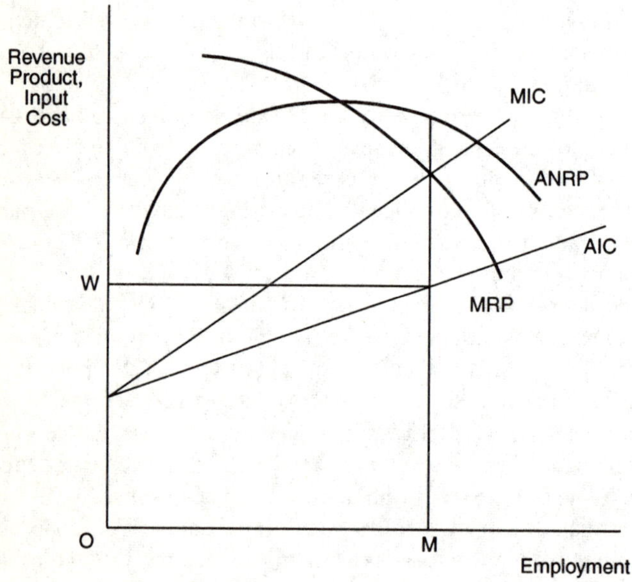

Figure 4.16

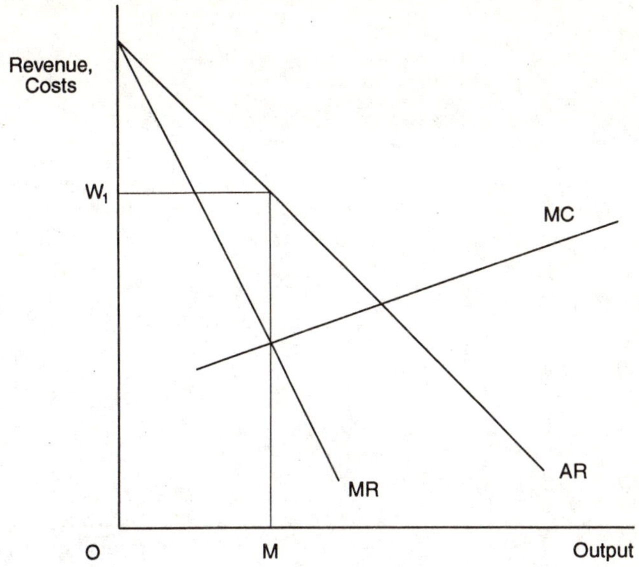

Figure 4.17

Bilateral Monopoly

We now move on to consider the final development of the treatment of monopoly: the situation where those who supply the input act in concert as a monopolist intent on securing the highest possible price for the input. The monopsonist purchaser of the earlier argument is now confronted by a monopolist seller of the input. Each side in the input market has only a single participant.

If we look at the problem from the standpoint of the monopsonist *purchaser,* the situation will be that outlined in Figure 4.15. The purchaser confronts positively sloped AIC and MIC curves, and a negatively sloped curve of MRP. Seen from the standpoint of the purchaser, the preferred solution is one where the level of employment offered is OM and the wage rate offered is W.

But if we look at the problem from the standpoint of the monopolist *seller* of the input, the picture is radically different. The MRP curve of the purchaser now appears as the AR (average revenue) curve of the seller; a curve which is negatively sloped and which must generate a negatively sloped curve of MR. Again, seen from the standpoint of the seller the AIC curve of the purchaser becomes the curve of marginal cost (MC). For the seller (Figure 4.17), the preferred solution is one where MR = MC – suggesting a level of employment of OM and a wage rate of W_1. In this case the wage rate lies above the point at which MR and MC intersect.

The total picture is summarised in Figure 4.18. Here we face an AIC curve and an MIC curve, together with the appropriate MRP curve, for the purchaser [P],

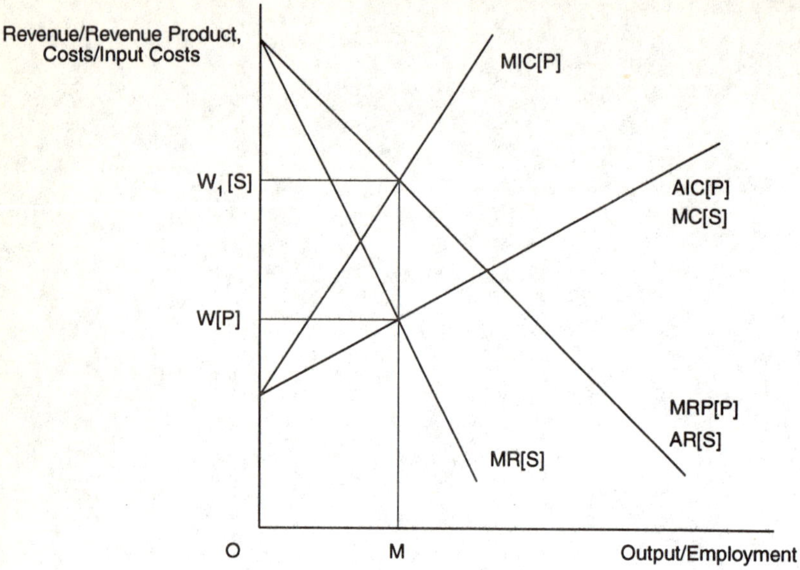

Figure 4.18

suggesting a wage rate of W[P]. For the seller, the AIC curve is seen to be the curve of MC[S] and the MRP curve as the curve of AR[S] to which there corresponds a curve of MR [S]. For the seller of the input, the preferred level of employment is OM (in the example chosen) at the higher wage rate of W[S].

The actual outcome will depend upon the bargaining position of the two participants. The model is thus indeterminate in the sense that it only permits us to identify a range within which a solution can be found. Given this it will be apparent that there will be as many positions for the monopolist's cost curve as there are values for the wage rate. Only when the bargain is struck can the position of the average cost curve be determined. If we now re-introduce the problems presented by limit-price analysis, it will become apparent that the range of discontinuity which we identified in the curve of MR must find a counterpart in the curve of MRP – a complication to which we will return in the treatment of oligopoly which is to follow.

Section B: Monopolistic Competition

The market situation which we address in this section is one where there is a monopoly element present, but also some degree of competition, arising from the presence of goods which are close, but not perfect, substitutes for the output of any given single seller. We are asked therefore to visualise the possibility that there may be an industry or group made up of a number of firms manufacturing a given type of product (say soap) but where the output of each firm is differentiated from that of others at least in the eyes of the consumer. The monopoly element arises because each firm is taken to be the sole seller of a particular brand of 'soap' the competitive element because no one seller has exclusive control over the supply of 'soap' as a commodity, and thus does not control the output of a product for which there are no close substitutes (the formal definition of monopoly).

In practice products may be differentiated from one another by virtue of trade marks, patents or copyright; design, specification or packaging. They may be further differentiated in the mind of the consumer through advertising – points which, taken together, suggest that in this market type, unlike perfect competition, the pairing of buyer and seller can no longer be regarded as random.

I. Modifications to the Demand and Cost Curves

Demand Curves

In a situation where the seller has a monopoly with respect to a brand of product that seller is likely to have some control over the price at which it is sold. The AR curve which faces the seller will therefore be negatively sloped, so that we can accept the relationships between AR and MR which have already been established. We are presented therefore with a contrast with perfect competition (where the AR curve was a horizontal straight line) but also something of a contrast to monopoly, in that the AR curve facing the firm must here be relatively elastic (reflecting the presence of a number of close substitutes in the market); certainly more elastic that the demand curve for the product of the industry of which the individual firm is a part. To put the same point in another way, there must be a difference between having exclusive control over the supply of a brand of soap, and control over the total output of the commodity; a difference which must be reflected in the contrasting elasticities of the relevant AR curves.

In order to express this difference we may work in terms of two AR curves, 'ARd' and 'ARD'. *The ARd curve is defined as that curve which traces out the way in which the revenue of the individual firm will change on the assumption that competing firms hold their prices constan*t. This curve will be relatively elastic in view of the presence of a number of close substitutes (Figure 4.19(a)).

The ARD curve is defined as that curve which traces out the way in which the

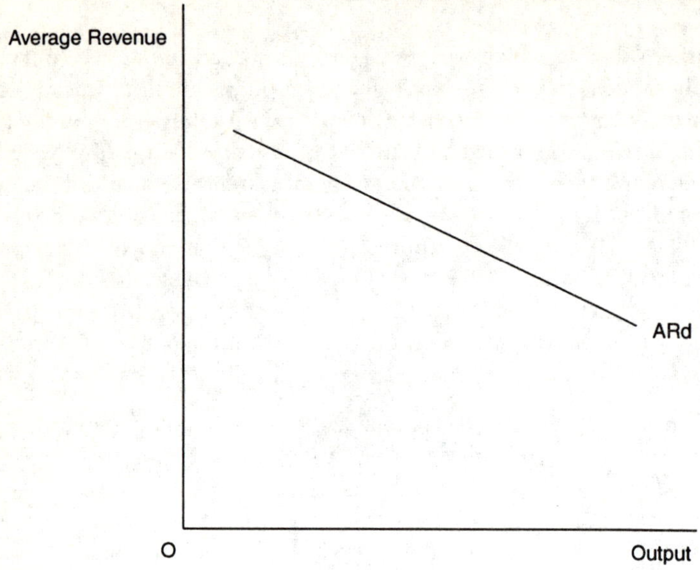

Figure 4.19(a)

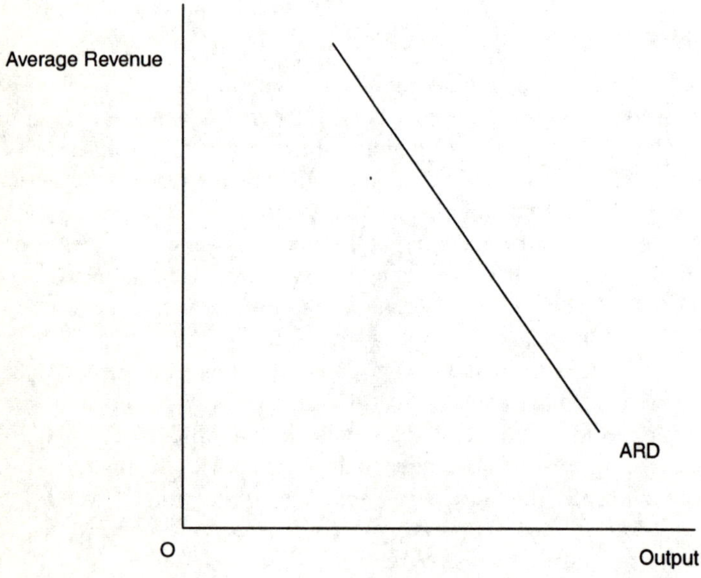

Figure 4.19(b)

revenue of the individual firm will change on the assumption that other firms alter their prices in the same direction. This curve is in effect the fractional part of the market demand curve which faces the firm – i.e. a part of the market demand curve for soap as a commodity. The ARD curve (Figure 4.19(b)) will therefore have the same elasticity as the market demand curve, while its position will be determined by the market share held by the firm. An increase in the number of firms in the industry would obviously tend to move the curve to the *left* and *vice versa.*

Relationships between ARd and ARD

To begin with, let us suppose that the slope of the ARd curve is the same for all members of the industry, thus allowing us to work in terms of a single curve which we can treat as representative of all firms in the group. Suppose further that the price actually charged is P so that each firm sells the quantity Oa (Figure 4.20(a)). In aggregate or market terms the prevailing price will also be P and the quantity sold will be equal to the contribution of each firm (Oa) multiplied by the number of firms (Figure 4.20(b)). It will be evident therefore that a point on the firm's ARd curve will correspond to a point on the fractional part of the market demand curve which faces it, so that ARD must pass through the ARd curve at that point where the firm is selling Oa units at the price P.

These relationships can be further clarified by taking an additional example. Suppose we start from the position shown in Figure 4.21 where the typical firm is selling the quantity Oa at the price P_1. Suppose further that this firm decides to cut price (for reasons yet to be fully explained) in the expectation that other firms will not do the same – i.e. in the expectation of selling Ob units by moving down the ARd curve. However, if other members of the group behave in the same way, for similar or different reasons, and cut their prices, then this will cause a movement down the ARD curve in effect. This kind of inter-relationship will be obvious on reflection: a cut in price by one firm could lead to a relatively large increase in sales, but if each firm cuts price in the same direction all firms will sell more at the lower price even although the first firm cannot sell as much more as it had previously assumed – Oc rather than Ob units in Figure 4.21.

The price charged by each firm is now P_2 and the quantity sold Oc; a price and quantity which must correspond to a point on the ARd curve which faces the firm – a curve which must now pass through ARD at the point C rather than B. The same sequence would be repeated if the firm under discussion cut price to P_3 in the expectation of selling Ob units – in this case rival firms could well be forced to cut price in the same direction and (possibly) to the same extent, resulting in sales of Od units per firm and a movement of the ARd curve downwards to cut the ARD curve at D. In terms of the example chosen it will be observed that the actual consequences of a reduction in price by a particular firm differ from those which were expected when the action was taken, and that the graphical result of a situation where each firm sells at progressively lower prices is a movement of the ARd curve down ARD. It will be noted that this is analogous to the situation in perfect

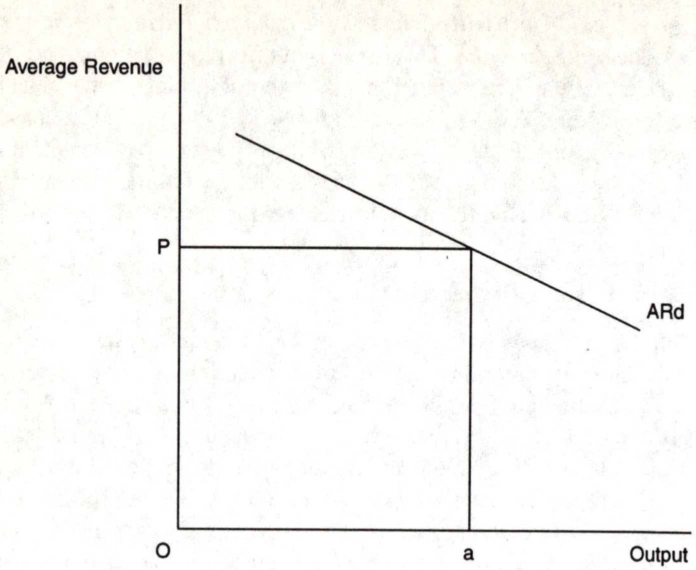

Figure 4.20(a)

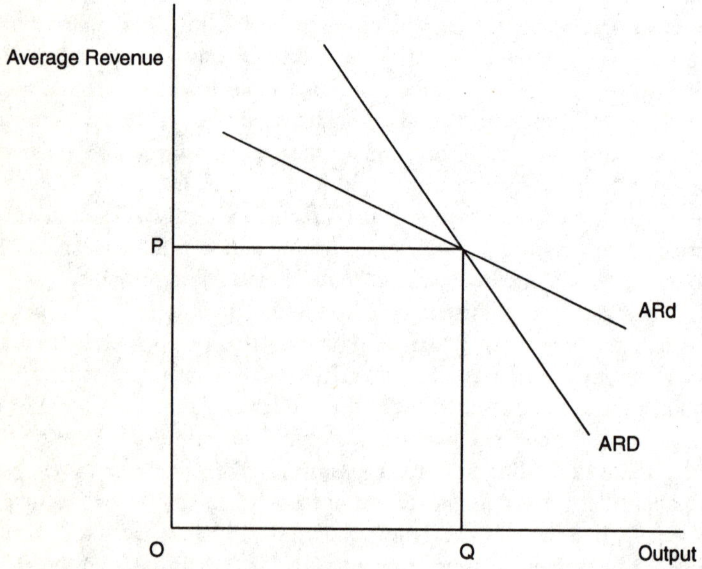

Figure 4.20(b)

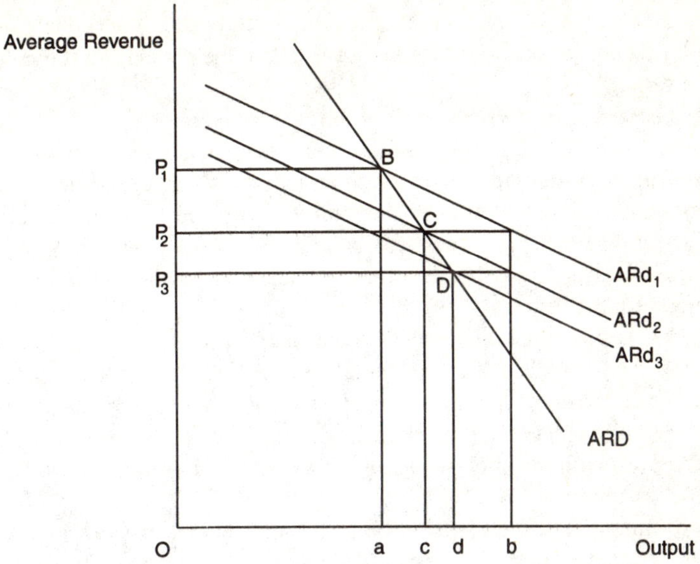

Figure 4.21

competition where lower prices result in a change in the position of the AR curve, and that in practice a fractional part of the market demand curve will face such firms also.

Cost Curves

As before, we can continue to make use of the results already established in the original discussion of this topic; that is, we continue to make use of the definitions of short and long run curves, their relationships to each other, their shapes and the characteristics of MC and AC curves where the latter are 'U' shaped. But evidently some modifications are required in order to take account of the means of product differentiation. These can be conveniently considered under two heads:

1. *Product Variation*: In this context the firm has a number of choices open to it with regard to the product it sells; a product which may be differentiated from others in the group by varying service, packaging or technical specification. In short, the firm which has already decided on the scale of its operations may still face a choice with regard to the specific cost curve on which it will operate – a choice which will be affected by the extent to which sales are expected to vary as a result. In the same way, patents or copyrights relating to production processes will affect the position if not the general shape of the cost curve which the firm chooses, and thus possibly the profits earned.

2. *Selling Costs*: Perhaps the most novel aspect of Chamberlin's analysis was

the introduction of selling costs as a distinct category from costs of production and his famous statement to the effect that costs incurred 'to adapt the product to the demand are costs of production; those made to adapt the demand to the product are costs of selling'[1].

Under the latter heading we can include the costs of advertising and salaries of sales personnel – in fact all those activities which are intended to improve information with regard to the product or to attract individuals to a specific brand of product through the manipulation of their preferences. Once again, the choice made with regard to selling outlays will be affected by the expected impact on sales – that is, their anticipated effect on the shape and position of the revenue curves which face the firm.

Obviously it is difficult to generalise about the shape of the curve of selling costs, since such costs will be affected by the size of the firm, the level of resources devoted to this purpose, the methods used and the choice of media, to name but a few. But if we take a single industry made up of firms which are similar in respect of size and type, then it may not be unrealistic to assume a long-run curve which is broadly 'U' shaped.

We could initially assume a period of increasing returns as sales inputs are increased followed by a period of decreasing returns, due for example, to gradually increasing sales resistance as the consumer is encouraged to sacrifice 'continually more important wants' (Chamberlin, p. 135). Such a curve is illustrated as SS in Figure 4.22. By adding the curve of production costs (LAC as previously defined) we arrive at the combined cost curve. In the diagram, for example, production costs at the output OL are LB, and selling costs (SS) are LP, so that if we add the distance AB (=LP) to the relevant point on the curve of production costs (PP) we establish a point on the combined cost curve (CC). Three points should be noted:

1. The vertical distance between the two curves indicates the selling cost at any output – for example, it is AB per unit where output is OL, and DC at an output of OM.
2. The general characteristics of the CC curve will be the same as those of the curve of production costs, given the assumptions made.
3. There is no necessary reason to suppose that the minimum point of the CC curve will correspond to the same level of output as the minimum point on the curve of production costs.

We could alternatively assume that the firm has made a choice at some point in the past with regard to the resources to be devoted to selling costs in the current period; that is, selling costs amount to a fixed cost as far as current operations are concerned. Here the curve of average selling costs will form a rectangular hyperbola. The combined cost curve can be established as before by a process of vertical addition which in this case is analogous to the way in which AFC was added

1 *The Theory of Monopolistic Competition*, 5th ed. (1948), p. 125.

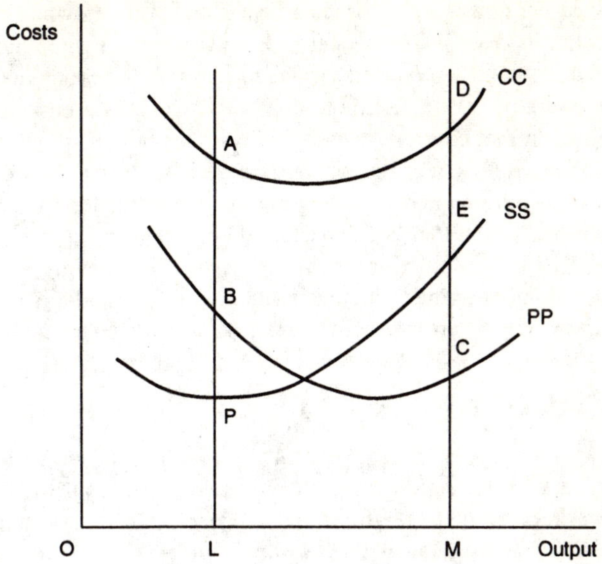

Figure 4.22

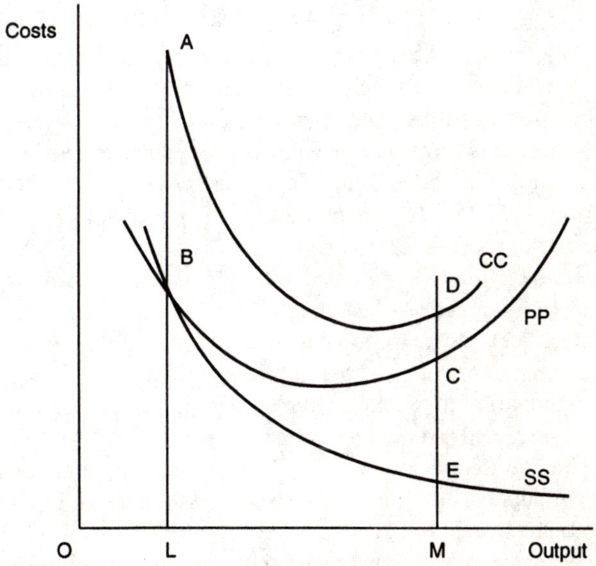

Figure 4.23

to AVC in the earlier discussion of production costs. This is shown in Figure 4.23.

In one sense, this discussion only reminds us that some simple modifications have to be made to familiar concepts before considering the problems of monopoly and competition. But at the same time it must be emphasised that something more is involved in that cost and revenue curves must now be regarded as interdependent with respect to their respective shapes and position. As we have seen, both the choice of product and of selling outlay will be made in the light of the revenue conditions which they are expected to generate, i.e. with regard to their impact on the shape and position of the AR curves which may face the firm. Unlike the situations examined previously, changes in demand conditions facing firm and industry may be created both exogenously and endogenously.

II. The Large Group

In considering the case of the large group we will continue to employ the hypothesis of rationality and the profit maximisation condition (MC = MR). We also take as our premisses the relationships which we have demonstrated to exist between average and marginal cost and revenue curves, using such curves in the modified forms which have just been considered. It will also be helpful to make use of a number of assumptions which fall into two broad categories: viz., those necessary to define the market type, and those which, without being essential to it, are justified on the ground that they simplify the analysis. The first group of assumptions include:

1. Large numbers of sellers; that is, a situation where the number of sellers is so large that the actions of any one cannot affect the circumstances of the market as a whole, or seriously affect the fortunes of its competitors.
   This assumption permits us to regard the ARd curve as having operational significance for the firm: in other words, in the context of the large group,the individual firm will act as if the ARd curve is the relevant AR curve, even although it is ultimately constrained by the fractional part of the market demand curve which faces it in fact.
2. Products which are differentiated through product variation and selling costs, but with high cross-elasticities.
3. Free entry and exit to or from the industry.

The second group of simplifying assumptions include:

1. Perfect competition in the factor market with inputs available to the firm at a constant price and without variation in quality.
2. Perfect competition among buyers of the commodities so that no one buyer or group of buyers can have a significant impact on the price.
3. Single product firms.
4. We neglect the problems associated with spatial competition or transport costs (see below, Chapter 6).

The final simplifying assumption is among the most important: namely, the 'heroic assumption that both demand and cost curves for all the products are uniform throughout the group' (Chamberlin, p.82). This is, of course, an 'heroic' assumption precisely because the whole point of the analysis of monopolistic competition is to draw attention to *diversity*: for example, to the diversity of products and preferences all of which tend to result in heterogeneity of prices, and variation over a wide range of outputs (scales of production) and in profits. However, this assumption permits us to use a single set of cost and revenue curves and to treat these as representative of all firms in the group (just as we did in the case of perfect competition). The justification of the assumption is that it permits us more easily to explain the nature of those processes by virtue of which individual firms, and the group as a whole, attain a position of equilibrium.

Equilibrium of the Individual Firm

The situation which has been outlined may be seen to present the firm with a number of choices regarding product, selling costs, and price. In practice it will be convenient to consider these cases separately by examining situations where product may vary with price and selling outlays constant; selling costs may vary with product and price held constant; and finally, where price may vary with selling costs and product specification constant.

Chamberlin supplies a simple illustration of some of the issues involved in dealing with the first problem (op. cit., pages 79–81; 167–68). Suppose that the price at which the commodity will be sold is known and constant, so that the problem is to select the product whose cost and market result in the greatest profit. In Figure 4.24, OE is the fixed price; AA′ and BB′ are the cost curves for two products A and B. If the market for A is such that OG units can be sold at the price OE, and for B such that OH units could be sold at the same price, then product B will obviously be chosen since the total profit available, NQDE, is greater than the area MECR.

It is worth noting that the product selected need not be the one whose cost of production is lowest, nor necessarily that for which demand is greatest. It will also be evident, in a competitive situation, that any excess profits generated by product variation will produce responses which will tend to eliminate them, either through firms altering product specification in the same direction as the innovating firm, or changes in supply which have the effect of lowering the price at which the commodity is sold.

Secondly, we can treat product and price as constant and consider the choice of selling outlay. In Figure 4.25 the curve of production costs is PP′, and the combined costs of production and selling at the given price are represented by CC′. If the price is in fact OF (a price line of FZ), then selling costs will be taken to that level which maximise profit. In Figure 4.25 output will be OB, with GN attributed to selling costs per unit, where the latter are expressed as before in terms of the difference between combined costs and production costs at a given level of output. Once again, we might expect surpluses generated by selling activity to be competed away, the limiting case being reached where the price at which the

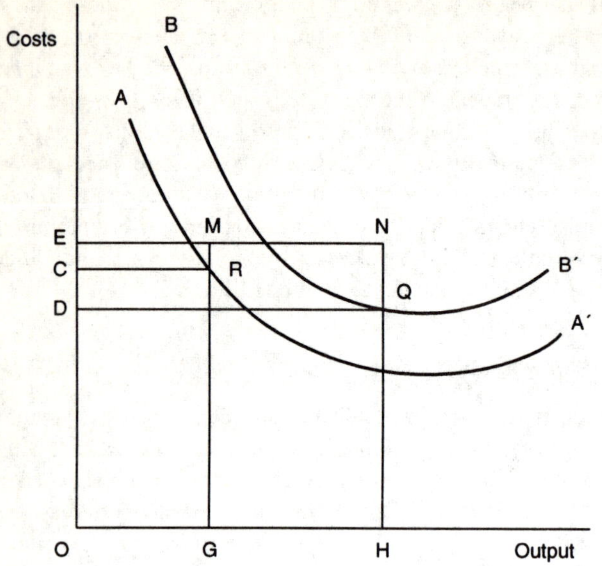

Figure 4.24

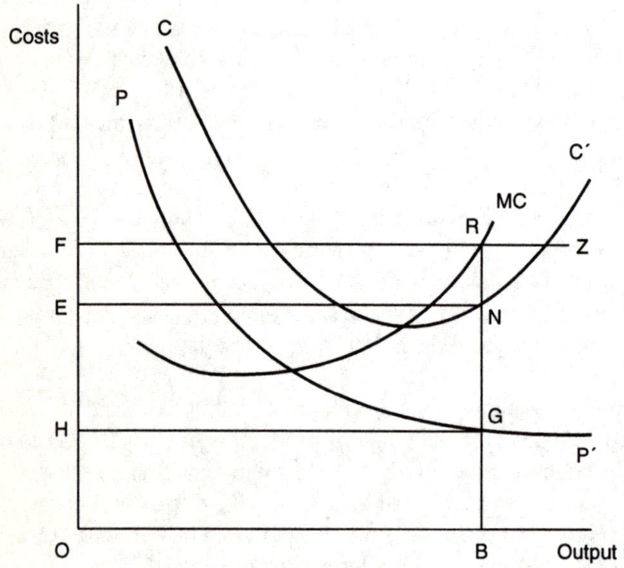

Figure 4.25

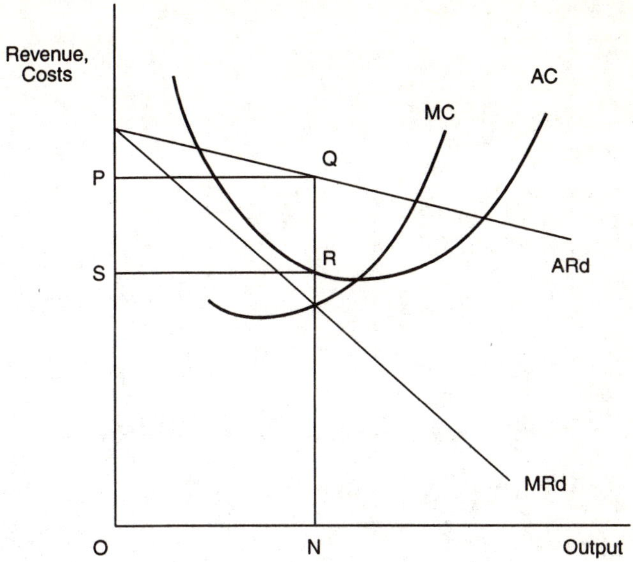

Figure 4.26

commodity is sold is equal to the cost per unit incurred.

The most typical textbook case is that which involves price adjustment with selling outlays and product held constant, and it is to this situation that we now turn.

Price Adjustment

To begin with, assume that the representative firm has reached a decision on product specification and selling costs and that the ARd curve generated by these decisions is such that excess profits may be earned. In Figure 4.26 price will be OP and the quantity sold ON. At this level of output MR = MC and it will not therefore pay the firm to offer more than this amount, (since MC lies above MR at greater levels of output) or less, (since MR exceeds MC). In the case shown, average cost per unit is NR and excess profit per unit is RQ. Total receipts are represented by the area ONQP, total costs by ONRS, and total excess profit by PQRS.

The parallels with the monopoly case considered in the previous section are obvious: the AR curve for example is negatively sloped, excess profits are earned, while in addition the firm will be operating on a range of the AR curve where elasticity is necessarily greater than one. On the other hand there are equally important differences. Notably, the ARd curve is highly elastic (reflecting the presence of a number of close substitutes) while in a competitive situation these excess profits are likely to be competed away as a result of new entry.

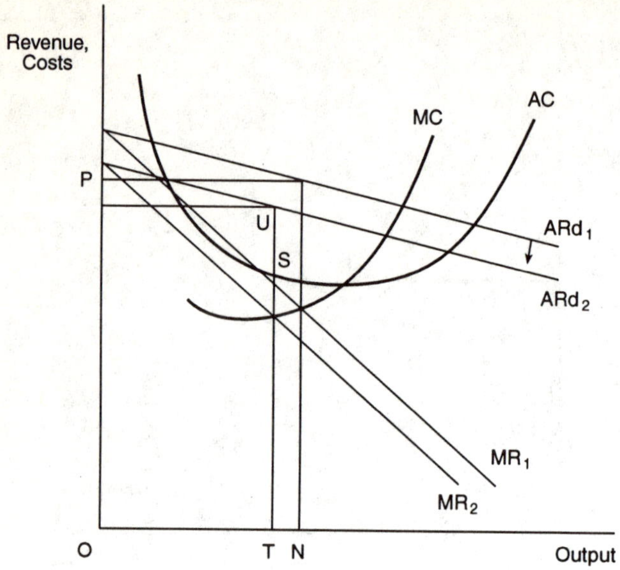

Figure 4.27

Long-Run Equilibrium

We assume, initially at least, that adjustment in the long run is in terms of changes in the number of firms rather than in terms of scale changes undertaken by member firms, and further that new firms can enter the industry under conditions of cost identical to those faced by existing firms. The latter assumption permits us to continue to employ a single set of cost curves representing the conditions faced by each firm. Given these assumptions, we would expect the number of firms to increase, attracted by the possibility of earning excess profits, and that such an increase in the number of firms would cause an expansion of supply and hence a general reduction in the price at which each firm can sell its product. In Figure 4.27 this situation is represented by a downward shift in the position of the typical ARd curve and a reduction in the output of the firm examined from ON to OT. It will be noted that although each firm produces OT at the new price, output in the aggregate will have risen as a result of the increase in the number of firms. At the original price P for example, total output is given by the contribution of each firm (ON) multiplied by the number of firms. In the second case, aggregate output is given by OT multiplied by the increased number of firms, say n + 1.

From the standpoint of the individual firm the situation illustrated is one of 'equilibrium' in the sense that each satisfies the profit maximisation condition (MC = MR), but it cannot represent a position of equilibrium for the group due to the continuing presence of excess profits of SU per unit. In short, the process out-

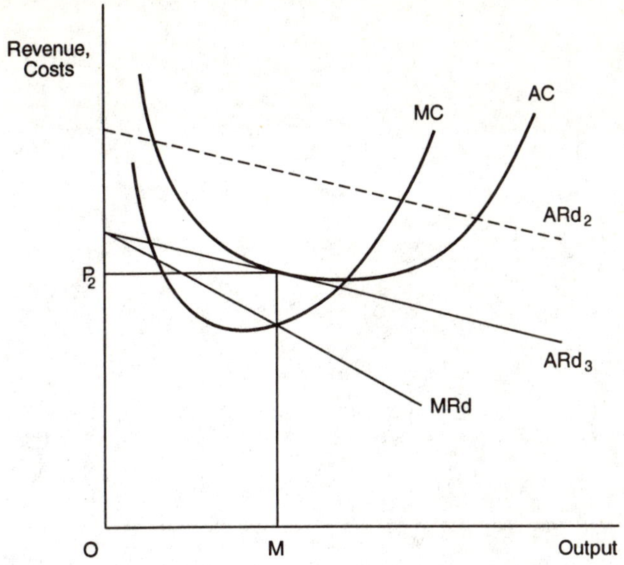

Figure 4.28

lined above will be repeated until a situation is reached where it is not in the interest of any member firm to change the level of output (i.e. where MC = MR) and where it will not pay any firm which remains external to the group to enter it (i.e. where AC = AR). This situation is illustrated in Figure 4.28 where as a result of the continuing inflow of firms, and consequent reduction in selling price, the ARd curve has been forced down to a position of tangency with the AC curve. Here the selling price is P_2 and output is OM. The situation as depicted presents a contrast with monopoly, since excess profits have not been sustained, and a parallel with the perfectly competitive solution, since AR = AC. The contrast with the latter market type lies in the fact that price is no longer equal to marginal cost, the equilibrium condition being that AR = AC and MR = MC but without the average and marginal values being equal to each other.

The Distinction between ARD and ARd

It may be helpful to repeat the above results by reference to the two types of revenue curve. It will be remembered that the ARD curve is the fractional part of the market demand curve which faces the firm in fact (whether or not it is recognised) and that its position indicates market share. Suppose a situation where the price charged by each firm was P_1 and that the ARd curve intersects the ARD at A. In the case shown MR is not equal to MC (Figure 4.29(a)). Given that each firm faces the same cost conditions, each will act to equalise MC and MR thus increasing the

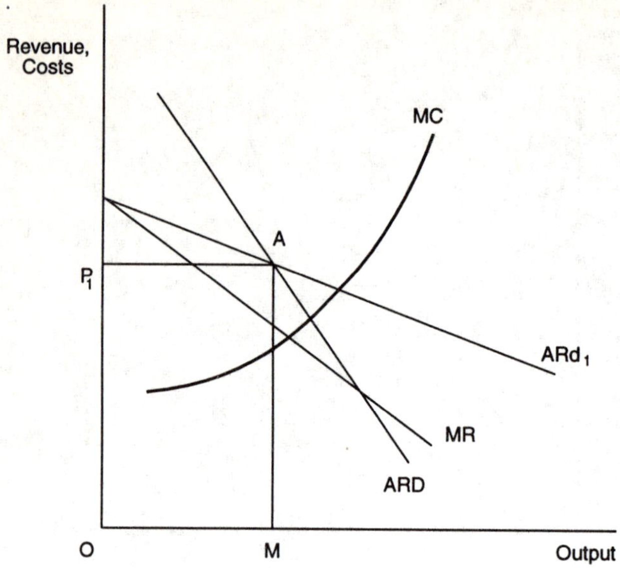

Figure 4.29(a)

quantity sold and reducing the price in the market.

In other words, the ARd curve would in effect slide down the ARD until a situation is reached where it would not pay any member firm to adjust output – i.e. where for each firm MC = MRd. The outcome is illustrated in Figure 4.29(b) where each firm sells OM and the situation is apparently stable.

In Figure 4.30(a) the AC curve is added to illustrate a situation of short run equilibrium where each firm earns excess profits. We can represent the movement to long run or group equilibrium in terms of a series of downward shifts in the position of the ARd curve as before, but with the addition of a movement to the left of the ARD – exactly what we would expect from an inflow of firms (Figure 4.30(b)). An additional point should be noted: strictly speaking, long run equilibrium for the group will require that there be no tendency for new firms to enter employment, and no tendency for firms within that employment to alter the scale of production. It requires therefore that AR = AC and MR = MC, where SAC = LAC and SMC = LMC – conditions which have already been discussed in dealing with both perfect competition and monopoly[2].

The situation is summarised by saying that not only will the ARD curve pass through the appropriate point on ARd but also that in equilibrium the level of output chosen will necessarily be sub-optimal, due to the negative slope of the latter

2 This exposition owes much to K J Cohen and R M Cyert (1965), *Theory of the Firm*, Prentice-Hall, Chapter 11.

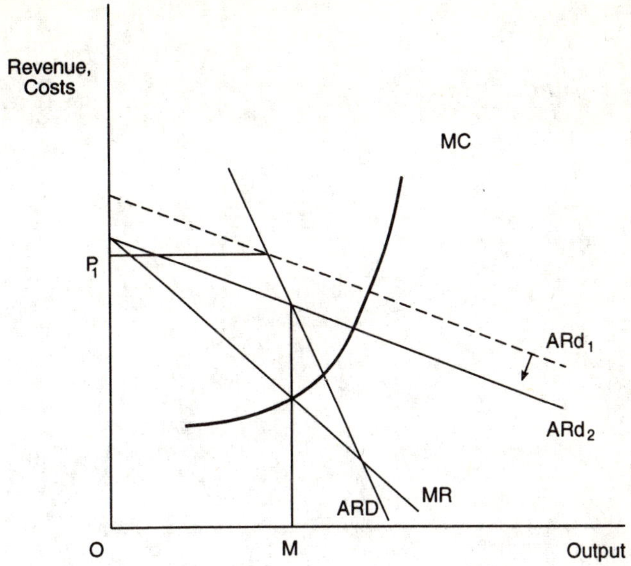

Figure 4.29(b)

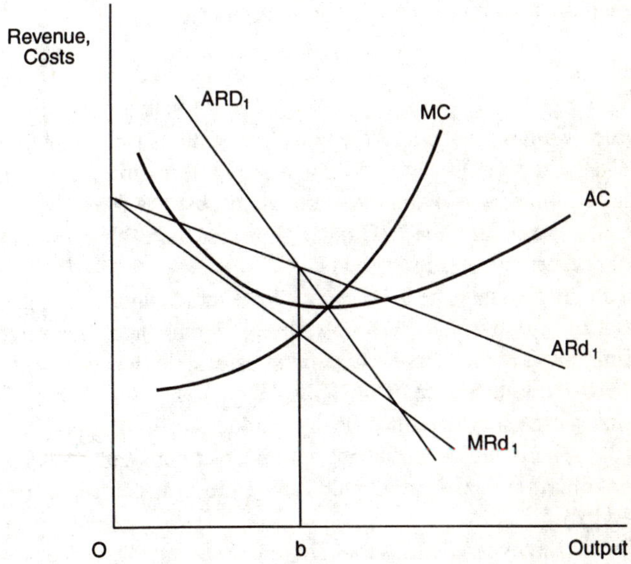

Figure 4.30(a)

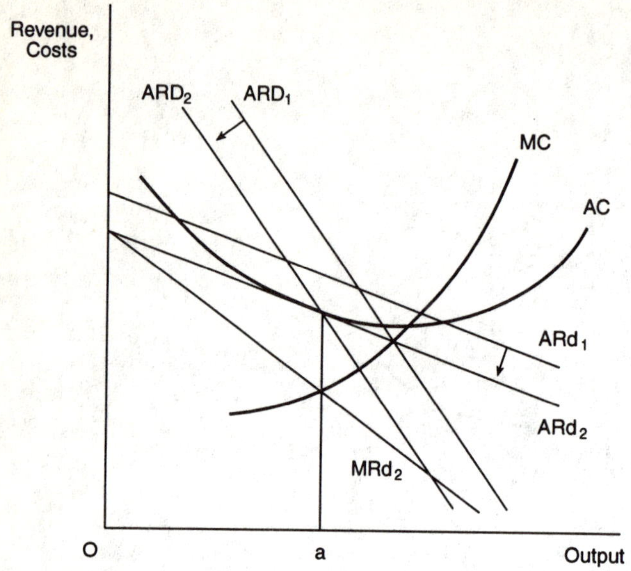

Figure 4.30(b)

curve; a curve which is of course that which the firm regards as having operational significance, given the assumptions made about numbers.

Input Analysis

The analysis which we have just considered has implications for the treatment of input analysis. On the supply side, the situation is straightforward in the sense that we assumed that the input was available at constant cost. As in the case of our earlier account, this means that the AIC line is horizontal and that the MIC line must therefore coincide with it (Figure 4.31).

The situation on the demand side is however a little more complicated. Here we must observe that the curve of ARd has operational significance where numbers are large, meaning that it is this curve which must determine the *perceived shape* of the curve of ANRP and therefore of MRP.

In this situation increasing quantities of the product are sold at progressively diminishing prices. There is thus a contrast with perfect competition (where the AR curve is horizontal) and with monopoly (since the firm confronts the more elastic curve of ARd).

In turn, this means that where ARd is thought to be relevant, the curve of ANRP will be steeper over its declining range as compared to perfect competition. As compared to monopoly, the curve of ANRP will decline less rapidly over the decreasing range.

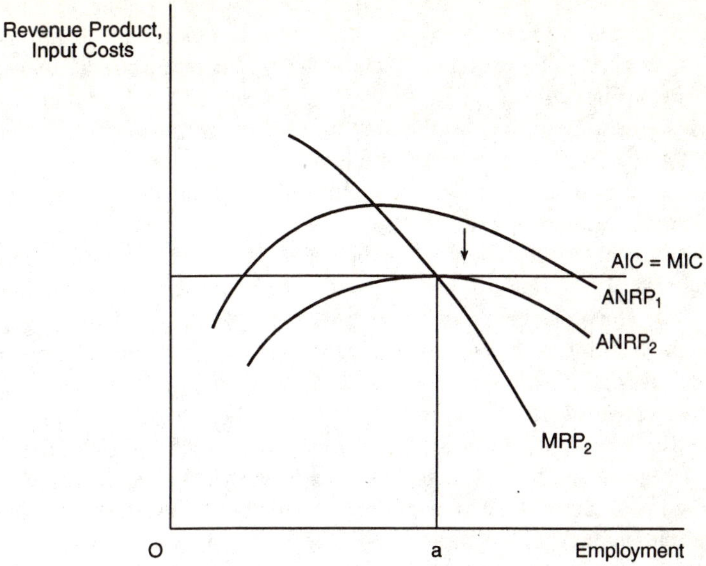

Figure 4.31

The mechanics of attaining a position of equilibrium feature a situation where, as the ARd curve progressively changes in its position, so too will the curve of ANRP until a position of tangency is reached with AIC. In equilibrium ANRP = AIC = MRP = MIC and the level of employment offered by each firm is Oa in Figure 4.31.

It will be noted that the outcome is similar to that obtained under conditions of perfect competition. But there is one important difference, namely that the curve of ANRP has a different set of characteristics, arising from the fact that the curve of ARd is perceived to be the relevant function.

Equilibrium and Allocation

The argument which we have just considered obviously permits us to establish a link between the equilibrium of the firm and of the industry. For example, it has already been determined that the firm must satisfy certain conditions in both the output and input markets if the situation facing the industry is to be regarded as stable.

On the output side, the conditions required are that ARd = AC and MRd = MC. On the input side, given the assumption of a horizontal AIC line, the required conditions are that ANRP=AIC, and MRP=MIC where both the average and marginal values are the same.

In Figure 4.32(a) equilibrium for the firm is shown to be established where Oa units are sold at the price P, while in Figure 4.32(c), the equilibrium level of employment offered is Oa at the wage rate W. The situation with regard to the industry is illustrated in Figures 4.32(b) and 4.32(d). Where the output offered by each firm is Oa (Figure 4.32(a)), aggregate output is given as OA, i.e. the contribution of each firm multiplied by the number of firms (Figure 4.32(b)). On the input side, the aggregate level of employment offered to maintain this level of output is OA, made up of the contribution of each firm multiplied by the number of firms (Figures 4.32(c) and 4.32(d)).

It will be evident that the analysis can be extended from this point to consider the consequences of an upward or downward shift in the position of the market demand curve. The argument can also be extended to take account of exogenous changes in the position of the aggregate demand curves in a manner analogous to that used when dealing with the model of perfect competition (see above, pages 102-113). At one level the only apparent differences between the two models is that in one case we work in terms of a horizontal curve of AR, while in the other the curve is negatively sloped. But such a conclusion would be misleading.

1. In Figures 4.32(a), 4.32(b) and 4.32(d) some curves are shown as dotted lines. This reminds us that the curve of ARD (Figure 4.32a) is a 'shadow' curve by which the firm is constrained but which it does not regard as having operational significance. In Figure 4.32(b) the 'supply curve' is shown as a dotted line, reminding us that in this market type (as in the case of monopoly) there is no longer an unambiguous relationship between price and output. Similarly in Figure 4.32(d) we are reminded that there is no longer an unambiguous relationship between the wage rate and the level of employment offered.

2. It should be emphasised that the model draws attention to the diversity of cost and revenue conditions facing member firms. A situation where products are differentiated draws attention to the fact that firms are different and that the cost and revenue functions which they face are interdependent.

3. The fact that firms are likely to face different conditions of cost and revenue means that in reality the relevant functions are likely to show variations in their position and shape. This means in turn that 'monopoly' profits are likely to obtain even in the long run due to specific advantages enjoyed by particular firms, for example, in regard to patents, entrepreneurial skills or locational elements. The 'heroic' assumption of similarity is 'heroic' precisely because it abstracts from the major characteristic of the model, namely diversity. Equally, the heroic assumption is an abstraction which can be dropped without damage to the analysis of the processes by virtue of which positions of equilibrium tend to be attained.

4. It is worth noting that we really meet the problem of competition for the first time within the framework of this model. In 'perfect competition', for example, firms do not strictly speaking compete so much as they react in a similar way to a particular set of known signals. Much in the manner of a group of people running a race they only compete in terms of the speed with which they arrive at their destination – but significantly, speed of reaction is not a prominent feature of the model. This is true to some extent of the large group case of imperfect competi-

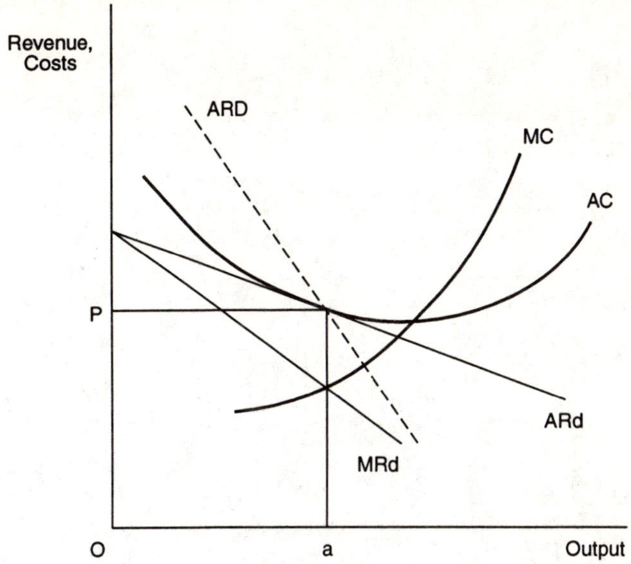

Figure 4.32(a)

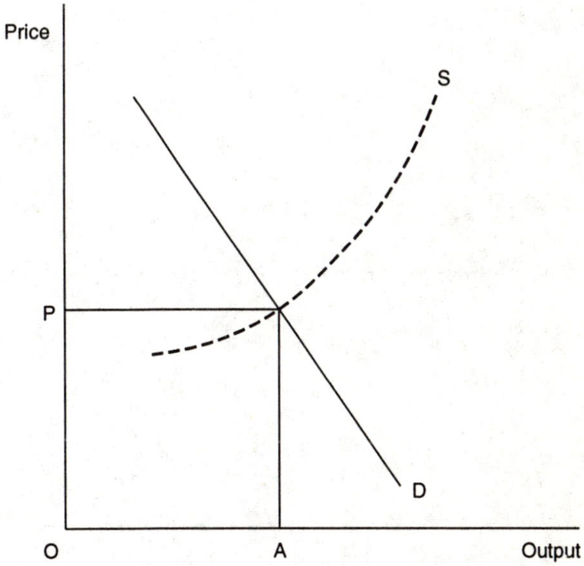

Figure 4.32(b)

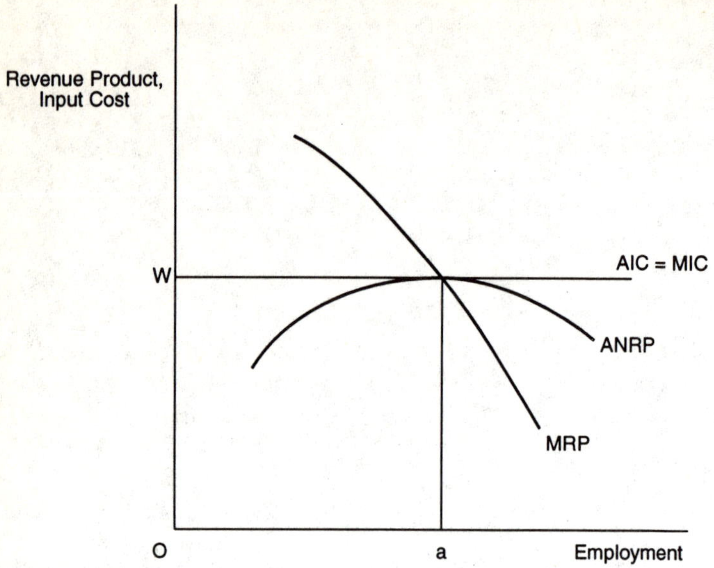

Figure 4.32(c)

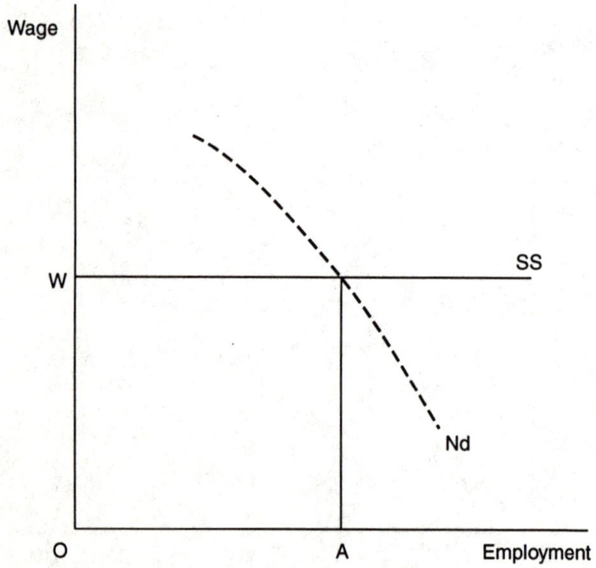

Figure 4.32(d)

tion, although there is one notable new dimension. In monopolistic competition firms compete by changing the conditions which face them and their rivals, i.e. they compete through the introduction of new products, or the manipulation of demand conditions, both of which are designed to create positions of advantage, however temporary. This is in fact the logical implication of the increased number of variables with which the model deals. To put the point in another way, the counterpoint to the tangency solution is the emphasis on the causes of change; causes which are shown to be possibly exogenous but largely endogenous. Looked at in this way, the original specification of the model invites attention to disequilibrium as a special and essential feature of the competitive process in the situation examined.

III. The Small Group

In the first two market situations which we examined, a single determinate solution was found to obtain with regard to the price/output decisions of the firm. In the case of monopoly, if we ignore the problems presented by 'limit price' analysis, the model prompts the conclusion that a particular level of output will be established where MC = MR; a condition which is normally compatible with excess profits. In the same way where perfect competition prevails the typical firm will equate the relevant average and marginal values in producing a particular output at a particular price. There is obviously a parallel here with the large group case of monopolistic competition although, as we have just seen, a number of additional problems arise there due to the interdependence of the cost and revenue functions.

The small group situation shares all the complexities of the large group case with one notable addition – the problem of interdependence between firms which arises simply because the number involved is taken to be small. In the large group it is legitimate to assume that each firm may act as if its decisions will have no impact – that is no direct impact – on the fortunes of its rivals. But where numbers are small we face the problem that decisions taken by one firm may profoundly affect others; a problem which may or may not be considered by the firm when framing policy.

The Small Group: Oligopoly

Since the large and small group cases of monopolistic competition are but two variations on a single theme we would expect a number of similarities; similarities which are reflected in the characteristics of the models. Thus, for example, we continue to use the hypothesis of rationality and the profit maximisation condition of MC = MR in the more complex situation of the small group. Again, we take as our premisses the relationships already established between average and marginal cost and revenue curves, suitably modified to take account of selling costs and the distinction between ARD and ARd (see above, pages 151-153). Once more, we employ two kinds of assumption: those necessary to define the market type and those which help to simplify the analysis.

The first group of assumptions include:

1. Small numbers of sellers, so that the activities of any one may have an important effect on its rivals.
2. Products which are differentiated through product variation and selling costs, but with high cross-elasticities.
3. Free exit from, but blocked entry to, the industry.

The second group of simplifying assumptions include:

1. Perfect competition in the factor market, with inputs available to the firm at a constant price and without variation in quality.
2. Perfect competition among buyers of the commodity.
3. Single product firms; and
4. No transport costs.

As before, the final simplifying assumption is among the most important: the 'heroic' assumption that the cost and revenue conditions facing the firms are the same – an assumption which permits us to use a single set of cost and revenue curves as representative of the circumstances and activities of all members of the group.

Now it will be evident that the critical points of difference between the two examples of monopolistic competition relate to the assumption of blocked entry and to the issue of numbers. Where numbers are small, the actions taken by one firm may have an important effect on the fortunes of its rivals. A number of assumptions can therefore be made relating to the possible behaviour of some or all members of the group. For example, interdependence may be immediately recognised, or consistently ignored, or initially ignored and subsequently recognised.

Conjectural Variations

To illustrate the nature of these possibilities we initially ignore the complication presented by the cost curves, and recall the definitions so far used with regard to the ARD and ARd curves. It will be remembered that the ARD curve is the fractional part of the market demand curve which faces the firm; i.e. that curve which shows how revenue will change on the assumption that all member firms are changing price in the same direction. The ARd curve, as we have seen, represents the demand curve for the product of the individual firm and indicates the way in which revenue would alter on the assumption that rival firms do not alter their prices. Now in the large group case it can be assumed, by virtue of the numbers involved, that the ARd curve will be taken to have operational significance – the complication presented by oligopoly is that this may or may not be the case, depending on the assumptions made with regard to the behaviour of firms. In Figure 4.21 (p.153), for example, suppose price is P_1 and that the quantity sold by the typical firm is Oa. If the firm ignores its likely impact on its rivals it will regard

ARd_1 as the relevant curve and may cut price with a view to increasing sales to Ob. Such a price cut will generate a response where numbers are small, probably forcing all firms to follow suit – thus in effect causing the ARd curve to move down the ARD. Thus we face a particular situation where the firm acts in the expectation that ARd is the relevant revenue curve, but in so doing produces a response which indicates that as the single firm reduces price its competitors will follow, which means that in fact ARD is relevant. It will be evident that where mutual dependence is continually ignored, a price-cutting firm, despite the lessons of experience, will persist in reducing price (at least until it meets the constraint represented by its costs). Diagrammatically, this would be represented by a continuous downward movement in the ARd. Here the ARd has operational significance at least in the eyes of the firm and the ARD is in effect a 'shadow' curve – a function by which the firm is ultimately constrained but whose real significance, indeed existence, it does not recognise.

If, on the other hand, member firms in fact appreciate the nature of the problems which we have just outlined, they may from the outset understand that the consequence of price reduction will be a movement down the ARD – in this case the latter curve is perceived to be that which has operational significance, with the ARd curve ignored.

The most probable outcome would seem to be the intermediate solution, namely where mutual dependence is initially ignored or not appreciated, but subsequently recognised on the basis of experience. Suppose in Figure 4.21 (p. 153) that price is cut to P_2 with a view to increasing sales to Ob – i.e. operating on the assumption that ARd is relevant. If other firms respond by cutting price in the same direction, each firm will sell Oc units and ARd will have moved to position 2. If, as seems likely, the price cutting firm appreciates that this is likely to be the response made by its rivals to such a policy, if repeated, it may decline to cut price further, appreciating that such a policy will in effect involve a movement down the ARD. In this example, the firm begins by regarding ARd as relevant, but subsequently appreciates its limited significance as compared to ARD.

It is at least conceivable, once the situation is appreciated, that the firm may decline to cut price below P_2; a point which is associated with the idea of a composite or kinked demand curve. In Figure 4.33 suppose the price charged is P_2. Any subsequent decision to lower price will be seen to involve a movement down the fractional part of the market demand curve facing the firm, i.e. a movement down the ARD. On the other hand, it is supposable that a firm deciding to increase price would not induce its rivals to follow suit – a change which would involve a movement along the ARd in an upward direction, given the definition of that curve. In short, the average revenue curve may be perceived to be a composite curve made up of a part of ARd and part of ARD – AC and CD in Figure 4.33. It will be noted that there is nothing in what we have said so far which allows us to say at what point the importance of ARD will be recognised, i.e. to predict the position of the 'kink' or the range over which that position may move.

We also face a further difficulty which arises from the fact that we visualise the

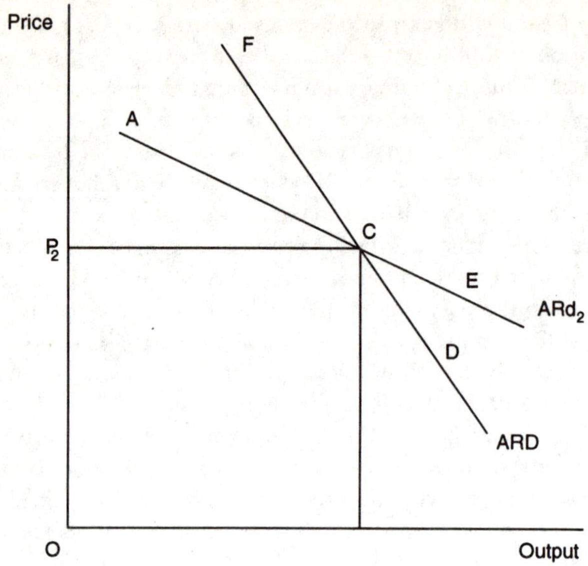

Figure 4.33

firm as forming a judgement of demand conditions which in turn incorporates a judgement as to what its rivals may do in response to a particular action. The composite AR curve of ACD represents one such judgement. But it is possible that a decision to increase price might be followed by rivals while a decision to decrease price might not. On this set of assumptions the composite demand curve (i.e. the curve of AR) would be seen as made up of FC and CE (Figure 4.33).

It is also plausible to suggest that where a firm recognises the problem of interdependence it may decide to sell as much as possible at the price P_2 and to avoid any further cuts in price on the ground that such a policy would involve a movement down the curve of ARD. In this case, the composite curve is identified as P_2CD – essentially a variant of the case of 'limit pricing' which we considered when dealing with monopoly.

Average and Marginal Revenue Curves

If the position of the 'kink' in the demand curve is taken as given, at least for the moment, it will be evident that the marginal revenue curve must also have a composite character.

In dealing with the large-group case only the MRd curve was mentioned since this curve alone had operational significance for the firm. But in the new situation of the small group both ARD and MRD must be considered. In Figure 4.34 MRd is drawn to correspond to ARd and MRD to correspond to the fractional part of

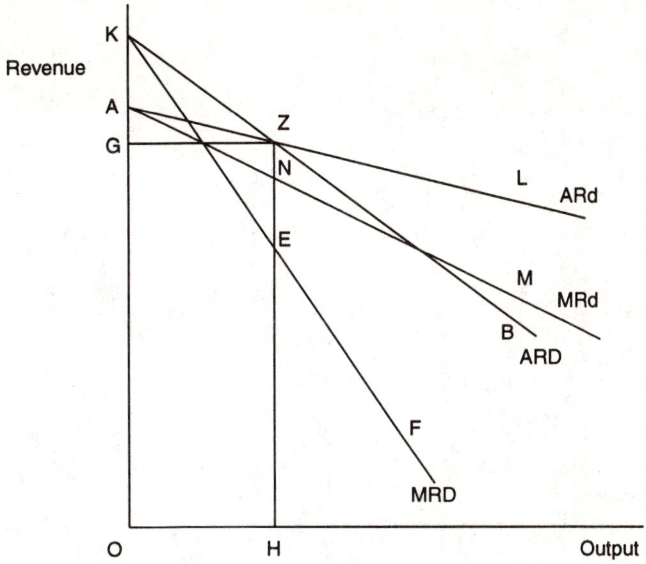

Figure 4.34

the market demand curve (ARD).

Let us suppose that the composite curve of AR is perceived to be AZB in Figure 4.34. Where this is the case, the composite MR curve will correspond to those sections of the curves of AR which are perceived to be relevant. For example, if the firm believes that a decision to *increase* price will not be followed by its rivals then the relevant section of MR will be given by AN. If the firm believes that a *reduction* in price will be matched by its rivals, then ZB is perceived to be relevant. The corresponding section of the curve of MR is thus EF. In short the composite AR curve will be associated with a composite curve of MR, given in this case by AN and EF with a vertical range of discontinuity given by NE.

If the composite AR curve was perceived to be KZL, then we face a situation where the firm believes that its rivals will match an increase in price, but decline to follow a reduction in price. In this case the composite MR curve is given by KE (the relevant section of MRD) and NM (the relevant section of MRd). It will be noted that the range of discontinuity remains the same even given the dramatic alteration to the perceived characteristics of the curve of MR.

If on the other hand the composite curve of AR is taken to be GZB then the curve of MR would change yet again. On this set of assumptions the firm proposes to sell what it can at a given stable price. Here the AR curve is made up of GZ and ZB. The curve of MR will now be given by GZ (since AR=MR) and EF (the range of MRD which corresponds to the relevant range of ARD). If the 'limit price' variant of the kinked demand curve is likely to be the most plausible in the

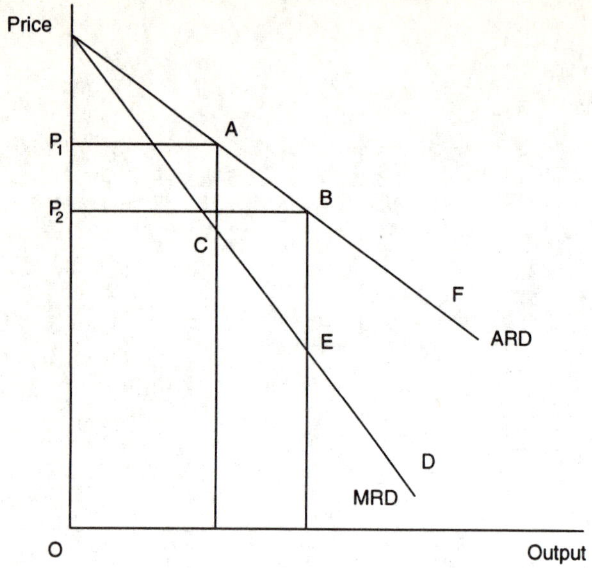

Figure 4.35

context of oligopoly, then it should be noted that it has the effect of *widening* the range of discontinuity to ZE as compared to NE.

Finally it should be noted that any change in the price at which the commodity is sold will involve a change in the position of the 'kink' in the demand curve which the firm believes to be relevant and, therefore, a change in the position of the composite curve of MR. Figure 4.35 considers the simplest of the three possibilities we have so far reviewed.

Suppose the price charged is P_1 and that the perceived AR curve is P_1AB. The corresponding curve of MR will then by given by P_1ACD. Suppose the price now falls to P_2. In this case the perceived AR curve could be P_2BF generating an MR curve of P_2BED. The position of the range of discontinuity (AC and BE) thus moves downwards and to the right. It will be observed that the number of firms is assumed to remain constant so that we may work in terms of a single representative curve of ARD.

Equilibrium with Zero Costs

The three possible behavioural situations which we have so far considered can now be illustrated by taking the relationships between cost and revenue into account. We do this in the first instance by reference to the simplest case where MC is zero, i.e. where the curve of MC coincides with the x-axis.

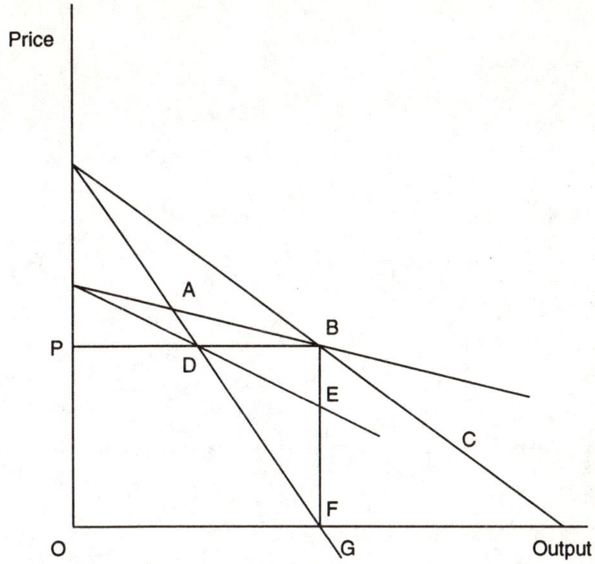

Figure 4.36

1. Mutual Dependence Recognised

Where mutual dependence is recognised immediately and fully appreciated by all members of the group, MRD will be seen to be the relevant curve. Under such circumstances the profit maximisation condition requires that MRD = MC. This case is illustrated in Figure 4.36. It will be seen that this solution is similar to that expected under monopoly, the only difference being that we are here referring to the policy followed by a typical firm, rather than that followed by the single seller. In Figure 4.36 the price charged will be OP and the output per firm will be OF, so that the total output will be given by the output of each firm multiplied by the number of firms. This solution represents the upper limit as far as price is concerned, and the lower limit with regard to output.

2. Mutual Dependence Ignored

Where mutual dependence is consistently ignored, a series of price reductions will take place indicating that the final price and the quantity sold would be respectively lower and higher than in the situation previously examined. Suppose, for example, that the process begins from the kind of situation illustrated in Figure 4.36, but that at least one of the member firms decides to cut price in the belief that its rivals will not follow suit. On this assumption, the firm would regard ARd as relevant and would consider it appropriate to reduce price precisely because MRd is not equal to marginal cost. Evidently price cutting of this kind could continue

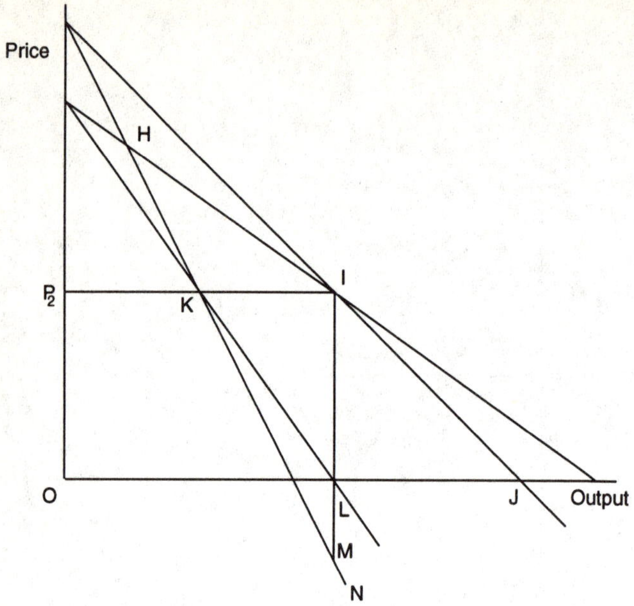

Figure 4.37

if mutual dependence is ignored, the lower limit being reached where MRd = MC so that no firm would find it in its interest to cut price further. This case is illustrated in Figure 4.37 where the output chosen is OL, selling at the price P_2. Evidently it would not pay the firm to offer an amount greater than OL, since MRd becomes negative at this point while MC = 0; nor would it offer less than this quantity since MRd is positive while MC = 0. Two points arise:

First, where MC is zero, the firms which immediately recognise their mutual dependence (Figure 4.36) will operate at that point on the ARD curve where elasticity is equal to 1, and at a point on the ARd curve where elasticity is greater than 1 (see above, p.134). Where mutual dependence is consistently ignored and the MRd is taken to be relevant, (Figure 4.37), the firm will operate at a point on the ARd curve where elasticity is equal to 1 and the elasticity of the fractional part of the market demand curve is less than 1.

Secondly, it will be observed that while the latter solution is the one which will typically obtain in the large group case given the assumption of large numbers, it will only obtain in the small group case given a particular assumption about the behaviour and knowledge of the firms involved. While logically possible, the latter solution seems to be unlikely in practice due to the learning effect and is really only of value in that it permits us to isolate a lower limit for price and an upper limit for quantity sold.

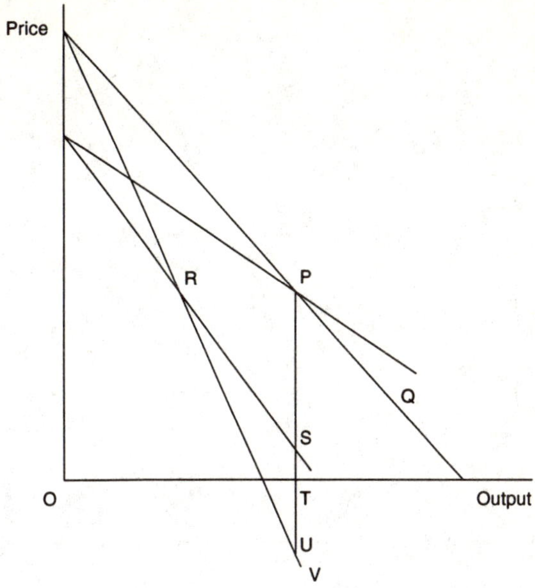

Figure 4.38

3. Mutual Dependence initially Ignored but subsequently Realised

Starting once more from the price charged and quantity sold as shown in Figure 4.36, suppose that a member firm decides to cut price in order to test the reaction of its rivals, thus causing a downward movement of ARd and establishing the position of the kinked demand curve. In this case the price chosen would be lower than the 'monopoly' solution and would inevitably mean that MRD and MC were no longer equal – in fact any departure from the monopoly solution will mean that MC will exceed MRD at any given level of output. By the same token, if the process of price cutting stops at the point chosen, then the price charged will be higher than would be the case in the large group situation, with a smaller quantity offered for sale. In this case, therefore, MRd will not be equal to MC and will in fact lie above it. In short, a solution intermediate between the monopoly and the competitive outcomes will mean that while output may be stable, MC will be equal neither to MRD nor MRd. Graphically, the MC curve (still assumed to be zero) will pass through the range of discontinuity in the composite MR curve – SU in Figure 4.38. This, however, could be a stable solution, if all members of the group recognise the consequences of a further reduction in price.

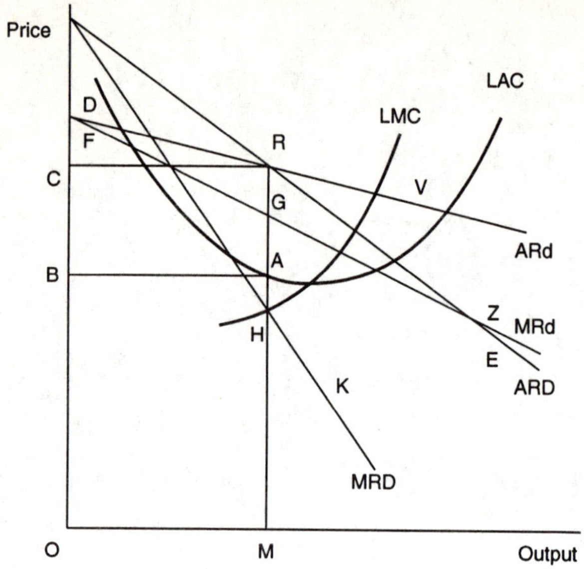

Figure 4.39

Equilibrium with Positive Costs

Since all the principles discussed above apply when we make allowance for positive average and marginal costs the three main possibilities may be quickly summarised.

1. Mutual Dependence Recognised

Where the 'monopoly' solution obtains, each firm is assumed to be fully appraised of the opportunities presented by the competitive structure. Here each firm enjoys in effect the advantage of perfect knowledge meaning that each firm decides to adopt a pricing strategy which allows the members of the group to share the available (monopoly) profits. In such a situation MRD is perceived to be relevant and output for each firm will be OM (Figure 4.39) sold at the price R. In the situation illustrated, the 'kinked demand curve' is perceived to be DRE; the composite MR curve is FGHK yielding a range of discontinuity of GH. As before, the MC curve cuts the range of discontinuity at its lowest limit where MC=MRD (at the point H).

2. Mutual Dependence Ignored

If we start from the previous solution, but drop the first behavioural assumption, this would mean that one or more firms considers that it or they could cut price without generating a reaction from its rivals. If one or more firms now thinks in

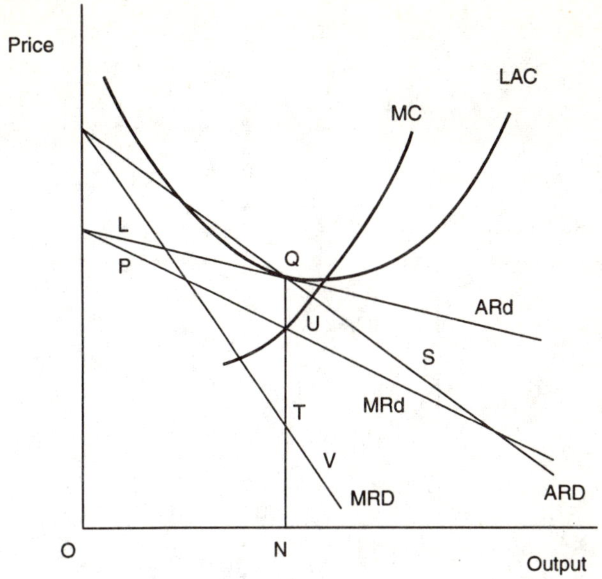

Figure 4.40

terms of ARd and therefore of MRd, the situation would change as a result of these firms endeavouring to bring MRd and MC to equality. If the process of action and reaction already outlined were to continue, the lowest limit would be reached where MRd and MC were equal. In Figure 4.40 this situation is reached where ARd is tangent to the long run average cost curve (LAC) at the point Q. This is the outcome which we would expect under the conditions of the large group. But it is also an outcome which *could* occur in the small group if we assume that mutual dependence is consistently ignored.

In the case illustrated (Figure 4.40), the kinked demand curve is shown as LQS, the composite MR curve is PUTV and the range of discontinuity as UT. Where MRd = MC, the MC curve cuts the relevant range of discontinuity at the top. Output for each firm is now ON, and the selling price is Q.

3. Mutual Dependence initially Ignored but subsequently Realised

The contrasting solutions just considered can be summarised in a single diagram (Figure 4.41) thus serving to delineate the boundaries of a range within which price may settle. The points R and Q also define the range over which the position of the discontinuity in the curve of MR may be located. It will be observed that the range of lateral movement in the position of the range of discontinuity will be determined by the shape of the curves of cost and revenue.

The technical point just made serves to remind us of the fact that the most likely outcome will be *within* the range of RQ, reflecting the plausible assumption that

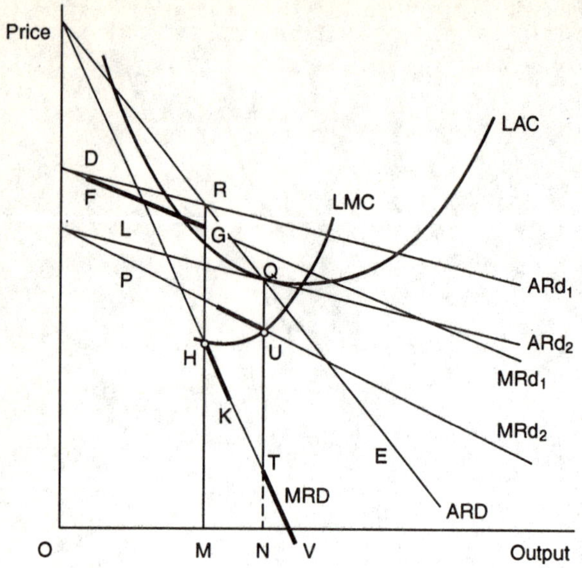

Figure 4.41

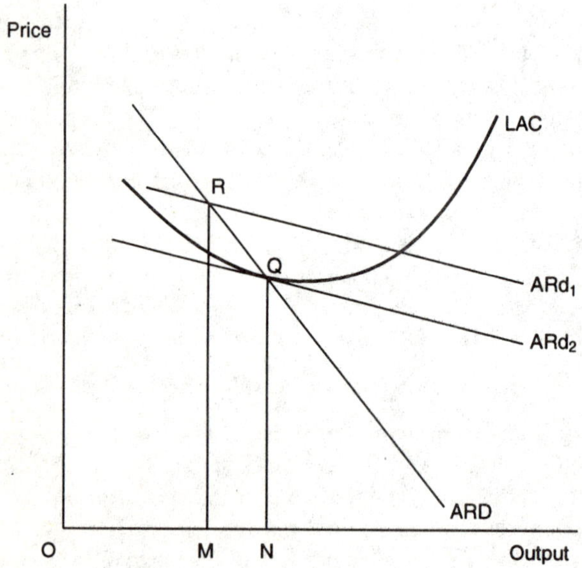

Figure 4.42

price-cutting will produce a learning effect. The most likely outcome will be one where neither MRd nor MRD is equal to MC, i.e. where the MC curve passes through the range of discontinuity. But the model does not permit us to identify a specific solution; it only permits us to identify a range within which a decision as to price and therefore output will be located. Figure 4.42 summarises the possibilities using only the curves of AC, ARd and ARD.

At the same time it should also be noted that the stability of an intermediate solution will be affected by uncertainty on the part of the firm: uncertainty regarding the intelligence of rivals, the extent to which a price cut could be introduced without provoking a response and with respect to buyers' preferences. A particular firm might also be uncertain as to the extent to which its rivals may regard price or output as the major variable.

Input Analysis

It is now a familiar fact that where we face an AR curve which is negatively sloped, then the curve of average net revenue product (ANRP) will slope downward more rapidly in its decreasing phase than would be the case under conditions of perfect competition. But we now face two possible versions of the AR curve, the familiar ARd and ARD. This means in turn, that the ANRP curve based upon ARD will slope downwards more rapidly in its decreasing phase than would be the case where ARd was thought to be relevant.

1. Mutual Dependence Recognised

If we assume a horizontal AIC curve, then the results just stated may readily be applied to the small group case. Take first the 'monopoly' solution outlined in Figure 4.39. In this case, as we have seen, output is OM sold at the price R. Here the kinked demand curve is given by the range DRE and the curve of MR by FGHK. On the input side (Figure 4.43), the curve of ANRP and that of MRP have a shape determined by the curve of ARD (Figure 4.39) while the curve PR, $ANRP_1$ is determined by the shape of ARd. In the case shown, a decision to produce OM units of the commodity is matched by a decision to use OA units of the variable input. The fact that monopoly profits of RA per unit (Figure 4.39) obtain is reflected in the fact that ANRP exceeds AIC by RH. On the output side, MRD = MC while on the input side MRP = MIC at the point H in Figure 4.43. It will be noted that we have abstracted so far from the complicating feature that a curve of MRP must correspond to the curve of $ANRP_1$.

It will also be noted that this solution will be stable so long as the behavioural assumptions used in constructing the 'monopoly' solution hold good.

2. Mutual Dependence Ignored

Where mutual dependence is consistently ignored (Figure 4.40), the outcome, as we have seen, is a situation where the curve of ARd is forced downwards to a position of tangency with LAC at the point Q. In this situation MRd = MC and the

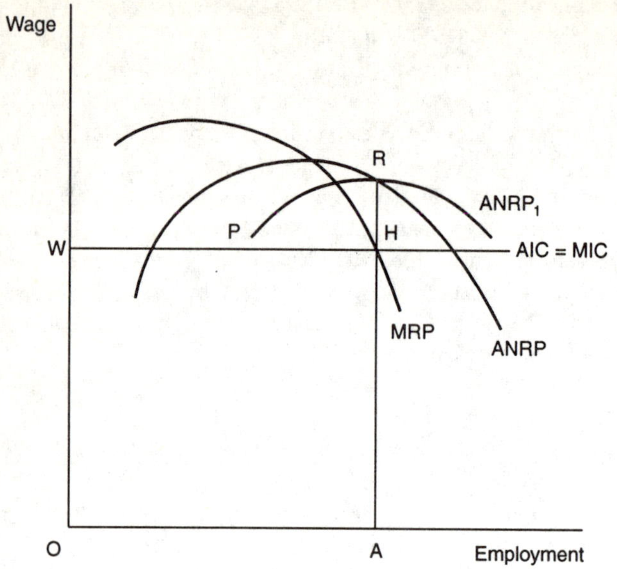

Figure 4.43

level of output attained is ON, sold at the price Q where ARd and LAC are equal.

On the input side (Figure 4.44), the curve of $ANRP_2$ (based on ARd) has been forced downwards until a position of tangency has been established at the point Q. In this case, excess profits have been eliminated (since ANRP = AIC) while in addition MRP = MIC. The level of employment offered is OB. In the case illustrated it will be noted that we work in terms of ANRP (based on ARD in Figure 4.40) while concentrating attention on the curve of $ANRP_2$ (based upon ARd) and on the MRP curve which corresponds to it.

3. Mutual Dependence initially Ignored but subsequently Realised

The range of possible solutions on the output side has been summarised in Figure 4.41. Here, as we have seen, we are able to identify a 'monopoly' solution where output is OM and MRD = MC. In this case we have been able to identify the composite or kinked demand curve (DRE) and the composite MR curve (FGHK) which are based upon the relevant sections of ARD, ARd, MRD and MRd.
These results find their counterpart in terms of input analysis. In Figure 4.45 the monopoly solution is reflected in the fact that the firm offers OA in terms of employment. Here MNRP = MIC, (while in equilibrium ANRP exceeds AIC by RH).

On the output side, the kinked demand curve is given as DRE (Figure 4.39). In terms of the analysis of the input market, the curve of ANRP must also be a composite curve, here given as GRN (Figure 4.44). The corresponding curve of

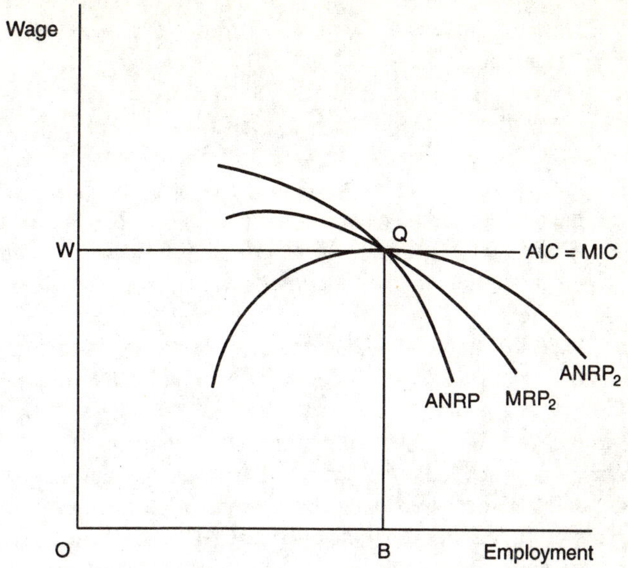

Figure 4.44

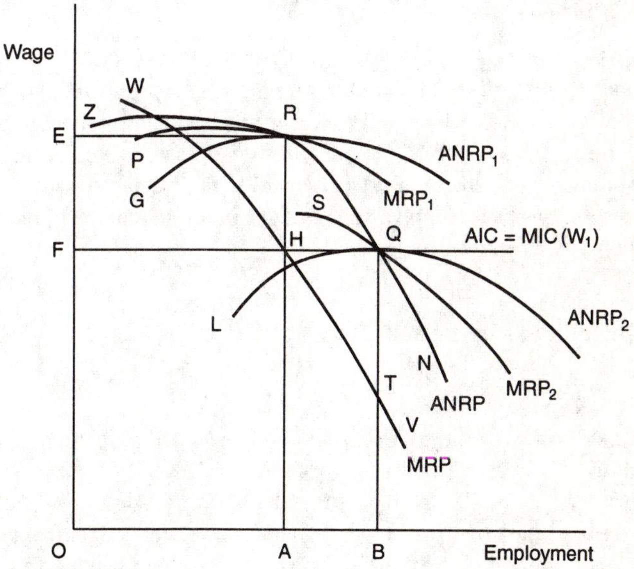

Figure 4.45

MNRP now appears as PRHV. This yields a range of discontinuity of RH and a solution where the MIC curve cuts the range at its lowest relevant point (i.e. where MRP = MIC at the point H).

In Figure 4.41 we also took account of a situation where the behavioural assumptions generated an outcome such that ARd was forced into a position of tangency with LAC. In this case, MRd = MC. As before, the perceived kinked demand curve is LQE while the composite marginal revenue curve is PUTV. On the input side, the process outlined forces the curve of $ANRP_2$ (based upon ARd) to a position of tangency with AIC where in addition, MRP_2 (based on ARd) equals MIC. This result mirrors the outcome on the output side where all excess profits are eliminated.

In the case illustrated, the kinked demand curve is perceived to be LQE while, as we have noted, the composite MR curve is given by PUTV (Figure 4.41). On the input side, the composite ANRP curve emerges as LQN and the composite MRP curve as SQTV (Figure 4.45). The level of employment offered is now OB at the prevailing wage rate. In both cases, it will be noted that the composite curves of ANRP and of MRP are based upon the sections of these curves which correspond to the appropriate sections of the curves of AR and MR in Figure 4.41.

Just as in the case of the output analysis, it will be evident that the most likely outcome will be located within the range RQ. This means of course that the most likely outcome will be one where the curve of MIC passes through the range of discontinuity in the curve of MRP.

4. Further Extensions

It is of course perfectly possible that the oligopolistic firm may face a positively sloped supply curve for labour and therefore a positively sloped curve of MIC. It is equally possible that a generalised model of bilateral monopoly may be relevant in oligopolistic situations – thus lending a further element of indeterminacy to the model outlined above. Uncertainty with regard to the wage rate (at least until the bargain is struck) will, as we have seen, render indeterminate the position of the firm's cost curve (see above, pages 147-148).

Some Implications of the Argument

1. The Entry of New Firms

In outlining the model of the small group it was assumed that entry was blocked; an assumption which permitted us to work in terms of a single curve of ARD and to consider only the problems involved in determining price. It will be recalled that the fractional part of the market demand curve which 'confronts' the firm indicates the way in which revenue is expected to change when all firms follow the same pricing strategy. The slope of the curve is therefore the same as that of the market demand curve, while its position indicates the share of the market enjoyed by the firm.

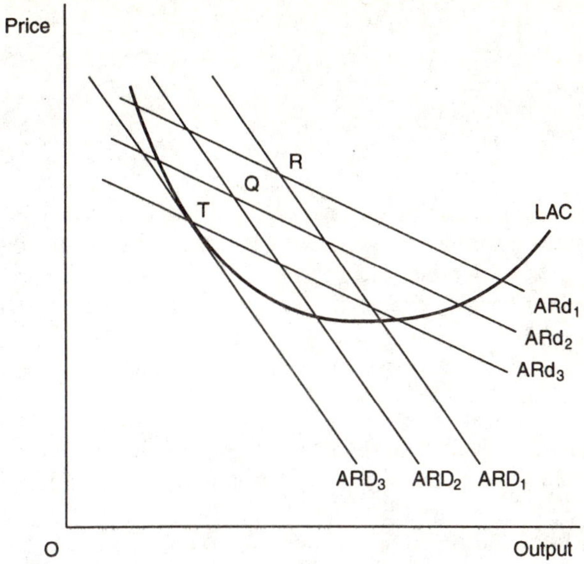

Figure 4.46

It is equally clear that the assumption of blocked entry could be relaxed indicating that the position of both the ARD and the ARd confronting the existing 'representative' firm could change. To illustrate the case let us suppose that new 'firms' can enter the employment under identical conditions to those facing existing firms. For the moment we continue to assume that we can work in terms of a single set of cost and revenue functions treating these as typical of all firms (including new firms) in the group. Suppose further that all firms adopt a conservative pricing policy, i.e. that they accept a series of outcomes such as the points R, Q and T in Figure 4.46. In this case we generate a number of different positions for the kinked demand curve as a consequence of allowing for new entry. Once again this new situation will produce corresponding changes in the shape and position of the curves of ANRP.

2. Price Cutting and the Size of the Group

The example reminds us of another difficulty. We have presented a model based on constant numbers with a view to identifying a range within which an equilibrium price might be found. The implications of such a model is that price-cutting is irrational, i.e. that it will result in a less profitable outcome. But clearly there are circumstances under which price-cutting could be construed as a competitive strategy designed to improve the profitability of the remaining firm or firms. A position of tangency of the ARD curve with AC (point T in Figure 4.46) for example could be followed by a process of price-cutting with a view to driving rivals from the group and of allowing the market share of the survivor(s) to increase. Where this occurs, the fractional part of the market demand curve facing the sur-vivor(s) could move progressively to the right, carrying the curves of ARd with it.

3. Diversity of Firms

We have assumed throughout the analysis of monopolistic competition that all firms are the same – thus permitting the use of a single set of cost and revenue conditions. In doing so we follow the example of E. H. Chamberlin and for the same reasons; namely, that it simplifies the argument and avoids the necessity of drawing a set of functions for each firm. But in reality firms will vary in their characteristics and not least in terms of size. The point is well put in Chamberlin's *Theory of Monopolistic Competition* (1948, pages. 81–2) where it is noted that:

> Each product has distinctive features and is adapted to the tastes and needs of those who buy it. Qualitative differences lead to wide divergences in the curves of cost of production, and buyers' preferences account for a corresponding variety of demand curves both as to shape ... and as to position... The result is a heterogeneity of prices, and variation over a wide range of outputs (scales of production) and in profits... To a very considerable extent the scheme of prices is the result of conditions unique to each product and to its market.

From one point of view the recognition of diversity of conditions makes the problem of oligopoly more manageable. For example, variation in size may lead to a situation where one firm is dominant with regard to the market as a whole. Such a firm may set prices and allow others to sell what they can at that price – presenting them in effect with a horizontal AR curve. It has also been observed that barometric price leadership occurs. In this situation one firm, not necessarily the largest, is conventionally the first to announce price changes where these are related to changes in style, quality or costs.

But from other points of view the recognition of diversity does present problems. We are reminded for example of the need to construct a set of diagrams covering each firm; of the difficulty of constructing a model such as that illustrated in Figure 4.41 which identifies a single range within which a price/output decision may be located and of the problems of actually constructing the demand curve for an industry (and therefore of identifying the fractional part of that curve which we assumed would confront the firm).

4. Space and Interdependence

A further difficulty is presented by the issue of space in the sense that firms and markets are spatially distributed. Firms which are spatially distributed may be members of a large group and at the same time confirm that even in this case we are likely to find evidence of interdependence; i.e. a situation where the firm cannot abstract, or would be advised not to abstract, from the possibility that its decisions as to price may have repercussions on its rivals.

For example, retail stores or filling-stations may be members of a large group while forming a network of inter-related markets. In this case, a retailer of petrol may cut price, forcing adjacent sellers to follow suit. A more extensive cut, on the other hand, could force a like response from rivals within the relevant area and even from those on the boundaries of neighbouring areas. The so-called 'chain linking effect' in fact suggests that even where numbers are large, consideration of indirect influence may be relevant when settling on a pricing strategy.

A related problem arises when we consider the importance of spatially distributed markets in the sense that the decision to alter price for one product may have an impact on the demand for quite different products, thus suggesting that an important area of concern relates to inter- (as distinct from intra-) industry competition. This general problem serves as a reminder of the earlier treatment of consumer demand where the focus of attention was directed to the problem of choice between different goods, as distinct from the choice between different brands of a particular type of product.

Recognition of issues such as these has led to an appreciation of the point that the phenomenon of interdependence is more general than the model of oligopoly itself – which means in turn that the problems of indeterminancy which are so usefully illustrated by this model are of even wider application than we might suppose.

5. Uncertainty

Finally, attention should be drawn to one of the most important features of the model, that is, the attention given to the problem of perceived interdependence and of the prominence given to the role of the behavioural assumptions which we employ. In this connection we should recall the definitions which were given earlier with regard to the curves of ARD and of ARd. ARD was defined as tracing the changes in revenue which would occur on the assumption that all firms cut price in the same direction, i.e. on the assumption that all firms would react in the same way to a price cut introduced by any one. ARd on the other hand was defined as the curve which indicates changes in revenue given a particular assumption about the way in which rivals will behave: both represent extreme cases and provide us with an understanding of the boundaries within which choices may be made.

But in practice, pricing policy will be affected by uncertainty, for example, as to the direct influence of each seller upon price, the intelligence of rivals, the extent to which a pricing strategy will produce responses from firms in this or other industries, and with respect to the timing of the response when it does come. Under such circumstances, the curves of ARD and ARd like those of ANRP are *imagined curves, projections made in the face of an uncertain future*. The curves are fluid boundaries which are liable to change in the light of experience of price-cutting and non-price competition.

One response to this situation shows an appreciation of the point that monopolistic competition and especially the treatment of oligopoly are best treated in terms of analogies which, unlike the model of perfect competition, are not drawn from Newton's laws of motion. Historically, the treatment of oligopoly has been dominated by an analogy with chess. Game Theory emerges as one way of dealing with the problems of decision-making in a competitive environment dominated by the problems of uncertainty and interdependence. But an apparatus which allows us to *deal* with a problem does not mean that it is capable of supplying *solutions*.

Chapter 5

Oligopoly and Game Theory

Introduction

This chapter extends our analysis of theories of competition to consider more fully the situation where there are only a few firms in an industry. As is usual in economics our analysis of oligopolistic industries will be based on a number of assumptions. The use of assumptions has the advantage of clarifying exactly what conditions must hold in order to achieve certain results or outcomes. At the same time assumptions have the disadvantage that they are frequently unrealistic. This disadvantage will not bother the theorist who is keen to discover the intricacies of the model regardless of its empirical relevance, but it will bother the economist who endeavours to make sense of the world or the policy maker who wishes to draw policy conclusions. The study of oligopoly theory goes some way towards satisfying both the theorist and the pragmatist. Oligopoly theory assumes that there are only a few firms in the industry and thereby relaxes the extreme postulates of both perfect competition – which assumes an infinitely large number of firms – and monopoly – which considers but a single firm. The relaxation of these assumptions has the dual effect of injecting greater realism – something that should please the pragmatist, and of complicating the analysis thus leading to a plethora of assumption dependent results – something that should satisfy the theorist. Moreover, having acquired a taste for the effects of relaxing the firm numbers assumption, it is possible to go on to consider the effects of relaxing other assumptions, such as, perfect information, rationality and so on. Not surprisingly, the nature of the effects is similar: greater realism purchased at the price of greater complexity.

The assumption of a small number of firms implies that oligopoly may be distinguished from the extreme cases of both perfect competition and monopoly, by virtue of the fact that the fortunes and actions of all firms are interdependent. The question of interdependence does not arise in the case of perfect competition since the infinitesimally large number of firms ensures that each firm is insignificant in the face of the total market or industry. The actions of any individual firm have a negligible effect on industry variables, such as, market output and price. Firms are atomistic and anonymous amongst a multitude of identical competitors: they do not have to consider the possible reactions of rivals to changes in their output, since changes in the output of an individual firm are so small as to go unnoticed by the rest of the industry.

The lack of interdependence between firms in perfectly competitive markets is shared by firms operating under conditions of monopoly for the rather obvious reason that in the case of monopoly (when entry is blocked) there are no other firms with which to be interdependent. Hence, despite the fact that the models of perfect competition and monopoly are two polar extremes they share in common the absence of any interdependence with rival firms. This common feature of the two models is largely to blame for their lack of realism: competition in the perfectly competitive model can exist only between unidentifiable rivals while in the case of monopoly competition is non-existent. Modelling actual competition between recognisable rivals requires a more complex approach. In recent years this complexity has been handled by the use of game theory. Game theory was developed by von Neumann and Morgenstern in the 1940s as a means of modelling situations of interdependent decision making. In this chapter we will look at the basics of game theory and at a number of applications of the theory to oligopoly.

The chapter is organised as follows: section A outlines Cournot's famous model of duopoly and shows how the relaxation of Cournot's assumptions about firm numbers and the beliefs or conjectures of firms yields a spectrum of oligopoly results that lie between the two extremes of perfect competition and monopoly. In this section emphasis is placed on firm's beliefs about rivals' reactions and the possibilities for collusion. Section B provides an introduction to game theory. The section starts with a brief review of the basic rules and terminology of game theory and a description of one of the most famous games: the prisoners' dilemma. In this section we also discuss a number of other games that have become standards in the literature. In the context of these games a number of themes that are central to this chapter, such as, multiple equilibria and rationality, are highlighted. Section C considers applications of the prisoners' dilemma and other games to oligopolistic competition and strategic entry deterrence. In this section we deal with a number of important aspects of oligopolistic interaction that have been emphasised by the game theoretic approach. In particular, we consider the effects of time, imperfect information, strategic commitment, threats and credibility. Section D picks up a major theme running throughout this chapter: rationality. In this section we outline a number of limitations of the standard model of instrumental rationality and discuss the alternative models of bounded, procedural and expressive rationality. The final section draws some conclusions on the significance of the application of game theory to oligopoly and economic analysis.

Section A : Cournot's Model of Duopoly

Antoine Augustine Cournot was a mathematician and philosopher who paved the way for the application of mathematics to economics. In 1838 he published his main economic treatise, *Recherches sur les Principes Mathématiques de la Théorie des Richesses*. In this work Cournot examines a number of models of competition including monopoly, unlimited (or perfect) competition and his now famous model of duopoly. Cournot considered the case of two firms (firm 1 and firm 2) producing a homogeneous product – mineral water. For simplicity he assumed that costs of production were zero for both firms. In the analysis that follows we will consider the more general case of positive costs but in order to keep our diagrams simple we will assume that unit costs, denoted, c, are constant. This implies that average and marginal cost coincide and are represented by a straight line as shown in Figure 5.1. Industry demand is given by the downward sloping average revenue demand curve D, which for simplicity we also assume to be linear. Associated with this average revenue curve is a marginal revenue curve that cuts the quantity, Q, axis half way between the demand curve and the origin.

Faced with this cost and demand structure and driven by profit maximisation, the problem facing each firm is to find that level of output that maximises profits. Note that Cournot explicitly assumed that firms choose to set output rather than price. Of course, firms cannot set both output and price since these are related by the demand curve. Changing the choice variable of firms from output to price significantly changes the results attained. If firms that produce a homogeneous product set price rather than output then it can be shown following Bertrand (1883) that in equilibrium industry price and quantity will be equal to the perfectly competitive levels. However, we will ignore this complication and consider only the case where firms set output.

The key difference between duopoly, on the one hand, and both perfect competition and monopoly, on the other, is that now each firm must consider its rival's strategy. Industry price and hence, each firm's profit, is only determined after total industry output (equal to the sum of firm 1's and firm 2's outputs) is determined: the fortunes of both firms are interdependent. Given that this is the case each firm must hazard a guess or conjecture about its rival's output strategy before it can calculate its own profit maximising output. Cournot made the simplifying assumption that each firm's conjecture or belief about its rival's output response was set equal to zero. That is, as any firm adjusts or changes its own output it does so in the belief that its rival will keep its output level constant. More formally we can write firm 1's conjectural variation as:

$$CV_1 = \frac{\Delta \text{ 2's Output}}{\Delta \text{ 1's Output}} = 0 \qquad (1)$$

where delta denotes 'change in'. This expression shows that firm 1 conjectures that as it changes its output, firm 2's output remains unchanged. Likewise firm 2's conjecture is given by

$$CV_2 = \frac{\Delta\ 1\text{'s Output}}{\Delta\ 2\text{'s Output}} = 0 \tag{2}$$

Using these behavioural assumptions it is possible to determine industry equilibrium price and quantity levels. Note that since the model is symmetric (that is, there are no differences in costs or product between the two firms) total industry output is split equally between the two firms.

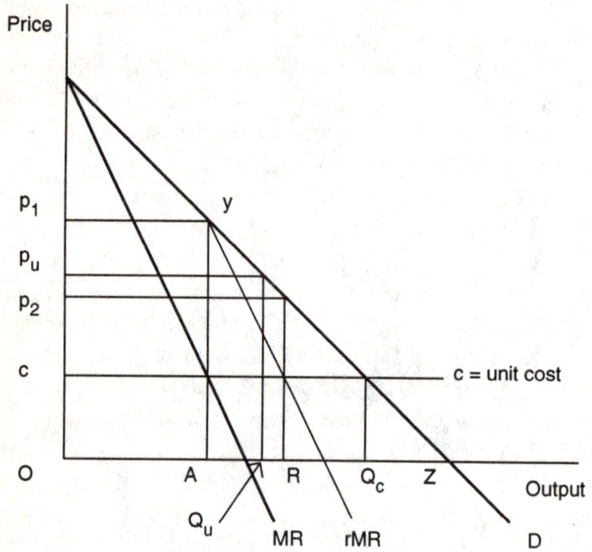

Figure 5.1: Cournot Oligopoly

The attainment of equilibrium can be viewed as an iterative process. Assuming initially that firm 1 is the only firm with production up and running, it maximises profits in the belief that firm 2's output (equal to zero) will remain unchanged. Hence firm 1 will choose to produce where marginal revenue equals marginal cost and will supply half the perfectly competitive output (1/2 Q_c, denoted in Figure 5.1 by the distance OA), at a price p1. When firm 2 commences production it observes that firm 1 is supplying OA and believes (according to equation (2)) that firm 1 will continue to produce at this level. On this basis firm 2 calculates a residual demand curve that has the line Ay as its vertical axis so that the operative demand curve for firm 2 is given by yD. Associated with this residual demand curve is a residual marginal revenue curve (rMR) that (by virtue of the linearity of the AR curve) cuts the horizontal axis half way between A and Z. The profit maximising rule for firm 2 is the familiar one of equating marginal revenue with marginal cost, the only difference in this case is that given the existence of firm 1, firm 2 is effectively operating on its residual average and marginal revenue curves. Hence firm 2 produces at the point half way between A and Q_c and supplies 1/4 of the total market ($1/4Q_c$). Total supply is now equal to OR and industry price is reduced to p2. Once firm 2 has entered the market (producing $1/4Q_c$), firm 1's output of OA is no longer the profit maximising level. In order to return to an optimal level of production firm one must choose an output level that maximises its profit given that firm 2 is supplying 1/4 of the market. To attain its objective of profit maximisation under Cournot oligopoly firm 1 will apply the profit maximising rule of equating its residual marginal revenue with marginal cost.

One way of viewing the profit maximising rule under Cournot duopoly (assuming a zero conjectural variation) is that each firm must produce half of unsatisfied market demand. Note that this is equivalent to equating marginal revenue and marginal cost, given that firms calculate their residual demand curves.

Hence, at the outset firm 1 maximises profits by producing $1/2Q_c$. When firm 2 sets up production it maximises profits by producing $1/2(1/2Q_c) = 1/4(Q_c)$. Normalising Q_c by setting it equal to 1, it can be seen that firm 1 initially supplies half the market, $1/2(1 - 0)$ and when firm 2 enters it initially supplies a quarter of the market, $1/2(1 - 1/2)$. Of course, this is not the end of the matter since once firm 2 has entered the foray, firm 1 is no longer in a profit maximising position. In order to restore its profit maximising output, firm 1 must now produce $1/2(1 - 1/4) = 3/8$. This adjustment by firm 1 implies that firm 2 must now produce $1/2(1 - 3/8) = 5/16$. This process of adjustment, with firm 1 gradually contracting its output and firm 2 gradually increasing its output, will continue until both firms produce 1/3 of the perfectly competitive output Q_c.

Cournot equilibrium is thus characterised by an industry output of Q_u equal to 2/3 Q_c, and an industry price of p_u. Note that given the modified profit maximising rule of producing half of unsatisfied market demand there is no tendency to change output (ie equilibrium is attained) only when each firm produces a third of the market, since $1/2(1 - 1/3) = 1/3$. Note also, that despite the fact that on the adjustment path to equilibrium each firm's belief about its rival's reaction is incorrect, in equilibrium each firm's belief or conjecture is plausible since neither firm has an incentive to change output.

Cournot equilibrium can also be illustrated with the use of reaction curves as shown in Figure 5.2. These curves depict the best response of each firm to different quantities of output produced by its rival. Cournot reaction curves are drawn on the assumption of a zero conjectural variation and are derived from the profit maximising or first order conditions.

In Figure 5.2 the distance OA corresponds to the distance OA in Figure 5.1. Consider Figure 5.2 and assume as before that initially there is only one firm (firm 1) in the market. On the basis that firm 2 is initially producing zero, firm 1 reads off its best response to this output level from its reaction curve and produces OA equal to half of the total market. Firm 2 enters the market taking firm 1's output

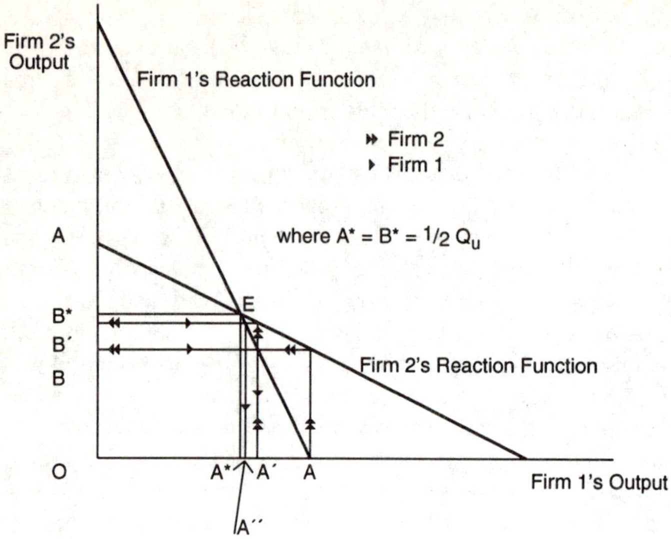

Figure 5.2: Cournot Reaction Curves and Cournot Equilibrium

of OA as given and reads off its best response from its reaction curve on the vertical axis, hence firm 2 now produces OB equal to 1/4 of the total market. Firm 1 now takes 2's output as given at OB and selects its best response by reading across from point B to its reaction curve and down to the horizontal axis to the point A′. This process of adjustment continues until Cournot equilibrium is reached at point E. At this point, with each firm supplying 1/3 of the total market there is no incentive for either firm to adjust its output. The point E, with its associated industry price and quantity, p_u, Q_u, is also known as a Nash equilibrium. We shall discuss this equilibrium concept in more detail shortly. For the moment it is sufficient to note that in Nash equilibrium each firm's output strategy is a best response to its rival's output strategy.

As before it is apparent that the adjustment process belies each firms belief that its rival will not change its output level and this would appear to constitute a weakness of the model. There are 3 responses to this view. The first is that if the model is solved mathematically then the first order conditions attained from maximising each firm's profit function can be rearranged to attain the equilibrium level of output for each firm without any recourse to a process of adjustment. This is the virtue of the comparative static approach and it proves that the model is formally consistent. A second response would be that firms theoretically work out the adjustment process ex-ante (in much the same way as it has been described above) before producing a single unit of output. In this case each firm will realise that there is only one stable equilibrium output and will choose this output level straight-off. A third possibility is that firms learn the equilibrium output by experience and apply this experience to the problem at hand. Again, the effect is the same since experience tells firms that output levels other than 1/3Qc are unstable and it is therefore advisable to produce this level from the outset. The important point to note is that all three of these responses remove the need for the actual adjustments in output described above to take place so that there is no violation of firms' beliefs.

Another feature of Cournot's model that is worthy of discussion and is of central importance to the main theme of this chapter is the question of collusion and the role of the belief system that underlies each firm's strategy choice. From Figure 5.1 it can be seen that while both firms are making some excess profits in Cournot equilibrium, both firms would be better off if they restricted their combined output to the monopoly level Q_m represented by the distance OA. Hence, there is an incentive for firms to collude. Attainment of the joint profit maximising output (with each firm producing 1/4Qc) requires firms to co-ordinate their output plans. Perfect co-ordination of output plans demands that every change in firm 1's output is matched by an identical change in firm 2's output. This requires that the behavioural rule underlying firm's strategies is changed from Cournot's original assumption of a zero conjectural variation to a conjectural variation equal to 1. Hence,

$$CV_1 = \frac{\Delta \text{ 2's Output}}{\Delta \text{ 1's Output}} = 1 \qquad (3)$$

and

$$CV_2 = \frac{\Delta \text{ 1's Output}}{\Delta \text{ 2's Output}} = 1 \qquad (4)$$

Suppose we started from Cournot equilibrium and firm 1 decided to reduce its output slightly in an attempt to reach the joint profit maximising output (see Figure 5.1). Under perfect co-ordination, that is when each firm's conjectural variation is equal to 1, this reduction in output will be matched by firm 2. In response firm 1 will reduce its output once more and so on, the process continuing until firm 1 has no incentive to carry on reducing output. This will occur at an industry output of OA with each firm producing 1/2OA.

We have now considered two possible equilibrium outcomes: Cournot equilibrium which is based on a zero conjectural variation and the joint profit maximising or collusive outcome based on a conjectural variation equal to 1. However, Cournot argued that despite the possibility of multiple equilibria, only the Cournot equilibrium is stable. Cournot offered no formal proof of this proposition but he reasoned that at the joint profit maximising (collusive) output there would be a temptation for the profit maximising firm to cheat and produce slightly more than its rival in order to undercut the market price. As Cournot wrote:

> Why is it then that, for want of an understanding, the producers do not stop, as in the case of a monopoly or of an association, at the value of p derived from equation (4) [in Cournot's text equation (4) determines the monopoly price and hence the joint profit maximising output], which would give them the greatest income?
>
> The reason is that producer 1 having fixed his production at what it should be according to equation (4) and the condition that q1 = q2 [i.e. firms produce equal quantities of output], the other will be able to fix his own production at a higher or lower rate with a temporary benefit. To be sure, he will soon be punished for his mistake, because he will force the first producer to adopt a new scale of production which will react unfavourably on producer 2 himself. But these successive reactions, far from bringing both producers nearer to the original condition [of joint monopoly], will separate them further and further from it. In other words, this condition is not one of stable equilibrium; and, although the most favourable for both producers, it can only be maintained by means of a formal engagement; for in the moral sphere men cannot be supposed to be free from error and lack of forethought any more than in the physical world bodies can be considered perfectly rigid, or supports perfectly solid, etc. (Cournot 1838, 1960: 83; text in square brackets added for clarification).

This passage makes it clear that in Cournot's view a collusive equilibrium can only be sustained if firms are party to some form of binding contract. Without such a contract, greed and the temptation to cheat will force the firms back to the Cournot or non-cooperative equilibrium. It is for this reason that collusive contracts are illegal in most advanced industrialised countries. As mentioned above, Cournot offered no formal proof of his proposition that a belief system characterised by a zero CV dominates a belief system that has each firm's CV equal to one, but the recent application of game theory to oligopoly has proved this proposition to hold true under certain conditions.

As a final point we should note that Cournot's analysis did not consider the possibility of entry by rival firms. Once we acknowledge the existence of potential entrants then firms may choose an output strategy that takes account of the existence of both incumbent competitors and the existence of potential entrants. In general the possibility of entry by rival firms will limit the extent to which incumbent firms restrict output and earn oligopoly profits, since the existence of such profits may attract new firms into the industry. Before leaving this section to turn to a discussion of game theory it is worthwhile summarising our analysis of models of competition by incorporating the models discussed above in a single diagram in order to draw out the relationships between them.

Perfect competition and monopoly provide two bench marks between which all other models of competition/oligopoly lie. In Figure 5.3 the equilibrium solution for monopoly is p_m, Q_m while the perfectly competitive industry would price at

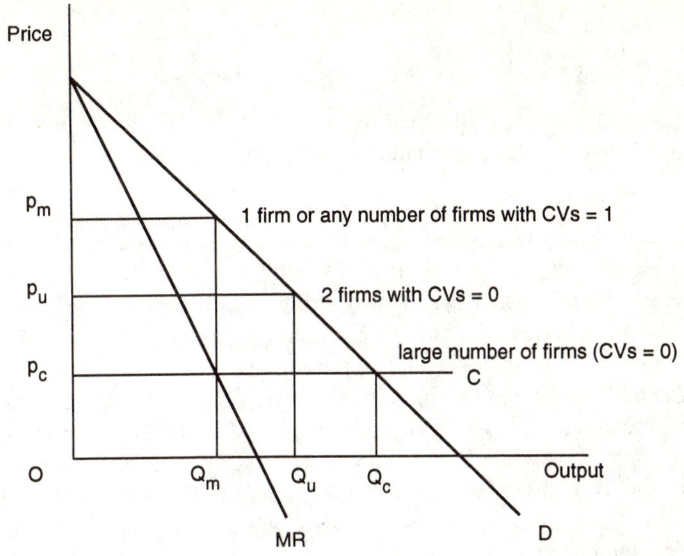

Figure 5.3: Models of Compretition: Equilibria under Different Market Structures and Behavioural Rules (Beliefs)

p_c, and supply a quantity, Q_c. It should be noted that the perfectly competitive solution cannot be derived from this diagram since under constant (or increasing) returns to scale, the theory of perfect competition breaks down (Sraffa (1926)). Nevertheless, as an abstract exercise it is possible to take the perfectly competitive pricing result (i.e. price = MC) and superimpose it on Figure 5.3.

The juxtaposition of perfect competition and monopoly depicted in Figure 5.3 delineates the outer limits between which the outcomes from all oligopoly models must lie. This is one of the main values of the theories of perfect competition and monopoly: based as they are on extreme assumptions, they define the two extremities of a spectrum of models of competition. Our analysis of static oligopoly models results in outcomes which fall between these two points. For example, the Cournot equilibrium derived above on the basis of 2 firms and a zero conjectural variation results in an equilibrium price of p_u and an equilibrium quantity of Qu. As we have seen, Cournot's model can be extended to take account of collusion between firms by letting each firm's CV = 1. Under this assumption the equilibrium solution will be Q_m, p_m, with each firm supplying $1/2Q_m$. It should also be noted that it is possible to allow a degree of collusion (rather than perfect collusion where CV = 1) by letting the CV of firms vary between 0 and 1. Such variation allows us to attain equilibrium price and quantity solutions that lie between Q_u and Q_m and p_u and p_m. In this way the CV can be viewed as an index of the degree of collusion as shown in Figure 5.4.

It is also possible to relax another of Cournot's assumptions to attain equilibrium

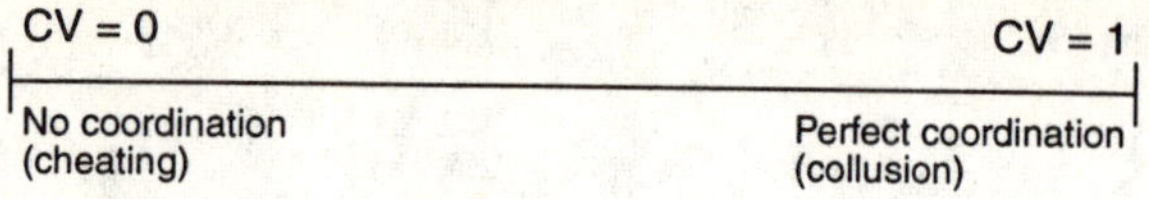

Figure 5.4: The Conjectural Variation as an Index of Collusion

outcomes that lie between Q_u and Q_c, and p_u and p_c. If we assume a zero CV and gradually increase the number of firms in the industry from 2 to 3, to 4 to 10 and so on, the solutions for price and quantity will gradually shift to the right of Q_u on the quantity axis and downwards from p_u on the price axis. Indeed, as we increase the number of firms it can be shown that the equilibrium solution converges to the perfectly competitive price and quantity. It is only necessary to increase the number of firms to about 10 in order to get reasonably close to the perfectly competitive equilibrium. Of course, this is on the assumption that firms do not collude (that is, CV = 0). It should be noted that regardless of the number of firms in an industry, if collusion can be sustained, it is possible for any oligopolistic market structure to attain the joint profit maximising or collusive outcome, Q_m, p_m. However, it is obvious that it is easier for firms to collude the fewer they are in number. Hence, the degree of collusion is likely to be positively related to the degree of market concentration.

Oligopoly Theory and Indeterminacy

It should be clear from the discussion above that whereas both perfect competition and monopoly have unique equilibrium outcomes, oligopoly suffers from a degree of indeterminacy. This indeterminacy arises as a result of two factors: firm numbers and beliefs. As far as the first factor is concerned indeterminacy disappears as soon as we make an assumption or observation about the number of firms in an industry. However, the second source of indeterminacy is far more intractable since in order to solve it we must know which set of beliefs firms operate under: in essence we need to know something about the psychology of firms. It is this feature of oligopoly that distinguishes it from its perfectly competitive and monopolistic counterparts. Once we leave the abstract worlds of perfect competition and monopoly we need a theoretical framework for analysing how firms interact with each other. Game theory has gone a long way towards providing such a framework.

Section B: The Theory of Games

Early work on the mathematical theory of games was carried out by John von Neumann (von Neumann, 1928). He continued working in this area throughout the next decade and during the late 1930s and early 1940s collaborated with Oskar Morgenstern to publish the first text on game theory and economics: *Theory of Games and Economic Behaviour* (von Neumann, Morgenstern, 1944). The book had two main objectives. The first was to provide an exposition of the theory of games and provide a number of applications or examples to illustrate the theory. The second was to focus on the application of the theory to economic and sociological problems. Of these two objectives the authors made it clear that the latter captured the main focus of their interest:

> Our major interest is, of course, in the economic and sociological direction. Here we can approach only the simplest questions. However, these questions are of a fundamental character. Furthermore, our aim is primarily to show that there is a rigorous approach to these subjects, involving, as they do, questions of parallel or opposite interest, perfect or imperfect information, free rational decision or chance influences. (von Neumann and Morgenstern 1944: v)

As is frequently the case in the development of theories (Cournot's contribution is another example) von Neumann and Morgenstern's work on game theory and its application to economics went largely unrecognised by mainstream theory[1] for a considerable time and was only fully assimilated into mainstream economics in the 1980s.

In this section we start by providing a brief exposition of the theory of games using applications or examples that have become standards in the literature. Once the basic concepts of game theory have been discussed we will then go on to consider the application of game theory to oligopolistic interaction.

I. Introduction to Game Theory

Game theory has a precise formulation and a precise terminology. The term 'game' refers to a situation of interdependent decision-making governed by a number of rules. For example, one of the rules governing most oligopoly games is that it is illegal for firms to make collusive contracts. In addition it is stated at the outset who has access to which information. Games have at least two participants called players and a set of possible outcomes, where each outcome depends on the

1. This is not to say that considerable progress was not made in this area during the 1950s, 60s and 70s as a number of economists and social scientists made substantial contributions to the theory and its applications eg Nash (1951), Luce and Raiffa (1957), Shubik (1959), Shapely (1953), Harsanyi (1967/8), Harsanyi and Selten (1972), Selten (1978).

actions or moves of the players[2]. Players are assumed to have a clearly defined preference ordering over all the possible outcomes of the game that is consistent with their objective (eg profit maximisation). In general, players are assumed to be instrumentally rational in the sense that given their objectives they choose the most efficient way of achieving them. Each player receives a payoff (which may be positive or negative) from playing the game. The most common payoff in oligopoly games is profit. A game consists of a sequence of actions or moves where a move is defined as a choice between a number of alternatives. With the exception of games that consist only of 1 move, a move must be distinguished from a strategy. A strategy constitutes an overall game plan that details what a player would do in any situation in which she might find herself.

Knowledge, Information and Certainty

An important assumption underlying most games is common knowledge. Assumptions about knowledge and common knowledge are distinct from assumptions about information. Common knowledge refers to a situation where information or knowledge is known by all players and all players know not only that all other players know this information but also that all players know that all other players know this information and so on *ad infinitum*.

Games may be characterised by various information structures. Under perfect information all players know their own payoffs and the payoffs of their rivals and observe all moves made by rival players. Under imperfect information one or more players cannot observe either the payoffs of their rivals and/or the moves of their rivals. Where the information structure is imperfect some players may have access to more information than others. For example, in a two player game, asymmetric information refers to a situation where one player is uncertain about her rival's payoffs or moves, while the other player has perfect information (knows the payoffs and can observe the moves of all players).

Games may be characterised by certainty or uncertainty. Under certainty there are no moves of chance in the game, in other words, Nature (or chance) does not play a role. By way of contrast, in games characterised by uncertainty Nature plays a part and there are moves of chance. For example, if two players play a game of tossing a coin and calling either Heads or Tails, Nature moves to determine which side of the coin faces upwards.

Finally, and it would seem just to confuse matters, games may also be characterised by complete or incomplete information. As Rasmusen notes,

> In a game of incomplete information, Nature moves first and is unobserved by at least one of the players. Otherwise the game is one of complete information....Two kinds of games have complete but imperfect information: games with simultaneous moves, and games where late in the game Nature

2. It should be noted that in some games there are chance moves by Nature and that Nature may be viewed as a player.

makes moves not immediately revealed to all players. (Rasmusen 1989:53,54]

Zero-sum Games and Non-Zero-sum Games

Broadly speaking there are two type of games: zero-sum games and non-zero sum games. In the former, one player's gain is another player's loss so that at the end of the game the sum of each players' benefits or payoffs is zero. As von Neumann and Morgenstern have pointed out games of entertainment, such as, Bridge or Chess, are usually of this type. By contrast non-zero sum games are characterised by the fact that the sum of all payments or payoffs will usually not be zero and in general will not even be constant since it will depend on the course of action or strategies chosen by players. Most types of economic interaction are characterised by this type of payoff structure. As a result this chapter is concerned solely with non-zero-sum games.

Non-zero-sum games may be classified according to whether they are cooperative or non-cooperative. In the former, participants in the game are free to make legally binding agreements, hence players in a cooperative oligopoly game would be free to make collusive contracts. In the latter, participants are not free to cooperate in this way, instead they are usually in competition with other players and the use of legally binding collusive contracts is ruled out. Plainly, non-cooperative games conform closely to situations of oligopoly in economies where collusive contracts are illegal and thus, non-enforceable. In the light of this fact this chapter is concerned only with non-cooperative games. We start by considering one of the most famous games: the prisoners' dilemma.

II. The Prisoners' Dilemma

The prisoners' dilemma summarises a situation of simultaneous interdependent decision-making between two prisoners who are being held and questioned by the police. The police believe that they have committed a fairly major crime such as armed robbery but do not have sufficient evidence to convict them. As a result they question the prisoners separately and offer them the following choices. If neither of them confesses they will both be convicted for 1 year on a trumped-up minor charge, such as, possession of a fire arm. If both of them choose to cooperate by confessing to armed robbery their case will be treated leniently by the Judiciary and they will each receive a sentence of 10 years. Finally, if one of the prisoners chooses to confess while the other remains silent, then the confessor will receive a suspended sentence for turning Queen's evidence and enabling a conviction, while her/his accomplice will receive a maximum prison sentence of 15 years. Notice that the prison sentences or payoffs reflect negative levels of utility. The objective of each player is to maximise their utility, that is, minimise their prison sentence (payoff) and these objectives are common knowledge.

		PLAYER 2	
		Confess	Don't Confess
PLAYER 1	Confess	(10, 10)	(0, 15)
	Don't Confess	(15, 0)	(1, 1)

Table 5.1: Payoff Matrix for the Prisoners' Dilemma Game

The payoffs for this game can be summarised in the payoff matrix shown in Table 5.1. The matrix adopts the standard convention of showing player 1's payoffs as the first term in each bracket and player 2's payoffs as the second term. The payoff matrix relates moves or strategies to payoffs and outcomes: this type of representation is known as the strategic or normal form.

An alternative form of representation is the extensive form: in this case the game is shown as a decision tree as shown in Figure 5.5. Each node of the decision tree is labelled to indicate which player is making an action choice or move at that node. The branches from the node represent the choices or moves available to that player. Ultimately, the branches of the decision tree lead to terminal dots and associated payoffs.

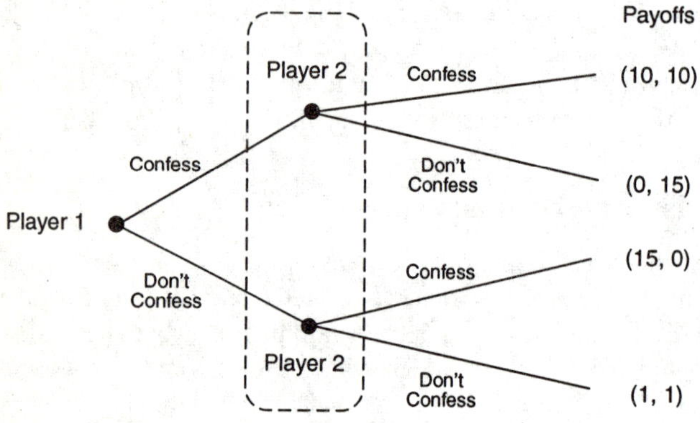

Figure 5.5: The Prisoners' Dilemma in Extensive (Game Tree) Form

Since the prisoners' dilemma is a simultaneous move game this is shown on the decision tree by a broken frame around player 2's two decision nodes. The broken line indicates that player 2 does not know the choice of player 1 at the previous decision node, in other words the game is one of imperfect information since neither player knows the choice of the other before making their own move. In the discussion that follows we will concentrate on the normal or strategic form representation of the prisoners' dilemma. In the following section, which deals with sequential move games, both the normal and extensive forms will be employed.

It can be seen from Table 5.1 that each player has two choices (*Confess,* or *Don't Confess*). As this game will only be played once, a move is identical to a strategy and the strategy space is therefore confined to the above two choices. It should be noted that when a game is only played once it is referred to as a one-shot game and that changing the time horizon (that is, the number of times the game is played) can significantly alter the results attained.

As we have seen, since players make their moves simultaneously and neither knows the choice of the other before making their own choice, the prisoner's dilemma is characterised by imperfect information. That is, although both players know all the payoffs associated with different outcomes, they cannot observe the move of their counterpart before making their own move. However, it should also be noted that the game is one of common knowledge in that both players know that each of them knows the payoffs shown in Table 5.1. In addition both players know that the objective of each of them is to maximise their utility, that is, it is common knowledge that both players are instrumentally rational. When encountering the prisoners' dilemma for the first time, many people implicity object to this assumption on the basis that if the prisoners had committed the crime together they would be bound by the moral code 'honour among thieves'. There are three responses to this view. The first is that it is not necessary that the two prisoners' actually have collaborated or indeed even committed the crime: the history of the story prior to them being held and questioned separately and offered 'deals' by the police is, in fact, irrelevant. Here it is enough to note that in reality innocent people have been known to confess under police questioning. The second response is that the suspects are indeed collaborators in crime but the payoffs have already been adjusted to reflect the fact that players may feel some guilt or disutility from confessing. The third is that players are not instrumentally rational but follow a value-based model of rationality which permits adherence to rules such as 'honour among thieves'. We postpone a discussion of this final option until Section D.

As shown in Table 5.1 there are 4 possible outcomes to the one-shot prisoners' dilemma game. Each player has a preference ordering over these outcomes and will prefer the outcome that best satisfies their preferences. Given that both players have the same objective of maximising their utility they both have the same preference ordering which is given in Table 5.2

Plainly this ordering over outcomes is driven by the value of the payoffs given in the right hand column of Table 5.2 and the fact that the motivating objective of players is to maximise utility, that is, minimise prison sentence. Table 5.2 exposes the essence of the prisoners' dilemma, namely, that both player's would prefer to confess while their opponent stays silent. The problem is that the outcome of the game depends on the strategy choice of both players and each player has no con-

Preference Ordering	Required Strategy Combination	Payoff
1st Best Outcome	Confess while other player Doesn't Confess (Confess, Don't Confess)	0 years
2nd Best Outcome	Don't Confess while other player Doesn't Confess (Don't Confess, Don't Confess)	1 year
3rd Best Outcome	Confess while other player Confesses (Confess, Confess)	10 years
4th Best Outcome	Don't Confess while other player Confesses (Don't Confess, Confess)	15 years

Table 5.2: The Preference Ordering of a Prisoners' Dilemma Player

trol over the strategy choice of her/his rival. Here, it is important to recall that we are considering a non-cooperative game and have therefore ruled out the use of contracts, such as an enforceable agreement not to confess.

The solution to this game is easily worked-out. Each player must look at the possible payoffs associated with each strategy. For example, consider the game from the point of view of player 1. If player 1 adopts the strategy *Don't Confess*, she/he will receive a payoff of 1 or 15 depending on the strategy choice of player 2. Alternatively, if player 1 chooses the strategy *Confess*, she/he will receive a payoff of 0 or 10. In order for player 1 to calculate which strategy is best it is sufficient

Payoff from choosing Don't Confess	1 or 15
Payoff from choosing Confess	0 or 10

Table 5.3: Payoff Possibilities for Player 1

to compare the possible payoffs from each strategy as shown in Table 5.3.

Of course, whether player 1 receives a payoff of 1 or 15, or 0 or 10, depends on what strategy player 2 adopts. However, it should be apparent that regardless of the strategy choice of player 2, player 1 is always better of choosing *Confess* since reading down the columns it is obvious that: 0 is less than 1 and 10 is less than 15! By the same reasoning player 2's best strategy choice is also *Confess.* As a result the equilibrium outcome for this game is *Confess, Confess* and both players receive a payoff of 10.

The equilibrium solution *Confess, Confess* (10, 10) is called a Nash equilibrium. A Nash equilibrium is an outcome where each player's strategy is a best response to its opponent's strategy. Nash equilibrium also refers to a situation of fulfilled expectations by players. For example, in the above game each player expects her/his rival to try to 'win' the game. Both players know or can infer the preference ordering since they know the motivation (utility maximisation) of the other by virtue of the assumption of common knowledge rationality. As a result both know they are carrying out the same type of calculation and will end up with the same strategy choice – *Confess.* This is the utility-maximising strategy for both players, so they both adopt it and find that their expectation about their rival's strategy choice is correct. It is also the case that in Nash equilibrium no player could attain a better payoff given the strategies adopted by the other player(s).

A further characteristic of the equilibrium solution to the prisoners' dilemma game described above is that it is unique. This is the case because the game possesses *a strictly dominant strategy*. A strictly dominant strategy can be defined as a strategy choice that is the best choice regardless of the strategy choice of one's rival(s). In a game with a strictly dominant strategy both players will always adopt this strategy and there is a unique equilibrium outcome. Many games do not possess dominant strategies and are characterised by multiple equilibria.

Before concluding our discussion of the prisoners' dilemma something must be said about the nature of the equilibrium outcome. It should be obvious that the result itself presents something of a dilemma. After all, both players would be better off if they each chose the strategy don't confess. In this case they would both receive a payoff of 1. In other words the equilibrium solution is Pareto sub-optimal. The sub-optimality of the prisoners' dilemma result is particularly uncomfortable given that is derived from instrumentally rational behaviour. As Luce and Raiffa point out, 'two so-called irrational players would fare much better than two so-called rational ones.' (Luce and Raiffa 1957: 96). We will pick-up this theme of rationality later on in the discussion.

Many socio-economic situations contain elements of the prisoners' dilemma. The arms race between the USA and the old USSR was an example of two players engaged in the costly accumulation of nuclear weapons. Both players would clearly be better off not having to continue to compete in this race, but neither player could afford to fall behind for fear of being the victim of a first strike attack. It is notable that in this instance the two players saw that there would be mutual benefit if both could be party to a legally binding agreement to limit the appropriation of arms – hence both players were signatories to the Strategic Arms Limitation Treaties (SALT). In effect the players changed the nature of the game from non-cooperative to cooperative. In most economic situations, particularly in the case of oligopoly, the legal system rules out this option.

Trade Union membership is another example. Clearly, in terms of wage bargaining, or negotiations over employment conditions, workers would be better off if they were all union members. In this case the union would be more representative, it would have greater funds and more bargaining power vis-a-vis the employer. However, while it is in the collective interests of all workers to join the union, individually it pays workers to free-ride and reap the benefits of union negotiated wage increases and improvements in working conditions without paying the union membership fee. If all workers were instrumentally rational none would belong to the union and all would be worse off! The old closed-shop system (which was all but abolished under the 1982 Employment Act) was an attempt to overcome this free-rider problem.

A number of other situations such as pollution control and the protection of the ozone layer, or the provision of public goods provide examples of the free-rider problem. For example, all of us probably have a preference for clean air and the protection of the ozone layer but as individuals we realise that we cannot limit the extent to which other people use their cars or generate pollutants. Acting as instrumentally rational agents each of us would sacrifice the common good for the convenience of using a car!

Team work also opens up the possibility for the type of opportunistic behaviour that is the hallmark of the prisoners' dilemma. Consider the payoff matrix shown in Table 5.4. Players 1 and 2 are two members of a firm and work jointly to produce a particular good. Each player's utility is a positive function of the level of production and a negative function of effort. If both exert high effort the output level is high and each receives a payoff of 3. If one player puts in high effort while their co-worker free-rides (exerts low effort) production is reduced. In this case the free-rider gets a payoff of 4, while the player that works hardest receives a payoff of 1. Finally, if both players attempt to free-ride simultaneously then production is reduced even further and each player receives a payoff of 2. The Nash equilibrium for this game is (low effort, low effort). Both players attempt to free-ride simultaneously and production falls to its lowest level.

		PLAYER 2	
		Low Effort	High Effort
PLAYER 1	Low Effort	(2, 2)	(4, 1)
	High Effort	(1, 4)	(3, 3)

Table 5.4: Team Work Game

These examples lead to two observations. The first is that despite the fact that instrumental rationality predicts that no-one should belong to a trade union, bear personal costs to limit pollution, pay taxes to finance public goods or participate equally in team work, casual observation assures us that such behaviour is commonplace. Either, large numbers of people are 'irrational' or there is something too restrictive about the rationality concept we have employed. The second is that given the temptation to free-ride there is frequently a role for legislation to ensure that the common good prevails.

Finally, perhaps the most pertinent example in the context of oligopoly theory is the oil industry. Most of the major oil producing countries are members of OPEC; the UK is an exception. One of the objectives of OPEC (which as an international organisation is not subject to national legislation on restrictive practices) is to reach formal agreement on production quotas with a view to manipulating the price of oil. As a non-member, the UK free-rides on OPEC agreements and reaps the benefit of higher prices without being constrained by an output quota. In the following section we will consider the relevance of the prisoners' dilemma for games of collusion between rival oligopoly firms where such agreements are not possible.

III. Multiple Equilibria

As we have seen the prisoners' dilemma yields a unique equilibrium outcome. In general, socio-economic games are not uniquely determinate but furnish a number of possible equilibria. To illustrate the possibility of multiple equilibria we will consider two games: Chicken and the Battle of the Sexes. In both cases we will consider a one-shot play of the game.

Chicken

Chicken (or the crossroads game) describes a situation where two players drive cars towards each other and must choose between keeping a straight course (a strategy choice denoted stay) and swerving away for fear of collision (a strategy choice denoted swerve). A game of this type featured in the film *Rebel Without a Cause* when James Dean, the new kid in town, is challenged by the incumbent gang leader, Buzz.[3] In this scene both protagonists must drive their car along a cliff-top towards the edge, the first player to jump out of their car is 'chicken' and loses the game. As one of the actors in the film remarked 'I'd never had a chickie run like that. When we played "chickie" we just drove our own cars down the street at each other and whoever swerved lost.'[4] The payoff matrix for this latter more conventional version of the game is shown in Table 5.5 and reflects the following preference ordering. Each player prefers to stay while her/his rival swerves. In this case the 'stayer' achieves hero status while the 'swerver' experiences humiliation. The second best outcome for either player is that both players choose swerve. In this case no-one can claim victory but equally neither player has been humiliated and both escape the certain death associated with head-on collision. The third best outcome for each player occurs when they choose to swerve while their rival chooses stay. In this case the 'swerver' loses face while the 'stayer' gains victory. Finally, the worst possible outcome occurs when both players choose to stay simultaneously. In this case they crash or end up over the edge of

3.'*Rebel without a Cause* tells a story as old as *Tom Brown's School Days*: a boy's adventures, travails and triumph on his first day at a new school. James Dean plays the part of the fledgling Jim Stark, a new boy at Dawson High. On the first day of classes, he tries to make friends by offering a ride to the girl next door (Natalie Wood). She snubs him. And when he arrives at school, he finds it is dominated by a group of bullies (the gang) who persecute weaker boys. The hero then befriends the weakling (Sal Mineo), defends him from the others and emerges vindicated and triumphant ... Most of *Rebel* takes place ... late at night in a teenage world of violence, romance and death.'(Dalton, 1975, p 221).

4. Frank Mazzola, who played one of Buzz's gang. Cited in Dalton (1975) p 251.

		PLAYER 2	
		Stay	Swerve
PLAYER 1	Stay	(–3, –3)	(2, 0)
	Swerve	(0, 2)	(1, 1)

Table 5.5 Chicken (or the Crossroads) Game

the cliff.

This game does not possess a dominant strategy. Instead, there are two Nash equilibria – (swerve, stay) and (stay, swerve) where player 1's strategy choice is the first term in the brackets. Note that each of these equilibria has the property that one player's strategy choice is the best response, given the strategy choice of her/his rival. That is, if player 1 chooses to stay, player 2's best response is to swerve and vice-versa. The existence of two possible equilibria implies that we have no way of knowing which equilibrium will actually be played out. In other words it is not clear which is the best strategy to adopt.[5]

The Battle of the Sexes

A similar situation arises in another game that is frequently cited in the literature, the Battle of the Sexes. In this game there are two players – a man and a woman who must decide over two possible venues – a boxing match or a concert – for an evening out. It is assumed that the preferences of each player are stereotypical so that the woman prefers the concert to the fight, while the man prefers the fight to the concert. However, both the man and the woman prefer to be together at their least preferred event rather than alone at their preferred event. Of course, the worst possible outcome is that both go to their partner's preferred event – in this case they are not together and they are at an event that they do not favour. The payoffs for a one-shot version of this simultaneous move game are shown in Table 5.6.

Again, there are two possible Nash equilibrium solutions to this game, either (fight, fight) or (concert, concert). Plainly, the woman would prefer (concert, concert) while the man prefers (fight, fight). As the game stands we have no way of knowing which equilibrium will actually be played out. However, the game can be used to illustrate several points. Firstly, it is apparent that if either player can make a pre-commitment to either event and disclose it to the other player then they may gain advantage. For example, suppose the woman announces that she intends to go to the concert and nothing will alter this decision, then so long as the man

5. As it turns out in *Rebel Without a Cause* the game is not played out as planned: 'during the run Buzz catches his sleeve on the door handle and can't get out. Trapped in his car, he careers over the side, and his life ends in a "burst of gas and flames."' (Dalton (1975) p 252). In the parlance of game theory the game switches from one of certainty to one of uncertainty. Recall that in games of uncertainty there are moves of chance. In the film Nature moves to prevent Buzz jumping out of the car.

		MAN	
		Fight	Concert
WOMAN	Fight	(1, 2)	(–1, –1)
	Concert	(0, 0)	(2, 1)

Table 5.6 : Battle of the Sexes

believes this to be true he has no choice but to go to the concert as well. As Luce and Raiffa (1957) point out,

> it is advantageous to disclose one's strategy first and to have a reputation for inflexibility. It is the familiar power strategy: "This is what I'm going to do; make up your mind and do what you want." If the second person acts in his own best interests, it works to the first player's advantage. (Luce and Raiffa 1957: 91).

Similarly, if players can make some pre-play act of commitment, such as buying tickets, they may gain advantage, since it indicates they are set on a particular course of action. However, as Luce and Raiffa acknowledge pre-play communication has not been included in the payoffs shown above and it can have the effect of altering the preference ordering and hence the relative structure of the payoffs. For example, suppose that the man tries to gain a first-mover advantage by buying two tickets for the boxing match without consulting the woman. This act may be viewed adversely by the woman as unacceptable power play. In this case the woman's preference ordering (and payoffs) may change such that she prefers to pass over both the boxing match and the man and go to the concert alone. In most of the games in this chapter we do not consider pre-play communication and the complications it involves.

IV. Pure Strategies and Mixed Strategies

Chicken and Battle of the sexes have two features in common. First, they both possess pure strategy Nash equilibria and second they both result in multiple equilibria. In order to understand the first point we must define a pure strategy and distinguish it from a mixed strategy. A pure strategy consists of a single strategy. In the two games above the strategies, stay, swerve, fight and concert are all pure strategies and the four pure strategy equilibria are:

(stay, swerve)
(swerve, stay)
(concert, concert)
(fight, fight)

A mixed strategy consists of a probability distribution over pure strategies. For example, one possible mixed strategy (though not the optimal or best one) in the

Chicken game would be to toss a coin and if it comes down heads choose stay, tails choose swerve. By varying the probability with which each strategy is chosen, players can vary their expected payoff. An optimal mixed strategy occurs when the expected payoff is maximised. Mixed strategies can be useful when: (i) pure strategy equilibria do not exist, (ii) there are multiple pure strategy equilibria, and/ or (iii) in cases where a mixed strategy yields a higher expected payoff than a pure strategy.

In the two games described above pure strategy equilibria exist but it is impossible to tell which of the two equilibria in each game will actually be played out. One response to this problem is to adopt an optimal mixed or randomised strategy. Such strategies can be derived by each player setting-up an expected payoff function for her/his rival and maximising it with respect to the probability of choosing a given strategy. In a mixed strategy equilibrium, players are indifferent between pure strategies. Following Rasmusen (1989) we may use this property to calculate the mixed strategy equilibria for the Chicken game, shown in Table 5.5.

In order to make each player indifferent between staying and swerving we must set the expected payoffs from each of these two strategies equal to each other. Let's calculate the expected payoff for player 1. If the probability of Player 2 staying is denoted p_W – then the probability of player 2 swerving is given by the complementary probability, $(1 - p_W)$. The expected payoff of player 1 from choosing the strategy stay is given by:

$$(-3)\, p_W + 2\,(1 - p_W) \tag{5}$$

and the expected payoff from choosing the alternative strategy swerve is given by:

$$(0)\, p_W + 1\,(1 - p_W) \tag{6}$$

In order to satisfy the property of indifference between alternative pure strategies that characterises an optimal mixed strategy we must set the expected payoffs from the two choices stay and swerve equal to each other, as shown below.

$$(-3)\, p_W + 2\,(1 - p_W) = (0)\, p_W + 1\,(1 - p_W) \tag{7}$$

Solving for p_W it can be seen that the mixed strategy equilibrium implies that player 1 should stay with probability 0.25 and swerve with probability 0.75. Since, the game is symmetric a similar calculation for player 2 would reveal the same probabilistic strategy choice. Hence, both players stay with probability 0.25 and swerve with probability 0.75. It should be noted that if both players adopt the optimal mixed strategy then any of the four outcomes shown in Table 5.4 is a possible equilibrium outcome. The most likely outcome is that both players will swerve – the probability of this occurring is 0.75(0.75) = 0.5625. The two outcomes (stay, swerve) and (swerve, stay) occur with equal probabilities of 0.25(0.75) = 0.1875, while the probability of (stay, stay) is given by 0.25(0.25) = 0.0625. Since there are only four possible outcomes these probabilities must sum to 1.

There are a couple of points that are worth noting about this result. The first is that the expected return from playing the optimal mixed strategy is 0.75. Players could clearly do better than this if they could co-ordinate their actions, say by taking it in turns to stay and swerve. Secondly, it is apparent that the mixed strategy equilibrium (stay, stay) has a positive probability of 0.0625, hence there is a positive chance that both players die, which in economic terms, implies that inefficient outcomes are not ruled out. Clearly, if conventions or procedures could be established this outcome might be avoided.

V. Coordination, Multiple Equilibria and Focal Points

Chicken (or Crossroads) and Battle of the Sexes can both be viewed as games of coordination. If players can coordinate their actions then inefficient outcomes can be avoided and the problem of multiple Nash equilibria can be solved. However, as they stand, the games offer no insight into how such coordination might be bought about. This problem of coordination is of direct relevance to oligopoly as we will see in the following section. For the moment, recall the problem facing Cournot's duopolists: if both firms can coordinate their output strategies then they are able to attain the joint profit maximising output.

Schelling (1960) has considered a number of games of coordination with multiple equilibria and has shown that certain equilibria form focal points, in that, they are more likely to be played out than others. Schelling conducted experiments with the following games. The games shared the common feature that in order to win the game each player must match their strategy (move) with that of all the other players. In the first game players are told to call 'heads' or 'tails', if all players call the same they each win a prize. In the second game players are asked to circle one of the following numbers:

7 100 13 261 90 555

You win this game if you circle the same number as all the other players. In the third game players were asked to tick one of sixteen squares shown below. Again

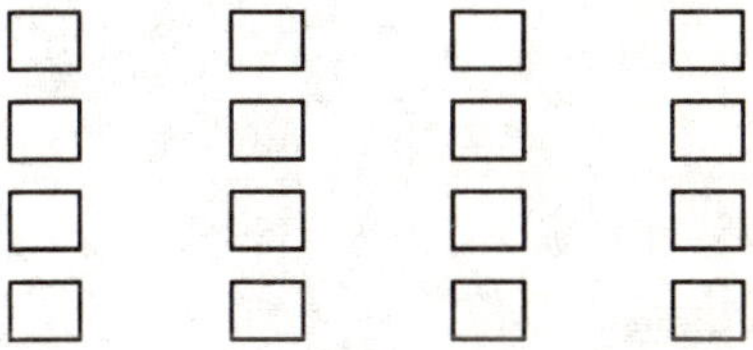

players win by matching their choice to that of the other players.

In the fourth game players are told that they must choose a meeting place in New York City and a meeting time. The aim of the game is to try to make your strategy choice coincide with that of others.

Schelling specified a number of other games in a similar vein. The important point to note about these games is that they all possess multiple Nash equilibria. In all the games described above any of the outcomes is a possible best response to the strategy choice of other players. For example, in the second game if all other players circle the number 7, then this strategy choice constitutes a Nash equilibrium.

The results from Schelling's experiments revealed that certain equilibria formed focal points. In the first game 36 people out of 42 choose 'heads'. In the second game 37 players out of 41 choose one of the first 3 numbers and of these three numbers, the number 7 led 100 by a small margin. In game three the upper left square received 24 votes out of 41, while game four showed a majority of people meeting at the information booth of Grand Central Station and virtually all of them chose the time: 12 noon. Of all the possible Nash equilibria, these strategy choices turned out to be more likely candidates than the others and Schelling argued that they formed focal points. As Schelling wrote,

> These problems are artificial, but they illustrate the point. People can often concert their intentions or expectations with others if each knows that the other is trying to do the same. Most situations – perhaps every situation for people who are practiced at this sort of game – provide some clue for co-ordinating behaviour, some focal point for each person's expectation of what the other expects him to be expected to do. (Schelling 1960: 57)

Of course, the problem is to find the key. In games with multiple equilibria, the determination of the actual equilibrium outcome is likely to be strongly influenced by the cultural background of the players and the institutional environment. Recall the game of Chicken described above and suppose that this game is played as the crossroads game with both players approaching adjacent corners of a crossroads and with the strategies stay and swerve replaced by the strategies speed-up and slow-down as shown in Table 5.7. It is important to note that the game is not subject to the highway code – to stress this point Schelling has set the game in the desert where no legal system applies. As we have seen this game has two possible Nash equilibria (speed-up, slow-down) and (slow-down, speed-up). However, it is arguable that one is more likely than the other.

		PLAYER 2	
		Speed-up	Slow-down
PLAYER 1	Speed-up	(–3, –3)	(2, 0)
	Slow-down	(0, 2)	(1, 1)

Table 5.7: The Crossroads Game

To see this it is sufficient to note that the convention, 'give way to the right', will save players from the inefficient outcome (speed-up, speed-up). One of the players (for the sake of argument let's say player 2) must approach the crossroads to the right of the other (player 1). As Schelling notes,

> The conventional priority system lacks legal or moral force; but it is so expedient when coordination is needed that the one discriminated against may yield to its discipline, recognizing that he should be grateful for an arbiter, even though it discriminates against him, and recognizing also that he is trapped by the other's acceptance of...and expectation that both will comply. (Schelling 1960: 300, 301)

A further possibility is that signalling via stereotypes may give some clue to players about the type of opponent they are facing. For example, if you notice that the car approaching you is a Ford Escort, with two dice dangling in the windscreen and a teenage male behind the wheel you might be more inclined to slow-down than if the car were a Metro driven by a Nun or a BSM dual control vehicle with 'L' plates and a learner driver at the wheel! The economic analogue of these applications is found in games of economic interaction that possess multiple equilibria. In such cases, instrumentally rational behaviour associated with maximising expected utilities can lead to inferior outcomes. Hence, behaviour based on standard procedures, such as, following the convention 'give way to the right', or attempts to signal whether you're a speed-up or slow-down type of player by the type of car you drive lead to Pareto improvements compared to the instrumentally rational mixed strategy approach.

What this suggests is that the standard model of rationality applied to economics may provide less of a guide to how people do and should behave compared to other models of rationality such as procedural or expressive rationality, which will be discussed in more detail below. The need for analysis of different types of rationality has been stressed by Schelling,

> As a matter of fact, many of the critical elements that go into a model of rational behaviour can be identified with particular types of rationality or irrationality. The value system, the communication system, the information system, the collective decision process, or a parameter representing the probability of error or loss of control, can be viewed as an effort to formalize the study of 'irrationality'. (Schelling 1960: 16, 17)

Before closing this introductory section we shall briefly consider one other game that has become a standard in the literature: The Centipede Game. The centipede game is a sequential move game, that is, player 1 moves first, player 2 moves second and the moves continue to alternate in this fashion until the end of the game. Each player's move is represented by a dot at a decision node as shown in Figure 5.6. At each move a player must choose between moving down or moving across. The payoffs at each stage of the game are shown in parenthesis with player 1's payoff shown first. If at any stage of the game a player chooses down then the game ends and the players receive the payoffs indicated at that stage. It is assumed that it is common knowledge that both players are instrumentally ratio-

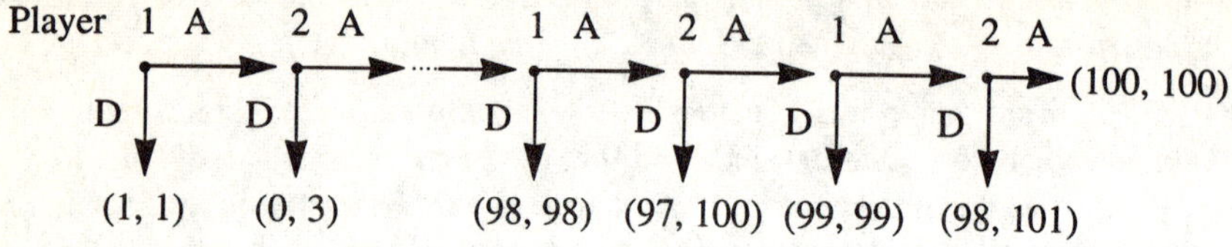

Figure 5.6: The Centipede Game

nal.

In order to determine the Nash equilibrium[6] solution to this game players must look forward and work backwards. Player 1 moves first and calculates that if the game reaches the final decision node then player 2 would move down, and this would give player 1 a worse payoff than if player 1 moved down at the penultimate decision node. But looking at the previous decision node it is obvious that player 2 would not move across to reach this node, but down. This reasoning continues backwards until the first decision node, hence, the perfect Nash equilibrium has player 1 moving down with her/his first move, so that the players receive payoffs of (1, 1) respectively.

The Nash equilibrium is dictated by the essential feature of the prisoners' dilemma: opportunism. If both players could trust each other and coordinate their moves then cooperative behaviour could yield the payoffs (100, 100). However at later stages of the game there is room for opportunism and instrumentally rational players are unwilling to expose themselves to such behaviour – in effect player 1 forecloses this possibility by moving down on the first available occasion.

The outcome predicted by instrumentally rational behaviour can be compared with actual outcomes attained from experimental data. Data from real life trials of this game show that typically players do not move down at the first opportunity but succeed in reaching later decision nodes. We will return to a discussion of this game in Section D.

This concludes our introduction to the basic principles and problems of game theory. In the sections that follow we will continue to extend this analysis of game theory but all of the applications will be confined to situations of oligopolistic interaction.

6. In fact the equilibrium solution described here is known as a perfect Nash equilibrium. A perfect Nash equilibrium is defined in detail on page 204.

Section C: Game Theory and Oligopoly

In this section we look at the application of game theory to aspects of oligopolistic competition. In particular we will focus on Cournot's model of oligopoly and show how this model and the problems of collusion and oligopolistic coordination can be analysed using game-theoretic techniques.

I. Cournot and Collusion

It will be recalled from Section B that the problem facing Cournot's two duopolists is to find an output strategy that is consistent with each firms' objective of profit maximisation. This problem is complicated by the fact that each firm must profit maximise on the basis of a belief or conjecture about its rival's output response to changes in its output strategy. If one is prepared to accept Cournot's assumption that firms operate under a zero conjectural variation then it is easily shown that for a normalised output strategy space that includes all possible outputs between 0 and 1, Nash equilibrium is achieved when each firm produces 1/3.

However, we saw that one of the problems with this solution is that it is belief dependent, in so far as a change in each firm's conjectural variation from zero to one would change the equilibrium outcome from the Cournot solution (1/3, 1/3) to the collusive solution (1/2, 1/2). Cournot argued that the collusive equilibrium was unstable as each firm faced a temptation to cheat and produce slightly more, selling it at a lower price.

This problem of collusion can be analysed using game theory and is in fact an example of the prisoners' dilemma discussed above. Consider a version of the Cournot game that limits each firm's strategy choice to two possible output levels: low output – consistent with collusion or a conjectural variation equal to 1, and high output consistent with Cournot equilibrium and a conjectural variation equal to zero. The payoffs shown in Table 5.8 are broadly consistent with these strategy choices. That is, although the absolute numbers are somewhat arbitrary they reflect the relative payoffs associated with low and high output.

		FIRM 2	
		High Output (CV = 0)	Low Output (CV = 1)
FIRM 1	High Output (CV = 0)	(1, 1)	(5, 0)
	Low Output (CV = 1)	(0, 5)	(3, 3)

Table 5.8: Payoff Matrix for the Prisoners' Dilemma Game

If both firms choose to restrict output by adopting the collusive low output strategy, they will each receive a payoff of 3. Alternatively if both firms adopt the high output or Cournot strategy they will each receive a payoff of 1. The worst possible outcome for an individual firm is to produce a low output (and attempt to sell it at a high price) while its rival produces high output and sells it at a lower price. Of course, this is the mirror image of the best outcome for an individual firm (high output, low output). In this case the high output firm undercuts its rival's price and steals the market.

It should be apparent that the collusion game described above has all the features of the prisoners' dilemma described earlier. High output is, in fact, a dominant strategy so that in a one-shot play of the game the Nash equilibrium solution is (high output, high output). Moreover, the Nash equilibrium (1, 1) is Pareto inferior to the collusive outcome (3, 3). Both firms would be better off if they adopted the collusive (low output) strategy but since this strategy is strictly dominated by the high output (or cheating strategy) tacit collusion is ruled out. One way of viewing this outcome is that while firms realise that they would be better off colluding (that is choosing low output) the temptation to cheat and pick-up the payoff 5 is too great for the profit maximising firm. As both firms cheat simultaneously, they end up at (1, 1). It was precisely this intuition that Cournot used to rule out the possibility that firms have a CV = 1 thus justifying the assumption of a zero CV. Game theory proves that for a one-shot play of the game this intuition was indeed correct since the high output strategy (consistent with the belief that CV = 0) strictly dominates the low output strategy (consistent with belief that CV = 1).

This is an important result because it implies that the second source of indeterminacy, highlighted at the end of section A (page 198) is removed. Thus, it would seem that the application of game theory to the question of collusion suggests that the collusive equilibrium can be ruled out because the belief system necessary to sustain it (CV = 1) is strictly dominated by the non-collusive belief system (CV = 0). In other words, it would seem that game theory resolves the indeterminacy problem that is an essential feature of oligopolistic interaction. This is an important result but as we shall see its relevance is strictly limited to one-shot games and known finite repetitions of a game.

To end this discussion of collusion in a one-shot game we will briefly consider the welfare properties of the collusive and non-collusive outcomes shown in Table 5.8. Here, it is important to distinguish the utility of the players from the utility of society at large, or the common good. That is, it is important to distinguish between private and public interest. In the case of oligopoly, collusion is in the interests of firms but against the public interest since it restricts output and raises price. In this case the dilemma implicit in the collusion game is the other side of the coin to the paradox of self-interest emphasised by Adam Smith. Smith argued that self-interested behaviour in the commercial world results in competitive pressure that has the effect of lowering price and raising social welfare. This process can be seen quite clearly in the Collusion game outlined above. Opportunistic behaviour on the part of each individual player actually results in an outcome that is Pareto superior from the point of view of society.

Not all of the examples of the prisoners' dilemma discussed in Section II contain the paradox that self-interested behaviour results in outcomes that are Pareto superior for society as a whole. For example, consider the cases of pollution or team work. In these examples self-interest leads to high levels of pollution and low levels of production. The outcomes, whilst containing the opportunism inherent in the original prisoners' dilemma game, are against the public interest of society as a whole. In short, while the collusion game described above results in a superior outcome for society at large this property is not common to all prisoners' dilemma type games. Indeed, it is the peculiarity of the outcome from the collusion game that was implicitly recognised in Smith's paradox of self-interest.

II. Repeated Games

The results we have attained so far have all been derived from single plays of a game. This raises the objection that were the game to be repeated a number of times the results attained may be very different. Repetition of the game opens up the possibility of learning as well as the use of threats and punishment strategies. For example, in the collusion game discussed above, firms might learn that self-interested behaviour does not result in maximum (Pareto optimal) profits. Hence, after a few repetitions of the game, one might expect to see the firms adopting the collusive low output strategy. Suppose the game were repeated 20 times, surely after a few plays both firms will see the obvious advantage of collusion and start producing low output?

Unfortunately, this argument does not bear scrutiny. The problem is that any known finite repetition of a game (where the number of plays is known with certainty before play commences) has a final play or terminating game. This final play will be played out exactly as if it were a one-shot game. Hence, in the last period, players will revert to the use of the dominant strategy: high output. But once players recognise that this is the inevitable outcome in the final play of the game, then they will soon see that there is no point in colluding in the 19th play since there are no future plays remaining where a reputation for trust might count. Thus, collusion is also ruled out in the 19th play of the game. With no prospect of collusion in either the ultimate or penultimate plays, there is little purpose of colluding in the 18th play; again this play will be played as if it were a one-shot game and both firms will adopt the high output strategy. This argument, known as the backward induction argument, continues unravelling throughout the entire 20 plays. The fact that there is a final play means that it is impossible to build up interdependence between successive plays of the game: each play is played as if it were a single game and opportunism rules the day. Again, Cournot's insight that cheating (or a CV = 0) dominates other strategies (beliefs) appears to be vindicated.

It seems, therefore, that repeating the game a finite number of times does not allow a resolution of the prisoners' dilemma. This leaves open the question of what would happen if the game were repeated an infinite or an indefinite number of times? In an infinite repetition the game is assumed to continue forever, while in an indefinite repetition the length of the game is uncertain but there is still a positive probability that the game could be repeated indefinitely. Hence, an indefinite repetition includes the possibility of an infinite repetition. More importantly, an infinite or indefinite repetition opens up the possibility of the use of threats and punishment strategies designed to facilitate collusion since, with the prospect of an indefinite time horizon, there is always the possibility of recouping the cost of punishment strategies that damage both players now if the strategy leads to future collusion.

Consider an indefinite repetition of the collusion game using the payoffs given in Table 5.8. In this case each player's strategy set will consist of a number of strategies which outline what it will do in response to any strategy its rival chooses. Given that the game is being played into the indefinite future the number of such strategies is vast. Each strategy consists of a series of moves stating what a player will do at any stage of the game. The crucial question is, does this change in the time horizon of the game make collusion more likely?

Two strategies designed to promote collusion are the trigger strategy (TS) and the tit-for-tat (TFT) strategy. Let's look at the trigger strategy first. A player, playing the trigger strategy starts by choosing 'collude' and will choose 'collude' at every stage in the game provided that her/his rival does not play the opportunistic strategy 'cheat'. If at any stage of the game the rival player is observed 'cheating' then a TS player will punish this move by playing 'cheat' in all subsequent plays of the game. As Vickers (1985) points out under the TS 'cheating triggers perpetual non-collusion.'

It can be shown that as long as players attach sufficient weight to future profits then it pays to adopt the TS rather than the cheating strategy (ie always playing high output) which we now denote 'always cheat' (AC). In comparing the payoffs from these two strategies we must discount future profits by the discount factor, w, where,

$$w = \frac{1}{(1+r)} \qquad (8)$$

and r is the discount rate. Whether or not it pays to play the trigger strategy or the alternative strategy AC depends on which strategy yields the highest discounted stream of future profits. The payoff from adopting the trigger strategy when playing another TS player is:

$$3 + 3w + 3w^2 + 3w^3 + \ldots = \frac{3}{(1-w)} \qquad (9)$$

while the payoff from adopting the non-cooperative strategy AC when playing a TS player is:

$$5 + 1w + 1w^2 + 1w^3 + \ldots = 5 + \frac{w}{(1-w)} \qquad (10)$$

In order to ascertain under what conditions it pays to play the TS it is sufficient to compare the two payoffs given in equations (9) and (10) as shown below:

$$\frac{3}{(1-w)} > 5 + \frac{w}{(1-w)} \qquad (11)$$

That is, in order for collusion to occur the payoff from the trigger strategy must exceed that from the strategy always cheat. Hence, we set up equation (11) as an inequality in order to determine under what conditions the inequality will hold. Solving equation (11) for w shows that the payoff from playing the TS will exceed the payoff from AC so long as $w > 1/2$. As long as this condition holds collusion is sustained by the use of the TS.

Notice that w has two interpretations besides its function as the discount factor. The first is that w is the weight that players attach to the future. If $w = 0$ this implies that players attach no weight to the future: all that matters is the present. In this case, it can be seen from equations (9) and (10) that the payoffs from cheating and collusion revert to those of a one-shot play since all terms after the first term in each equation are reduced to zero. The second interpretation of w is that it reflects the probability that, at any given play, the game will continue. Under both interpretations it follows that the higher is, w, then the greater the likelihood of collusion.

The above analysis reveals one way of resolving the prisoners' dilemma. Under the threat of the TS, and assuming an indefinite repetition in which players attach sufficient weight to the future, it would seem that economic agents overcome the opportunistic behaviour that is the characteristic feature of Prisoner Dilemma-type games.

Despite the fact that the use of the trigger strategy can be used to resolve the prisoners' dilemma, there are a number of problems with this resolution. The first is that it relies on the fact that players must believe that there is a chance, however small, that the game will last forever. As Hargreaves Heap (1989) has pointed out, players must believe in their own immortality! Clearly, this is irrational. Second, while the threat implicit in the trigger strategy does the trick in enabling collusion to dominate (provided $w > 1/2$, given the payoffs in Table 5.8), it is not the only strategy that does so.

Another strategy that can be used to sustain collusion is the tit-for-tat strategy (TFT). A player following the tit-for-tat strategy starts by choosing collude and then adopts the strategy that her/his rival played in the previous period. The use of the TFT strategy against a player who also adopts TFT will yield a payoff of:

$$3 + 3w + 3w^2 + 3w^3 + \ldots = \frac{3}{(1 - w)} \tag{12}$$

This may be compared with the payoff from playing the TFT strategy against a player adopting the strategy AC. In this case the payoff is given by:

$$5 + 1w + 1w^2 + 1w^3 + \ldots = 5 + \frac{w}{(1 - w)} \tag{13}$$

Again, collusion will be sustained under the use of the TFT strategy as long as $w > 1/2$. Hence, not only are there now two possible collusive equilibria (one being TFT plays TFT, the other, TS plays TS) but for values of $w > 1/2$, it is impossible to tell from observation of the outcomes (payoffs) at each stage of the game which strategies are actually being played out.

So far we have identified 3 possible Nash equilibria that are solutions to the collusion game: AC plays AC, TS plays TS and TFT plays TFT. All of these strategies are straight forward in that they depend on very simply rules to determine what will happen at each stage of the game. However, in an infinitely repeated game there are many other strategies that may result in Nash equilibria. In fact, any feasible stream of payoffs that yields players a return at least as great as they would get from playing the strategy AC, which offers a security level of payment equal to

$$\frac{1}{(1 - w)} \tag{14}$$

can form part of an equilibrium strategy. Hence, there is any number of possible Nash equilibria. This finding is known as the Folk Theorem, so called, because the main result of the theorem was well-known in the literature before anyone formalised it.[7] Essentially, the logic behind the Folk Theorem is that since the game may be repeated indefinitely, there is always a sufficient number of plays remaining for players to use some threat or punishment strategy that is going to yield them a better payoff than that given by the strategy AC. That is, you can invest in a punishment strategy today in the knowledge that there is an infinite time horizon over which it is possible to recoup the cost by inducing collusion in the future. The main implication of the Folk Theorem for oligopoly theory is that oligopolistic interaction will be characterised by indeterminacy whenever the time horizon of the game (interaction) is indefinite and players attach sufficient weight to future payoffs.

7. The theorem has subsequently been extended by Friedman (1971) to take account of discounting and subgame perfect Nash equilibria (which we will discuss later).

The existence of multiple equilibria immediately raises the question of which strategy is best? Are all equilibrium strategy combinations equally plausible, or are some more likely to be played out than others? This question has been addressed by Axelrod (1981), who has shown that under certain conditions the TFT strategy emerges as a stable strategy. Axelrod adopts two approaches to the question of determining what strategy, if any, is likely to dominate.

The first approach was a tournament or experimental approach. In this approach Axelrod (1980a) asked game theorists, in economics, psychology, sociology, political science and mathematics to submit strategies for a repeated version of a game characterised at each stage by a payoff matrix like that shown in Table 5.8. The length of the game was set at 200 moves. Each strategy that was submitted was played against all the others and a randomly generated strategy in a round-robin tournament. The highest average score was attained by the TFT strategy. Having attained this result Axelrod then circulated the results of the game and invited entries for a second round. In the second round 62 different strategies were submitted and the game was played with an indefinite time horizon. The expected median length of the game was 200 moves, achieved by setting $w = 0.99654$. Again, the TFT strategy, which was one of the simplest strategies submitted, emerged as the clear winner. Axelrod put the success of the TFT strategy down to the fact that it was 'nice', 'provocable' and 'forgiving'. That is, it is never the first to cheat, it punishes opportunistic behaviour and, unlike the TS, a TFT player is prepared to follow a cue to re-establish collusion.

The second approach was a general theoretical approach based on evolutionary theory that drew on the influential work of the biologist Maynard Smith (1974). Maynard Smith considered the conditions under which a population of 'meanies', all playing the strategy always cheat, could be invaded by a single 'mutant' player, playing another strategy, let's call it strategy 'X'. Strategy X can be said to invade the strategy AC if it yields a higher expected payoff than AC. Maynard Smith then turned this around to define a strategy that cannot be 'invaded' by any other strategy. Such a strategy is known as an evolutionary stable strategy. It follows that if all players adopt an evolutionary (or collectively) stable strategy then no player can attain a higher payoff by playing any other strategy, hence the strategy can persist as a long-run equilibrium strategy.[8]

As Axelrod points out,

> The biological motivation for this approach is based on the interpretation of the payoffs in terms of fitness (survival and fecundity). All mutations are possible, and if any could invade a given population it would have had the chance to do so. Thus only a collectively stable strategy is expected to be able to maintain itself in the long-run equilibrium as the strategy used by all. (Axelrod 1981: 310)

8. Collective stability is a refined version of Maynard Smith's concept of evolutionary stability. For a discussion of the distinction see Hughes and Oughton (1993).

The economic interpretation of this approach is that given instrumentally rational agents, players will try any strategy designed to maximise profits, hence the only means by which a strategy can survive in the long-run is if it yields a higher return than any other. Put another way, both players adopt a strategy because neither could do any better by adopting any other strategy.

Axelrod's contribution to the literature was to determine the conditions under which strategies are collectively stable. In order to discuss Axelrod's proof in relation to the TFT strategy we must first re-express the payoff matrix for our collusion game in general terms as shown in Table 5.9.

		FIRM 2	
		Low Output (CV = 1)	High Output (CV = 0)
FIRM 1	Low Output (CV = 1)	$(\pi_m/2, \pi_m/2)$	(π_j, π_i)
	High Output (CV = 0)	(π_i, π_j)	(π_c, π_c)

Table 5.9: Collusion Game Expressed in General Terms

where

$$\pi_i \quad > \quad \pi_m/2 > \quad \pi_c \quad > \quad \pi_j$$

Axelrod has shown that the TFT strategy is collectively stable provided that

$$w \quad > \quad \max\left(\frac{\pi_i - \pi_m/2}{\pi_i - \pi_c}\,, \quad \frac{\pi_j - \pi_m/2}{\pi_m/2 - \pi_j}\right) \qquad (15)$$

Hence, for the values of the payoffs shown in Table 5.8 it can be seen that the TFT strategy is collectively stable if w > 2/3. As Axelrod notes,

> The significance of this theorem is that it demonstrates that if everyone in a population is cooperating with everyone else because each is using the TFT strategy, no one can do better using any other strategy provided the discount parameter is high enough. (Axelrod 1981: 312)

However, TFT is not the only collectively stable strategy. The strategy AC is also collectively stable. Although the number of collectively stable strategies is less than the number of possible equilibrium strategies this still raises the question of which collectively stable strategy is likely to dominate. Axelrod has attempted to provide an answer to this question by showing that some collectively stable strategies can be invaded by groups of players adopting another collectively stable strategy. More precisely, consider the situation where a group of players are playing the strategy AC. This strategy is collectively stable and therefore cannot be invaded by a single player arriving and trying to play TFT. However, if a small cluster of TFT players arrive at the same time then TFT can emerge as a stable strategy provided that the proportion of TFT invaders, p, is greater than:

$$p \quad > \quad \frac{\pi_c/\delta - (\pi_j + (1-\delta)\,\pi_c/\delta\,)}{\pi_m\,/2\delta - (\,\pi_j + (1-\;\delta)\,\pi_c/\delta)} \qquad (16)$$

Given the values of the payoffs shown in Table 5.8 and setting $\delta = 0.1$ (which implies that two interacting players have a 90 per cent chance of meeting again) then collusion can be established in a market of less than 21 firms by the entry of just two firms playing the TFT strategy. This is a powerful result, as Axelrod notes,

> Suppose a business school teacher taught a class to give cooperative behaviour a chance, and to reciprocate cooperation from other firms. If the students did, and if they did not disperse too widely (so that a sufficient proportion of their interactions were with others from the same class), then the students would find their lessons paid off.
>
> When the interactions are expected to be of longer duration (or the time discount factor is not as great), then even less clustering is necessary. For example, if the median game length is 200 moves (corresponding to w = 0.99654) and the payoff parameters are as given in Figure 5.1 (our Table 5.8), even one interaction out of a thousand with a like-minded follower of TIT FOR TAT is enough for the strategy to invade a world of 'meanies'. Even when the median game length is only two moves (w = 0.5), anything over a fifth of the interactions by the TIT FOR TAT players with like-minded types is sufficient for invasion to succeed and cooperation to emerge. (Axelrod 1981: 316)

The intuition behind this result is that TFT does as well against AC as AC does against itself, but better than AC does when playing a TFT player. In addition Axelrod has shown that while AC can protect itself from individual players entering the market one at a time but not from clusters of TFT players entering simultaneously, the same is not true for TFT. TFT cannot be invaded by an AC player entering individually nor can it be invaded by a cluster of AC players.

The significance of Axelrod's results is that they show that starting from a group of self-interested firms each seeking to maximise their own profit, collusion can emerge provided a small cluster of firms are prepared to collude. In this case the prisoners' dilemma is resolved. This result raises several issues. The first is that it overturns Adam Smith's view of the invisible hand as a device that ensures that firms price competitively. Indeed, Axelrod's theory of the emergence of cooperation among egoists is precisely the opposite of Smith's view of the emergence of competition out of self-interested greedy behaviour. Of course, Smith was well aware of the temptation for firms to collude and has fairly lengthy passages that discuss explicit collusion and the need to control monopolies. However, the results discussed above refer to tacit rather than explicit collusion and suggest collusive practices may emerge from instrumentally rational behaviour even when firms are not in cahoots.

Second, it shows that provided a small proportion of firms are willing to collude then collusion – equivalent to each firm having a conjectural variation equal to 1 – can emerge as a stable strategy. Hence, this undermines Cournot's belief that a conjectural variation of zero is likely to dominate.

Third, a degree of indeterminacy over the strategy choice of players remains. However, some progress has been made in that we know that the indeterminacy is driven by (i) the expected median length of the game and (ii) the proportion of players willing to collude.

Finally, there is the issue of rationality. Axelrod's theoretical and experimental analysis shows us that TFT is likely to emerge as a collectively stable strategy provided there is at least a small number of players willing to cooperate. To this extent it provides a way of choosing between equilibrium strategies and shows that under certain conditions TFT can emerge as collectively stable. These results are attained using the assumption of instrumental rationality. However, one problem with these theoretical results is that they require players to believe that there is a small chance that the game will continue forever. As we have seen, players must believe in the possibility of their own immortality and this does not sit comfortably with the assumption of instrumental rationality. The theme of rationality will be picked up in Section D. Before turning to this topic we consider a number of applications of game theory to strategic entry deterrence. The first of these games looks at predatory pricing and reputation effects.

Strategic Entry Deterrence

A limitation of Cournot's model of duopoly is that it fails to take account of competition from potential entrants. In Cournot equilibrium both industry price and industry profits will be above their competitive levels. In the absence of entry barriers the existence of excess profits will attract new firms into the industry. If incumbent firms foresee this possibility then they may attempt to adopt an output or pricing strategy designed to limit entry. In this section we will look at three such strategies: (i) predatory pricing and reputation building, (ii) limit pricing and (iii) advertising.

Sequential Move Games: Predatory Pricing and the Chain Store Paradox

Predatory pricing occurs when a firm cuts price below cost in order to dispense with rival firms or new entrants. The objective behind predatory pricing is that firms incur short-run losses in order to maximise long-run profits. It should be noted that predatory pricing is not part of normal competition since the object is not simply to lower price towards cost but to lower price below cost with the clear intention of raising price above cost as soon as the objective of eliminating competitors has been achieved. Hence, the long-run effect of predatory pricing is anti-competitive and as a result it is illegal under US and EU competition law. Famous cases of predatory pricing include Freddie Laker's Sky Train. Laker entered the air travel market offering cut price fares between London and New York in competition with the two leading incumbent firms British Airways and Pan-Am. The two incumbents cut prices in retaliation and the Sky Train Company faced bankruptcy. Although no formal investigations were published it is widely reported that Laker received out of court settlements as compensation for unfair pricing practices.

Predatory pricing can be modelled in a game theoretic framework by considering the strategy choices of an incumbent firm and a potential entrant. The game is a sequential move game because the potential entrant moves first choosing between the two strategies 'enter' the market and 'stay out' of the market. Once the potential entrant has made her decision the incumbent firm chooses between two strategies 'fight' entry by lowering price below cost, and 'acquiesce' to entry. The payoffs for a single play or a one-shot version of this game are shown in extensive form in the game tree in Figure 5.7. The normal or strategic representation of the same game is shown in Table 5.10.

It is not difficult to see what the Nash equilibrium outcome would be for a single play of this game. To solve the game players should look forward and work backwards. The potential entrant moves first and calculates that if she forces the game to the second decision node this reduces the incumbent's choice to a payoff of –1 or 1. Given that both players share the common knowledge of their rationality, the potential entrant knows that faced with the fact of entry the incumbent firm

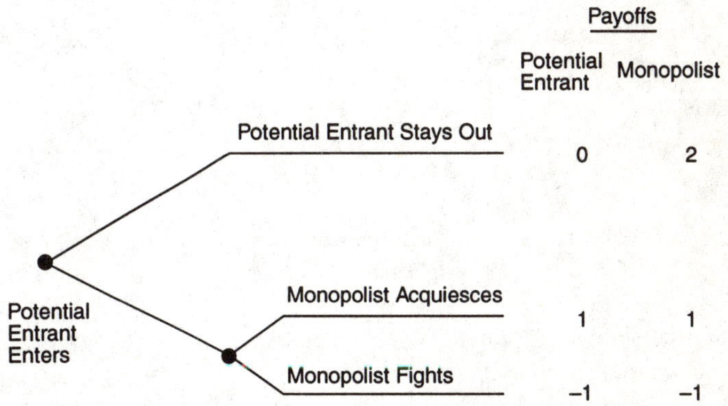

Figure 5.7: Predatory Pricing in Extensive Form

will be forced to acquiesce. Hence the (perfect) Nash equilibrium solution to this game is that the potential entrant chooses 'enter' and the incumbent firm chooses 'acquiesce'. Both players receive a payoff of 1. This Nash equilibrium is described as a perfect Nash equilibrium to distinguish it from other Nash equilibria that are not subgame perfect. In order to be subgame perfect a strategy must be the best response to a rival's strategy in all subgames of the whole game. A subgame is simply a move or sequence of moves that constitutes a part of the entire game. The game above consists of two moves and the sub-game consists of the second move (ie the strategy choice of the incumbent).

The importance of distinguishing between a perfect Nash equilibrium and other Nash equilibria is that the former rules out the use of non-credible threats. To illustrate this point, suppose that the incumbent firm issues the following threat: 'enter this market and I will fight entry with predatory pricing'. If this threat is believed by the potential entrant then she will stay out of the market and the equilibrium outcome will be 'potential entrant stays out' – this yields payoffs to the potential entrant and the incumbent of 0 and 2, respectively as shown in the strategic representation of the game given in Table 5.10. However, such a threat is obviously non-credible since we know that faced with the fact of entry rational behaviour dictates that the incumbent firm should acquiesce. In other words, the threat to fight entry is evidently non-credible because the strategy 'fight' is not rational in the subgame that occurs after the potential entrant has made her/his move. In terms of Table 5.10 this implies that the Nash equilibrium (stay out, fight if potential entrant enters) is not a perfect Nash equilibrium.

		MONOPOLIST	
		Fight if Potential Entrant Chooses IN	Acquiesce
POTENTIAL ENTRANT	Enter	(–1, –1)	(1, 1)
	Stay Out	(0, 2)	(0, 2)

Table 5.10: Predatory Pricing Represented in Normal or Strategic Form

The game tree shown in Figure 5.7 illustrates one of the essential features of predatory pricing, namely that it imposes short-run losses on both the entrant and the incumbent. Hence, in a one-shot play predatory pricing is irrational. Plainly, predatory pricing is only an attractive option in a repeated game where the costs incurred in the short run can be offset against future benefits. Scherer (1980) considered the use of predatory pricing by a chain-store that operates in a number of distinct geographic markets. In this case Scherer argued that it would pay the monopolist to fight entry in one or two towns as a demonstration effect to deter potential entrants in other towns from entering. As Scherer argued,

> If rivals come to fear from a multimarket seller's actions in Market A that entry or expansion in Markets B or C will be met by sharp price cuts or other rapacious responses, they may be deterred from taking aggressive actions there. Then the conglomerate's expected benefit from predation in Market A will be supplemented by the discounted present value of the competition-inhibiting effects its example has in Markets B and C. (Scherer 1980: 338)

This intuitively plausible line of argument which relies on the multimarket seller establishing a reputation for playing tough with entrants so as to deter entrants in other markets, has been called into question by Selten who has formalised the situation described above in a finitely repeated game. Selten (1978) analysed the role for reputation building via the use of predatory pricing in a formal game theoretic model. The game can be summarised as follows. A monopolist chain store has branches in 20 different towns. In each town there is a potential entrant contemplating setting up a rival chain store. The game is played over 20 time periods – one time period for each town/potential entrant. In period 1, entrant number 1, in town number 1, decides whether to enter or not, and the monopolist chain store decides whether to fight entry or acquiesce. This scenario is repeated sequentially in all 20 towns with the 20 potential entrants in turn. What is the equilibrium outcome of this game? Is there a role for reputation-building as suggested by Scherer?

It is clear that in the last play of the game there is no point in the chain store fighting entry. Fighting is costly to the monopolist and since there are no more plays of the game remaining there is no point in investing in a reputation that is designed to influence future play. At the same time the potential entrant knows that it is irrational for the monopolist to fight and so she will enter. Thus, the final play of this game is played as if it were a one-shot game with the potential entrant choosing enter and the monopolist choosing acquiesce. Given that this is the outcome of the final play it quickly becomes apparent that in the penultimate (nineteenth) play of the game there is no future play remaining where play might be influenced by the chain store's previous actions or reputation (since both players know that in the last play of the game the potential entrant will enter and the monopolist will acquiesce). Hence, the penultimate play is played just as if it were the last play with the outcome (enter, acquiesce). By the same reasoning the outcome is identical in the eighteenth play and indeed in every play stretching right back to the first. As was seen to be the case in the repeated prisoners' dilemma, the outcome of this game is dictated by backward induction. Each sequential play is played as if it were a one-shot game and it is impossible to build interdependence between time periods. As a result 'fighting entry' is ruled out as a rational strategy since the success of predatory pricing depends crucially on the link between present and future plays of the game.

This result is known as the Chain Store Paradox; the paradox being that the perfect Nash equilibrium outcome seems intuitively unreasonable compared with

Scherer's suggestion that the chain store should play tough in the early stages of the game in order to build a reputation for being strong and thus scare off future potential entrants (Friedman 1986).

There are two ways of resolving the paradox. First, it is apparent that changing the time horizon of the game from a finite to an infinite horizon implies that there is no final play of the game and so the backward induction argument cannot be brought into play. In this case a role for reputations can be established but it rests on the premise that players believe that the game will continue forever. Again, players must believe in their own immortality. This is clearly a technical resolution which depends on the assumption of an infinite time horizon.

Second, it is possible to inject some asymmetries into the information structure of the game so that potential entrants are uncertain of the payoffs of the monopolist, and hence of the type of monopolist, that they are facing. This resolution of the paradox has been suggested by Kreps and Wilson (1982).

Kreps and Wilson (1982) suggest that whenever there is a degree of doubt about the type of player or monopolist that potential entrants face, then the incumbent firm can exploit this doubt by the strategic use of reputation building. To illustrate their argument Kreps and Wilson introduce a second type of monopolist into the chain-store game. More precisely, Kreps and Wilson introduce the possibility of the existence of a strong monopolist for whom it is always rational to fight entry. The payoffs for the strong monopolist are shown in Figure 5.8a below. Given the conditions on the size of the payoffs shown below the matrix, it is apparent that if entry occurs it will pay the strong monopolist to fight since this yields a payoff of 0 rather than –1 which is what the monopolist would receive if she/he chose the alternative strategy acquiesce. If potential entrants know the payoffs of the strong monopolist then they would know that if they enter, the monopolist will fight and they will receive a payoff of (b – 1) which is negative since $0 < b < 1$. As a result the best strategy for the potential entrants is to stay out of the market.

Kreps and Wilson now inject asymmetric information into Selten's chain-store game by assuming that potential entrants do not know the payoffs of the monopolist they face with certainty. Instead, potential entrants are unsure as to whether they face a strong monopolist, for whom it is always rational to fight, or a weak monopolist, with a relative payoff structure that is the same as that shown in Figure 5.7 for whom it is always rational to acquiesce (these payoffs are shown in generalised form in Figure 5.8b). The potential entrant's uncertainty about the type of monopolist they face, opens the way for a weak monopolist to exploit this information asymmetry by mimicking the behaviour of a strong monopolist. This provides a rationale for Scherer's intuition that a monopolist may engage in predatory tactics as part of a reputation-building strategy designed to deter entry in the future.

Kreps and Wilson have modelled the use of reputation building in the following way. There are N + 1 players, consisting of N potential entrants and the chain-store monopolist. Nature moves first in the game to determine whether the monopolist is a strong monopolist whose payoffs are given by Figure 5.8a or a

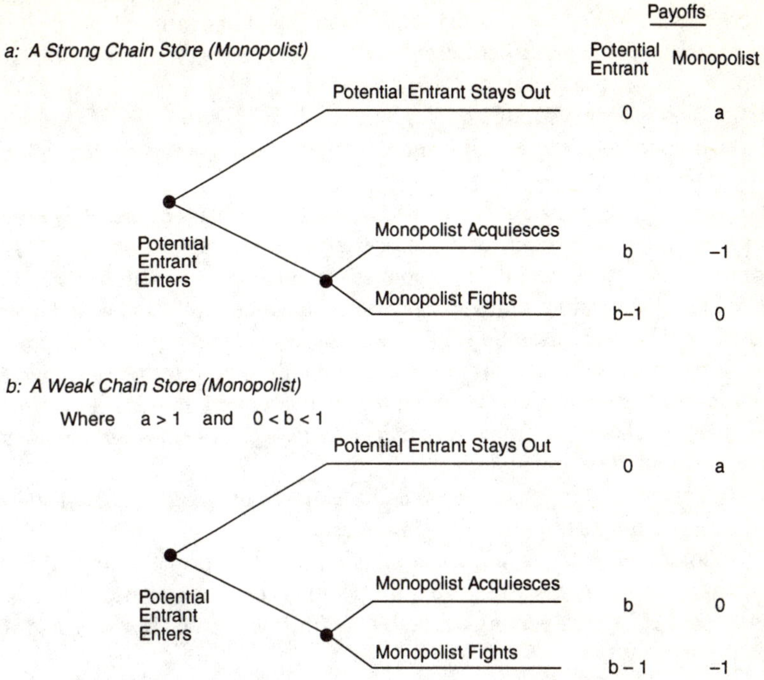

Figure 5.8: A Strong Chain Store and a Weak Chain Store

weak monopolist whose payoffs are given by Figure 5.8b. The monopolist plays the n period game with each potential entrant in turn, starting with potential entrant number n, then $n - 1$, $n - 2$ and so on down to potential entrant number 1. In other words time is indexed backwards from period n to period 1.

Since the potential entrants are uncertain about the type of monopolist they are facing they must form a probabilistic assessment of the nature of the incumbent. Potential entrants start with a prior belief (or guess) about the chance or probability that the monopolist is strong – we denote this probability p_n, where n is the stage of the game (eg in a 20 stage game with 20 potential entrants, one in each time period, $n = 20, 19, 18, 17, \ldots 1$). As the game is played out potential entrants at later stages observe the actions of previous potential entrants and the monopolist and use this information to update their belief (or probabilistic assessment) that the monopolist is strong. In other words potential entrants waiting for their turn to play, learn about the nature of the monopolist as the game goes on. Kreps and Wilson assume that the learning rule that players use to update their beliefs is the Bayesian learning rule. Bayes rule can be applied to situations where a given observation or action (fight) may arise as a result of various causes. Bayes rule uses conditional probabilities to determine the probability that a given action is caused by a given event (the monopolist is strong). As new information is generated these probabilities are updated resulting in Bayesian learning.

For example, in the game just described it is apparent that there are two reasons why the monopolist may fight:

(i) the monopolist is strong and

(ii) the monopolist is weak but is mimicking the behaviour of a strong monopolist in order to build a reputation for being strong.

The potential entrants gain information as the game is played since they observe whether the monopolist fights or acquiesces at different stages of the game. If the monopolist acquiesces then the monopolist's true nature is revealed since only a weak monopolist would acquiesce. However, if the monopolist fights at any stage of the game this is consistent with the two motives (causes) given in (i) and (ii) above. If potential entrants observe the monopolist fighting they are therefore faced with the problem of ascertaining the motive underlying this action/move. Bayes rule calculates the probability that (i) is true given that the monopolist is observed playing the strategy fight.

At each stage of the game, the potential entrants update their belief that the monopolist is strong using the following rules:

(a) If there is no entry at stage n + 1, then no new information regarding the monopolist's action is revealed to future potential entrants. Hence, there is no informational basis for updating the belief that the monopolist is strong and so

$$p_n = p_{n+1} \tag{17}$$

(b) if there is entry at stage n + 1 and entry is met with the response acquiesce, or if $p_{n+1} = 0$, then

$$p_n = 0 \tag{18}$$

that is the monopolist's reputation is blown as soon as it acquiesces and the chain-store is known with certainty to be a weak chain-store. In this case potential entrants will choose the strategy enter and the chain-store will respond by choosing the strategy acquiesce, in all remaining plays of the game. Finally, in case (c) uncertainty about the true nature of the monopolist remains but potential entrants observe the monopolist fighting and must use this new information to update their belief that the monopolist is strong:

(c) if there is entry at stage n + 1 and entry is fought, and $p_{n+1} > 0$ then

$$p_n = \max(b^n, p_{n+1}) \tag{19}$$

that is, p_n equals the greater of the two values b^n and p_{n+1}. The rule that is used to update p_n is Bayes rule which is given by equation 20:

$$\begin{aligned} p_{n-1} &= \frac{\text{prob(fights|strong).prob(strong)}}{\text{prob(fights|strong).prob(strong) + prob(fights|weak).prob(weak)}} \\ &= b^{n-1} \end{aligned} \tag{20}$$

The intuition behind this formula is straightforward. As we have seen there are two reasons a chain-store may fight: either it is a strong chain-store with payoffs given by Figure 5.8a or it is a weak chain endeavouring to establish a reputation for being strong. The sum of the probabilities of these 'causes', which may both give rise to the observation of 'fighting' by the chain-store, is given by the denominator of Equation 20. The numerator of the equation reflects the possibility that strength is the factor dictating the strategy choice fight. The ratio thus reflects the probability that the monopolist is fighting because it is strong. The terms in Equation 20 are either given *a priori* (as in the case of prob(fight|strong) which is equal to 1, and prob(strong) and prob(weak) which are equal to p_n and $(1 - p_n)$ from the previous period) or are determined by the strategies of the players, as in the case of prob(fights|weak) which reflects the strategy choice of the chain-store in the face of entry (see below). Plainly, the return to a weak chain store from investing in a reputation for playing tough changes as the game progresses (*ceteris paribus* it diminishes as the game is played), as a result the chances of a weak chain store finding it profitable to fight also change and this is reflected in changes in the term prob(fights|weak). In order to determine this term we must look at the strategies of the monopolist.

Strategies of the monopolist

The first point to note is that if the monopolist is strong it always pays to fight entry. Hence, for $p_n = 1$ the best response to entry is fight. If the monopolist is weak and entry occurs at stage n then the monopolist should respond in the following way:

(i) if $n = 1$ (last play) the monopolist should acquiesce since fighting is costly and there are no future plays of the game remaining in which to recoup this loss.

(ii) If $n > 1$ and $p_n \geq b^{n-1}$ then the monopolist should fight.

(iii) If $n > 1$ and $p_n < b^{n-1}$ then the monopolist should adopt a random or mixed strategy and fight with probability

$$\frac{(1 - b^{n-1})p_n}{(1 - p_n)\, b^{n-1}} \qquad (21)$$

and acquiesce with 1 minus this probability. Note that as the game progresses b^{n-1} increases (since b is less than 1 and n is declining). Hence for a given value of p_n fighting becomes less likely as the game progresses.

At this point we should also consider the strategies of the potential entrants. These can be summarised by the following decision rules:

Strategies of the potential entrants

(i) If $p_n > b^n$ then the potential entrant should stay out.

(ii) If $p_n < b^n$ then the potential entrant should enter. Note that as the game progresses b^n increases so that for any p_n entry becomes more likely.

(iii) If $p_n = b^n$ then the entrant chooses a random or mixed strategy, entering with probability $(1 - (1/a))$ and staying out with probability $1/a$.

These strategies are consistent with the updating of beliefs described above and with each potential entrant maximising its expected payoff given these beliefs. Taken together, the beliefs and strategies of potential entrants and the monopolist can be shown to be consistent and to constitute a sequential Nash equilibrium.[9]

It follows from the strategies outlined above that if $p_n > b^n$ in the last play of the game the entrant will stay out. As Hargreaves Heap (1989) has pointed out once entry is uncertain in the last play, the backward induction argument cannot be bought into play and other results, such as reputation building, are now possible. The significance of this model is that it demonstrates the importance of asymmetric information in determining the equilibrium solution to the chain-store game. Only a tiny amount of uncertainty regarding the nature of the incumbent firm is needed in order for the reputation effect to surface. That is, even with a very small p_n the chain store may successfully exploit this tiny doubt in the minds of the potential entrants by building a reputation for playing tough.

It should also be noted that if the monopolist is weak, then in order to build a reputation for being strong it needs entrants to enter so that it can fight and thus raise p_n. Otherwise, p_n stays constant while b^n increases as the game progresses. The importance of introducing imperfect information is that it allows a role for reputation building or predatory pricing as a rational strategy. Kreps and Wilson's analysis has been influential in the economics literature and may be adapted to other situations where reputation is important in determining outcomes. For example, reputation was an important factor underlying the credibility of the government's commitment to the central parity in the Exchange Rate Mechanism. Even if a government is actually weak and therefore prepared to consider devaluation, it makes sense for the government to pretend to be strong ie committed to the current parity come what may.

Limit Pricing and Strategic Commitment

Limit pricing is designed to prevent or limit entry. Firms that enjoy some degree of monopoly power may choose an output level other than the short run profit maximising level in order to avoid attracting new firms into the industry. When analysing games between incumbent firms and potential entrants it is necessary to consider the expected strategic response of rival firms. For example, the incumbent firm must form a belief or conjecture about the potential entrant's response to its output (and implicit price) strategy. Assuming that it is common knowledge that both players are instrumentally rational then the incumbent firm knows that if potential entrants know that they can earn excess profits post-entry, they will enter

9. The sequential Nash equilibrium described by Kreps and Wilson (1982) is a refined version of the perfect Nash equilibrium concept.

the market. In order to calculate its profits in the post-entry game a potential entrant must form a conjecture about the response of the incumbent firm if it enters the market. In the literature the most famous conjecture or belief is the Sylos postulate, named after the Italian industrial economist Sylos-Labini. The Sylos postulate states that potential entrants believe that the incumbent firm will continue to produce the same level of output post-entry as it was producing pre-entry. This conjecture on the part of potential entrants is assumed to be common knowledge in that the incumbent firm maximises its profits on the basis of the Sylos postulate. In effect the postulate assumes a no response 'reaction' by the incumbent firm following entry by a potential entrant. This postulate is therefore akin to Cournot's assumption of a zero conjectural variation – the main difference is that now the game is being played between an incumbent firm (monopolist) and a potential entrant rather than between two incumbent firms.

Assuming that firms set output in order to maximise profits then the incumbent firm will choose that output level that maximises profits and leaves no incentive for potential entrants operating under the Sylos postulate to enter the industry. The determination of the equilibrium limit price and its associated output level will differ according to whether the incumbent firm has a cost advantage or not. In the case of a cost advantage and assuming constant unit costs then it can be seen from Figure 5.9 that profit maximisation leads to a limit price of p_L. That is, in order to maximise profits and successfully limit entry the incumbent simply sets its price

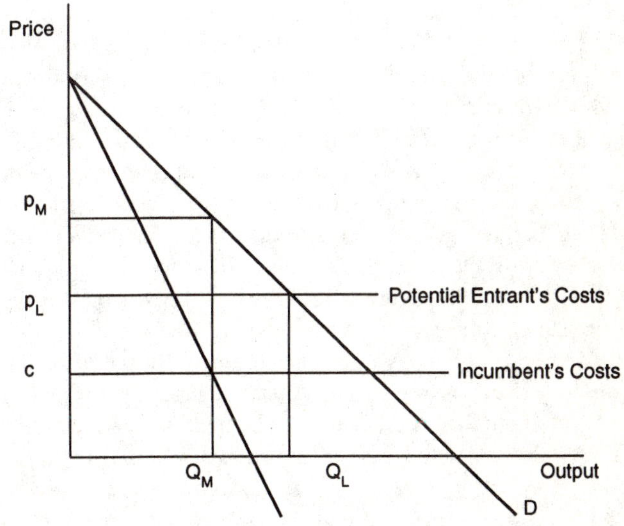

Figure 5.9: Limit Pricing with a Cost Advantage

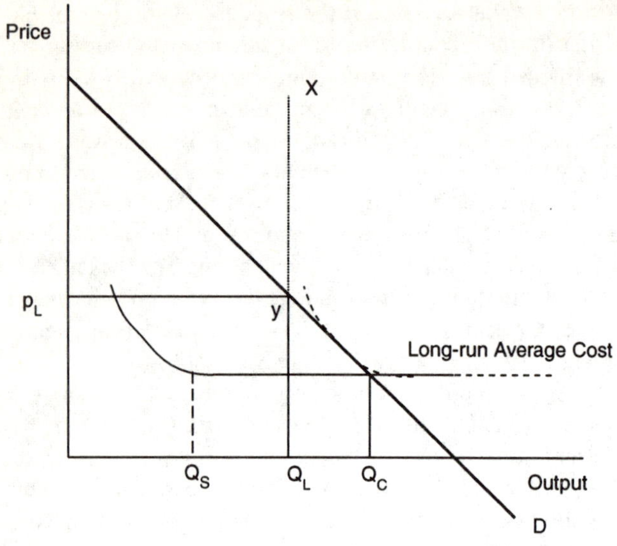

Figure 5.10: Limit Pricing with Increasing Returns to Scale and Identical Costs

equal to the potential entrants unit cost, thus leaving no scope for profitable entry by rival firms.

In the more interesting case of identical costs and economies of scale the determination of the limit price hinges on the minimum efficient scale of production. If both the incumbent firm and potential entrants have access to the long run average cost curve shown in Figure 5.10 then it can be seen that in order to compete with the incumbent firm on equal cost terms the potential entrant must produce at least Q_S. Given that both players know that the potential entrant is operating under the Sylos postulate, the best output strategy for the incumbent is to produce a quantity Q_L such that the residual demand curve facing the potential entrant, yD, lies everywhere below the potential entrant's long-run average cost curve as shown by the dotted line in Figure 5.10. It is now impossible for the potential entrant to supply any quantity of unsatisfied market demand ($Q_C - Q_L$) at a positive level of excess profit, hence there is no incentive for the potential entrant to enter. The limit price is therefore p_L and is read off from the demand curve D.

It is important to note that in order for this strategy to be successful the potential entrant must believe that the incumbent firm will continue to produce Q_L following entry. Hence, the incumbent firm has more chance of successfully limiting entry if it can make some form of strategic commitment to produce Q_L come what may. Of course, it may not be in the interests of the incumbent to continue to produce Q_L in the post-entry game. If potential entrants perceive this, which would amount to an abandonment of the Sylos postulate, then they will enter the indus-

		POTENTIAL ENTRANT	
		Enter	Stay Out
INCUMBENT	Continue to Produce Q_L	(0, 0)	(3, 0)
	Reduce Output below Q_L if entered	(1, 1)	(3, 0)

Table 5.11: Limit Pricing and Entry Deterrence

try. Thus the credibility of the Sylos postulate depends on the irreversibility of the incumbent's decision to produce Q_L.

To see these points more clearly the situation described above can be modelled using game theory. In order to simplify the analysis we will restrict the strategy set of the incumbent to two strategies: (i) continue to produce Q_L and (ii) reduce output below Q_L if entered. The strategy choices of the potential entrant are: enter and stay out. The payoffs shown in the matrix in Table 5.11 are fairly arbitrary but they do reflect the essential characteristics of the limit pricing game described in Figure 5.10.

The matrix shows that in a one-shot play of this game the potential entrant will enter and the incumbent firm will accommodate entry by reducing its output. This can be seen from the extensive form of this sequential move game shown in Figure 5.11. If the potential entrant enters, this forces the incumbent firm to choose between a payoff of 0, if she maintains output, or 1 if she reduces output. Plainly, a profit-maximising producer will choose the latter strategy. In other words the threat to continue to produce Q_L is non-credible since the potential entrant knows that if she should enter, it is not in the incumbent's interests to maintain the pre-entry level of output. The perfect Nash equilibrium for this game is, therefore, (enter, reduce output). If, however, the incumbent can convince the potential entrant that it is in its interests not to reduce output then it may successfully deter entry. It is tempting to think that the existence of other potential entrants may be sufficient to make the incumbent's threat to maintain output credible. This is equivalent to considering a repetition of the game where the incumbent firm maintains the output level Q_L in order to deter future potential entrants. However, as we have seen unless the game is repeated infinitely the backward induction argument comes into play and the outcome of the game reduces to that of a one-shot play.

In a finite repetition, credibility of the incumbent's commitment to Q_L could only be introduced by some change in the payoff matrix that made it more profitable for the incumbent to continue to produce Q_L rather than reduce output. One such device for engineering such a change might be investment in industry specific fixed capital equipment In this case the incumbent firm may find it more

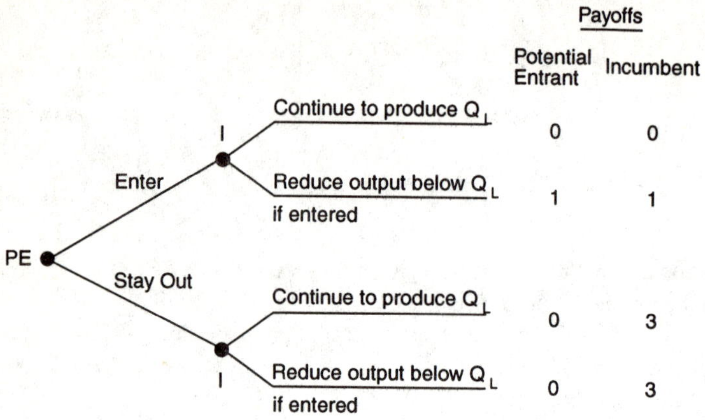

Figure 5.11: Game Tree for Limit Pricing with Increasing Returns to Scale and Identical Costs

profitable to maintain output instead of reducing output since reduced output may result in higher unit costs and lower profitability. Moreover, such an investment might signal to potential entrants that the incumbent is committed to produce Q_L. In this case the payoff matrix would change to that shown in Table 5.12.

Alternatively, if we assume increasing returns and a slight cost advantage for the incumbent then the incumbent firm can threaten to increase output in the face of entry to a level which would result in industry price falling below the cost curve of the incumbent. In this case the payoff matrix would be adjusted to yield a negative payoff to the entrant should she choose Enter.

		POTENTIAL ENTRANT	
		Enter	Stay Out
INCUMBENT	Continue to Produce Q_L	(0, 0)	(3, 0)
	Reduce Output below Q_L if entered	(–1, 1)	(3, 0)

Table 5.12: Limit Pricing with Industry-specific Fixed Capital

This payoff matrix assumes that the reaction time of the incumbent is less than the set-up time for the potential entrant

		POTENTIAL ENTRANT	
		Enter	Stay Out
INCUMBENT	Increase Output to reduce P below PE's AC if entered	(2, –1)	(3, 0)
	Maintain Output at Q_L	(0, 0)	(3, 0)

Table 5.13: Limit Pricing under Increasing Returns and a Cost Advantage

An incumbent with the payoffs given in Table 5.13 could be referred to as a strong incumbent. If potential entrants are uncertain about the cost and payoff structure of the incumbent (that is, they are uncertain about the type of incumbent they face) then Kreps and Wilson's analysis for predatory pricing follows through to the case of limit pricing and it may pay weak incumbents with payoffs shown in Table 5.11 to increase output (reduce price) in order to mimic the behaviour of strong incumbents.

Advertising and Credibility

The question of credibility and strategic commitment also arises in the case of advertising. Advertising expenditure can be used as an entry deterring strategy because it raises rival's costs. Consider the following game that is based on Salop (1983). An incumbent monopolist wishes to deter entry by potential rivals and can adopt one of two strategies: (i) no advertising or (ii) spend *a* on advertising. The potential entrant also chooses between two strategies: (i) enter matching advertising expenditure of the incumbent or (ii) stay out. The payoffs for this game are shown in Table 5.14.

Clearly, if the incumbent does not advertise the potential entrant will enter and both firms will receive a payoff of π_d. If the incumbent firm chooses to advertise it should set a equal to or slightly greater than π_d since this reduces the potential entrant's profits to zero. It follows that it pays the incumbent to advertise as long as,

$$(\pi_m - a) \geq \pi_d \qquad (22)$$

Since a must equal, at least, π_d this expression can be written as,

$$\pi_m \geq 2\pi_d \qquad (23)$$

Theoretically this condition can be seen to hold since, with a linear demand curve and constant unit costs, monopoly profits will always be at least equal to (under collusion), and more normally, greater than, duopoly profits (see Figure 5.3 above). However, in order for advertising to be a successful entry deterring strategy the incumbent firm must convince potential entrants that it will continue to spend a on advertising in the post-entry game. In the absence of a credible com-

		INCUMBENT	
		No Advertising	Spend a on Advertising
POTENTIAL ENTRANT	Enter Matching Advertising Expenditure	(π_d, π_d)	$((\pi_d - a), (\pi_d - a))$
	Stay Out	$(0, \pi_m)$	$(0, (\pi_m - a))$

Table 5.14: Advertising Game

mitment to spend a on advertising the potential entrant will enter in the knowledge that the incumbent's best response is no advertising, and the strategy choices (enter, no advertising) form the perfect Nash equilibrium. If the incumbent can make a credible commitment to spending a on advertising, perhaps through the use of a paid up contract with an advertising agency, then the potential entrant will find that its most profitable strategy is stay out and the incumbent will receive a payoff of $(\pi_m - a)$. In this case the perfect Nash equilibrium is (stay out, advertise). Again, the success of this strategy depends on the irreversibility of the decision to spend a on advertising. The significance of this game is that it demonstrates the importance of strategic commitment in determining the equilibrium solution.

Section D: Rationality

The question of rational choice has been a recurring theme throughout this chapter. The importance of rationality stems from the need to model the behaviour of economic agents. The application of game theory to the question of oligopoly highlights the fact that equilibrium outcomes are belief dependent. This implies that it is not sufficient to construct a theory that predicts rational strategy choices (or actions), what is also required is a theory that can explain why agents operate with the belief system that characterises a particular equilibrium outcome.

The standard assumption regarding rationality, that has become synonymous with the term itself, is instrumental rationality. This model of rationality assumes that agents have well behaved preferences and act to satisfy their preferences in the most efficient way possible. As Hargreaves Heap notes, 'This person is no stranger to most economists; he/she is the ubiquitous maximiser. [Instrumental] rationality is located in the means-end framework as the choice of the most efficient means for the achievement of given ends.' (Hargreaves Heap 1990: 4). That is to say, agents maximise the attainment of 'ends' - or payoffs - and the 'means' are only of significance in so far as they reflect efficiency criteria. Hence, the instrumentally rational agent has no qualms about playing the dominant strategy in prisoners' dilemma-type games since this is viewed as the most efficient means of maximising one's utility.

As we have seen there are a number of difficulties with this approach and the prisoners' dilemma result. For example, the non-cooperative outcome to the prisoners' dilemma game is Pareto inefficient and runs counter to the empirical evidence concerning the apparent unwillingness of many economic agents to free-ride (manifest in the existence of Trades Union, individual participation in pollution control, etc). In addition, predictions attained from the instrumentally rational model of individual behaviour run counter to experimental data attained from games such as the Centipede game where contrary to the prediction of a downward move by player 1 at the first stage of the game, the data reveal that players typically progress a good way along the Centipede before one of them plays the opportunistic 'down' move.

One possibility is that games are characterised by some degree of imperfect information. Indeed, if imperfect information is injected into the repeated prisoners' dilemma then collusion can be sustained by instrumentally rational behaviour within the confines of a finite game. In a similar vein it is possible to resolve the chain-store paradox by injecting a degree of imperfect information into the model. This provides an appealing account of reputation building as an instrumentally rational entry-deterring strategy. However, in the case of games with perfect information the limitations of instrumental rationality are exposed.

A further possibility is to preserve the assumption of perfect information and show that cooperative outcomes are possible in indefinite repetitions of the game where players choose to cooperate now for the sake of a better future. We have looked at a number of these models, for example, the repeated collusion game and the evolution of cooperation based on the tit-for-tat strategy. This shows that instrumentally rational agents can attain Pareto superior outcomes provided that there is some positive probability that the game will be repeated indefinitely. However, this solution is problematic for instrumental rationality since it requires agents to believe that there is some positive probability that the game will go on forever. As Hargreaves Heap (1990) notes, this belief in the possibility of one's own immortality does not sit comfortably with the model of instrumental rationality, which is rather weak when it comes to specifying what constitutes rational belief. Moreover, as we have seen, the Folk Theorem indicates that multiple equilibria are prevalent in repeated games, which suggests that the standard model of rational choice lacks a theory of equilibrium selection. Finally, as we indicated at the beginning of this chapter, empirical observation and experimental evidence shows that players frequently cooperate in finitely (and indefinitely) repeated games. Hence, either large numbers of economic agents are 'irrational', or there is something too restrictive about the model of instrumental rationality. This last possibility suggests that alternative models of rational behaviour are required. Three broad approaches to modelling rational behaviour are: (i) bounded rationality, (ii) procedural rationality and (iii) expressive rationality. We will look at each of these approaches in turn.

Bounded Rationality

This model of rationality has its roots in the work of Simon (1982). It suggests that agent's rationality is bounded by some form of computational or informational limitation. As a consequence outcomes differ from those that would be attained by unbounded maximising behaviour. While the outcomes based on this model differ from those attained from strictly instrumental rational behaviour the model itself does not break fundamentally with its instrumentally rational counterpart in the sense that: (i) agents would like to be instrumentally rational if only computational ability would allow it; and (ii) the short-cuts players use are specific to the individual.

Procedural Rationality

This model is sometimes viewed as an adjunct to bounded rationality. Faced with computational limitations agents follow well established procedures or norms rather than following strictly maximising behaviour. In the literature on rationality such behaviour has been described as satisficing rather than maximising. However, Hargreaves Heap (1990) has argued that there is more to procedural rationality than this. In particular procedural rationality is most relevant when there are multiple equilibria and no amount of additional computational power will help agents in ascertaining which equilibrium will actually be attained. For example, consider the game of chicken outlined above. Increased computational ability will be of no help to agents in determining which equilibrium (stay, swerve) or (swerve, stay) will be played out. Hence, Hargreaves Heap (1990, 1992) argues that procedural rationality must be viewed in a historical and social context: historical norms and customs are used in a deterministic way to help avoid inefficient outcomes in games with multiple equilibria. In this way procedural rationality is distinct from bounded rationality because it shows how shared value systems, beliefs and norms are functional in resolving indeterminacy. This adds a clear historical and social dimension to the theory of choice and equilibrium selection. By contrast Simon's (1982) account of bounded rationality places emphasis on norms and conventions that provide short-cuts in situations where computational ability is found lacking but the commonality of these rules does not feature as an integral part of his theory.

In order to appreciate the importance of the historical and social context in which shared beliefs and conventions are functional recall the crossroads game discussed above. Players avoid the inefficient outcome (speed-up, speed-up) by appealing to the standard convention 'give way to the right'. The significance of procedural rationality is that it provides a common foundation for coordinating activity. It is because the social, historical and institutional context provides common conventions, procedures or norms that procedural rationality is useful in determining equilibrium outcomes in games with multiple equilibria.

Expressive Rationality

Expressive rationality is grounded in an existentialist view of economic interaction. Economic agents are self-consciously reflective about their preferences and have a desire for self respect and 'to make sense of the self'[10] (Hargreaves Heap (1990, 1992)). Under expressive rationality,

> we have a picture of the individual who is groping for what is worthwhile; She/he experiments with and discusses this or that, much as a natural scientist would, when trying to make sense of something like subatomic physics which is as hidden from the naked eye as life is opaque.

According to this model of rationality the 'means' or strategies that agents follow matter just as much as the 'ends'. Actions take on particular significance because they express or reveal what agents view to be worthwhile in the world. As Hargreaves Heap (1990) notes, the power of this view of rationality becomes

10. It may be argued that this desire could be incorporated into the standard model of instrumental rationality by including the desire 'to make sense of the self' in the objective function of the individual. However, it has been argued that this misses the true nature of the desire where,

> The objective actually reflects a central source of doubt and uncertainty within the individual. People are not sure about what they should value in themselves. Indeed, without this doubt there would be no project of 'making sense of the self'. The self would be understood and the ends of the individual could be specified. Instead, it is precisely because they cannot be specified that we have an objective of 'making sense of the self'. (Hargreaves Heap ,1992, p 23).

apparent when it is linked with procedural rationality. Under procedural rationality the norms, conventions and rules that agents follow generate information about the values of players and therefore about the type of players one faces. Given the existence of shared value systems agents can associate themselves with different value systems by virtue of their actions or strategy choices. Hence,

> Action is no longer a means to a given end. Action is implicated in the choice of ends; it is part of a groping towards who to be, what ends to have; and it would be better described as activity which is its own end. (Hargreaves Heap 1990: 5).

Two examples can be used to illustrate this view. The first is based on a reformulation of the centipede game suggested by Hollis (1992). In this example the centipede game is played as a walk along the *Enlightenment Trail* with its six historic pubs. As the players reach each of the pubs in succession they take it in turns to decide whether to drink in that pub, in which case the walk ends, or to continue with the walk. Each player has a preference ordering over the six pubs – a zero refers to a player's least preferred pub and a 5 to her/his favourite pub. The map of the route is shown in Figure 5.12 with the value of each player's payoff at each pub reflecting their order of preference over the pubs. So, for example, The *Rational Choice* is ranked fifth by player 1 and last by player 2. By way of contrast, *The Triumph of Reason* is ranked second by player 1 and is player 2's favourite pub.

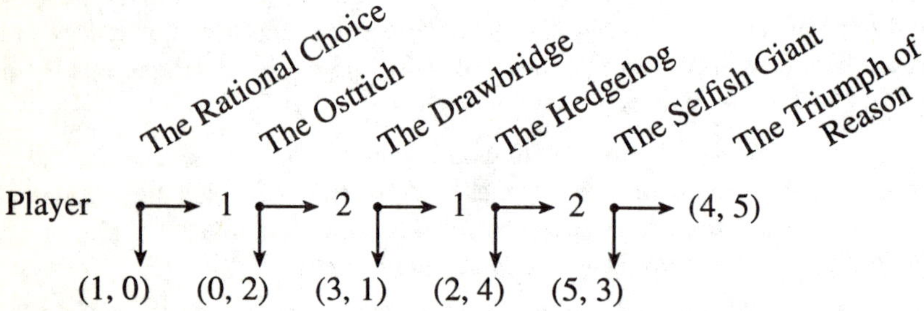

Figure 5.12: The Enlightenment Trail

Now if players 1 and 2 are instrumentally rational they will end up drinking at *The Rational Choice* – adjudged a rotten dive of a pub by both players. As we saw above this result is attained by players looking forward to the last decision node and working backwards. Instrumental rationality gives rise to this result because it is 'ends' driven and player 1's 'action' of choosing a rotten pub is inconsequential. However, if actions matter as well as ends then the selfish choice of a rotten pub is no longer inevitable. Hollis (1992) appeals to a Kantian account of reason that allows agents to distance themselves from their preferences so that reason overcomes inclination. According to Kant (1788) the purpose of reason is not merely to achieve ends that are beneficial but also to produce actions that are beneficial in themselves Indeed, if human action were concerned only with attaining certain ends then Kant argues that instinctive inclination is a superior motivating force than reason. However, Kant argued that as humans beings we are creatures of reason as well as instinct and we reason in order to make our actions worthwhile. Hence, two Kantians playing the Enlightenment Trail are able to reach the superior outcome and drink in the final pub (*The Triumph of Reason*) because they value the action that is necessary to further the common good (that is, avoid opportunism and choose a pub that both players adjudge to be good) whereas their instrumentally rational counterparts will end up at *The Rational Choice.* The Kantians are able to do better than instrumentally rational agents because they follow universalisable principles and adhere to a value system where actions are valued for their own sake. Moreover, these actions provide signals to other players that convey information about the type of player they are dealing with.

To take another example, consider the question of collusion that is central to the theory of oligopoly. Here, a player may choose to collude because they value this action more highly than 'cheating'. The attainment of Pareto optimal outcomes in other prisoners' dilemma-type games, such as trade union membership, pollution control etc, can also be seen to flow from the Kantian concept of universalisable principles and/or expressive rationality.

Finally, we should note that taken together procedural, and Kantian expressive rationality can be used to choose between equilibrium outcomes in games with multiple equilibria. In the collusion game outlined above the strategy space is restricted to 2 choices – collude and cheat. However, as we saw in Section B there are degrees of collusion and the conjectural variation (or index of collusion) may vary between 0 and 1 thus giving rise to multiple equilibria. The precise determination of the degree of collusion and of industry price and quantity may depend on historical norms and conventions established in the industry. In effect a given price-cost margin may become the norm and the strategy choice facing players is to follow the norm by producing a quantity consistent with it or adopt a competitive high-output strategy which undercuts the standard price. In essence the norm provides the focal point of the game and a positive price-cost margin may be sustained by an industry value system that values trust over opportunism. Of course, we have also seen that the collusive equilibrium may be attained by instrumentally rational agents following the tit-for-tat strategy. However, the success of the TFT strategy depends on the belief that there is some, albeit small, probability that the game will go on forever. The advantage of explaining cooperative behaviour in terms of expressive or Kantian rationality is that it is not strictly dependent on the time horizon of the game (Hargreaves Heap (1990)). In addition it demonstrates the importance of historical, cultural and institutional factors in determining economic outcomes.

As a final cursory example consider the team work game depicted in Table 5.4. The outcome of team work games can be shown to be culture dependent. In Japan, where culture dictates that high effort is valued while low effort is despised, the inefficient outcome (low effort, low effort) is likely to be avoided. The prevalence of the high effort equilibrium in Japanese firms is evidenced by recent reports which highlighted overwork and an unwillingness to take leisure time as a problem in the Japanese way of life. Indeed some commentators have suggested that a change in the value system, giving greater priority to leisure time, is required to prevent social and health problems related to over-work.

Conclusion

As we have seen, one of the main attractions of oligopoly theory is the diversity of models that the theory has produced. Many of the models discussed above take Cournot's original analysis as a starting point and consider extensions of the model based on the relaxation of certain assumptions. For example, models of limit pricing and even predatory pricing extend the analysis of oligopoly to take account of potential competition. Similarly, the analysis of advertising is an attempt to study the effects of increasing the range of strategic variables that firms have at their disposal. The models of limit pricing, predatory pricing and advertising discussed above provide just a few examples of recent attempts to model different types of oligopolistic interaction. These models represent just the tip of the iceberg in oligopoly theory, (for example, in this chapter we have not even started to discuss the vast literature on product differentiation, technology, multinationality, international trade etc), however our analysis has served to illustrate two important features of oligopoly theory: indeterminacy and strategic interdependence.

As we saw at the beginning of this chapter both of these factors are inherent features of Cournot's original analysis of duopoly. This is because they can both be traced to the need for firms in oligopolistic industries to incorporate a conjecture about rivals' strategies into their own strategy choice. A complete theory of oligopoly requires something to be said about the belief system inherent in firms' strategy choices. Cournot satisfied himself about the determinacy of his duopoly model because he argued that a belief system characterised by a zero conjectural variation would dominate all other conjectural variations. However, as we have seen this assumption does not necessarily hold in dynamic models of oligopoly. One of the main values of game theory is that it provides a framework for the discussion of conjectures and beliefs and it allows economists to formalise the conditions under which certain belief systems, and hence certain equilibria, dominate. At the same time game theory has highlighted the belief dependent nature of equilibrium in oligopolistic models with multiple equilibria and has thereby made explicit the need for economists to say something about the factors affecting belief formation. Hence, game theory has accentuated the need for economics to take account of the historical, social and institutional environment in which economic agents operate and in this respect alone, quite apart from its substantial contribution to other aspects of economics, it has made a valuable contribution to the discipline in general and oligopoly theory in particular.

Authorities

Axelrod, R (1980a) Effective Choice in the Prisoners' Dilemma, *Journal of Conflict Resolution*, 24, 3-25.

Axelrod, R (1980b) More effective choice in the prisoners' dilemma, *Journal of Conflict Resolution*, 24, 379-403.

Axelrod, R (1981) The emergence of cooperation among egoists, *American Review of Political Science*, 75, 306-318.

Bertrand, J (1883) Théorie Mathématique de la Richesse Sociale, *Journal des Savants*, pp 499-508.

Cournot, A A (1838) *Recherches sur les Principes Mathématiques de la Théorie des Richesses*. English edition (1960) translated by N T Bacon, New York, Kelly.

Dalton, D (1975) *James Dean*.

Friedman, J (1986) *Game Theory with Applications to Economics*, Oxford, Oxford University Press.

Hargreaves Heap, S (1990) *Rationality in Economics*, Oxford, Blackwell.

Hargreaves Heap, S (1992) Rationality in Hargreaves Heap S, Hollis, M, Lyons, B, Sugden, R and Weale, *The Theory of Choice*, Oxford, Blackwell.

Harsanyi, J C (1967/8) Games with Incomplete Information Played by 'Bayesian' Players, I: The Basic Model, *Management Science*, 14, 159-82 and Games with Incomplete Information Played by 'Bayesian' Players, II: Bayesian Equilibrium Points, *Management Science*, 14, 320-34.

Harsanyi, J C and Selten, R (1972) A generalised Nash solution for two-person bargaining games with incomplete information, *Management Science*, 18, 80-106.

Hollis, M (1992) A rational agent's gotta do what a rational agent's gotta do, *Royal Economic Society Newsletter*, January.

Hughes, K and Oughton, C (1993) Diversification, multi-market contact and profitability, *Economica*, May.

Kant, I (1788) *Critique of Practical Reason*, translated and edited by Beck L W, *Critique of Practical Reason and Other Writings in Moral Philosophy*, Cambridge, Cambridge University Press.

Kreps, D (1991) *A Course in Microeconomic Theory*, London, Harvester Wheatsheaf.

Kreps, D and Wilson, R (1982) Reputation and imperfect information, *Journal of Economic Theory*, 27, 253-79.

Luce, R and Raiffa, H (1957) *Games and Decisions*, New York, John Wiley.

Maynard Smith, J (1974) The theory of games and the evolution of animal conflicts, *Journal of Theoretical Biology*, 47, 209-221.

Maynard Smith, J (1982) *Evolution and the Theory of Games*, Cambridge, Cambridge University Press.

Nash, J (1951) Non-Cooperative Games, *Annals of Mathematiques*, 54, 286-95.

Rasmusen, E (1989) *Games and Information*, Oxford, Basil Blackwell.

Salop, S C (1979) Strategic Entry Deterrence, *American Economic Review*, 69, 335-338.

Schelling, T (1960) *The Strategy of Conflict*, Cambridge Mass., Harvard University Press.

Scherer, F M (1980) *Industrial Market Structure and Economic Performance*, Chicago, Rand McNally.

Selten, R (1978) The chain store paradox, *Theory and Decision*, 9, 127-59.

Shapely, L (1953) A Value for n-Person Games, in Kuhn, H and Tucker, A. (eds) *Contributions to the Theory of Games* Vol II, Princeton, Princeton University Press.

Shubik, M (1959) Edgeworth Market Games, in Tucker, A and Luce, R (eds) *Contributions to the Theory of Games* Vol IV, Princeton, Princeton University Press.

Simon, H (1982) *Models of Bounded Rationality*, Cambridge, Mass. MIT Press.

Smith, A (1976) *An Inquiry into the Nature and Causes of the Wealth of Nations*.

Sraffa, P (1926) The laws of return under competitive conditions, *Economic Journal*.

Vickers, J (1985) Strategic Competition Among the Few, *Oxford Review of Economic Policy*, 1, 39-62.

von Neumann, J (1928) Zur Theorie der Gesellschaftsspiele, *Mathematische Annalen*, 100, 295-320.

von Neumann, J and Morgenstern, O (1944) *Theory of Games and Economic Behaviour*, Princeton, Princeton University Press.

Chapter 6

Conclusion: A Re-orientation of the Theory of Value?*

As noted at the outset, this study is intended to provide *a* perspective on price theory. It began with Paretian analysis before proceeding to construct the necessary Marshallian functions which themselves reveal a pattern of interdependence. The interaction of these functions was addressed in the context of an allocative model based upon the assumption of perfect competition, and then extended to a simple statement of a self-regulating economic system. In all of these cases, results can be said to be determinate in the context of models which are essentially mechanistic.

But these arguments were intended to pave the way for a study of monopolistic competition, where the world we confront is no longer mechanistic and where the problems involved have to be addressed using much more complex analogies and pieces of apparatus. In a sense therefore the preceding chapter marks the conclusion of the study. But it may be useful to add a few words more.

The theory of the firm on which this text has concentrated owes a great deal to E.H. Chamberlin. It may be appropriate therefore to say something about the background to, and content of, the theory as it was originally stated. It may also be instructive to be reminded of Chamberlin's assessment of what the theory was designed to achieve and the direction for further research which he thought it prompted. The argument of this concluding section also allows us to take a retrospective view of the bulk of the analysis addressed in previous chapters in so far as it relates to the apparatus and content of the theory of the firm.

I. The Background

This story may be said to begin with Alfred Marshall who early recognised that the use of what may be called the mathematical *mode* produces an enormous gain in precision (Schumpeter 1954: 960) if only because it helps the thinker 'to make sure that he has enough, and only enough, premises for his conclusions' (Marshall

* This Chapter is based upon Skinner (1984, 1986).

1956: ix). The use of the *language* of mathematics emphasises this gain.

In his *Essays in Biography*, J.M. Keynes reminded us of Marshall's warm regard for Edgeworth (Keynes 1951: 159) and for Jevons, with the latter reverenced 'as among the very greatest of economists' (*ibid.*: 289). Keynes also recalled that passage in the preface to the first edition of the *Principles* where Marshall reported that the *form* in which his ideas had been cast was 'most affected by mathematical conceptions of continuity, as represented by Cournot's *Principles*' (Marshall 1956: viii). It was under Cournot's guidance, and to a lesser extent that of von Thünen, that Marshall had come to appreciate the importance of the margin,'and that in particular the demand for a thing is a continuous function, of which the marginal increment is, in stable equilibrium, balanced against the corresponding increment of its cost of production' (*ibid.*: viii-ix). Marshall added that: 'It is not easy to get a clear full view of continuity in this aspect without the aid either of mathematical symbols or of diagrams' - passages and practices which led Keynes to claim him as the founder of 'modern diagrammatic economics' (Keynes 1951: 157).

Perhaps none of this is surprising when we recall Marshall's own expertise in the quantitative field, or the enthusiasm for mathematics felt by one whose earlier intention had been to study molecular physics. Yet at the same time it should be recalled that if the *form* of Marshall's work owed much to Cournot, its *substance* was more profoundly affected by contemporary work on biology, history, and philosophy, where the authorities cited included Spenser and Hegel. The perspective thus supplied contributed to give Marshall a distinctive grasp of the inherent complexity of economic phenomena which in turn caused him 'to banish his mathematics from the surface of his argument' (Schumpeter, 1954: 956). The same considerations may help to explain his preference for diagrammatic representations (themselves confined to footnotes) over mathematical symbols (Marshall 1956: ix).

In Marshall's case, the result of this concern was some degree of imprecision.

It is not hard to see how this came about, even if we look only at the restricted field which is the subject of the present argument. One obvious area of difficulty emerges when we consider that Marshall's main attention was focussed on the industry, which was assumed in turn to be made up of a number of firms all at different stages of their life cycle. As he noted 'at any particular moment some businesses will be rising and others falling' (Marshall 1956: 314). In this context the representative firm, whose situation determines the supply price of the commodity in question, is apparently rather loosely defined as one which:

> ... has had a fairly long life, and fair success, which is managed with normal ability, and which has normal access to the economies, external and internal, which belong to (the) aggregate volume of production; account being taken of the class of goods produced, the conditions of marketing them and the economic environment generally (*ibid.*: 265).

Little wonder, perhaps, that R.L. Bishop should have complained of Marshall's 'fuzzy device of the representative firm (Bishop 1964: 34).

Similar problems affected Marshall's treatment of competition, which is never stated to be 'perfect' but rather as 'open' or 'free' - a term which 'neither seeks nor affords much precision in definition' (Hutchison 1953: 76). Monopoly too presents its own problems even if Marshall did isolate the extreme case (Marshall 1956: 395) and comment on the phenomenon of 'a severely monopolistic pricing policy' (Marshall 1920: 396). But Marshall also observed that 'there is much to be learnt from a study of the relations on which the interests of the monopolist stand to those of the rest of society' (Marshall 1956: 395) before going on to consider the importance of long-run pricing policy and situations where the monopolist may be sensitive to the benefits which accrue to himself and to the consumer (*ibid.*: 402). Marshall was alive to the problems of pricing policy in the light of 'sources of possible competition', noting that even where 'large and strong', the monopolist 'will not make full use of his power but will adjust his prices to obtaining a firm hold on the market before he can be caught by competitive supply' (Marshall 1920: 396-97). The reference to competitive supply is an interesting one, believing as Marshall did, that:

> ... though monopoly and free competition are ideally wide apart, yet in practice they shade into one another by imperceptible degrees; that there is an element of monopoly in nearly all competitive business; and that nearly all monopolies that are of any practical importance in the present age, hold much of their power by an uncertain tenure; so that they would lose it ere long, if they ignored the possibilities of competition, direct and indirect (*ibid.*: 397).

Into this rather loose set of classifications, Marshall was to fit the problems presented by time, risk, and the issue of information; the role of innovation, advertising and the structure and management of the firm (O'Brien 1981, 1984). It is hardly surprising that Schumpeter should have referred to 'Marshall's broad and deep comprehension of the monopolistic and quasi monopolistic phenomena of his age' (Schumpeter 1954: 978n), or to find Keynes describing *Industry and Trade*, like the *Principles*, as 'a mine rather than a railway'; 'the fruits of Marshall's learning and ripe wisdom' (Keynes 1951: 213).

Marshall's concern with realism presented some problems, leading to Samuelson's claim, *in contrast to his assessment of Adam Smith*, (Samuelson 1977: 42-3) that the 'ambiguities of Alfred Marshall paralysed the best brains in the Anglo-Saxon branch of our profession for three decades' (Samuelson 1967: 109).

In fact, much of the work done in the post-Marshallian period reflected the application of 'more rigorous academic standards of logical and terminological tidiness and precision' (Hutchison 1953: 315; cf. Robinson 1971: 15).

Three major developments are to be noted. First, it may be recalled that the move from the study of competition in the Marshallian manner to that of perfect competition involved an attempt to recapture the mathematical precision of

Francis Edgeworth who was perhaps the first writer 'to attempt a systematic and rigorous' definition of the model (Stigler 1965: 246; Shackle 1967: 26). In an interesting article entitled 'Perfect Competition Historically Considered', Stigler attributed the initial reformulation to J.B. Clark's *Distribution of Wealth* (1899), while it is also well known that H.L. Moore (Moore 1906), fittingly a commentator on Cournot, also complained of the 'bewildering vagueness of a fundamental term' (Hutchison 1953: 309). But perhaps the classic statement of the *assumptions* of the theory occurs in F.H. Knight's *Risk, Uncertainty and Profit* (1921) where it is noted, significantly, that:

> The argument is to be regarded as a condensed summary of classical theory, with especial reference to and emphasis upon those premisses and implications which have not been adequately emphasised in the theory itself ... Aside from this *special emphasis*, the argument will not differ a great deal from that of J.S. Mill and very little from Marshall's *Principles* (*ibid*.: 51).

Knight's statement of the necessary conditions includes the now familiar references to rationality, perfect knowledge, large numbers, product homogeneity, costless intercommunication, and perfect mobility in all economic adjustments (*ibid*., Part 2, chapters 3 and 4), moving Stigler to remark that:

> It was the meticulous discussion in this work that did most to drive home to economists generally the austere nature of the rigorously defined concept and so prepare the way for the widespread reaction to it in the 1930s (Stigler 1965: 256).

But greater precision not only involved attention to the necessary *conditions* of the model. It also involved a second major development: a *technical* advance in the shape of the concept of marginal revenue which, for the Cambridge (England) economists, constituted the 'clue and catalyst that transformed everything' (Shackle 1967: 64), thus lending a further degree of accuracy to the models of perfect competition and monopoly. Something of the flavour of the period is to be gained from Joan Robinson's introductory remarks:

> There are many occasions, ... when several explorers are surprised, and somewhat pained, on meeting each other at the Pole. Of such an occasion the history of the 'marginal revenue curve' presents a striking example ... I was not myself one of the many explorers who arrived in rapid succession at this particular Pole. I first learnt of it from Mr. C.H.P. Gifford of Magdalene College, who was then reading for the Economics Tripos. Shortly afterwards Mr. P.A. Sloan, of Clare College, showed me an unpublished essay in which it occurred. Next it was published by Mr. R.F. Harrod in the *Economic Journal* of June 1930, in an article which must have been written almost simultaneously with Mr. Sloan's paper ... Meanwhile a number of explorers were added to the rapidly growing crowd at the Marginal Revenue Pole. Professor T.O. Yntema (who also anticipated Mr. Harrod's formula for the

relation of average to marginal value) had, unknown to me, arrived there long before (*Journal of Political Economy*, December 1928). Dr. E. Schneider, Dr. H.V. Stackelberg, and Professor Mehta, amongst many others, appear to have discovered it independently. Even the naming of this concept presented a minor coincidence. I was dissatisfied with Mr. Gifford's and Mr. Harrod's titles for it, and it was christened for me by Mr. Robinson as 'marginal revenue' some time before Professor Viner published an article (in the *Zeitschrift für Nationalokonomie*, September 1931) in which he refers to it by the same name (Robinson 1933: vi-vii; 26 and note).

The statement just cited helps to explain Samuelson's complaint: 'That grown men (or women?) argued seriously in 1930 about who had first used or named the curve that we now call 'marginal revenue' is a joke. Cournot had settled all that a century earlier' (Samuelson 1967: 110). This is the reaction of a mathematician. The significant development seems to have been that the marginal curves were *drawn* in this period (Boulding 1942: 792) as, for example, in Harrod's 1930 article which deployed both revenue and cost curves in the discussion of equilibrium. The most remarkable example, however, is surely Viner's 'Cost Curves and Supply Curves' (Viner 1931), where he claimed to have been presenting 'fundamental charts' (drawn by a *specialist,* Y.K. Wong) long before the date of publication.

The developments above noted marked a major change of emphasis which witnessed not only the translation of diagrammatic representations from the notes to the main text, but also a renewed preoccupation with the *firm* (as distinct from the industry). As P.W.S. Andrews noted:

> The implications of the definition of a perfect market ... when explored by puristic mathematical theorists, made it necessary to argue in terms of the individual business. Requiring the full, short or long run, atomistic equilibrium of the industry, their methodology made explicit the necessity for the equality of marginal cost and marginal revenue (Andrews 1964: 18).

Equally important was the emergence of a new orthodoxy of which Mrs. Robinson and Chamberlin were to become the leading critics; an established image of the economic process which, in Shackle's words:

> ... showed a smooth sea of perfectly competitive firms in equilibrium, interrupted here and there by a few monopolist whirlpools obeying a different law ... In a perfectly competitive world the laws of value would have approached the universal validity and beautiful simplicity of the law of gravity (Shackle 1967: 43).

The subsequent move from perfect competition in the direction of the analysis of monopoly, to take the third point was, to a large extent, a consequence of the contemporary discussion concerning the laws of return. This discussion was initiated by J.H. Clapham (Clapham 1922) and was given added point by Piero

Sraffa's article of 1926, 'The Laws of Returns under Competitive Conditions'. Two major points should be noted. First, Sraffa argued that:

> Everyday experience shows that a very large number of undertakings, - and the majority of those which produce manufactured goods - work under conditions of individual diminishing costs (Sraffa 1953: 189).

In these circumstances, the outcome is indeterminate under the rigorous conditions of perfect competition, from which it follows, secondly, that 'it is necessary to abandon the path of free competition and turn in the opposite direction, namely towards monopoly' (*ibid.*: 187). But monopoly was now defined in a new and particular way, as relating to a situation where the buyers of goods were *not* indifferent as between producers of similar products:

> ... long custom, personal acquaintance, confidence in the quality of the product, proximity, knowledge of particular requirements ... the reputation of a trade mark, or sign, ... such special features of modelling or design in the product as ... have for their principal purpose that of distinguishing it from the products of other firms (*ibid.*).

In short, Sraffa was drawing attention to the 'intermediate zone' between perfect competition and monopoly, narrowly defined, thus giving a considerable stimulus to the study of *monopoly* in the broadest sense (Galbraith 1948: 99).

But the work which most explicitly built on the Sraffa thesis, was Joan Robinson's *Economics of Imperfect Competition*:

> We have only to take the word monopoly in its literal sense, a single seller, and the analysis of monopoly immediately swallows up the analysis of competition (Robinson 1933: 5).

Mrs. Robinson's concern with the intermediate case, and something of the quality of her analysis, can be seen in her treatment of product differentiation, in the Sraffian manner, (*ibid.*: 89-90) and of the elasticity of the revenue curves where the latter are affected by the number of competing monopolists and the substitutability of their products. The analysis embraces a discussion of competitive equilibrium (*ibid.*: chapter 7) wherein the tangency solution is developed, yielding a case where a state of equilibrium is attained under conditions of decreasing cost. Further technical advances included the isolation of a *version* of the kinked demand curve with the attendant discontinuities in marginal revenue (*ibid.*: 215 and note) and the important attempt to explore the properties of monopoly and monopsony treated as the two sides of a single coin.

The book is also remarkable for its technical content. It is to Mrs. Robinson that we owe much of the geometry of modern price theory (developed in Part I), elaborated in a book which was 'presented to the analytical economist as a box of tools. It is an essay in the technique of economic analysis, and can make only an indirect contribution to our knowledge of the actual world' (*ibid.*: 1). The result was a re-affirmation of the mathematical (and geometrical) approach; a perspective which was in sharp contrast to that adopted by Marshall and by Marshallians such as Robertson and Shove (O'Brien 1984) who had sought to rehabilitate the representative firm in the face of Sraffa's criticism:

> They examined the existing world in a spirit of respect, they brought as much of it intact into their discourse as they could, they valued the contours and features of the landscape they beheld and tried to mould their arguments upon them rather than cut a path direct to rigorous conclusions. Mrs. Robinson did the opposite. Clear and definite questions cannot be asked about a vague, richly detailed, fluid and living world. This world must therefore be exchanged for a *model,* a set of precise assumptions collectively simple enough to allow the play of logic and mathematics ... The model is a work of art, freely composed within the constraints of a particular art form, namely the logical binding together of propositions (Shackle 1967: 47).

The approach, which owed much to techniques with which Marshall was familiar, and to which Chamberlin made some contribution, was to have a profound effect on the future assessment of the latter's work.

II. Chamberlin

The Preliminary Argument

To a very large extent E. H. Chamberlin stands apart from the developments just mentioned as he makes plain in the 'Origin and Early Development of Monopolistic Competition Theory' (Chamberlin 1961). Serious work on his thesis apparently began in 1924, was largely completed in 1926 and the study filed in the following year. This means that Chamberlin's 'discovery' of the curves of marginal cost and marginal revenue was made quite independently of his English and German colleagues. Further, as Chamberlin himself made clear, the thesis had no link with Sraffa's work 'Nor did the Book itself attack Marshall ... on any of the issues there involved' (*ibid.:* 532). Indeed he always insisted that his work was an attack 'not on Marshall, but on the theory of perfect competition' (*ibid.:* 540). He might have added that *The Theory of Monopolistic Competition* was essentially Marshallian both in its style of reasoning and in the pre-occupation with realism; a pre-occupation which led Chamberlin to play down the operational significance of the marginal curves while recognising their importance in a technical sense.

Unlike Mrs. Robinson, Chamberlin did not regard marginal revenue as the 'heart of the matter' (Chamberlin 1957: 274–75). As he observed:

> In my own attempt to blend monopoly and competition, the marginal revenue curve was discovered at an early stage and seen for what it is – a piece of pure technique unrelated to the central problem. It actually enters into my own

> exposition as a separate curve at only two points. *(ibid.*: 274).

The position was then clarified in the statement that:

> A major deficiency in the marginal revenue technique is that it does not by itself reveal the price. This means that the discussion of equilibrium takes place primarily in terms of *output*, the category so neatly determined by the intersection of the two marginal curves, instead of in terms of *price*, the category with reference to which business decisions are most usually taken.

Rather, Chamberlin cited three sources of inspiration. First, the 'Taussig-Pigou controversy as to whether charging what the market will bear in railway rates was to be explained in terms of joint costs' (Chamberlin 1961: 517). Secondly, he drew attention to the 'literature of business' and especially to the stimulus provided by Allyn Young (Blitch 1983). As Chamberlin recalled, Young had given particular attention to trade marks and patents in so far as they conferred a monopoly power which is also consistent with competition:

> ... each makes a product unique in certain respects; this is its monopolistic aspect. Each leaves room for other commodities almost but not quite like it; this is its competitive aspect (Quoted, Chamberlin 1961: 525).

A third source of stimulus was located in 'Business economics' with special reference to advertising and the operation of retail markets (*ibid.*: 529). Here Chamberlin drew attention to A. C. Pigou's perception that advertising was *peculiar* to what was in effect monopolistic competition, and to Marshall's distinction between 'constructive' and 'combative' advertising.

Chamberlin's task was to give the theory of value a different orientation – *having first defined the extremes of competition and monopoly* and explored some of the ground between them (duopoly).

In the initial stage of the argument, Chamberlin examined a situation where the product was homogeneous but numbers varied. Having defined *pure monopoly* (Chamberlin 1948: 63) as involving 'control over the supply of all economic goods' he concentrated attention on the case of the single seller who comprises the industry, making the point that in this type of case there is 'always competition between the product concerned and others' (*ibid.*: 64). This is the 'simple and familiar' example (*ibid.*: 15) involving control over price (*ibid.*: 7) in a situation where there are no *close* substitutes.

Chamberlin's solution is now well known making it necessary only to recall the state of knowledge in the 1920s; a state of knowledge which is reflected in the care with which marginal revenue and marginal cost are defined (*ibid.*: 14 and 24) and in the significance of their deployment in a single diagram (*ibid.*: 13, Figure 1, reproduced here as Figure 6.1). It is also interesting to note that Chamberlin took these steps as a means of freeing the reader from the normal association between equilibrium and the intersection of the curves of Demand and Supply (the point Q rather than P in Figure 6.1).

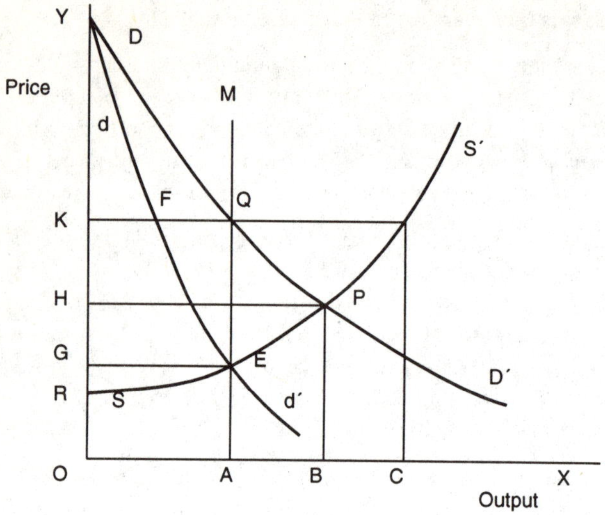

Figure 6.1

Pure Competition, a term which Chamberlin may have introduced to the literature (Schumpeter 1954: 973n):

> is taken as a point of departure, the adjective 'pure' being chosen deliberately to describe competition unalloyed with monopoly elements. It is a much simpler and less inclusive concept than perfect competition, for the latter may be interpreted to involve perfection in many other respects than in the absence of monopoly (Chamberlin 1948: 6).

Thus defined, pure competition is of interest 'because it describes a portion of economic activity' in the context of a highly organised market (*ibid.*: 11, 9). Chamberlin went on to argue that: 'in order to define the point of equilibrium ... it is necessary to examine the demand and supply conditions for the group'. He then proceeded to deploy the now familiar diagrams (reproduced here as Figure 6.2) concerning the operation of the firm and the situation in the market as a whole (*ibid.*: 17-25).

Common-place as the example now is, there are a number of points of interest arising from the concern with pure rather than with perfect competition. First, Chamberlin conducted his treatment of equilibrium by reference to the marginal *producer*, noting that the cost curve for *intra*-marginal firms will have the same minimum point, if rents are included as costs. Secondly, he allows for the fact that if the minimum point of the average cost curve *thus defined* may be at the same distance from the X axis, the curves for different producers may still vary in their

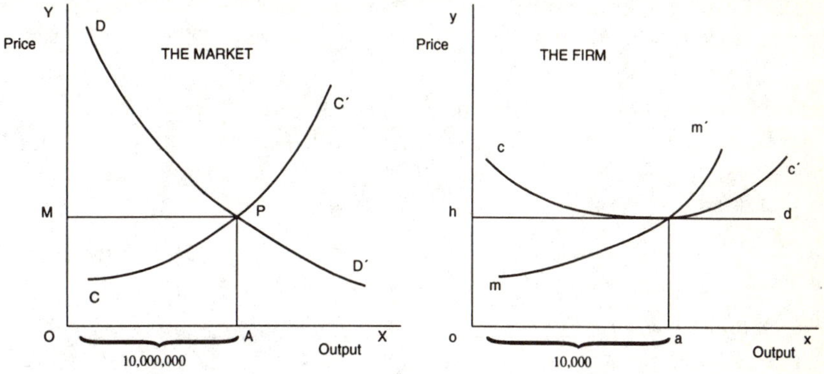

Figure 6.2

location with reference to the Y axis. Thirdly, formal allowance is made for the possibility that the process of new entry may affect the position of the average cost curve facing the firms.

But to the modern reader, as for Chamberlin himself, the third chapter on *Duopoly and Oligopoly* is among the most interesting in that it examines a situation which is intermediate between the extreme cases of monopoly and pure competition, where the products sold are not differentiated. The original material appeared in the *Quarterly Journal of Economics* for 1929. Chamberlin had been obliged to strike out a reference to Oligopoly at the insistence of F.W. Taussig, the then editor, who 'thought the term a monstrosity' (1957: 33) – a decision which must have caused the author some pain since he was unaware at that time of any prior use of the term in print.

It is impossible to review in this place the extensive history of duopoly theory or even the treatment which Chamberlin accorded to the subject in his third chapter (and Appendix A which deals with Mathematical Theories of Duopoly and Oligopoly). But it is appropriate to note that the Cournot model (1838) of two sellers offering an identical product is arguably the most important example chosen, at least for didactic purposes (see above, Chapter 5).

Basically, Chamberlin reviewed a case where the sellers were interdependent but pursued policies with regard to price or output on the assumption that their rival's reaction would remain unchanged – the case of *mutual dependence ignored.* In both cases (price and output), Chamberlin confirmed that the outcome would be determinate and accord with the situation which would have obtained under competitive conditions. The case of *mutual dependence recognised*, as Chamberlin reports the matter, was also consistent with a determinate result, namely the monopoly solution, and was associated with Young in his review of Bowley's *Mathematical Groundwork of Economics* published in the *Journal of the American Statistical Association* for 1925 (1948: 47 and note).

Writing in 1957, Chamberlin was to argue that:

> Everyone sought *the* solution, and I can recall no hint of my own general position that the problem is a manifold one with a large number of different answers depending on which of many possible assumptions are made (Chamberlin 1957: 36).

Chamberlin's own results are usefully summarised at pages 53–4 of the original publication (Chamberlin 1948) and were stated in this form:

> 1. Duopoly is not one problem, but several. The solution varies, depending upon the conditions assumed. Putting to one side the factor of uncertainty, it is (with minor exceptions) determinate for each set of assumptions made.
> 2. If sellers have regard to their *total* influence upon price, the price will be the monopoly one.
> 3. If sellers neglect their indirect influence upon price, each determining his policy as though his competitors were uninfluenced by what he did, the results vary ...
> 4. If sellers neglect both their indirect and direct influence upon price, the outcome will be the purely competitive price, *regardless of numbers*.
> 5. Uncertainty, where present, as to (a) whether other competitors hold their amounts or their prices constant, (b) whether they are far sighted, (c) the extent of the possible incursions upon their markets, and (d) in the case of a time lag, its length, renders the outcome indeterminate.

In Chamberlin's view, the 'real problem' was the development of the dependence recognised case and the exploration of the consequences of uncertainty (1957: 38). It is no exaggeration to claim that this theme became an increasingly dominant one in the context of a further phase of the problem, that of product differentiation where numbers are both large and small.

Essentials of the Theory

Chamberlin's main interest was in that situation where the pairing of buyers and sellers is no longer random; that is, where goods are differentiated in the mind of the consumer. Here the firm may control price, product specification and selling costs where the latter are 'incurred to alter the position or shape of the demand curve' (Chamberlin 1948: 117). The problems which are exposed by such a perspective are wide ranging so that it is important to note at the outset that

Chamberlin concerned himself almost solely with intra- rather than inter-industry competition and that he retained something very like the Marshallian industry in so doing. As he put it:

> The group contemplated initially is one which has *ordinarily* been regarded as composing one imperfectly competitive market: a number of automobile manufacturers, or producers of pots and pans, or magazine publishers, or of retail shoe dealers (*ibid.*: 81).

Even this restrictive perspective, however, meant that the technical apparatus had to be altered as compared to the treatment of pure competition.

The firm now has a choice of cost curve arising from the capacity to alter product specification (*ibid.*: 94–100) while in addition selling costs have to be added to costs of production. Chamberlin thought that it would be difficult to generalise about the curve of selling costs since its shape would be affected by the nature of the product, the level of planned expenditure, and the choice of media, but gave it a 'U' shape in both short and long run (*ibid.*: 133–35, 138).

An equally important innovation resulted from Chamberlin's appreciation of the point that:

> A monopoly of "Lucky Strikes" does not constitute a monopoly of cigarettes, for there is no degree of control whatever over the supply of other substitute brands' (*ibid.*: 65).

He thus introduced two revenue curves. The DD curve is defined as the fractional part of the Market Demand curve (e.g. for cigarettes) which 'shows the demand for the product of any one seller at various prices on the assumption that his competitors prices are always identical with his' (*ibid.*: 90). In contrast, the *dd* curve provides 'a rough index of buyers preferences for the product of one seller over that of another' (*ibid.*: 93) and indicates the 'increase in sales which he could realise by cutting his price provided others did not also cut theirs' (*ibid.*: 90).

In the context of the large group, the relatively elastic (as compared to DD) dd curve is relevant since it is legitimate to assume that any adjustment 'by a single producer spreads its influence over so many of his competitors that the impact felt by any one of them is negligible' (*ibid.*: 83) – i.e., the *diffusion* effect.

To ease the task of exposition, Chamberlin proceeded under the heroic assumption that both demand and cost curves for all products 'are uniform throughout the group' (*ibid.*: 82) thus permitting the use of a single set of revenue and cost functions.

Methodologically, the technique is classically Marshallian in that Chamberlin assumed price and product, product and selling costs, selling costs and price to be given, before allowing the third element in each case to vary (*ibid.*: Chapters 5 and 7). In fact Chamberlin spent a great deal of time in discussing product variation and selling costs (see above, pages 153-155) although there is little doubt that the analysis of price adjustment attracted most attention – perhaps because of the obvious parallels and contrasts with pure competition.

The procedure is familiar: if the typical seller faces a dd curve which is consistent with excess profits, new entry will force the curve to a position of tangency with the cost curve thus yielding an equilibrium position under conditions of decreasing cost – a variant of the Sraffa solution (see above, p. 253).

While Chamberlin makes allowance for changes in the position of the demand curve in consequence of new entry, an interesting example is where numbers are assumed constant and excess profits obtain. In this case, the (unintended) consequence of *each* seller seeking to cut price with a view to maximising profit, is a *general* reduction in the market price so that *dd´* 'slides' down *DD´* until the position of tangency is reached (Figure 6.3). Equilibrium is defined by two conditions:

(a) *dd´* must be tangent to PP´, and
(b) *DD´* must intersect both *dd´* and PP´ at the point of tangency (*ibid.*: 93).

But the emphasis on tangency obscures the real purpose, and one may sympathise with Chamberlin's repeated complaint that this solution had come to be regarded, in the typical text book account as 'the central principle involved' (*ibid.*: 195). In fact Chamberlin recognised that decisions on cost, price, and selling outlay were closely linked, and therefore that the cost and revenue functions facing the firm were interdependent. The reader was in fact presented with a market situation where in practice the 'result is heterogeneity of prices, and variation over a wide range of outputs (scales of production) and in profits'(*ibid.*: 81) which are unlikely to be completely eliminated even in a competitive environment.

Chamberlin's treatment of *the small group* was no less important at the time of writing, particularly since the argument brought to the fore a problem which is implicit in the large group case (with its interdependent functions) – that of determinancy. Building on the analysis of Chapter 3 (duopoly), Chamberlin argued that the particular outcome would depend on the behavioural assumptions made. The monopoly (Figure 6.3) solution will obtain if each seller 'sought to maximise his profit with regard to his full influence, direct and indirect, upon the situation (*ibid.*: 100), i.e., at point Q in the figure. The competitive solution will obtain 'If sellers neglect their indirect influence upon the price, each assuming the others to be unaffected by his own actions' but forcing a reaction which results in each firm arriving at the point R. The most probable solution (dependence recognised) might be expected within these extremes (with *dd* lying at a point intermediate between Q and R), but with its stability affected by uncertainty:

> the same elements of uncertainty are present here as under the simpler hypothesis of a standardised product ... Each seller may be in doubt as to his rival's policy, and therefore as to his own, because he does not know (a) whether, if his rival's present policy continues, it will continue with respect to his price or with respect to his output, (b) how intelligent and far-seeing his rival is, and (c) how large would be the incursions made upon him by his own price cut. This last factor is augmented by a new unknown – the extent of the buyers preferences for his own product over others, expressed by the

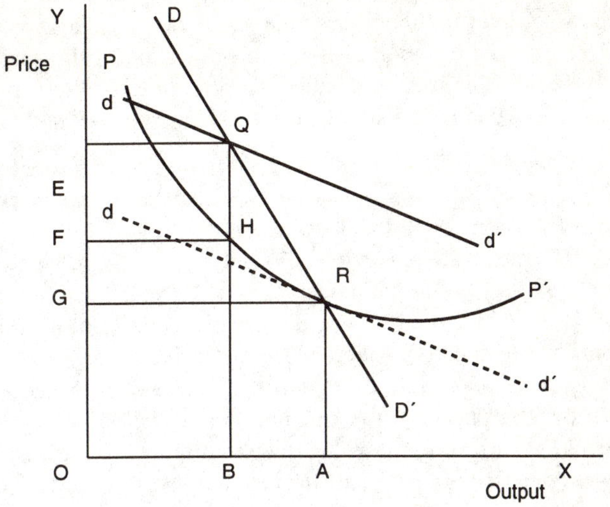

Figure 6.3

shape of the demand curves for individual products (*ibid.*: 101).

But concentration on an *identifiable* range within which a solution may be found (such as RQ in the figure) is itself misleading, depending as it does on the 'heroic assumption' of similarity of cost and revenue curves which is not a necessary feature of the model. The material point is that there are as many solutions as there are behavioural assumptions to be made – all in the context of a situation where the demand curves in question are essentially 'imagined' ones (since their anticipated shape depends upon judgements as to the future reaction of rivals) and where the cost curves may differ in both location and shape (cf. Sweezy 1939).

While it seems a short step from the analysis just considered to the 'kinked demand' curve model, P.W.S. Andrews only found in *The Theory of Monopolistic Competition* 'an ingenious piece of analysis' which should 'now be recognised as a general background to the theory' (1951: 159). On the other hand, Hall and Hitch acknowledged that Chamberlin's 'two demand curves' were based on the same assumptions as their own 'illustrative curves' (1951: 122n). In noting the point, Chamberlin was to argue, quite correctly, that the version associated with Hall and Hitch was 'merely a combination of my own d and DD curves, with the more elastic d portion lying above the ruling price' (1957: 288). But Chamberlin did *not* develop the kinked demand curve model in its now familiar form, and may well have believed that under most circumstances, the more elastic section of *dd* which lay above the ruling price was irrelevant; a variant of the 'limit price' solution (see above, p. 140):

> business men may set their prices with reference to costs rather than to demand, aiming at ordinary rather than at maximum profits, and more or less taking it for granted that they will continue to enjoy about their usual share of the total business ... In this case, since the prices of all move roughly together, ... the curve dd is of no significance (Chamberlin 1948: 105).

It is this which explains Chamberlin's contention that he had anticipated the 'full cost' principle in his *Theory of Monopolistic Competition* and his belief that this principle was fully consistent with his analysis.

But the most striking difference of all surely arises from the fact that Chamberlin's analysis of the *DD* and *dd* curves was developed *without reference* to MRD or MRd (see above, p. 173). The discontinuous range of the composite marginal revenue curve which is implied by the argument was in fact only made explicit in 1939 with the analyses of Sweezy and of Hall and Hitch who, working quite independently, also presented the kink not as a logical possibility based on a series of conjectural variations but as 'an ingenious rationalisation of the price rigidities that were reported in many statistical studies' (Stigler 1965: 404).

General Implications of the Argument

Chamberlin offered a number of general conclusions in the context of his treatment of oligopoly.

Firstly, Chamberlin noted that the case of oligopoly was consistent with conflict; with the attempt by firms to drive rivals from the market. This example, in effect, makes the important point that price-cutting is not always the 'irrational' behaviour that the *dependence ignored* case, taken in isolation, might at first sight suggest (Chamberlin 1948: 92–3).

Secondly, he argued that dependence recognised does not of itself involve collusion (*ibid.*: 106). As he noted elsewhere, 'this is a *legitimate* solution of *oligopoly,* consistent with complete independence of the sellers'; a point which carried with it some important policy implications:

> if a chess player decides against a particular move because the responses to it which his rival would make would be damaging to him, he cannot be accused of 'spontaneous co-operation'; and he should hardly be *required* by the rules to make the move on the ground that otherwise he would be entering into a 'conspiracy in restraint of chess'; or into an agreement with his rival. Why, then, should a businessman who acts with equal (and rather ordinary) intelligence in deciding not to make a price cut, be accused (either by economists or by attorneys general) of collusion, or of *tacitly* co-operating with someone? The point is that the idea of co-operation in *any* sense is *unnecessary* to the result (Chamberlin 1957: 39).

The chess analogy had also been noted by Irving Fisher (1898):

> As a matter of fact, no businessman assumes either that his rival's output or price will remain constant any more than a chess player assumes that his opponent will not interfere with his effort to capture a knight ... his whole thought is to forecast what moves the rival will make in response to one of his own (Hutchison 1953: 313–14).

The point is an important one since Chamberlin was moved to observe that his own case of mutual dependence recognised , which he described as 'a new phase of the problem' (Chamberlin 1948: 46) had been anticipated by Fisher's article. But it should be observed that Chamberlin employed the *analogy* of a game, as distinct from the *theory* of games, noting almost in passing that 'game theory' had an application in dealing with the problems which he had identified (Chamberlin 1957: 37). The development of game theory was a major feature of the subject in which Chamberlin played no part.

Thirdly, Chamberlin advanced the interesting proposition that the phenomenon of *oligopolistic interdependence*, and thus the relevance of the model, was likely to be more general than the distinction between the large and small group might at first sight suggest. Even in the context of the *large* group, he observed that almost 'any general class of product divides itself into sub-classes'. In such a case:

> any individual seller is in *close* competition with no more than a few out of the group, and he may seek to avoid price competition for the very reason given as applying to small numbers – that his cut will force those in closest competition with him to follow suit (*ibid.*: 103).

The *associated issue of space* is equally interesting. Chamberlin always recognised, as Wicksell had done (Schneider, in Kuenne 1967: 139–40), that the issue of location 'has been held in undue isolation from the rest of economics' and that 'spatial differentiation is the general rule' (Chamberlin 1957: 6). He announced his intention to give the matter greater prominence in his 1951 manifesto, 'Monopolistic Competition Revisited' and later made the point that spatial issues had featured more prominently in his thesis than in the first edition of the book (Chamberlin 1961: 522). Chamberlin later added two important appendices to his work (from his thesis), one dealing with the contribution of Hotelling (Appendix C), while the other addressed the question of Urban Rent (Appendix D).

Yet Chamberlin did confront the problem which is presented by spatially distributed firms, which may be members of a *large group* operating under conditions of monopolistic competition. For example, retail stores or filling stations, may form a network of interwoven markets. A (retail) seller of petrol may cut price to a limited extent, forcing adjacent rivals to make some response. A more extensive cut, on the other hand, could force a like response from rivals within the relevant area and hence from those who are on the boundary of *neighbouring* areas – the 'chain linking effect', which suggests that even if the numbers selling physically similar (or indeed identical) products are large, consideration of indirect influence may enter in when account is taken of location (see above, p. 187).

To clarify the point Chamberlin later commented on the phenomenon of the 'isolated monopolist' who is not subject to repercussions in that when he cuts price 'he makes his gains from a large number of others, so that no *one* of them is appreciably affected by what he does' (Chamberlin 1957: 54) – a condition (isolation) which can also be extended to pure competition (*ibid.*: 56). This case was contrasted with the *non-isolated* seller (*ibid.*: 57), covering 'the problem commonly known as oligopoly' and also the *relationship* between firms which are likely to obtain when allowance is made for spatial distribution.

But the specific case in which Chamberlin became increasingly interested was the one identified by Nicholas Kaldor who was concerned with the problem of competition between quite *different* products. Kaldor cited the case of demand for cigarettes in a given location as being more affected by the price of beer in the same location than by the price of cigarettes in a distant place – thus rendering the demand curves indeterminate (Kaldor 1934: 340; 1935: 40). In noting the problems involved Chamberlin recognised the possible applications of the model of price discrimination (which had been mentioned in the thesis but *not* the book) (Chamberlin 1961: 519). At the same time, he also came to believe that the 'subject needs to be re-written in terms of that extremely useful concept which originated, I believe, with Mr. Kaldor, of cross elasticity of demand, rather than in terms of the number of sellers in a market' (Chamberlin 1957: 61).

It should be observed that the discussion of choice, with which the analysis of this book began, was primarily concerned with decisions to consume quantities of *different* (and competing) goods.

But the point which Chamberlin wished to convey is an important one, namely that 'When any seller is so situated that he knows that what he does will have a substantial influence on others and thereby may lead them to alter their present policies, he would be short-sighted indeed not to take all of this into account' (*ibid.*: 57). What Chamberlin had done was gradually to widen his understanding of 'sources of influence', notably as a result of introducing the problem of the spatial distribution both of customers and firms. This in turn led to an appreciation not just of oligopoly but of the phenomenon of *oligopolistic interdependence*, thus giving a new meaning to the original claim:

> it seems evident to me that oligopolistic elements are very general in the economic system and that economic study must be increasingly concerned with their influence upon prices and other economic categories (Chamberlin 1948: 61).

In short we face an economic *system* (not just a single model) which is characterised by interdependence and thus by uncertainty and conjecture.

Finally, it is interesting to note that Chamberlin had perceived (like Joan Robinson) the need to develop the analysis of input markets in the light of his treatment of output.

Chamberlin not unnaturally concentrated on the output side when developing his theory, but without entirely neglecting the analysis of factor returns. The main argument appeared in his 'Monopolistic Competition and the Productivity Theory of Distribution' (1934); an article which subsequently appeared as chapter 8 of the *Theory of Monopolistic Competition* and in *Explorations in Economics* (1936). It was in this work that he set out to explore the problem which is presented by the fact that 'even a slight element of monopoly necessarily reduces the remuneration of all factors employed in a given firm below the value of their marginal products' (Chamberlin 1948: 181). As a result, Chamberlin chose to emphasise the distinction between marginal product and *marginal revenue product*, indicating that it is the latter which is brought to equality with the marginal input cost. Writing in 1957 he was to claim:

> In the field of incomes, the discovery that productive services are paid their marginal *revenue* products instead of their marginal products as defined under pure competition is sweeping in its generality, and (properly interpreted) would seem to the writer to be one of the truly revolutionary features of the new analysis (Chamberlin 1957: 7).

Chamberlin also pointed out that the application of his analysis to the labour field 'was in its infancy', in itself an interesting statement for the time.

Chamberlin did not develop this case, but he did explore the implications of a positively sloped supply curve for the factor (Chamberlin 1948: 84). Later he was to develop an argument more commonly associated with J. K. Galbraith's *Concept of Countervailing Power* (1952) – namely, that in the context of monopolistic competition, broadly defined, the relevant relationship is that of bilateral monopoly (Chamberlin 1957: 255) 'more or less restricted by competitive elements on both sides' (*ibid.*: 260). An article written in 1951 gives some idea of the novelty of the thought and its attendant implications:

> Economists as well as the public are fooled by the fact that the adjective 'monopoly' is always attached to the noun 'profit' and never to the noun 'cost'. But economists at least should not be fooled in a matter as straightforwardly technical as this appears to be *(ibid.*: 266).

In fact, the case of bilateral monopoly (as developed by Edgeworth) received a good deal of attention in Haley's survey (1948), albeit *without reference* to the Chamberlinian treatment of *Monopolistic Competition* and the implied suggestion that wage rates and therefore the position of the firm's cost curve(s) are unknown – at least until the bargain is struck (see above, pages 147-148, 184). The links between output and input analysis were temporarily obscured.

Conclusion

Writing in the introductory essay of *Towards a More General Theory of Value* nearly 25 years after the original publication, Chamberlin repeated his claim that the 'purpose of the theory is to do a better job of explanation by presenting a continuum between two extremes rather than two sharply distinguished and mutually exclusive categories' (Chamberlin 1957: 5). He then went on to summarise the characteristics of the approach as compared to pure competition:

1. Monopolistic competition is more general than pure competition in that it includes monopoly as well as competition, and combines both in all degrees.
2. Monopolistic competition is more general than pure competition in that it embraces heterogeneity of the product in all degrees, and not merely in the lowest, or zero, degree to which the theory of pure competition is restricted.
3. Monopolistic competition is more general than pure competition in that it ranges in the field of numbers over the one, the few, and the many, thus embracing oligopoly wherever it is present, instead of assuming it away.
4. Monopolistic competition is more general than pure competition in that it embraces selling activity, instead of assuming that goods are sold automatically and costlessly, as does the theory of pure competition.
5. The expansion of monopolistic competition beyond the range of problems envisaged by pure competition is perhaps nowhere so dramatically in evidence as in its admission of the product itself as a variable.
6. Finally, monopolistic competition is more general than pure competition in that it embraces policy objectives other than profit maximisation; and specifically the full cost principle (*ibid.*: 16–24).

The basic pre-occupations remained unaltered, although Chamberlin did indicate that there would have been some changes in exposition if the opportunity had been present to re-cast the book:

> The present formulation is much simpler. It begins with the individual seller and uses the spatial example to illustrate how the entire economic system may be viewed as an elaborate network of inter-related firms, each one being able to adjust from the beginning either its price, product or selling outlay. The uniformity assumption is used only momentarily, and diversity appears at once in the form of concentration of buyers. The individual firm is either isolated or related oligopolistically to others. The group has disappeared from the formulation here given, and with it the concept of large numbers, since the individual seller in this latter instance is again correctly described as isolated, even in the special case of pure competition (*ibid.*: 68).

Little of the *formal* structure of *Monopolistic Competition* would appear to survive, even if there had been no change in Chamberlin's understanding of the characteristics of the market as a type.

However, Chamberlin had no compelling reason to drop the concept of the group ('if it had meant an industry, the word industry would have been used', (*ibid.*: 68n) or sub-group (Chamberlin 1948: 102–03) in the context of small numbers. There are as a matter of fact 'industries' as the term is ordinarily understood (*ibid.*: 81) composed of a small number of identifiable firms, such as automobile manufacturers or supermarkets, and which provide classic examples of oligopoly as Chamberlin originally defined the term. But it is quite clear from the appendices which were gradually added, and from the articles published in collected form in 1957 that Chamberlin's thinking in the field had progressively developed in a positive way. The 'manifesto' of 1951 and the retrospective review of 1961 amply testify to his intentions. Yet the book was never re-written in a way which would have reflected the evolving plan with the result that the reader is left to re-interpret the original, in the light of later developments, and to alter the weighting to be attached to its component parts.

In retrospect it is now clear that Chamberlin intended his readers to ascribe increasing importance to the problems presented by *small* numbers and further to the phenomenon of *oligopolistic interdependence* – a condition which may prevail quite generally where numbers are large but firms are spatially distributed. To this problem, Chamberlin added those presented by Kaldor, who as we have seen, indicated that the pricing policies of firms selling quite different products could be affected by the fact that they are located in the *same* place.

In *all* of these cases we confront the problem of interdependence and a situation where the curves of revenue *and* of revenue product are conjectural. Brian Loasby added a further point in noting the problems of decision making under conditions of uncertainty. In the situations described above there is no clearly defined path to equilibrium; 'in this fog of ignorance, there is no equilibrium' (Loasby 1976: 189).

As Shackle noted in a passage cited in the Introduction:

> When economic theory elects to bring in imperfect competition and to recognise uncertainty, there is an end to the meaning of general equilibrium. Economics thereafter is the description, piece by piece, of a collection of fragments. These fragments may fit together into a brilliant, arrestingly suggestive mosaic, but they do not compose a pattern of unique, inevitable order (Shackle 1967: 295).

It is difficult to avoid the impression that the wreckage which Shackle identified has often been ignored (Shackle 1967: 27). In 1967 he wrote that after the lessons of the 1930s had been absorbed, economics provided an account 'of how men cope with scarcity and uncertainty' (*ibid.*: 7). But in another passage added to the Foreword of the 1983 edition he noted that in the years after 1945:

> Economics re-asserted its claim to be the science of rational conduct, able to inform itself adequately about the determining conditions in which its actions would work out their consequences. The 1970's have opened afresh the gulf between what we see around us and what the theory of business as a rational self-co-ordinating and fore-knowing action can explain (*ibid.*: vi).

As Paul Samuelson observed:

> Ironically, it was not until after World War II that economists generally began

> to think in terms of general equilibrium ... this represents an advance in logical clarity but something of a retreat in terms of realistic appraisal of actual imperfectly competitive market structures (in Kuenne 1967: 113).

Writing in 1961 Chamberlin noted that he could see no escape (and no reason to try to escape) from 'the conclusion that the ubiquitous forces of oligopoly (broadly defined) and of non-price competition (to namely only these) must be responsible for many loose ends, multiple optima and indeterminateness in one sense or another in groups and in the system' (Chamberlin 1961: 539). What we have to avoid is the temptation 'of formulating problems with the objective of assuring a determinate result' (Chamberlin 1957: 62). Yet in dealing with these problems, Chamberlin confronted a procedural difficulty which exercises in comparative statics as described in this volume also share.

In the world described by Chamberlin we confront a situation where firms effectively compete by *changing* the conditions which confront their rivals. Here the causes of change are *endogenous* so that in a sense the argument invites attention to the problem of disequilibrium as a special and essential feature of the economic process. It is hardly surprising that Chamberlin should have likened his own position to that of Schumpeter (Chamberlin 1957: 62–63). Elsewhere he observed that 'certain features of monopolistic competition would indicate that it is necessarily a theory of change to be associated with dynamics rather than with circular flows' (*ibid.*: 225).

The problem is one of change: the techniques used to solve that problem were however classically Marshallian. As Triffin has noted, 'Born and bred in a Marshallian environment, monopolistic competition has been, unto this day, encumbered by the fetters of particular equilibrium methodology' (Triffin 1956: 188). Chamberlin himself recognised the problem in remarking that he may have been misled, and proved misleading, by and through his application of a technique which, in Marshall's words, goes 'step by step, breaking up a complex question, studying one bit at a time, and at last combining ... partial solutions into a more or less complete solution of the whole riddle'.

In this context we should recall Joan Robinson's later appreciation of the point that a correct path would have entailed 'abandoning the static analysis and trying to come to terms with Marshall's theory of development' (Robinson 1951: vii–viii). Yet this is not the whole story.

Chamberlin undoubtedly recognised that theoretical structures have their limitations, wishing as he did to move the discussion in the direction of empirical research, so that Georgescu-Roegen was surely correct in emphasising his concern with 'the analysis of the actual' (in Kuenne 1967: 38).

The point has been widely made in the literature, notably by Galbraith (Galbraith 1948: 104, 107) and J. S. Bain (in Kuenne 1967: 152ff). In an interesting monograph on Chamberlin, Romney Robinson noted that he had 'pushed the whole of price analysis a major step towards that descriptive realism which had been so sadly lacking in post-Marshallian theory' (Robinson 1971: 42). He added that 'Chamberlin's monopolistic competition theory can fairly be described as an attempt to interpret more fully the world which Marshall discussed' (*ibid.*.: 10). In Chamberlin's own words, his book 'contains not a technique, but a way of looking at the economic system' (Chamberlin 1948: 204); in effect, a return to the perspective supplied by Marshall's *Industry and Trade* but by a circuitous and demanding route.

The theory of games, informative as it is, is of limited assistance here, which is possibly why Chamberlin did not choose to go down this route, despite the dramatic advances made in his lifetime.

Authorities

Andrews, P.W.S. (1964), *On Competition in Economic Theory*, London, Macmillan.

Bain, J.S. (1967), Chamberlin's Impact on Microeconomic Theory, in Kuenne (1967), chapter 7.

Blitch, C.P. (1983), Allan A. Young: A Curious Case of Professional Neglect, *History of Political Economy*, 15, 1–24.

Boulding, K. and Stigler, G.J. (1953), *Readings in Price Theory*, London, Allen and Unwin.

Chamberlin, E.H. (1948), *The Theory of Monopolistic Competition*, Cambridge, Harvard University Press.

Chamberlin, E.H. (1957), *Towards a More General Theory of Value*, Oxford, The University Press.

Chamberlin, E.H. (1961), The Origin and Early Development of Monopolistic Competition Theory, *Quarterly Journal of Economics*, 75, 515–543.

Demsetz, H. (1989), *Efficiency, Competition and Policy*, Blackwell.

Dewey, D. (1969), *The Theory of Imperfect Competition*, Columbia

Fellner, W. (1949), *Competition Among the Few*, New York, Alfred Knopf.

Fisher, I. (1898), Cournot and Mathematical Economics, *Quarterly Journal of Economics*, 12, 126–27.

Galbraith, J.K. (1948), Monopoly and the Concentration of Economic Power, in *A Survey of Contemporary Economics* ed. H.S. Ellis, Homewood, Richard D. Irwin, 1948.

Georgescu-Roegen, N. (1967), Chamberlin's New Economics and the Unit of Production, in Kuenne (1967), chapter 2.

Haley, B.F. (1948), Value and Distribution, in *A Survey of Contemporary Economics*, ed. H.S. Ellis, Homewood, Richard D. Irwin, 1948.

Hall, R.L. and Hitch, C.J. (1939), Price Theory and Business Behaviour, *Oxford Economic Papers*, 2, 12–45.

Hotelling, H. (1929), Stability in Competition, reprinted in Boulding and Stigler, chapter 23.

Kaldor, N. (1934), Mrs. Robinson's Economics of Imperfect Competition, *Economica*, I, 335–341.

Kaldor, N. (1935), Market imperfection and excess capacity, *Economica* 2, 33–50.

Keppler, J. (1994), *Monopolistic Competition Theory, Results and Implications*, Baltimore and London, The John Hopkins University Press.

Kuenne, R.E. (1967), *Monopolistic Competition Theory, Studies in Impact*, London, John Wiley.

Loasby, B.J. (1976), *Choice, Complexity and Ignorance*, Cambridge, The University Press.

Marshall, A. (1920), *Industry and Trade*, London, Macmillan.

Nikaido, H. (1975), *Monopolistic Competition and Effective Demand*, Princeton, Princeton University Press.

Phlips, L. (1983), *The Economics of Price Discrimination*, Cambridge, The University Press.

Pigou, A.C. (1924), *The Economics of Welfare*, London, Macmillan.

Rheinwald, T.P. (1977), The Genesis of Chamberlinian Monopolistic Competition Theory, *History of Political Economy*, 9, 522–534.

Robinson, Joan (1933), *The Economics of Imperfect Competition*, London, Macmillan 1951.

Robinson, J. (1951), *Collected Economic Papers*, Oxford, Basil Blackwell.

Robinson, R. (1971), *Edward H. Chamberlin*, New York, Columbia University Press.

Rothschild, R. (1987), The Theory of Monopolistic Competition: E.H. Chamberlin's Influence on Industrial Organisation Theory over Sixty Years, *Journal of Economic Studies*, 14 (1).

Samuelson, P.A. (1967), The Monopolistic Competition Revolution, in Kuenne (1967), chapter 5.

Samuelson, P.A. (1977), A Modern Theorist's Vindication of Adam Smith, *American Economic Association Papers and Proceedings*, 67, 42–49.

Schneider, E. (1967), Milestones on the way to the Theory of Monopolistic Competition, in Kuenne (1967), chapter 6.

Schumpeter, J.A. (1954), *History of Economic Analysis*, London, George Allen and Unwin.

Shackle, G.L.S. (1967), *The Years of High Theory*, Cambridge, University Press.

Skinner, A.S. (1981), Of Factor and Commodity Markets: A Note on E.H. Chamberlin, *Oxford Economic Papers*, 33, 122–34.

Skinner, A.S. (1983), The Origins and Development of Monopolistic Competition, *Journal of Economic Studies*, 10, 52–67.

Skinner, A.S. (1984), Oligopoly and the Theory of the Firm (with M.C. MacLennan) in *Economic Analysis in Historical Perspective*, ed. J. Creedy and D.P. O'Brien, London, Butterworths.

Skinner, A.S. (1986), Edward Chamberlin: The Theory of Monopolistic: A Re-orientation of Theory of Value, *Journal of Economic Studies*, 13, 27-44.

Sraffa, P. (1926), The Laws of Returns under Competitive Conditions, *Economic Journal*, 36, reprinted in Boulding and Stigler (1953), chapter 9.

Stigler, G.J. (1950), *Five Lectures on Economic Problems*, New York, Macmillan.

Stigler, G.J. (1965), Perfect Competition Historically Considered, *Essays on The History of Economics*, Chicago, University Press.

Sweezy, P.M. (1939), Demand Under Conditions of Oligopoly, reprinted in Boulding and Stigler (1953), chapter 20.

Triffin, R. (1956), *Monopolistic Competition and General Equilibrium Theory*, Cambridge, Harvard University Press.

Young, A. (1925), Review of Bowley's Mathematical Groundwork, *Journal of the American Statistical Association*, 20, 134.

Appendix

Mathematical Notes

The purpose of this Appendix is not to teach elementary mathematical economics. That purpose is already served by any one of a number of existing texts. Instead it is to offer some helpful commentary on the way mathematics has been employed at various steps in the main text and, in particular, to supply the intervening steps in the manipulation which was omitted from some of the derivations employed there. This should not only enable the reader who already has some grounding in the relevant mathematical techniques to develop a more confident understanding of their use, but also assist the reader who presently lacks such grounding to identify more precisely the areas where reference to a mathematical economics text would be beneficial.

The Appendix takes the form of a series of Notes on specific topics, with appropriate cross-referencing to the main body of the text, principally to the sections of it enclosed in square brackets. In general those sections offered a parallel treatment of specific technical parts of the argument, an alternative to the diagrammatic treatment more generally employed. The diagrammatic technique is an essentially visual device to help to resolve the problem of manipulating abstract concepts to obtain relevant results, frequently equilibrium outcomes. Thus, for example, equilibrium conditions can be specified in terms of tangencies or intersections between lines drawn in a graph. Its visual character hopefully makes the argument more easy to grasp. However, the diagrammatic approach has limitations, apart from obscuring the fact that lines in a graph are no more than visual representations of particular *mathematical* expressions. The diagrammatic approach lacks the greater generality of the mathematical approach. Greater generality is not just a matter of permitting the argument to be extended into situations which cannot be represented visually (i.e. beyond three dimensions). It is also a matter of providing greater insights into the nature of the concepts being employed. For example, the mathematical approach can reveal the significance of some of the special characteristics which have been given to the lines in the graphs: for example, the use of curves of particular shapes, in particular relationships to each other. Consequently, in terms of the pure logic of the argument, the mathematical approach obliges us to become aware of the full range of assumptions from which the abstract argument has been constructed, the assumptions necessary and just sufficient for the conclusions which have been obtained.

1. The Functions Representing Preferences and Production Possibilities

The key to the application of the mathematical method and its accompanying diagrammatic representation is a basic proposition: that consumers' preferences (in respect of combinations of quantities of different goods) and producers' production possibilities (in respect of combinations of quantities of different inputs) can be represented by a general class of continuous and differentiable mathematical functions. For example, in the case of preferences (see page 7):

$$U = f(X,Y)$$

where U is an indicator of preference and X and Y are quantities of two goods.

The other characteristics of these functions are prescribed only in very broad respects, although the manner in which the functions representing consumer preferences and production possibilities are separately manipulated allows the derivation of some distinctive conclusions.

Adoption of the basic proposition requires certain assumptions to be made about the nature of preferences and of production possibilities. The inherent (cardinal) measurability of quantities of inputs and outputs readily accommodates the representation of production by a numerical function, leaving the assumption of infinite divisibility (for the function to be continuous) of both inputs and outputs as the most obvious departure from reality. The matter is less straightforward in the case of preferences. Since declaring a 'preference' involves a comparison of only two items, further assumptions are necessary to develop the concept to allow a more general representation of preferences by a function: all pairs of items (bundles of quantities of goods, the 'baskets' of page 3) must be comparable on the same basis, and the comparison must be extendable in a particular respect from pair to pair – if A is preferred to B and B is preferred to C then this must imply A is preferred to C. These are respectively the assumptions of completeness of preferences and transitivity of preferences, two of the so-called axioms of choice.

The functions are initially assumed to lack global maxima, beyond which either preference or output would decline in response to additional quantities of goods or inputs. In the case of preferences this involves the further 'axiom' of insatiability ('more is always preferred to less'); in the case of production possibilities it may involve limiting the domain of the function on the grounds that the production of a particular level of output by the use of more inputs than the minimum physically necessary is uneconomic, or simply by assuming that if a global maximum of output exists it is unattainable, lying beyond the specific constraint.

That is, in the case of preferences:

$$\frac{\partial U}{\partial X}, \frac{\partial U}{\partial Y} > 0$$

In economic terminology marginal utilities (and marginal physical products) are always positive.

The functions are also assumed to have the property that contour lines (in the two variable case) on the surface are convex to the origin, at least locally. The 'axiom' of convexity provides the necessary feature in each case, interpreted economically as the 'imperfect substitutability' of either quantities of goods or quantities of inputs (see pages 7 and 25):

$$\frac{d^2Y}{dX^2} < 0 \text{ for a given value of the corresponding function.}$$

It will be appreciated that the concept of substitutability on which the logic of choice crucially depends thereby rests on the assumed existence and properties of the functions (i.e. the assumptions about preferences and production possibilities) and not directly on the intrinsic properties of the goods or inputs themselves: movement along a contour is simply a mathematical matter of different values of the arguments of the functions thus defined yielding the same value of the function.

2. The Total Differential

The concern for optimisation focusses attention on incremental changes in the value of the defined functions, which must in turn be due to changes in the values of the arguments of the functions. Incremental change in the value of a *single* variable, *holding all others constant*, produces a change in the value of the function, the relation defining the *partial derivative* of the function with respect to that variable. However, it is useful to have an expression which links a change in the value of the function to changes in all the independent variables. Thus the *total differential* (see page 8) defines a change in the value of the function as the sum of components arising from change in each of the variables, with each separate component being the product of the incremental change (the difference) in the particular variable concerned and the corresponding partial derivative. Thus given $U = f(X,Y)$ the total differential is

$$dU = \frac{\partial U}{\partial X}dX + \frac{\partial U}{\partial Y}dY$$

In effect, any change in the value of the function can be described as the resultant of a combination of movements due to independent changes in the values of each of the independent variables of the function. The intuition here may be supported by a simple analogy involving discrete changes: a distance from an origin to a location lying in, say, a northwesterly direction can be expressed as a combination of movements in a northerly and in a westerly direction, with the movement in each direction expressed in turn as a number of steps (the difference) times a particular length of stride (the partial derivative).

Given the concept of substitutability it is possible for the particular combination of movements (changes in the values of the independent variables) to be such as to leave the value of the function (the level of preference or the level of output) unchanged, whereupon manipulation of the total differential permits a conclusion to be drawn about the slope of the corresponding contour (indifference curve, price opportunity line, isoquant or transformation curve; see pages 8, 10, 28 and 33). This can usefully be extended to provide a link with constrained optimisation.

Setting the total differential of U = f(X,Y) equal to zero (which is the normal first-order condition for a relative extremum)

$$dU = \frac{\partial U}{\partial X}dX + \frac{\partial U}{\partial Y}dY = 0$$

By rearrangement

$$\frac{dX}{dY} = -\frac{\frac{\partial U}{\partial X}}{\frac{\partial U}{\partial Y}} \quad \text{for a given value of U}$$

This defines the slope of the indifference curve. The shape of the curve (i.e. how its slope changes as X and Y change, subject to U remaining constant) will be revealed by the derivative of this:

$$\frac{d\left(\frac{dY}{dX}\right)}{dX} = \frac{d^2Y}{dX^2} = -\frac{\frac{\partial U}{\partial Y}\frac{d\left(\frac{\partial U}{\partial X}\right)}{dX} - \frac{\partial U}{\partial X}\frac{d\left(\frac{\partial U}{\partial Y}\right)}{dX}}{\left(\frac{\partial U}{\partial Y}\right)^2}$$

$$= -\frac{\frac{\partial U}{\partial Y}\left(\frac{\partial^2 U}{\partial X^2} + \frac{\partial^2 U}{\partial X \partial Y}\frac{dY}{dX}\right) - \frac{\partial U}{\partial X}\left(\frac{\partial^2 U}{\partial X \partial Y} + \frac{\partial^2 U}{\partial Y^2}\frac{dY}{dX}\right)}{\left(\frac{\partial U}{\partial Y}\right)^2}$$

Now it was established (see pages 11–13) that for a constrained relative extremum

$$\frac{dY}{dX} = -\frac{\frac{\partial U}{\partial X}}{\frac{\partial U}{\partial Y}} = -\frac{Px}{Py}$$

By rearrangement

$$\frac{\partial U}{\partial X} = \frac{\frac{\partial U}{\partial Y} Px}{Py} \;;$$

Substituting in the expression for $\frac{d^2Y}{dX^2}$

$$\frac{d^2Y}{dX^2} = -\frac{\frac{\partial U}{\partial Y}\left(\frac{\partial^2 U}{\partial X^2} + \frac{\partial^2 U}{\partial X \partial Y}\left\{-\frac{Px}{Py}\right\}\right) - \frac{\frac{\partial U}{\partial Y} Px}{Py}\left(\frac{\partial^2 U}{\partial X \partial Y} + \frac{\partial^2 U}{\partial Y^2}\left\{-\frac{Px}{Py}\right\}\right)}{\left(\frac{\partial U}{\partial Y}\right)^2}$$

By rearrangement

$$= -\frac{\left(\frac{\partial^2 U}{\partial X^2} Py^2 - \frac{\partial^2 U}{\partial X \partial Y} PxPy - \frac{\partial^2 U}{\partial X \partial Y} PxPy + \frac{\partial^2 U}{\partial Y^2} Px^2\right)}{\frac{\partial U}{\partial Y} Py^2}$$

$$= \frac{2\frac{\partial^2 U}{\partial X \partial Y} PxPy - \frac{\partial^2 U}{\partial X^2} Py^2 - \frac{\partial^2 U}{\partial Y^2} Px^2}{\frac{\partial U}{\partial Y} Py^2}$$

Now the assumption of convexity of the indifference curve ensures that $\frac{d^2Y}{dX^2} > 0$ (that is, the negative slope of the indifference curve becomes less so as X increases). Since the denominator of the right-hand expression must be positive (prices are positive and the assumption of insatiability ensures that the marginal utility of Y is positive) it follows that the numerator must be positive. This conclusion will be of significance later.

3. The Lagrangean Method of Constrained Optimisation

The functions representing preferences and production are initially assumed to have no operationally relevant global maxima, so optimisation (choosing the most preferred combination, or maximising output) must involve relative or local extrema or turning points. However, the functions are defined to be monotonic – always increasing – over their relevant domains; they also lack relative extrema. So the existence of relative extrema (i.e. optimal outcomes) rests on the interaction between these functions and other functions representing operative constraints on the permissible combinations of values of the independent variables.

The Lagrangean method (see page 12) is a means whereby the objective function (representing preferences or production) may be combined with the constraint function (the price opportunity line or the isocost line) such that the standard mathematical approach to finding relative extrema may still be employed. The standard approach involves finding the first-order partial derivatives of a function, setting them equal to zero and then solving for the corresponding values of the independent variables. These values are then substituted in the second-order derivatives, the sign of which is sufficient to identify the nature of the relative extrema: maximum, minimum or point of inflection. The manner in which the objective function and the constraint are combined in the Lagrangean expression (a new function), through the introduction of a new variable (an arbitrary or undetermined variable termed the Lagrangean multiplier), means that one of the partial derivatives of the new function, when set equal to zero, involves satisfying the constraint. And when that constraint is satisfied, the Lagrangean expression itself collapses to become simply the original objective function. In other words a particular value of the objective function has been found where a relative extremum exists due to the interaction of the constraint with the objective function; the function has been optimised in relation to the given constraint.

Thus given the preference function $U = U(X,Y)$ and the constraint $R = PxX + PyY$ where R is the budget and Px and Py the prices of X and Y respectively, then the corresponding Lagrangean expression can be created by introducing a new variable λ (the Lagrangean multiplier), and giving it a particular coefficient obtained from the rearrangement of the constraint $R - PxX - PyY = 0$. Let L represent the new Lagrangean expression:

$$L = U(X,Y) + \lambda(R - PxX - PyY)$$

whereupon the first-order partial derivatives become:

$$\frac{\partial L}{\partial X} = \frac{\partial U}{\partial X} - \lambda P_x$$

$$\frac{\partial L}{\partial Y} = \frac{\partial U}{\partial Y} - \lambda P_y$$

$$\frac{\partial L}{\partial \lambda} = R - P_x X - P_y Y$$

These are set equal to zero, whereupon it becomes apparent from the nature of the third equation that the constraint is indeed satisfied. But if it is satisfied then the coefficient of the Lagrangean multiplier is zero, and the Lagrangean expression becomes the objective function U. The solution values of X and Y which define the relative extremum of L are values which define the corresponding value of U. Note, however, that *without the constraint* there is no relative extremum of U at these values of X and Y, given the assumptions which define the character of U.

There remain two issues: the question of the nature of the relative extremum, which may be maximum, minimum or point of inflection, and the economic significance of the Lagrangean multiplier. Both can be illuminated by the use of the total differential introduced in the preceding Note.

The Second Order Condition

The first-order condition can be written in terms of the total differentials of the objective function and the constraint, not just the partial derivatives of the Lagrangean expression: the condition is $dU = 0$ subject to $dR = 0$ (that is, in the case of a maximum, the budget has been used up to the point where there can be no further increase in U). The second-order condition (to discriminate between the possible types of extrema) requires that at the relative extremum d^2U has a particular sign, in terms of the second-order total differential: the requirement for a maximum is that $d^2U < 0$.

Now given $U = U(X,Y)$, and writing the constraint in general form as $R = R(X,Y)$, the respective total differentials are

$$dU = \frac{\partial U}{\partial X} dX + \frac{\partial U}{\partial Y} dY \text{ and}$$
$$dR = \frac{\partial R}{\partial X} dX + \frac{\partial R}{\partial Y} dY$$

Satisfying the first-order condition by setting these equal to zero, and rearranging

$$\frac{\dfrac{\partial U}{\partial X}}{\dfrac{\partial U}{\partial Y}} = \frac{\dfrac{\partial R}{\partial X}}{\dfrac{\partial R}{\partial Y}}$$

(Given that the constraint is specifically the linear relation $R = PxX + PyY$ it follows that the right-hand side is the ratio of the prices of the goods, this yielding the result of page 13).

In general terms the second-order total differential is

$$d^2U = \frac{\partial(dU)}{\partial X} dX + \frac{\partial(dU)}{\partial Y} dY$$
$$= \frac{\partial\left(\frac{\partial U}{\partial X}dX + \frac{\partial U}{\partial Y}dY\right)}{\partial X} dX + \frac{\partial\left(\frac{\partial U}{\partial X}dX + \frac{\partial U}{\partial Y}dY\right)}{\partial Y} dY$$

Just as the original involved changes in both X and Y so also must d^2U.

However for the constrained relative extremum $dR = 0$, in which case X and Y are not free to vary independently of each other: the constraint prevents that. Setting dR equal to zero it follows that dX and dY are linked such that

$$dY = -\frac{\frac{\partial R}{\partial X}}{\frac{\partial R}{\partial Y}}dX$$

Generally dX and dY are both constants in the total differentials. However, due to the constraint if one changes then the other must change as a result, making it a variable. This must be taken into account when deriving the second-order total differential.

Following this argument, and treating dY as dependent on dX, the second term in each bracket has to be treated as a product, since not only does the partial derivative change with respect to the relevant variable, so also does the difference dY.

$$d^2U = \left(\frac{\partial^2 U}{\partial X^2}dX + \frac{\partial^2 U}{\partial Y \partial X}dY + \frac{\partial U}{\partial Y}\frac{\partial(dY)}{\partial X}\right)dX + \left(\frac{\partial^2 U}{\partial X \partial Y}dX + \frac{\partial^2 U}{\partial Y^2}dY + \frac{\partial U}{\partial Y}\frac{\partial(dY)}{\partial Y}\right)dY$$

$$d^2U = \frac{\partial^2 U}{\partial X^2}(dX)^2 + \frac{\partial^2 U}{\partial Y \partial X}dXdY + \frac{\partial U}{\partial Y}\frac{\partial(dY)}{\partial X}dX + \frac{\partial^2 U}{\partial X \partial Y}dXdY + \frac{\partial^2 U}{\partial Y^2}(dY)^2 + \frac{\partial U}{\partial Y}\frac{\partial(dY)}{\partial Y}dY$$

$$= \frac{\partial^2 U}{\partial X^2}(dX)^2 + 2\frac{\partial^2 U}{\partial X \partial Y}dXdY + \frac{\partial^2 U}{\partial Y^2}(dY)^2 + \frac{\partial U}{\partial Y}\left(\frac{\partial(dY)}{\partial X}dX + \frac{\partial(dY)}{\partial Y}dY\right)$$

$$= \frac{\partial^2 U}{\partial X^2}(dX)^2 + 2\frac{\partial^2 U}{\partial X \partial Y}dXdY + \frac{\partial^2 U}{\partial Y^2}(dY)^2 + \frac{\partial U}{\partial Y}d^2Y$$

Now by the same line of reasoning

$$d^2R = \frac{\partial^2 R}{\partial X^2}(dX)^2 + 2\frac{\partial^2 R}{\partial X \partial Y}dXdY + \frac{\partial^2 R}{\partial Y^2}(dY)^2 + \frac{\partial R}{\partial Y}d^2Y$$

But the constraint requires $dR = 0$, so $d^2R = 0$. In addition, however, the linear form of the constraint ensures that

$$\frac{\partial^2 R}{\partial X^2} = \frac{\partial^2 R}{\partial Y^2} = \frac{\partial^2 R}{\partial X \partial Y} = 0$$

Consequently the final term of d^2R must also equal zero, and since $\frac{\partial R}{\partial Y} > 0$ it follows that $d^2Y = 0$.

In addition the form of the constraint yields the result that

$$dY = -\frac{\frac{\partial R}{\partial X}}{\frac{\partial R}{\partial Y}} dX \quad = -\frac{Px}{Py} dX$$

Substituting for d^2Y and dY

$$d^2U \;= \frac{\partial^2 U}{\partial X^2}(dX)^2 - 2\frac{\partial^2 U}{\partial X \partial Y}(dX)^2\left(\frac{Px}{Py}\right) + \frac{\partial^2 U}{\partial Y^2}\left(\frac{Px}{Py}\right)^2(dX)^2$$

Now the general rule for a maximum is that $d^2U < 0$, so

$$\frac{\partial^2 U}{\partial X^2}(dX)^2 - 2\frac{\partial^2 U}{\partial X \partial Y}(dX)^2\left(\frac{Px}{Py}\right) + \frac{\partial^2 U}{\partial Y^2}\left(\frac{Px}{Py}\right)^2(dX)^2 < 0$$

Dividing through by $(dX)^2$ and rearranging, it follows that the second-order condition for the constrained maximum is that

$$2PxPy\frac{\partial^2 U}{\partial X \partial Y} - Py^2\frac{\partial^2 U}{\partial X^2} - Px^2\frac{\partial^2 U}{\partial Y^2} > 0$$

Satisfaction of this condition is guaranteed by the assumption of convexity of the indifference curves, as is apparent from Note 2 above. Consequently the constrained relative extremum is indeed a maximum.

The Lagrangean Multiplier

The matter of the economic significance of the Lagrangean multiplier (λ) can also be illuminated by manipulating the relevant total differentials:

$$dU = \frac{\partial U}{\partial X}dX + \frac{\partial U}{\partial Y}dY$$
$$dR = \frac{\partial R}{\partial X}dX + \frac{\partial R}{\partial Y}dY$$

On this occasion they are first converted into total *derivatives* with respect to R, the budget, by dividing through by dR:

$$\frac{dU}{dR} = \frac{\partial U}{\partial X}\frac{dX}{dR} + \frac{\partial U}{\partial Y}\frac{dY}{dR}$$
$$\frac{dR}{dR} = 1 = \frac{\partial R}{\partial X}\frac{dX}{dR} + \frac{\partial R}{\partial Y}\frac{dY}{dR}$$

If the first-order conditions for a constrained relative extremum are satisfied, then:

$$\frac{\partial U}{dX} = \lambda Px \qquad \text{and} \qquad \frac{\partial U}{dY} = \lambda Px$$

Given the linearity of the budget constraint

$$\frac{\partial R}{dX} = Px \qquad \text{and} \qquad \frac{\partial R}{dY} = Px$$

Substituting in the expression for $\frac{dU}{dR}$

$$\begin{aligned}\frac{dU}{dR} &= \lambda Px \frac{dX}{dR} + \lambda Px \frac{dY}{dR} \\ &= \lambda\left(Px \frac{dX}{dR} + Px \frac{dY}{dR}\right) \\ &= \lambda\left(\frac{\partial R}{\partial X}\frac{dX}{dR} + \frac{\partial R}{\partial Y}\frac{dY}{dR}\right) \\ &= \lambda\left(\frac{dR}{dR}\right) \\ &= \lambda(1) \\ &= \lambda\end{aligned}$$

Thus in relation to the constrained maximum value of U, the Lagrangean multiplier turns out to be the contribution to that value from incremental variation in the budget. This can be variously called the marginal utility of income or (less satisfactorily) money, in the case of maximisation of preferences. Given the assumption of insatiability it follows that it is positive. In the case of output maximisation (subject to a cost constraint) it is analogously the marginal product of the cost outlay.

4. The Slutsky Equation

The mathematical derivation of the Slutsky Equation (which establishes that the Price Effect is the sum of a Substitution Effect and an Income Effect) commences with the first-order conditions for a constrained relative extremum (see page 13 and Note 3 above):

$$\begin{aligned}\frac{\partial L}{\partial X} &= \frac{\partial U}{\partial X} - \lambda P_x &= 0 \\ \frac{\partial L}{\partial Y} &= \frac{\partial U}{\partial Y} - \lambda P_y &= 0 \\ \frac{\partial L}{\partial \lambda} &= R - P_x X - P_y Y &= 0\end{aligned}$$

The ultimate objective is to explore the consequences for the particular values of X and Y which satisfy these conditions (say X* and Y*) of changes in the price of one of the goods (say Px). The procedure is to take the total differentials of these equations in respect of X* and Y*, initially allowing *all* the variables and parameters to change, and then to draw out the implications of the system of equations obtained. The procedure is somewhat cumbersome and lengthy without the use of matrix algebra, although it employs the now-familiar total differential; the same manipulation with the aid of matrix algebra can be found in more comprehensive texts on mathematical economics.

The required total differentials are as follows:

$$\frac{\partial^2 U}{\partial X^2}dX^* + \frac{\partial^2 U}{\partial X \partial Y}dY^* - Pxd\lambda - \lambda dPx = 0 \qquad (1)$$

$$\frac{\partial^2 U}{\partial Y^2}dY^* + \frac{\partial^2 U}{\partial Y \partial X}dX^* - Pyd\lambda - \lambda dPy = 0 \qquad (2)$$

$$dR - PxdX^* - PydY^* - X^*dPx - Y^*dPy = 0 \qquad (3)$$

The next step is to solve this set of simultaneous equations for the particular difference dX*. The first stage is to eliminate dY*; from (3):

$$dY^* = \left(\frac{dR - PxdX^* - X^*dPx - Y^*dPy}{Py}\right)$$

Substitute in (1) and (2)

$$\frac{\partial^2 U}{\partial X \partial Y}\left(\frac{dR - PxdX^* - X^*dPx - Y^*dPy}{Py}\right) + \frac{\partial^2 U}{\partial X^2}dX^* - Pxd\lambda - \lambda dPx = 0$$

That is, equation (4):

$$\frac{\partial^2 U}{\partial X \partial Y}(dR - PxdX^* - X^*dPx - Y^*dPy) + \frac{\partial^2 U}{\partial X^2}dX^*Py - PxPyd\lambda - \lambda PydPx = 0$$

And

$$\frac{\partial^2 U}{\partial Y^2}\left(\frac{dR - PxdX^* - X^*dPx - Y^*dPy}{Py}\right) + \frac{\partial^2 U}{\partial Y \partial X}dX^* - Pyd\lambda - \lambda dPy = 0$$

That is, equation (5)

$$\frac{\partial^2 U}{\partial Y^2}(dR - PxdX^* - X^*dPx - Y^*dPy) + \frac{\partial^2 U}{\partial Y \partial X}dX^*Py - Py^2d\lambda - \lambda PydPy = 0$$

The next step is to eliminate dλ, using (4) rearranged slightly and (5):

$$d\lambda = \frac{\frac{\partial^2 U}{\partial X \partial Y}(dR - PxdX^* - X^*dPx - Y^*dPy) + \frac{\partial^2 U}{\partial X^2}dX^*Py - \lambda PydPx}{PxPy} \qquad (6)$$

$$d\lambda = \frac{\frac{\partial^2 U}{\partial Y^2}(dR - PxdX^* - X^*dPx - Y^*dPy) + \frac{\partial^2 U}{\partial Y \partial X}dX^*Py - \lambda PydPy}{Py^2} \qquad (7)$$

Set (6) = (7) and cross-multiply the denominators:

$$Py^2\left(\frac{\partial^2 U}{\partial X \partial Y}(dR - PxdX^* - X^*dPx - Y^*dPy) + \frac{\partial^2 U}{\partial X^2}dX^*Py - \lambda PydPx\right)$$
$$= PxPy\left(\frac{\partial^2 U}{\partial Y^2}(dR - PxdX^* - X^*dPx - Y^*dPy) + \frac{\partial^2 U}{\partial Y \partial X}dX^*Py - \lambda PydPy\right)$$

Group the terms in dX* on the left-hand side:

$$Py^2\left(-\frac{\partial^2 U}{\partial X \partial Y}PxdX^* + \frac{\partial^2 U}{\partial X^2}dX^*Py\right) - PxPy\left(-\frac{\partial^2 U}{\partial Y^2}PxdX^* + \frac{\partial^2 U}{\partial Y \partial X}dX^*Py\right)$$
$$= -Py^2\left(\frac{\partial^2 U}{\partial X \partial Y}(dR - X^*dPx - Y^*dPy) - \lambda PydPx\right)$$
$$+ PxPy\left(\frac{\partial^2 U}{\partial Y^2}(dR - X^*dPx - Y^*dPy) - \lambda PydPy\right)$$

Extract dX* from the left-hand side:

$$dX^*\left(-\frac{\partial^2 U}{\partial X \partial Y}PxPy^2 + \frac{\partial^2 U}{\partial X^2}Py^3 + \frac{\partial^2 U}{\partial Y^2}Px^2Py - \frac{\partial^2 U}{\partial Y \partial X}PxPy^2\right)$$
$$= \left(PxPy\frac{\partial^2 U}{\partial Y^2} - Py^2\frac{\partial^2 U}{\partial X \partial Y}\right)(dR - X^*dPx - Y^*dPy) + \lambda Py^3dPx - \lambda PxPy^2dPy$$

Rearrange extracting –Py from both numerator and denominator:

$$dX^* = \frac{-Py\left(\left(-Px\frac{\partial^2 U}{\partial Y^2} + Py\frac{\partial^2 U}{\partial X \partial Y}\right)(dR - X^*dPx - Y^*dPy) - \lambda Py^2dPx + \lambda PxPydPy\right)}{-Py\left(-\frac{\partial^2 U}{\partial Y^2}Px^2 + 2\frac{\partial^2 U}{\partial X \partial Y}PxPy - \frac{\partial^2 U}{\partial X^2}Py^2\right)}$$

Cancel –Py and rearrange the numerator.

$$dX^* = \frac{\left(Px\frac{\partial^2 U}{\partial Y^2} - Py\frac{\partial^2 U}{\partial X \partial Y}\right)(dR - X^*dPx - Y^*dPy) - \lambda Py^2dPx + \lambda PxPydPy}{\left(-\frac{\partial^2 U}{\partial Y^2}Px^2 + 2\frac{\partial^2 U}{\partial X \partial Y}PxPy - \frac{\partial^2 U}{\partial X^2}Py^2\right)}$$

Note that the denominator of this expression has been encountered before (see Notes 2 and 3: the assumption of convexity of indifference curves ensured it had a positive value and thereby satisfied the second-order condition for a constrained maximum). For the sake of simplicity represent the denominator by D, noting that it has a positive value, and divide the quotient into two parts for ease of manipulation, to obtain equation (8):

$$dX^* = \frac{\left(Px\frac{\partial^2 U}{\partial Y^2} - Py\frac{\partial^2 U}{\partial X \partial Y}\right)(dR - X^*dPx - Y^*dPy)}{D} - \frac{\lambda Py^2 dPx - \lambda PxPydPy}{D}$$

The final stage is to examine the implications of this expression. Note that it shows the consequences for X* of change in all the relevant elements of the model; in that respect it is the total differential of X*. However, the effects of change in Px alone can be identified by substituting $dPy = dR = 0$. The consequences for X* are then found by dividing through by dPx:

$$\frac{dX^*}{dPx} = \frac{-X^*\left(Px\frac{\partial^2 U}{\partial Y^2} - Py\frac{\partial^2 U}{\partial X \partial Y}\right)}{D} - \frac{\lambda Py^2}{D} \tag{9}$$

which is in effect the *partial* derivative of X* with respect to Px, given the assumed constancy of the other variables Py and R.

However, a further insight can be obtained by holding both prices constant and varying the budget R instead: by substituting $dPx = dPy = 0$ and dividing through by dR:

$$\frac{dX^*}{dR} = \frac{\left(Px\frac{\partial^2 U}{\partial Y^2} - Py\frac{\partial^2 U}{\partial X \partial Y}\right)}{D} \tag{10}$$

Again this is in effect a partial derivative of X*, this time with respect to R, given the assumed constancy of Px and Py. Note that whether it is positive or negative depends on the relative magnitudes of the terms in the brackets, i.e. the extent to which the marginal utility of Y is affected by further change change in Y relative to change in X, and the relative prices).

Lastly consider a change in X* such that U remained unchanged (i.e. a movement along an indifference curve). Such a change would keep the total differential of $U = f(X,Y)$ equal to zero:

$$dU = \frac{\partial U}{\partial X}dX^* + \frac{\partial U}{\partial Y}dY^* = 0$$

Satisfaction of the first-order condition for the constrained maximum requires

$$\frac{\frac{\partial U}{\partial X}}{\frac{\partial U}{\partial Y}} = \frac{Px}{Py}$$

which implies

$$Px = \frac{\partial U}{\partial X} \text{ and } Py = \frac{\partial U}{\partial Y}$$

Substituting in the total differential:

$$PxdX^* + PydY^* = 0$$

But from equation (3)

$$dR - PxdX^* - PydY^* - X^*dPx - Y^*dPy = 0 \qquad (3)$$

Hence for such a change in X*

$$dR - X^*dPx - Y^*dPy = 0$$

Substituting this in (8), while assuming that Py is constant (i.e. dPy = 0), and dividing by dPx:

$$\left(\frac{\partial X^*}{\partial Px}\right)_{dU=0} = -\frac{\lambda Py^2}{D} \qquad (11)$$

Note that this is definitely negative since D and λ are positive by assumption.

Now it is possible to assemble the various implications of the expression for dX*. Combining equations (9), (10) and (11), and using the notation of partial derivatives, the result is obtained that

$$\frac{dX^*}{dPx} = \left(\frac{\partial X^*}{\partial Px}\right)_{dU=0} - X^*\left(\frac{\partial X^*}{\partial R}\right)_{dPx=dPy=0}$$

This is the Slutsky Equation. It shows that the effect on X* of a change in the price of X alone (the Price Effect) breaks down into two components: one is a consequential movement along an indifference curve (the first term, a Substitution Effect), the other being dependent on the effect which a change in the budget, prices held constant) would have had on X* (the second term, an Income Effect). However, the budget has changed only due to the change in Px under consideration. So the second term should be thought of as a total derivative, allowing the equation to be re-written as

$$\frac{dX^*}{dPx} = \left(\frac{\partial X^*}{\partial Px}\right)_{dU = 0} + \frac{\partial X}{\partial R}\frac{dR}{dPx}$$

the form employed on page 21.

Now given that D and λ are positive by assumption (of convexity and insatiability), it follows from (11) that the Substitution Effect is always negative. However, the sign of the Income Effect is indeterminate because it follows from (10) that the sign of $\left(\frac{\partial X^*}{\partial R}\right)_{dPx = dPy = 0}$ is indeterminate, depending on the relative magnitudes of two partial derivatives. Thus even although an increase in Px effectively *reduces* R (given Py) it is permissible for the Income Effect to yield an *increase* in X*.

5. Elasticities

The traditional focus within economics on comparative statics (comparison of equilibria arising from changes in selected parameters) has directed attention to the responsiveness of particular dependent variables to change in corresponding independent variables (e.g. the responsiveness of quantity demanded to change in price of the good concerned). This has led to an emphasis on the concept of elasticity (of demand, of supply). The mathematical concept of responsiveness is simply the derivative, either partial or total depending on context. The drawback shared by the mathematical concepts is that in their application to concrete cases they assume particular dimension, that is, they are measured in units peculiar to the application under consideration (notwithstanding their incremental nature). For example, the partial derivative of quantity of a particular good with respect to price is a measure of units of quantity of the particular good per unit price. This uniqueness prevents the comparison of derivatives from different applications. Accordingly a dimensionless measure would have advantages for that purpose: hence the usefulness of the concept of elasticity, a ratio of quotients of the same particular dimension, and thus a pure number.

(In the case of functions representing preferences there is a particular problem that, despite the function being understood to represent merely an ordering rather than a cardinal measure of preference, the derivative of the function (the marginal utility) still conveys an impression of cardinality given its implicit dimension. The role in the specification of the equilibrium solution of a *ratio* of marginal utilities (and thus a pure number) avoids that particular problem, in a manner analogous to that of the elasticity).

The particular ratio which defines an elasticity differs from the derivative in another significant respect: the latter is a measure (of the slope of the function) at a specific point in the domain of the function without regard to the co-ordinates of that point, while the former takes into account the relative position of that point, directly involving the values of the function and the independent variable(s).

This Note is concerned with the technical issue of revealing the association between the various forms which elasticity can take, and the mathematical properties of the functions. Some steps have already been taken in that direction (see pages 60–64), but there remain a few issues worth tackling.

The first of these is to provide the manipulation required to link the Slutsky Equation (see the preceding Note) with the corresponding elasticities.

The Slutsky equation previously derived is

$$\frac{\partial X^*}{\partial Px} = \left(\frac{dX^*}{dPx}\right)_{dU=0} - X^*\left(\frac{\partial X^*}{\partial R}\right)_{dPx=dPy=0}$$

First multiply both sides by the ratio $\frac{Px}{X^*}$, and multiply the second term of the right-hand side by $\frac{R}{R}$, hence:

$$\frac{\partial X^* Px}{\partial Px X^*} = \frac{Px}{X^*}\left(\frac{dX^*}{dPx}\right)_{dU=0} - \frac{Px R}{X^* R} X^*\left(\frac{\partial X^*}{\partial R}\right)_{dPx=dPy=0}$$

It should be apparent that the left-hand term is the own price elasticity of demand, previously represented by ε_{XX} (see page 61).

The second term of the right-hand side can be rearranged:

$$\frac{\partial X^* Px}{\partial Px X^*} = \frac{Px}{X^*}\left(\frac{dX^*}{dPx}\right)_{dU=0} - \frac{Px X^*}{R}\frac{R}{X^*}\left(\frac{\partial X^*}{\partial R}\right)_{dPx=dPy=0}$$

Now $\frac{PxX^*}{R}$ (part of the second term) is the proportion of the budget devoted to X, previously represented by α_X (see page 63), while $\frac{R}{X^*}\left(\frac{\partial X^*}{\partial R}\right)_{dPx=dPy=0}$ is the elasticity of X with respect to the budget R, i.e. the income elasticity of X previously represented by ε_{XR} (see page 61).

There remains the first term of the right-hand side. It is apparent that it has the same form as the own price elasticity except that it relates to a context where $dU = 0$, that is, where the change in price has been (notionally) accompanied by a change in the budget to provide compensation for the change in price. (The substitution effect, it will be recalled, involves a movement along an indifference curve, leaving U unchanged). This term can thus be defined as a compensated own price elasticity, ξ_{XX}.

Thus the first step has transformed the Slutsky equation into

$$\varepsilon_{XX} = \xi_{XX} - \alpha_X \varepsilon_{XR}$$

The next step is to give further consideration to the concept of the compensated elasticity, by introducing the compensated cross-price elasticity, ξ_{XY}. This is done by expressing the Slutsky equation in relation to change in the price of Y, rather than change in the price of X. (That is, in terms of Note 4, dividing equation (8) by dPy, with $dPx = dR = 0$):

$$\frac{\partial X^*}{\partial Py} = \left(\frac{dX^*}{dPy}\right)_{dU=0} - Y^*\left(\frac{\partial X^*}{\partial R}\right)_{dPx=dPy=0}$$

Now multiply both sides by the ratio $\frac{Py}{X^*}$, and multiply the second term of the right-hand side by $\frac{R}{R}$, hence:

$$\frac{\partial X^* Py}{\partial Py X^*} = \frac{Py}{X^*}\left(\frac{dX^*}{dPy}\right)_{dU=0} - \frac{PyR}{X^*R}Y^*\left(\frac{\partial X^*}{\partial R}\right)_{dPx=dPy=0}$$

which becomes, in terms parallel to the preceding manipulation:

$$\varepsilon_{XY} = \xi_{XY} - \alpha_Y \varepsilon_{XR}$$

The left-hand term is the cross price elasticity of X (see page 61), while the first term on the right is the compensated cross price elasticity of X.

Note 4 established the result that

$$\left(\frac{dX^*}{dPx}\right)_{dU=0} = -\frac{\lambda Py^2}{D} \qquad (11)$$

By a similar manipulation of equation (8) it follows that

$$\left(\frac{dX^*}{dPy}\right)_{dU=0} = \frac{\lambda PxPy}{D} \qquad (12)$$

These are converted into compensated elasticities by multiplication by the corresponding ratios:

$$\xi_{XX} = -\frac{\lambda Py^2}{D}\frac{Px}{X^*}$$

$$\xi_{XY} = \frac{\lambda PxPy}{D}\frac{Py}{X^*}$$

Consequently

$$\begin{aligned}\xi_{XX} + \xi_{XY} &= -\frac{\lambda Py^2}{D}\frac{Px}{X^*} + \frac{\lambda PxPy}{D}\frac{Py}{X^*} \\ &= \frac{-\lambda PxPy^2 + \lambda PxPy^2}{DX^*} \\ &= 0\end{aligned}$$

Returning to the results obtained for ε_{XX} and ε_{XY} it then follows that as

$$\varepsilon_{XX} = \xi_{XX} - \alpha_X \varepsilon_{XR}$$

and

$$\varepsilon_{XY} = \xi_{XY} - \alpha_Y \varepsilon_{XR}$$

it follows that

$$\begin{aligned}\varepsilon_{XX} &= \xi_{XX} + (\xi_{XY} - \alpha_Y \varepsilon_{XR} - \varepsilon_{XY}) - \alpha_X \varepsilon_{XR} \\ &= (\xi_{XX} + \xi_{XY}) - \varepsilon_{XY} - \varepsilon_{XR}(\alpha_X + \alpha_Y) \\ &= -\varepsilon_{XY} - \varepsilon_{XR} \\ &= -(\varepsilon_{XY} + \varepsilon_{XR})\end{aligned}$$

since, in the second line, the first bracketed term equals zero and the second (the sum of the proportions of the budget exhausted on the only two goods) equals unity. That is, the own price elasticity in respect of a particular good equals the negative of the sum of the cross price elasticity and the income elasticity, as noted on page 63.

The compensated price elasticities introduced a measure of responsiveness associated with movement along a contour of the relevant function (an indifference curve or an isoquant), in the specific context of a (notional) compensating change in the budget. A further measure of responsiveness connected with movement along these contours is the elasticity of substitution: it focusses on the responsiveness of the ratio of the values of the independent variables to the change in the slope of the contour in the vicinity of that point. (It will be recalled that the slope of the contour is either the Marginal Rate of Substitution or the Marginal Rate of Technical Substitution, depending on context).

The elasticity of substitution σ can be defined as follows, where S is, say, the slope of the indifference curve, i.e. the MRS:

$$\sigma = \frac{d\left(\frac{Y}{X}\right)}{dS} \frac{S}{\frac{Y}{X}}$$

In addition the following three relations are relevant:

$$d\left(\frac{Y}{X}\right) = \frac{XdY - YdX}{X^2}$$

$$dS = \frac{\partial S}{\partial X} dX + \frac{\partial S}{\partial Y} dY$$

$$dY = -\frac{\frac{\partial U}{\partial X}}{\frac{\partial U}{\partial Y}}dX \qquad \text{(See Note 3)}$$

$$= -SdX$$

Substituting these in the expression for σ

$$\sigma = \frac{\frac{XdY - YdX}{X^2}}{\left(\frac{\partial S}{\partial X}dX + \frac{\partial S}{\partial Y}dY\right)}\frac{S}{\frac{Y}{X}}$$

$$= \frac{(-XSdX - YdX)\ S}{XY\left(\frac{\partial S}{\partial X}dX - \frac{\partial S}{\partial Y}SdX\right)}$$

$$= \frac{-dX(Y + XS)}{-dX\left(XY\left(\frac{\partial S}{\partial Y}S - \frac{\partial S}{\partial X}\right)\right)}\frac{\frac{\partial U}{\partial X}}{\frac{\partial U}{\partial Y}}$$

Cancelling –dX and expanding $S = \frac{\frac{\partial U}{\partial X}}{\frac{\partial U}{\partial Y}}$:

$$\sigma = \frac{\frac{\partial U}{\partial X}\left(\frac{\partial U}{\partial X}X + \frac{\partial U}{\partial Y}Y\right)}{\frac{\partial U}{\partial Y}XY\left(\frac{\partial U \partial S}{\partial X \partial Y} - \frac{\partial U \partial S}{\partial Y \partial X}\right)}$$

Given the expression for S the bracketed term in the denominator can be manipulated as follows:

$$\left(\frac{\partial U}{\partial X}\left(\frac{\frac{\partial U}{\partial Y}\frac{\partial\left(\frac{\partial U}{\partial X}\right)}{\partial Y} - \frac{\partial\left(\frac{\partial U}{\partial Y}\right)}{\partial Y}\frac{\partial U}{\partial X}}{\left(\frac{\partial U}{\partial Y}\right)^2}\right) - \frac{\partial U}{\partial Y}\left(\frac{\frac{\partial U}{\partial Y}\frac{\partial\left(\frac{\partial U}{\partial X}\right)}{\partial X} - \frac{\partial\left(\frac{\partial U}{\partial Y}\right)}{\partial X}\frac{\partial U}{\partial X}}{\left(\frac{\partial U}{\partial Y}\right)^2}\right)\right)$$

$$= \frac{\left(\frac{\partial U}{\partial X}\frac{\partial U}{\partial Y}\frac{\partial^2 U}{\partial X \partial Y} - \frac{\partial U}{\partial X}\frac{\partial U \partial^2 U}{\partial X \partial Y^2} - \frac{\partial U}{\partial Y}\frac{\partial U}{\partial Y}\frac{\partial^2 U}{\partial X^2} + \frac{\partial U}{\partial X}\frac{\partial U}{\partial Y}\frac{\partial^2 U}{\partial X \partial Y}\right)}{\left(\frac{\partial U}{\partial Y}\right)^2}$$

$$= \frac{\left(2\frac{\partial^2 U}{\partial X \partial Y}\frac{\partial U}{\partial X}\frac{\partial U}{\partial Y} - \left(\frac{\partial U}{\partial X}\right)^2 \frac{\partial^2 U}{\partial Y^2} - \left(\frac{\partial U}{\partial Y}\right)^2 \frac{\partial^2 U}{\partial X^2}\right)}{\left(\frac{\partial U}{\partial Y}\right)^2}$$

Now the numerator of this expression is related to the expression which appeared in Note 2, and which in Note 4 was represented by D; let this new expression be represented by D'. Accordingly, this expression simplifies to

$$\frac{D'}{\left(\frac{\partial U}{\partial Y}\right)^2}$$

Hence,

$$\sigma = \frac{\frac{\partial U \partial U}{\partial X \partial Y}\left(\frac{\partial U}{\partial X}X + \frac{\partial U}{\partial Y}Y\right)}{XYD'}$$

D' (like D) is positive by assumption (embodied in the shape of the function); all the other terms are also positive, so the elasticity of substitution is positive. (This conclusion rests on taking S, the MRS, to be positive on the grounds that both marginal utilities are by definition positive. Were its significance as the slope of the indifference curve to be emphasised then S would be negative, given that the indifference curve has a negative slope).

The final step is to link this elasticity with the others which have been derived. These were specified in the vicinity of the equilibrium, allowing further manipulation to make use of the first-order conditions whereby

$$\frac{\partial U}{\partial X} = \lambda Px \text{ and } \frac{\partial U}{\partial Y} = \lambda Py.$$

First substituting these in the expression D':

$$\begin{aligned} D' &= \left(2\frac{\partial^2 U}{\partial X \partial Y}\frac{\partial U}{\partial X}\frac{\partial U}{\partial Y} - \left(\frac{\partial U}{\partial X}\right)^2 \frac{\partial^2 U}{\partial Y^2} - \left(\frac{\partial U}{\partial Y}\right)^2 \frac{\partial^2 U}{\partial X^2}\right) \\ &= \left(2\frac{\partial^2 U}{\partial X \partial Y}\lambda Px\lambda Py - (\lambda Px)^2\frac{\partial^2 U}{\partial Y^2} - (\lambda Py)^2\frac{\partial^2 U}{\partial X^2}\right) \\ &= \lambda^2 D \end{aligned}$$

Then substituting them in the expression for σ:

$$\begin{aligned} \sigma &= \frac{\frac{\partial U}{\partial X}\frac{\partial U}{\partial Y}\left(\frac{\partial U}{\partial X}X + \frac{\partial U}{\partial Y}Y\right)}{XYD'} \\ &= \frac{\lambda Px\lambda Py(\lambda PxX + \lambda PyY)}{XY\lambda^2 D} \end{aligned}$$

$$= \frac{\lambda PxPyR}{XYD}$$

Now multiply both sides by $(1 - \alpha_X)$, recalling that α_X is the proportion of the budget allocated to X:

$$\begin{aligned}
(1 - \alpha_X)\sigma &= \frac{\lambda PxPyR}{XYD}\left(1 - \frac{PxX}{R}\right) \\
&= \frac{\lambda PxPyR}{XYD}\left(\frac{R - PxX}{R}\right) \\
&= \frac{\lambda PxPy(PxX + PyY - PxX)}{XYD} \\
&= \frac{\lambda PxPyPyY}{XYD} \\
&= \frac{\lambda PxPy^2}{XD} \\
&= \frac{\lambda Py^2}{D}\frac{Px}{X} \\
&= -\xi_{XX}
\end{aligned}$$

That is,

$$\xi_{XX} = -(1 - \alpha_X)\sigma$$

The re-emergence of the compensated own price elasticity reveals that there exists a relationship between the elasticity of substitution and the own price elasticity. It will be recalled that the Slutsky Equation expressed in elasticity form is

$$\varepsilon_{XX} = \xi_{XX} - \alpha_X\varepsilon_{XR}$$

It follows, re-ordering the terms, that

$$\begin{aligned}
\varepsilon_{XX} &= -\alpha_X\varepsilon_{XR} - (1 - \alpha_X)\sigma \\
-\varepsilon_{XX} &= \alpha_X\varepsilon_{XR} + (1 - \alpha_X)\sigma
\end{aligned}$$

Ignoring the negative sign on the own price elasticity this can be transformed into the equation employed on page 57:

$$ep = KX.ei + (1 - KX).es$$

It follows that the placing of any condition on the elasticity of substitution (a property of the function concerned) such as requiring it to be constant has implications for the own price elasticity, making it a function of the income elasticity and the proportion of the budget devoted to the good in question. The choice of a *particular* mathematical function to represent preferences (or production possibilities) will have implications for elasticities of demand for the goods (or the inputs). This emphasises a general point: elasticities are particular perspectives on the properties of the functions employed to represent preferences and production possibilities.

It should be noted in conclusion that just as a movement along a demand function involves a combination of a substitution effect and an income effect, so it involves a combination of changes in each of the various elasticities which can be defined at the constrained optimum. Earlier in the argument (see pages 58 and 62) it was noted specifically that the own price elasticity generally changes along the demand function; now it should be evident that the other elasticities are similarly variable. Only if a function with very specific properties is used to represent preferences (or production possibilities) will exceptions to this exist. It is also worth recalling that all of these related elasticities are the product of the assumption of continuous and smooth differentiable functions, which supports the concept of incremental change in the values of variables (and thus the application of calculus); they are fundamentally theoretical rather than empirical concepts.

INDEX OF SUBJECTS

INDEX OF AUTHORITIES